Patrick Moore's
Yearbook of Astronomy
2014

Patrick Moore's Yearbook of Astronomy 2014

EDITED BY

Patrick Moore

AND

John Mason

MACMILLAN

First published 2013 by Macmillan
an imprint of Pan Macmillan, a division of Macmillan Publishers Limited
Pan Macmillan, 20 New Wharf Road, London N1 9RR
Basingstoke and Oxford
Associated companies throughout the world
www.panmacmillan.com

ISBN 978-1-4472-4396-0

1 3 5 7 9 8 6 4 2

A CIP catalogue record for this book is available from the British Library.

Typeset by Ellipsis Digital Limited
Printed and bound by CPI Group (UK) Ltd, Croydon, CR0 4YY

Contents

Monthly Notes 2014

Part Two

Article Section

Contents

Contents

Part Three
Miscellaneous

A Father Figure

Brian May
Astronomer and musician

For many years Patrick was a dear friend and a kind of father figure to me. I miss him terribly, as do all of his close friends and colleagues; the world has lost a priceless treasure that can never be replaced.

Patrick was the last of a lost generation – a true gentleman, the most generous in nature that I ever knew, an inspiration to thousands in his personal life and to millions through his fifty-five years of unique broadcasting. It's no exaggeration to say that Patrick, in his tireless and ebullient communication of the magic of astronomy, inspired every British astronomer, amateur and professional, for over half a century. Most astronomers I know will tell you that Patrick is the reason they first looked through a telescope. Through his countless books, articles and TV appearances, he somehow captured the adventure of the universe and brought it to us. He knew the universe in a way that will never be equalled. Patrick did not just know the facts – it was as if he lived out there, could find his way around it, knew it like the back of his hand. To the very end of his life he was actively distilling new discoveries into channels which made them not just accessible to astronomers, but also understandable to the general public – a rare gift, which he never tired of using to the full.

In his private life, Patrick was astoundingly giving. His dedication to young, aspiring astronomers was legendary. He replied to every letter, responded to questions, and helped young students both with gifts of equipment and the most precious gift of all: his time. He personally tutored some that he thought particularly promising, and sponsored others through higher education; in general, he gave away any income he ever made, to the point where he had no security himself, except that which his friends supplied. He was honoured by many universities with degrees and fellowships and, though he always insisted he was an amateur astronomer, his contribution to research was considerable. He made the first finely detailed map of the Moon's surface, which was

Brian and Patrick in his garden for the 2004 transit of Venus. (Image courtesy of the Sir Patrick Moore Collection.)

consulted by the first astronauts to walk on it. From the days before astrophotography was well developed, his notes and drawings from thousands of hours of pure observation are now a valuable archive.

Patrick was also a greatly caring human being, and a campaigner for the rights and welfare of animals. Privately, his cats were the loves of his life, and in public he was outspoken against cruelty of all kinds. His demolition of Theresa May's defence of fox hunting on the BBC is legendary. More recently, he spoke out against the Government's proposed massacre of badgers and attempts to repeal the Hunting Act.

Patrick had other talents too. He was a lifelong devotee of cricket, and bowled a mean googly in his day. He was an accomplished musician who played both piano and xylophone with great success in public. He composed music for these instruments and also for brass bands, much of which was recorded. He wrote science fiction novels, plays, spoof operas, and satirical commentaries on the foolishness of bureaucracy, under the assumed name of R. T. Fishall. He enjoyed good-naturedly ribbing those who believed in flying saucers or astrology, but had an open mind as to whether intelligent life might exist elsewhere in the universe.

The honour he was most proud of was being made a Fellow of the Royal Society – the only amateur astronomer ever to achieve this distinction – but he was also made a knight of the realm in 2001.

Patrick is mourned by the many to whom he was like a caring uncle, and by all who loved the delightful wit and clarity of his writings, or enjoyed his fearlessly eccentric persona in public life.

Patrick is irreplaceable. There will never be another Patrick Moore. But we were lucky enough to get one.

Editors' Foreword

Very sadly, following the death of Sir Patrick Moore on 9 December 2012, this foreword is being written by only one of us. Work on this *Yearbook* had already begun prior to Patrick's passing away, and the broad layout of the book and scope of the contributed articles had been jointly agreed, as usual, many months before the deadline.

Patrick invited me to join him in editing the *Yearbook* back in 2001 and it was always a joy to work on it with him every year. Although, in recent years, Patrick found it increasingly difficult to do much of the typing of the text because of his arthritis, he was at all times ready to provide advice and input when required and was always so incredibly enthusiastic about the *Yearbook*, which has endured for over fifty years. While working on this edition, I have missed his great friendship and companionship terribly, and also his incredible encyclopaedic knowledge of all things astronomical, which has made it more difficult than usual to draw everything together and complete the text. Whatever the time of day or night, and wherever in the world we both were at the time, Patrick was always willing and able to provide a ready answer to any queries I had while finalizing the content.

It was Patrick's wish that the *Yearbook* should continue for as long as it fulfilled a need, and so I have done my best to follow the long-established pattern, but with an important addition this year: I felt it was only right that some key contributors to the *Yearbook*, both past and present, should be able to express here what Patrick meant to them personally and pay tribute to his enormous contributions to astronomy and the popularization of science in general. My own tribute immediately follows this foreword.

I am, of course, indebted to all of the regular contributors for their support in completing this edition. Martin Mobberley has supplied the notes on eclipses, comets and minor planets, and Nick James has produced the data for the phases of the Moon, longitudes of the Sun, Moon and planets, and details of lunar occultations. As always, John Isles and Bob Argyle have provided the information on variable stars and double stars, respectively. Wil Tirion, who produced our stars maps for the Northern and Southern Hemispheres, has again drawn all of the line diagrams showing the positions and movements of the planets to accompany the Monthly Notes. These provide a detailed guide to what's happening in the night sky throughout the year, on a month-by-month basis.

We also have a fine selection of previously unpublished longer articles, both from our regular contributors and those new to the *Yearbook* this year. Following Patrick's long-established pattern, we have done our best to give you a wide choice of subject and technical level.

There have been many exciting and important developments in astronomy and astrophysics in recent years and several of these are featured in this edition. Stephen Webb looks at the most accurate observations ever made of the cosmic microwave background – the relic radiation left over from the Big Bang – recently completed by ESA's Planck mission, while David Harland looks at the nature of mass and the hunt by particle physicists for the elusive Higgs boson. In planetary science, David Rothery examines the planet Mercury and reviews the very latest findings from NASA's MESSENGER spacecraft, currently in orbit around the planet. For the amateur observer, Nick James describes the observations of comet C/2011 L4 (PanSTARRS), which became a naked-eye object in the spring of 2013, and Martin Mobberley gives some important advice on modern telescopic imaging of the giant planet Jupiter, which is at its best in 2014. On the centenary of the announcement by V. M. Slipher of his measurements of the radial velocities of spiral nebulae, William Sheehan describes the background to this remarkable piece of research, which led to the realization that the spiral nebulae (galaxies) are stellar systems seen at great distances. This, in turn, would lead to the discovery that the universe is expanding. We also have Richard Baum's fascinating tale of the mysterious object seen very close to the Sun in August 1921 by a number of independent observers in the US and Europe. Finally, as a fitting tribute to the lunar mapping work of the late Sir Patrick Moore, historian Allan Chapman provides an absorbing account of lunar cartography, the mapping of the Moon by telescopic observers from Thomas Harriot in 1609 to Sir Patrick himself.

I do hope you enjoy reading the range of articles that have been selected for you this year.

John Mason
Barnham, August 2013

The Patrick Moore That I Knew

John Mason

Co-Editor, *Yearbook of Astronomy*

I am quite sure that my story is fairly typical of those who came to know and love Patrick Moore, that I'm just another one of the countless people whom he enthused, inspired and encouraged over so many years. It is impossible to say just how many people there are across the world whose lives he touched in one way or another – probably millions, thanks to the medium of television and his longevity at the top of his field, as author, outstanding public speaker and broadcaster.

I became interested in astronomy at the age of seven when I witnessed a bright shooting star one summer's evening and wondered what it was. My mother found a number of books in the local library in an attempt to satisfy my innate curiosity about all things astronomical; and for my eighth birthday my sister bought me a copy of *The Observer's Book of Astronomy* (1962 edition) which cost 2s 6d (half a crown in old money, equivalent to 12.5p today). It was written by none other than Patrick Moore.

I read that book from cover to cover more times than I care to remember. I was totally captivated by Patrick's inimitable writing style and the incredible journey on which he took the reader. That book inspired me to learn as many of the brighter stars and constellation patterns as I could, and I read with great excitement and anticipation about events in the 'far future'; the return of Halley's comet in 1986, the total eclipse of the Sun visible from Devon and Cornwall in August 1999 and the probable Leonid meteor storm three months later that same year. I vowed to try and witness as many of these things as I could.

A couple of years after that, I wrote to Patrick after seeing him on BBC TV's *The Sky at Night*, asking his advice on buying a telescope. I had a postcard reply by return advising me to buy a pair of good binoculars (which I did) and to wait before buying a telescope (which I also did, buying one when I was fourteen years old).

In the summer of 1968, Patrick moved from Armagh to Selsey, only

John and Patrick enjoy a celebratory glass of champagne at a restaurant in Manchester on learning that John has had an asteroid named after him by the IAU. (Image courtesy of John Mason.)

a few miles from where I lived. Having telephoned beforehand, a school friend (Mark Savill) and I went round to his house to look through his telescopes. He lifted me up to the eyepiece of his 12½-inch reflector (lovingly called 'Oscar') to look at Saturn and I was completely hooked. If ever there was a life-changing moment, that was it!

Over the years, Patrick and I became good friends and I count myself as unbelievably fortunate to have known him and to have been able to travel around the world with him, to lecture and broadcast with him, to write books with him – but, most of all, to have enjoyed his wonderful company. He was a warm, gentle, highly intelligent man with seemingly limitless energy, and he was incredibly unselfish, introducing me to so many of his friends, most of whom I would never have had the chance to meet but for his initiation.

I was honoured when Patrick asked me to join him on various occasions on *The Sky at Night*, and when he invited me to co-write a book on Halley's comet with him in 1984 – and even more so when he asked me to become co-editor of this *Yearbook*, a volume that I had collected year on year since my youth.

Through his infectious enthusiasm, Patrick taught me how to enjoy and be amazed by the night sky and to become a curious and careful observer of it (although I could never match his skills), and also the great importance of communicating with others and encouraging them to do the same. He also taught me the value of a healthy scepticism where pseudo-scientific claims are concerned!

He was the most incredibly generous person that I have ever known, a walking encyclopaedia on all things astronomical, and such great fun to be with. I did not agree with everything he said, but I respected his views, and I miss his great friendship, his zany sense of humour, that booming laugh echoing through his home, and the staccato rattle of typewriter keys coming from the study as he pounded the keyboard.

After my parents, Patrick was the greatest influence on my early life. He was throughout my mentor, my inspiration and my champion, and I shall miss him for as long as I live.

Patrick by Peter

Peter Cattermole
Planetary geologist and volcanologist

I first met Patrick in 1953, when a school friend, whose mother ran the sub-post office at which he posted his mail, found out that I had an interest in the stars. We visited him at his request and immediately hit it off. I remember the smell of pipe tobacco and the thousands of books that crowded his study walls. He was at once friendly and enthusiastic. On the first evening he showed me his various telescopes and talked about observing the heavens, about cranks and science fiction he liked. He was then a well-known author but had yet to begin the amazing journey that became *The Sky at Night*.

He encouraged me to join him in observing the Moon and also the planets, particularly Mars and Jupiter; to join the JAS (now the SPA) and then the BAA. I couldn't believe my luck at having this amazing guy as a mentor. I spent long hours observing the Moon, and what was very obvious, right from the start of our friendship, was that he valued my observations and drawings just as much as his own. He encouraged in his inimitable enthusiastic way, and soon I had books filled with drawings of the Moon, Mars, Venus and the two gas giants. I particularly remember spending whole nights observing Mars when it was close in 1956. How lucky indeed was this callow youth!

I had wanted to be an astronomer for several years, but it was clear that my maths was never going to be good enough to achieve this goal. I left school at sixteen and took my first job in the Civil Service. This was not a great success and was never going to lead me in the direction of studying the Moon, a career that I so desired. Patrick knew of my dissatisfaction and suggested that I study for A-levels with a view to taking a geology degree. I thought this an almost reckless idea, but went along with it via a correspondence course. Patrick spent hours helping me and testing me on the syllabus. He also drove me around Britain in 'The Ark' (his ancient Ford Prefect), at his expense and in his time, to collect rocks and take photographs for the practical book I needed to

Patrick with Peter Cattermole on a geology field trip. (Image courtesy of the Sir Patrick Moore Collection.)

complete my exams. I got my A-levels and also a place at university. I know that I had to work for it, but without Patrick's encouragement I surely would have fallen short.

I got a degree and a doctorate, worked for NASA, and met hundreds of top scientists. At his invitation I appeared frequently on *The Sky at Night*, met my second-oldest friend, Iain Nicolson, and the three of us spent many a long, crazy weekend visiting the North Nibley Monument, a bizarre edifice to which Patrick retreated for a while when the pressures of work got too much for him. This was great fun and we continued to do this until he became too infirm – much to his chagrin. We also travelled to all kinds of exotic places, seeing Halley's Comet in Australia and total eclipses in Mexico and elsewhere. Travelling with Patrick was always interesting, liver-punishing and exhausting, but I would never have missed it for the world.

My enduring memory of my oldest friend is of an enthusiastic, completely eccentric man, with many views I abhorred but which I was prepared to ignore, a heart of gold – witness his charity work for the sick and disabled – an encourager of the young into the world of astronomy, generous to a fault, hugely knowledgeable and still considering himself as a rank amateur. Many a professional astronomer would have given their right arm to have his experience and knowledge. I will miss him for as long as I live, and I owe my fantastic professional life entirely to him. Who could wish for a dearer friend than he?

Remembering Patrick Moore

Iain Nicolson
Astronomer, lecturer and author

As a teenager in the late 1950s, I had been inspired by some of Patrick's earliest books and by that 'new' BBC Television programme, *The Sky at Night*. In 1960, I plucked up the courage to write to him for advice, and to my utter astonishment received by return a letter saying that he and a friend – Peter Cattermole – were about to head up to Scotland to look for a meteorite on the Isle of Lewis, and could they call in to see me on the way? They did, and thus began a close and hugely rewarding friendship with Patrick, and with Peter, that spanned more than half a century.

Shortly after that first encounter, I paid the first of many visits to his (then) home in East Grinstead, my abiding memories of which are of nights spent observing the Moon, planets and variable stars. He was a marvellous mentor from whom I learned a great deal, although I could never remotely match his skills. He did so much to shape the direction of my life – from commissioning my first *Yearbook* article (for the 1966 edition), recommending me to the publisher of my first books, and encouraging me, in 1969, to apply for a lecturing post in the newly created astronomy group at what is now the University of Hertfordshire. 'No chance,' I said. 'Bet you a bottle of Jameson's,' said he. I was astonished, and overjoyed, to lose that bet, and to embark on a career that I could not previously have dared to imagine.

Working with him over the years on books, lecture weekends, AstroFest and, from time to time, as a guest on *The Sky at Night*, made me acutely aware of his astonishing ability to grasp concepts instantly, store and recall masses of detailed information, crystallize the key points and communicate them with exemplary clarity through the written word, broadcast media and awe-inspiring lectures. His work rate was astonishing. Back in the early seventies, we wrote a little book together about black holes. My chapters took months to draft. We then got together at Farthings for a Jameson-fuelled weekend during which

Iain and Patrick sitting in Patrick's study at Farthings, his home in Selsey, 2005. (Image courtesy of Jean Nicolson.)

he wrote his entire contribution, and we put the book to bed. His phenomenal capacity for sustained hard work never diminished. Until late November 2012, when he was hospitalized for a couple of weeks, he was still working on book projects and revisions, having just completed a set of updates for the forthcoming paperback edition of his monumental *Data Book of Astronomy*.

Now and again, Peter Cattermole and I used to take him away for brief interludes during which nobody knew where he was. Free from the demands of press, media, publishers and the incessant ringing of the phone, he could relax completely, and just have fun. The focus of these excursions was to visit a conspicuous monument on a hill above the Gloucestershire village of North Nibley, which Patrick had deemed (tongue in cheek) to be the source of an intense aura of benevolence and well-being. Anytime he felt the need to get away from it all, he would ring us up and say, 'Time to visit the NNM', and we'd do our best to oblige. It gave him an excuse to do delightfully silly things – such as insisting that a passing young couple take a photograph of the three of us standing in the doorway of the monument clutching lighted sparklers; they obliged, then beat a hasty retreat!

Patrick was a truly inspirational character, talented in so many diverse ways. Eccentric, outspoken, kind, generous to a fault and intensely loyal, he had a tremendous sense of fun and a propensity for playing pranks, promulgating spoofs, berating authority and for sending himself up. Throughout his long career he gave freely and willingly of his time, energy, enthusiasm and resources to societies, organizations and individuals who sought his advice or help. With his infectious enthusiasm, boundless energy and unparalled communication skills, he inspired generations of astronomers – both amateur and professional – and raised the public awareness of, and involvement with, the science of astronomy to heights that had never before been achieved. Through his books, lectures and broadcasts, and over the fifty-five years during which he presented BBC Television's *The Sky at Night*, he became *the* public face of astronomy in the UK and beyond. He encouraged new generations of science communicators and set the bar very high for those who would follow in his footsteps. All of these things form part of his enduring legacy.

The Man Who Taught Me the Art of Visual Lunar and Planetary Astronomy

Paul G. Abel

Astrophysicist and visual observer of the Moon and planets

The summer of 1989 marked the start of my love of astronomy. I wasn't just bitten by the astronomy bug, I was completely ravaged by it, and it happened for two reasons. First, in August, not long after my ninth birthday, Voyager 2 was out at Neptune showing one magnificent picture after another. I'm quite sure that most of the science would have passed me by but for the fact that there was an utterly enchanting man (who was as exciting as Neptune itself!) speaking very animatedly about what each picture was telling us and what each discovery meant. He spoke quickly, but not a single word was wasted. In comparison, the other scientists spoke rather incoherently and looked shifty. I had just encountered Patrick Moore for the very first time.

Second, my mother pointed out that he was a famous astronomer, and if I wanted to get into astronomy, then I should go to the library to see if they had any of his books. So this is what I did, and, to my surprise, I found the small astronomy section at Burton Library had quite a few books, all written by him. I worked my way through them, but I was still unsure of a few things, so I decided to write to him. Alas, no one had his address! The lady at the library said we should try the BBC, but in the end I decided I would just put 'Patrick Moore' on the envelope and post it. Three days later came his reply!

His typed letter was gushing with enthusiasm, urging me not to rush into getting a telescope, but rather to get a pair of binoculars and make a start on learning the sky. He included a copy of his *Observer's Book of Astronomy* which he felt would be more useful than the other books I had mentioned. More importantly, the letter ended with the magical words, 'Keep in touch; I will do what I can to be of assistance.' I did just that.

Over the years, I corresponded with and telephoned Patrick quite a lot. During one such call, he urged me to join the British Astronomical Association, a fine institution dedicated to promoting astronomy. The BAA also makes good scientific use of the observations made by its members (if you're not a member, you should join!). Eventually, I obtained on loan a lovely 4.5-inch refractor from the BAA with which to observe the Moon and planets; again Patrick helped organize this for me.

After a brief absence of serious amateur astronomy during my undergraduate degree, I established an observatory here in Leicester and made plans to get back into planetary observing. I had always struggled with recording lunar and planetary detail, so, once again, I got in touch with Patrick. He invited me down to Farthings (I had had previous invites, but could never pluck up the courage to go!) and I went down and had a marvellous time. Patrick's advice was clear, though; the only way I would become skilled at this would be by putting in long hours at the telescope. He offered me the use of his 12½-inch reflector (called Oscar). It was a magnificent telescope on an alt-azimuth mount (Patrick had meant to upgrade it, but never got around to it). I had, of course, seen this famous telescope many times and now I was using it to train on. To this day that telescope has a special place in my heart.

I spent about a year, sometimes one weekend after the other, going down to Farthings and drawing the Moon and planets. I would often come in utterly frozen and Patrick would give me a whiskey and say, 'Right, now you have to make the neat copy!' My early drawings were rather crude but Patrick's enthusiasm for them kept me going. Sometimes the Selsey weather would produce clouds and mist. If this was the case I would spend hours poring over his log books which were in many ways autobiographical. The books contained not only his magical drawings of the Moon and Mars, but also the many accidents and mishaps which seemed to follow Patrick to a number of observatories. In recent years, Patrick was insistent that I should write a book about visual planetary astronomy. I agreed on one condition; that he would provide the foreword for my book. I wanted the opening of it to be from the man who got me started!

Eventually, I became a reasonable observer, and without a doubt I owe that to him. During the course of that year we became firm friends, and both my partner Matthew and I would escape to Farthings for weekends. Such weekends were always great fun and involved making

Paul and Patrick, both sporting monocles, in Patrick's study at his home in Selsey, after consuming several glasses of pea wine. (Image courtesy of Matthew Forman.)

wine, setting off Chinese lanterns in the hope of triggering UFO sightings and tasting his excellent collection of whiskeys. We would also bring down new wines and foods we had discovered for him to try. Farthings had a lovely large kitchen, and as we liked cooking, we would often cook local seafood dishes (Patrick preferred fish as he was 'reasonably confident' that they couldn't feel anything when caught). This was invariably washed down with a glass of 'pea wine', which Patrick would make just for the fun of asking people if they'd like a glass of 'pea'!

I should make it clear that there is nothing particularly unique about my story: Patrick did this with thousands of other people, young and old, across the country and further afield over many decades. He seemed to live for astronomy and encouraging people to get into it, and I am just one in a long line of professional astronomers who got started because of him. Even when confined to Farthings, he still wanted to see the latest observations and take part in any way he could. Quite frankly, if it hadn't been for Patrick, you would never have heard of me.

I would like to close this tribute to my dear friend with a letter which he wrote to me back in the 1990s. Patrick wrote fantastic letters which often seemed to contain whatever was in his head at the time. The amusing incident below is conveyed in a way that only Patrick could tell, so I will hand you over to him:

Dear Paul,

So glad to hear from you; it seems you have made a good start in astronomy! Alas I have not been able to observe Jupiter as, in a feat of efficiency on my part, I've somehow managed to lock myself out of my observatory! Thankfully, kind friends came to the rescue earlier this week and I have access once more. However, Spode's malign influence continues to be felt as the planet has now retired behind that infernal tree in Phyllis May's garden! I give up!!!

Best wishes,

PATRICK MOORE

P. S. Plastic!!!!! Your observatory roof should be as light as possible.

Patrick, the TV star

Jane Fletcher
Series Producer, *The Sky at Night*

I worked with Patrick on *The Sky at Night* from June 2002 until his death. There were only a handful of producers who worked with Patrick and who stayed with him for many years. I am afraid Patrick did not tolerate anyone he felt was not 'up to the mark' and they did not last long under his steely gaze and piercing intellect. We, the 'long serving producers', all formed close bonds with him and became part of his adopted family; always keeping in touch, a genuine friendship. The relationship was not unlike that of his RAF days: you all did your bit to make sure the mission was successful, but he was the Captain.

In his prime, Patrick was an extremely energetic man: tall, strong and very imposing. When I started working with him, his mobility was already in decline (the result of various war wounds), but he never, ever, let this get in the way of making the programme. As long as he could get out, he did, and he did what he could to make the best programme possible.

In the early days of my tenure, in May 2003, Patrick and I went to the very north of Scotland to see the annular eclipse off Caithness. Brian May met us there in his helicopter and came with us to see sunrise, with the eclipse already under way as the Sun came up. Patrick was calling out to some rowdy local lads who had been up all night drinking, telling them to behave themselves and be quiet. They politely obeyed! We also went down Boulby Mine, Europe's deepest mine, travelling out to the dark matter detectors installed under the North Sea. There Patrick played a short game of pool, which illustrated how dark matter is detected.

When Patrick could no longer get 'out and about' we brought the stars and people to him and his home in Selsey. I began filming in his garden, organizing star parties, where he could join in. He always enjoyed the camaraderie and would tell the astronomers that they must use his 15-inch telescope, especially to look at the planets.

Jane and Patrick by the seaside. (Image courtesy of the Sir Patrick Moore Collection.)

Patrick's love of a party was renowned. For the fiftieth anniversary the BBC allowed me to organize a special get-together of contributors who had helped make *The Sky at Night*. The cameraman and I spent a whole day arranging lights, planets and backdrops; the tent was draped around Patrick's 12½-inch telescope, which was specially lit. The whole scene looked wonderful. When we brought him in to see it, for once Patrick was 'almost' speechless! Everything went well, including our live link to the South African telescope.

Patrick was an astronomer, but he was also a showman and he loved performing, enjoying the 'fun' that television could bring. We recreated the set of the first programme, with Jon Culshaw being the young Patrick. Patrick engaged him in a bit of time-travelling banter and afterwards confessed it was all rather odd talking to a young version of himself and 'seeing that old set again after so many years'.

My routine when making the programme was to come down to his home, 'Farthings', twice a month. Our planning meetings were the most enjoyable. I would arrange lunch from his local restaurant, 'Seals', and we would enjoy some crab or other seafood delight brought by the owner Kiki. More than once his prawns seemed to spring back to life under his grip. Then we would settle down to write the script, phone the contributors and sort out the images. Sitting in his study, with Patrick bashing away at his Woodstock (later some unfortunate keyboard), with his cats around him, my memory now is that the sunlight always seemed to flood through his window.

Towards the end of his life, I was humbled by and greatly admired his resolve to keep going, no matter how much pain and discomfort he seemed to be in. I used to think that it was making *The Sky at Night* that gave Patrick purpose, but I now believe that he kept going for us. He realized how important the programme was for the people who worked on it, and above all the viewers who watched it.

The flickering images on television have only partly managed to capture the magical and magnificent man that was Sir Patrick Moore. At least they serve as a reminder of what a truly impressive person he was and the tremendous legacy he has left us all.

Preface

New readers will find that all the information in this *Yearbook* is given in diagrammatic or descriptive form; the positions of the planets may easily be found from the specially designed star charts, while the Monthly Notes describe the movements of the planets and give details of other astronomical phenomena visible in both in the Northern and Southern Hemispheres. Two sets of star charts are provided. The **Northern Star Charts** (pp. 7 to 31) are designed for use at latitude 52°N, but may be used without alteration throughout the British Isles, and (except in the case of eclipses and occultations) in other countries of similar northerly latitude. The **Southern Star Charts** (pp. 33 to 57) are drawn for latitude 35°S, and are suitable for use in South Africa, Australia and New Zealand, and other locations in approximately the same southerly latitude. The reader who needs more detailed information will find *Norton's Star Atlas* an invaluable guide, while more precise positions of the planets and their satellites, together with predictions of occultations, meteor showers and periodic comets, may be found in the *Handbook* of the British Astronomical Association. Readers will also find details of forthcoming events given in the American monthly magazine *Sky & Telescope* and the British periodicals *The Sky at Night*, *Astronomy Now* and *Astronomy and Space*.

Important note

The times given on the star charts and in the Monthly Notes are generally given as local times, using the twenty-four-hour clock, the day beginning at midnight. All the dates, and the times of a few events (e.g. eclipses), are given in Greenwich Mean Time (GMT), which is related to local time by the formula:

Local Mean Time = GMT – west longitude

In practice, small differences in longitude are ignored, and the observer will use local clock time, which will be the appropriate Standard (or

xxx

Zone) Time. As the formula indicates, places in west longitude will have a Standard Time slow on GMT, while places in east longitude will have a Standard Time fast on GMT. As examples we have:

Standard Time in

New Zealand	GMT + 12 hours
Victoria, NSW	GMT + 10 hours
Western Australia	GMT + 8 hours
South Africa	GMT + 2 hours
British Isles	GMT
Eastern ST	GMT − 5 hours
Central ST	GMT − 6 hours, etc.

If Summer Time is in use, the clocks will have been advanced by one hour, and this hour must be subtracted from the clock time to give Standard Time.

Part One

Monthly Charts and Astronomical Phenomena

Notes on the Star Charts

The stars, together with the Sun, Moon and planets, seem to be set on the surface of the celestial sphere, which appears to rotate about the Earth from east to west. Since it is impossible to represent a curved surface accurately on a plane, any kind of star map is bound to contain some form of distortion.

Most of the monthly star charts which appear in the various journals and some national newspapers are drawn in circular form. This is perfectly accurate, but it can make the charts awkward to use. For the star charts in this volume, we have preferred to give two hemispherical maps for each month of the year, one showing the northern aspect of the sky and the other showing the southern aspect. Two sets of monthly charts are provided, one for observers in the Northern Hemisphere and one for those in the Southern Hemisphere.

Unfortunately, the constellations near the overhead point (the zenith) on these hemispherical charts can be rather distorted. This would be a serious drawback for precision charts, but what we have done is to give maps which are best suited to star recognition. We have also refrained from putting in too many stars, so that the main patterns stand out clearly. To help observers with any distortions near the zenith, and the lack of overlap between the charts of each pair, we have also included two circular maps, one showing all the constellations in the northern half of the sky, and one showing those in the southern half. Incidentally, there is a curious illusion that stars at an altitude of 60° or more are actually overhead, and beginners may often feel that they are leaning over backwards in trying to see them.

The charts show all stars down to the fourth magnitude, together with a number of fainter stars which are necessary to define the shapes of constellations. There is no standard system for representing the outlines of the constellations, and triangles and other simple figures have been used to give outlines which are easy to trace with the naked eye. The names of the constellations are given, together with the proper names of the brighter stars. The apparent magnitudes of the stars are indicated roughly by using different sizes of dot, the larger dots representing the brighter stars.

The two sets of star charts – one each for Northern and Southern Hemisphere observers – are similar in design. At each opening there is a single circular chart which shows all the constellations in that hemisphere of the sky. (These two charts are centred on the North and South Celestial Poles, respectively.) Then there are twelve double-page spreads, showing the northern and southern aspects for each month of the year for observers in that hemisphere. In the **Northern Charts** (drawn for latitude 52°N) the left-hand chart of each spread shows the northern half of the sky (lettered 1N, 2N, 3N ... 12N), and the corresponding right-hand chart shows the southern half of the sky (lettered 1S, 2S, 3S ...12S). The arrangement and lettering of the charts is exactly the same for the **Southern Charts** (drawn for latitude 35°S).

Because the sidereal day is shorter than the solar day, the stars appear to rise and set about four minutes earlier each day, and this amounts to two hours in a month. Hence the twelve pairs of charts in each set are sufficient to give the appearance of the sky throughout the day at intervals of two hours, or at the same time of night at monthly intervals throughout the year. For example, charts 1N and 1S here are drawn for 23 hours on 6 January. The view will also be the same on 6 October at 05 hours; 6 November at 03 hours; 6 December at 01 hours and 6 February at 21 hours. The actual range of dates and times when the stars on the charts are visible is indicated on each page. Each pair of charts is numbered in bold type, and the number to be used for any given month and time may be found from the following table:

Local Time	18h	20h	22h	0h	2h	4h	6h
January	11	12	1	2	3	4	5
February	12	1	2	3	4	5	6
March	1	2	3	4	5	6	7
April	2	3	4	5	6	7	8
May	3	4	5	6	7	8	9
June	4	5	6	7	8	9	10
July	5	6	7	8	9	10	11
August	6	7	8	9	10	11	12
September	7	8	9	10	11	12	1

Local Time	18h	20h	22h	0h	2h	4h	6h
October	8	9	10	11	12	1	2
November	9	10	11	12	1	2	3
December	10	11	12	1	2	3	4

On these charts, the ecliptic is drawn as a broken line on which longitude is marked every 10°. The positions of the planets are then easily found by reference to the table on p. 64. It will be noticed that on the **Southern Charts** the ecliptic may reach an altitude in excess of 62.5° on the star charts showing the northern aspect (5N to 9N). The continuations of the broken line will be found on the corresponding charts for the southern aspect (5S, 6S, 8S and 9S).

Northern Star Charts

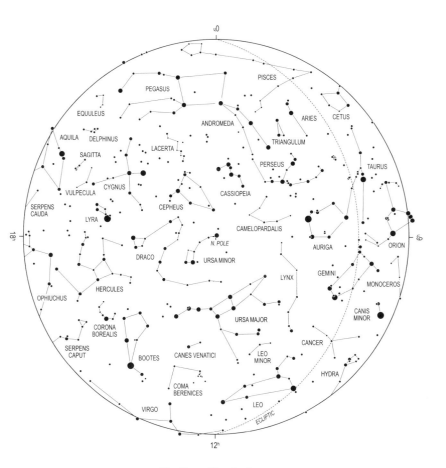

Northern Hemisphere

Note that the markers at 0ʰ, 6ʰ, 12ʰ and 18ʰ
indicate hours of Right Ascension.

1N

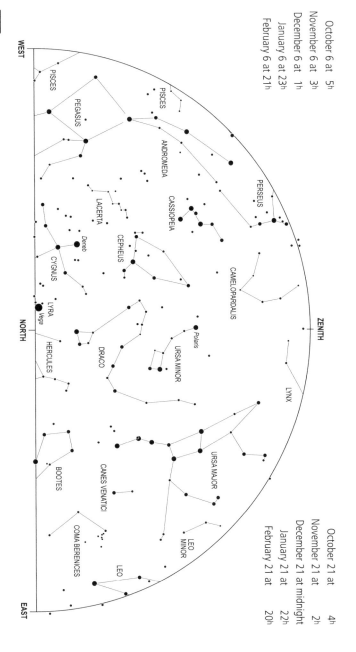

1S

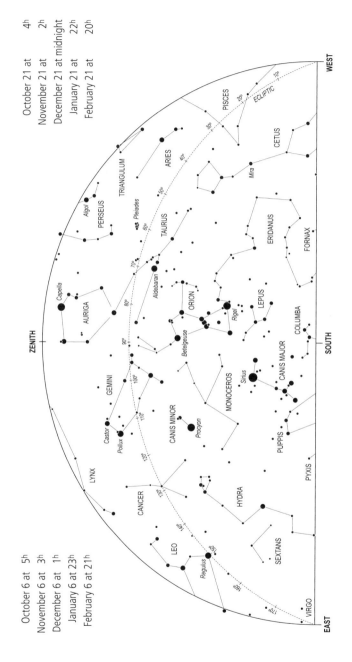

2N

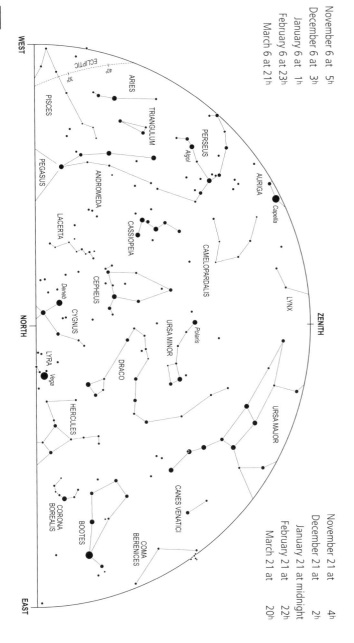

Northern Star Charts

2S

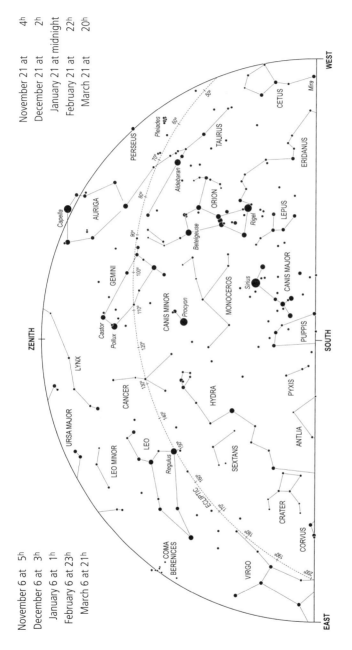

3N

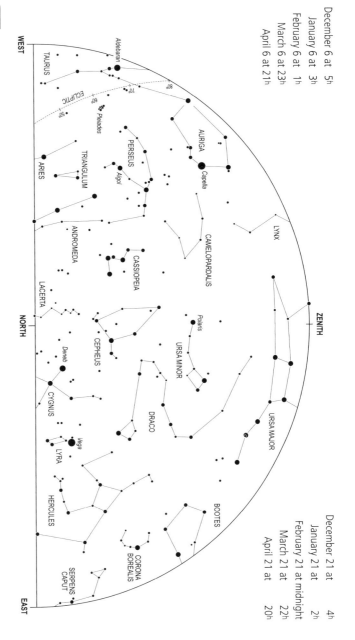

Northern Star Charts

3S

December 21 at 4ʰ
January 21 at 2ʰ
February 21 at midnight
March 21 at 22ʰ
April 21 at 20ʰ

December 6 at 5ʰ
January 6 at 3ʰ
February 6 at 1ʰ
March 6 at 23ʰ
April 6 at 21ʰ

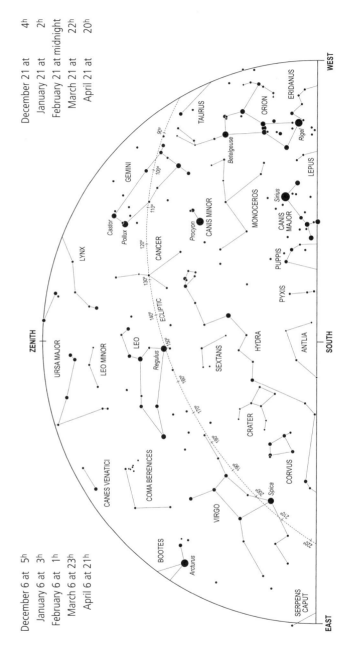

13

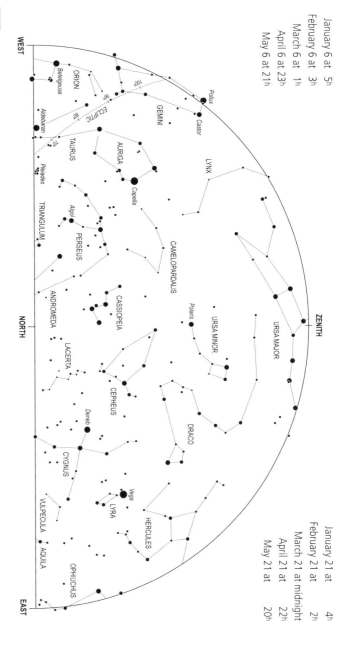

4N

4S

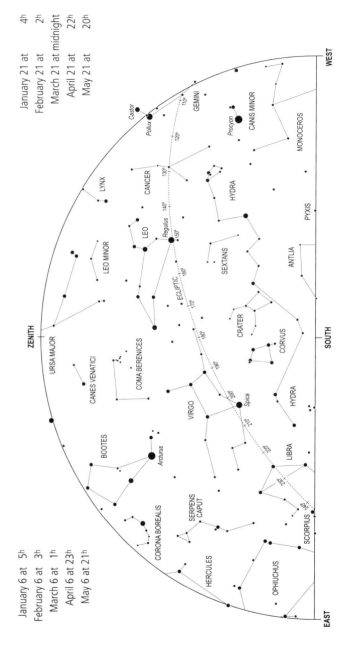

WEST

Castor
Pollux
GEMINI
110°
120°
Procyon
CANIS MINOR
MONOCEROS

LYNX
CANCER
130°
HYDRA
PYXIS

LEO MINOR
LEO
140°
Regulus
150°
SEXTANS
ANTLIA

160°
ECLIPTIC
170°

ZENITH

URSA MAJOR

CANES VENATICI

COMA BERENICES

CRATER
CORVUS
180°

190°
SOUTH

200°
HYDRA
Spica
210°

VIRGO

BOOTES

Arcturus

220°
LIBRA

SERPENS
CAPUT
230°

CORONA BOREALIS
240°
SCORPIUS

HERCULES
OPHIUCHUS

EAST

5N

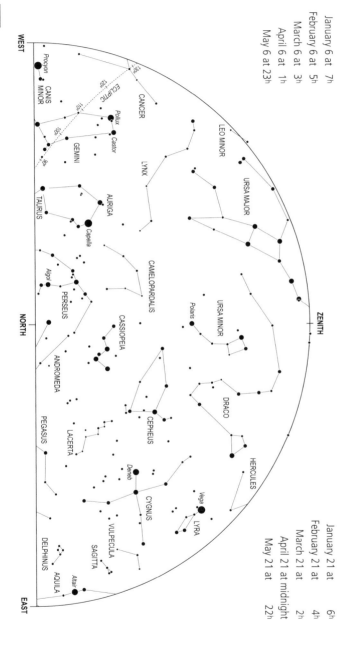

5S

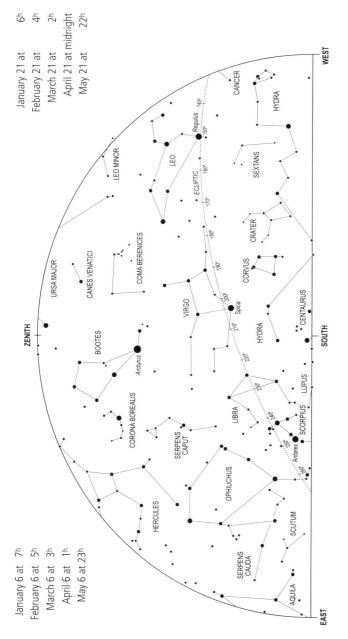

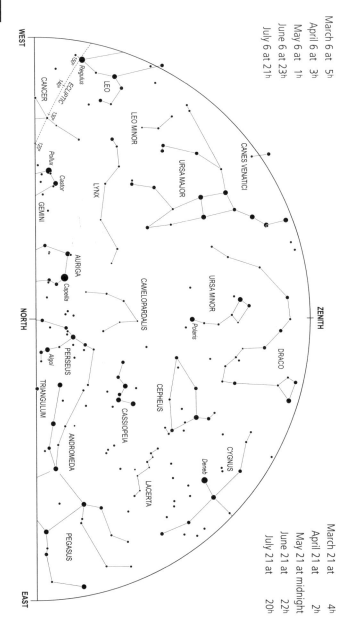

6N

Northern Star Charts

6S

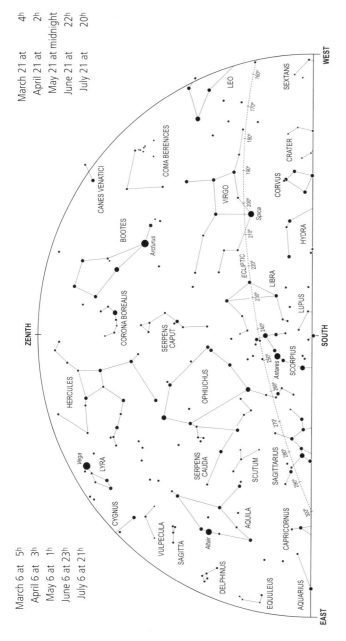

March 21 at 4ʰ
April 21 at 2ʰ
May 21 at midnight
June 21 at 22ʰ
July 21 at 20ʰ

March 6 at 5ʰ
April 6 at 3ʰ
May 6 at 1ʰ
June 6 at 23ʰ
July 6 at 21ʰ

WEST

ZENITH

SOUTH

EAST

LEO
SEXTANS
COMA BERENICES
CRATER
CANES VENATICI
VIRGO
CORVUS
BOOTES
Arcturus
Spica
HYDRA
ECLIPTIC
LIBRA
CORONA BOREALIS
LUPUS
SERPENS CAPUT
HERCULES
OPHIUCHUS
SCORPIUS
Antares
Vega
LYRA
SERPENS CAUDA
SCUTUM
SAGITTARIUS
CYGNUS
VULPECULA
AQUILA
CAPRICORNUS
SAGITTA
Altair
DELPHINUS
EQUULEUS
AQUARIUS

7N

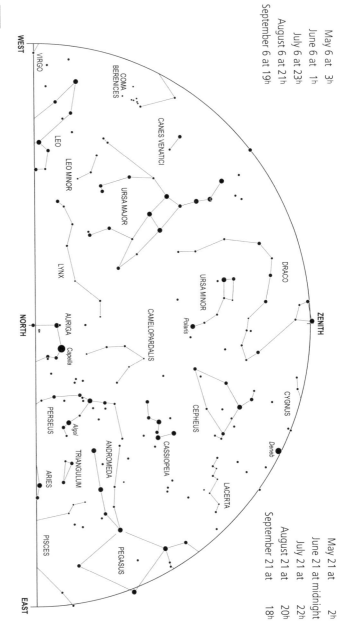

Northern Star Charts

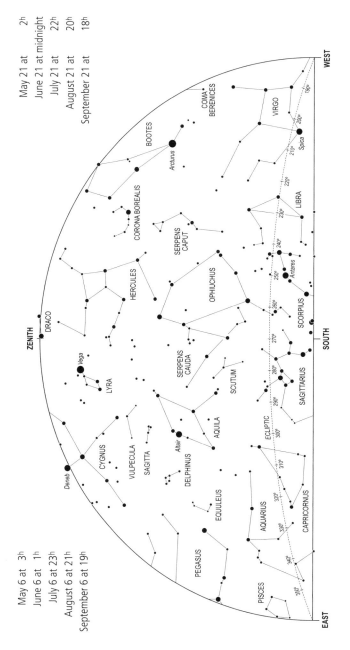

May 21 at 2h
June 21 at midnight
July 21 at 22h
August 21 at 20h
September 21 at 18h

May 6 at 3h
June 6 at 1h
July 6 at 23h
August 6 at 21h
September 6 at 19h

WEST

COMA BERENICES

BOOTES

Arcturus

VIRGO

Spica

190°

200°

210°

220°

CORONA BOREALIS

LIBRA

230°

SERPENS CAPUT

240°

HERCULES

OPHIUCHUS

Antares

250°

260°

ZENITH

DRACO

SCORPIUS

270°

SOUTH

Vega

SERPENS CAUDA

280°

LYRA

SCUTUM

SAGITTARIUS

290°

CYGNUS

VULPECULA

AQUILA

ECLIPTIC

300°

SAGITTA

Altair

310°

Deneb

DELPHINUS

EQUULEUS

320°

AQUARIUS

330°

CAPRICORNUS

PEGASUS

340°

350°

PISCES

EAST

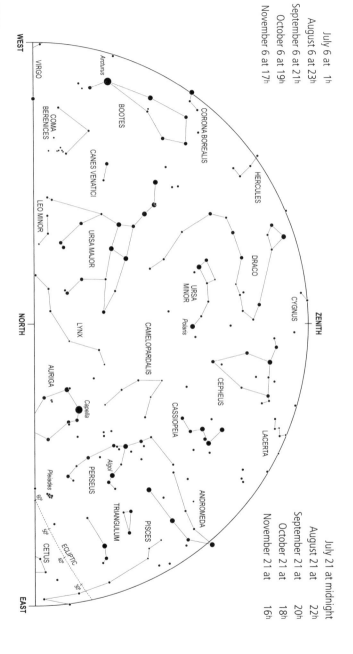

8N

Northern Star Charts

July 21 at midnight
August 21 at   22ʰ
September 21 at   20ʰ
October 21 at   18ʰ
November 21 at   16ʰ

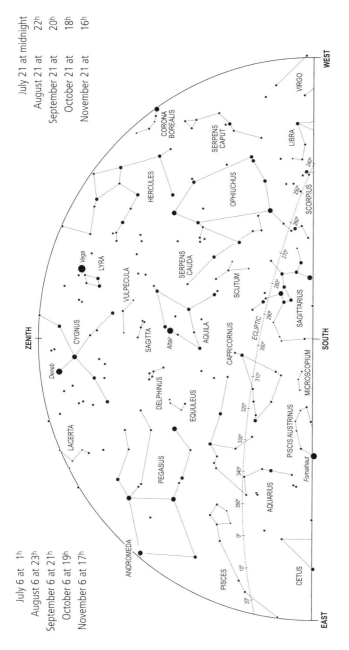

WEST

VIRGO

CORONA
BOREALIS

SERPENS
CAPUT

LIBRA

HERCULES

OPHIUCHUS

240°

SCORPIUS

250°

260°

Vega

LYRA

SERPENS
CAUDA

270°

ZENITH

VULPECULA

SCUTUM

280°

CYGNUS

280°

SAGITTARIUS

290°

Deneb

SAGITTA

Altair

AQUILA

ECLIPTIC

300°

SOUTH

CAPRICORNUS

DELPHINUS

310°

MICROSCOPIUM

LACERTA

EQUULEUS

320°

PEGASUS

330°

PISCIS AUSTRINUS

340°

Fomalhaut

350°

AQUARIUS

0°

ANDROMEDA

10°

PISCES

CETUS

20°

EAST

July 6 at   1ʰ
August 6 at   23ʰ
September 6 at 21ʰ
October 6 at 19ʰ
November 6 at 17ʰ

23

9N

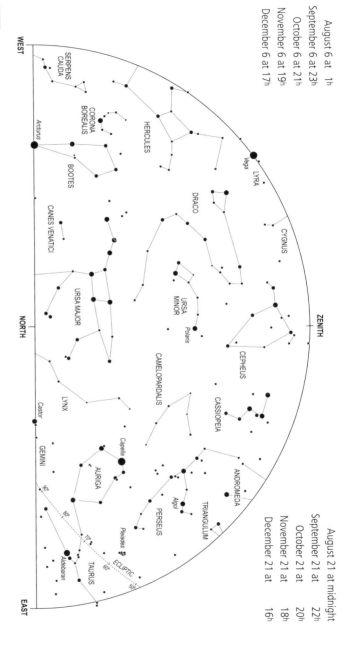

WEST

August 6 at 1h
September 6 at 23h
October 6 at 21h
November 6 at 19h
December 6 at 17h

SERPENS CAUDA

CORONA BOREALIS

Arcturus

HERCULES

Vega LYRA

BOOTES

CYGNUS

DRACO

CANES VENATICI

URSA MINOR

Polaris

URSA MAJOR

NORTH

ZENITH

CAMELOPARDALIS

CEPHEUS

LYNX

CASSIOPEIA

Castor

Capella

GEMINI

AURIGA

ANDROMEDA

Algol

TRIANGULUM

PERSEUS

Pleiades

ECLIPTIC

Aldebaran

TAURUS

EAST

August 21 at midnight
September 21 at 22h
October 21 at 20h
November 21 at 18h
December 21 at 16h

Northern Star Charts

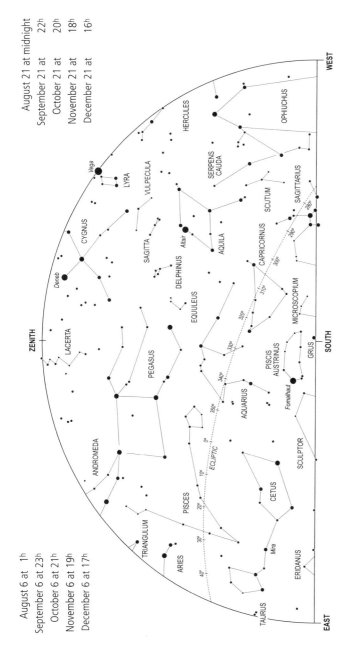

August 21 at midnight
September 21 at 22h
October 21 at 20h
November 21 at 18h
December 21 at 16h

August 6 at 1h
September 6 at 23h
October 6 at 21h
November 6 at 19h
December 6 at 17h

WEST

EAST

ZENITH

SOUTH

HERCULES
OPHIUCHUS
SERPENS CAUDA
Vega
LYRA
VULPECULA
SCUTUM
SAGITTARIUS
CYGNUS
SAGITTA
Deneb
Altair
AQUILA
CAPRICORNUS
DELPHINUS
LACERTA
EQUULEUS
MICROSCOPIUM
PEGASUS
ANDROMEDA
AQUARIUS
PISCIS AUSTRINUS
GRUS
Fomalhaut
SCULPTOR
PISCES
CETUS
TRIANGULUM
Mira
ARIES
ERIDANUS
TAURUS

ECLIPTIC

280°
290°
300°
310°
320°
330°
340°
350°
0°
10°
20°
30°
40°

25

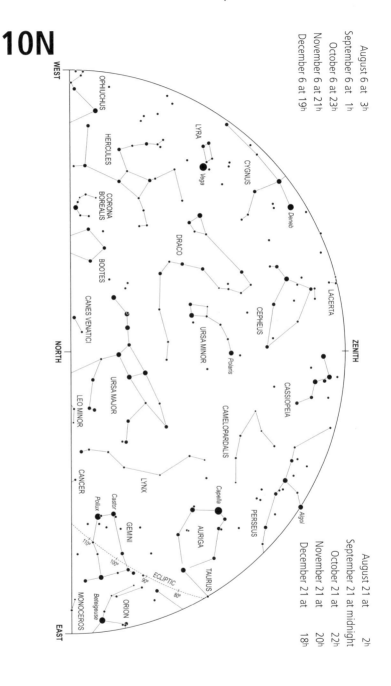

10N

WEST

OPHIUCHUS
HERCULES
LYRA
Vega
CYGNUS
Deneb
CORONA BOREALIS
BOOTES
DRACO
LACERTA
CEPHEUS
CANES VENATICI
URSA MINOR
Polaris
NORTH
CASSIOPEIA
ZENITH
LEO MINOR
URSA MAJOR
CAMELOPARDALIS
CANCER
LYNX
Capella
PERSEUS
Algol
Pollux
Castor
GEMINI
AURIGA
110°
100°
ECLIPTIC
90°
80°
TAURUS
MONOCEROS
Betelgeuse
ORION

EAST

August 6 at 3h
September 6 at 1h
October 6 at 23h
November 6 at 21h
December 6 at 19h

August 21 at 2h
September 21 at midnight
October 21 at 22h
November 21 at 20h
December 21 at 18h

Northern Star Charts

August 21 at 2ʰ
September 21 at midnight
October 21 at 22ʰ
November 21 at 20ʰ
December 21 at 18ʰ

August 6 at 3ʰ
September 6 at 1ʰ
October 6 at 23ʰ
November 6 at 21ʰ
December 6 at 19ʰ

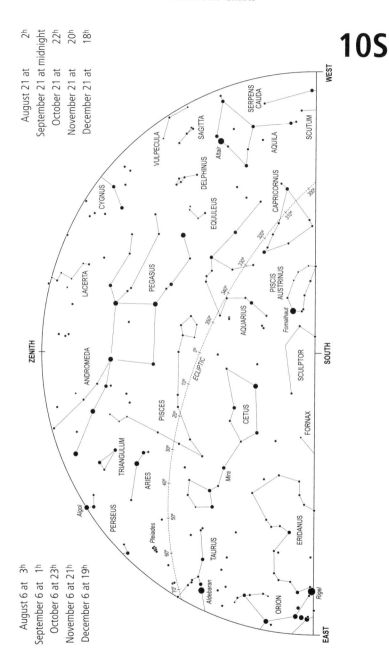

WEST

SERPENS CAUDA
SAGITTA
VULPECULA
DELPHINUS
Altair
AQUILA
SCUTUM
CYGNUS
EQUULEUS
CAPRICORNUS
310°
320°
330°
PEGASUS
PISCIS AUSTRINUS
LACERTA
340°
Fomalhaut
AQUARIUS
ANDROMEDA
350°
SCULPTOR
ZENITH
0°
ECLIPTIC
10°
SOUTH
PISCES
20°
CETUS
FORNAX
30°
TRIANGULUM
Mira
ARIES
40°
Algol
50°
ERIDANUS
PERSEUS
Pleiades
60°
TAURUS
70°
Aldebaran
ORION
Rigel

EAST

27

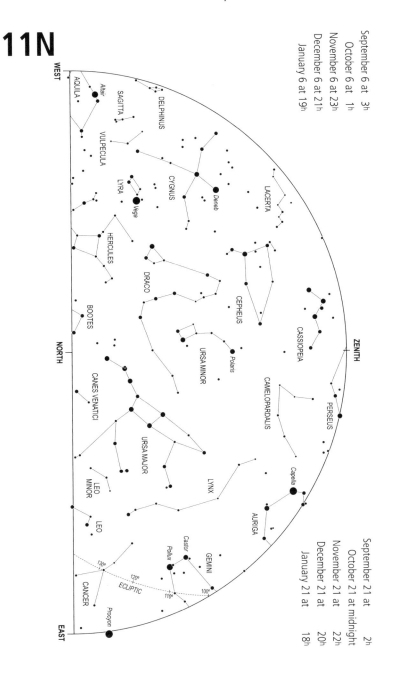

11N

11S

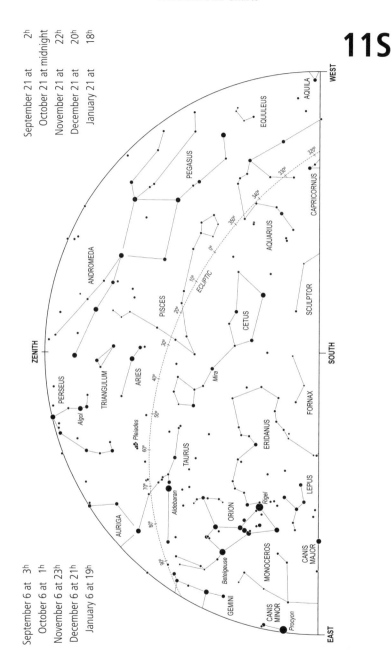

September 21 at 2ʰ
October 21 at midnight
November 21 at 22ʰ
December 21 at 20ʰ
January 21 at 18ʰ

September 6 at 3ʰ
October 6 at 1ʰ
November 6 at 23ʰ
December 6 at 21ʰ
January 6 at 19ʰ

WEST

AQUILA
EQUULEUS
PEGASUS
CAPRICORNUS
AQUARIUS
SCULPTOR
ANDROMEDA
PISCES
CETUS
ECLIPTIC
SOUTH
ZENITH
PERSEUS
Algol
TRIANGULUM
ARIES
Mira
FORNAX
Pleiades
TAURUS
ERIDANUS
AURIGA
Aldebaran
ORION
Rigel
LEPUS
Betelgeuse
MONOCEROS
CANIS MAJOR
GEMINI
CANIS MINOR
Procyon
EAST

320°
330°
340°
350°
0°
10°
20°
30°
40°
50°
60°
70°
80°
90°

29

12N

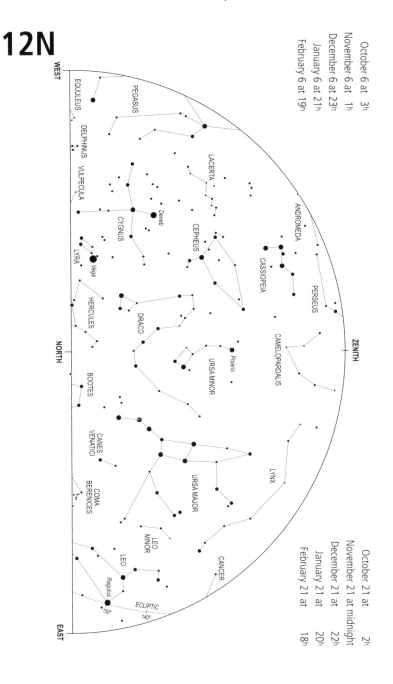

12S

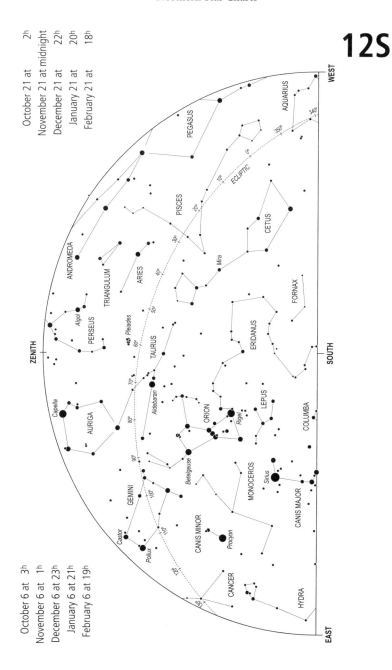

PEGASUS

AQUARIUS

WEST

340°

35°

ECLIPTIC

0°

10°

PISCES

20°

CETUS

30°

Mira

40°

ANDROMEDA

TRIANGULUM

ARIES

50°

FORNAX

PERSEUS

Algol

ERIDANUS

Pleiades

60°

TAURUS

ZENITH

70°

Aldebaran

ORION

LEPUS

Capella

80°

Rigel

COLUMBA

AURIGA

Betelgeuse

SOUTH

90°

MONOCEROS

Sirius

100°

GEMINI

CANIS MAJOR

Castor

110°

CANIS MINOR

Pollux

Procyon

120°

CANCER

HYDRA

130°

EAST

Southern Star Charts

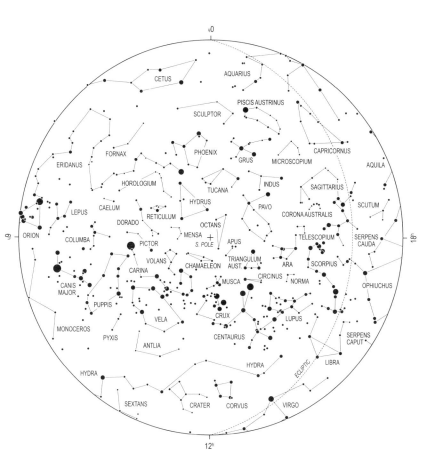

Southern Hemisphere

Note that the markers at 0ʰ, 6ʰ, 12ʰ and 18ʰ
indicate hours of Right Ascension.

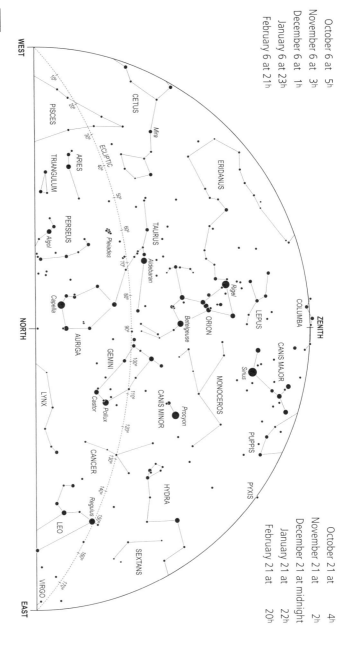

Southern Star Charts

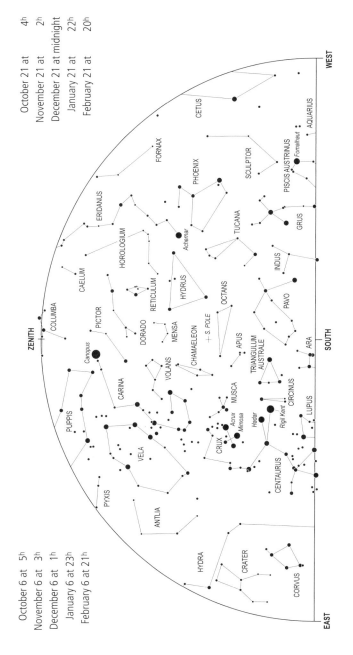

1S

October 21 at 4h
November 21 at 2h
December 21 at midnight
January 21 at 22h
February 21 at 20h

October 6 at 5h
November 6 at 3h
December 6 at 1h
January 6 at 23h
February 6 at 21h

WEST

EAST

SOUTH

ZENITH

CETUS
AQUARIUS
FORNAX
PHOENIX
SCULPTOR
PISCIS AUSTRINUS
Fomalhaut
ERIDANUS
TUCANA
GRUS
HOROLOGIUM
Achernar
INDUS
CAELUM
RETICULUM
HYDRUS
PAVO
COLUMBA
DORADO
MENSA
OCTANS
+ S. POLE
APUS
ARA
PICTOR
CHAMAELEON
TRIANGULUM AUSTRALE
Canopus
VOLANS
MUSCA
CIRCINUS
CARINA
CRUX
Acrux
Hadar
Rigil Kent
LUPUS
PUPPIS
Mimosa
VELA
CENTAURUS
PYXIS
ANTLIA
HYDRA
CRATER
CORVUS

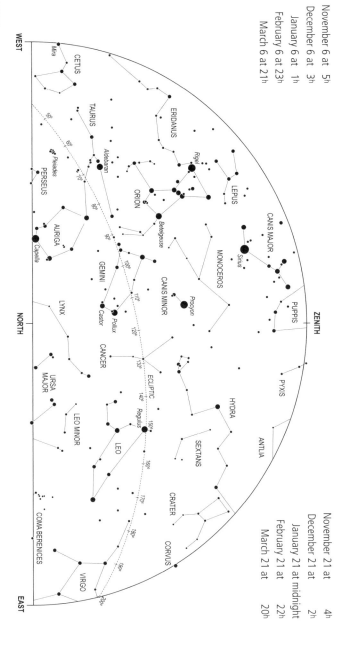

2N

2S

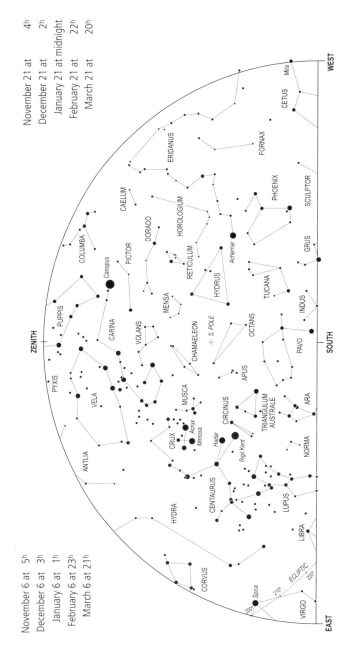

WEST

ZENITH

SOUTH

EAST

CETUS
Mira
FORNAX
ERIDANUS
SCULPTOR
PHOENIX
CAELUM
HOROLOGIUM
GRUS
DORADO
PICTOR
RETICULUM
Achernar
HYDRUS
TUCANA
INDUS
COLUMBA
Canopus
CARINA
MENSA
S. POLE
OCTANS
PAVO
PUPPIS
VOLANS
CHAMAELEON
PYXIS
VELA
MUSCA
APUS
ARA
CIRCINUS
TRIANGULUM AUSTRALE
Acrux
Mimosa
CRUX
Hadar
Rigil Kent
NORMA
ANTLIA
LUPUS
CENTAURUS
HYDRA
LIBRA
CORVUS
Spica
210°
ECLIPTIC
220°
200°
VIRGO

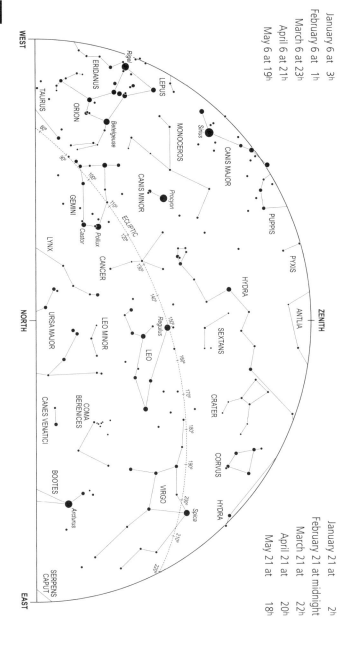

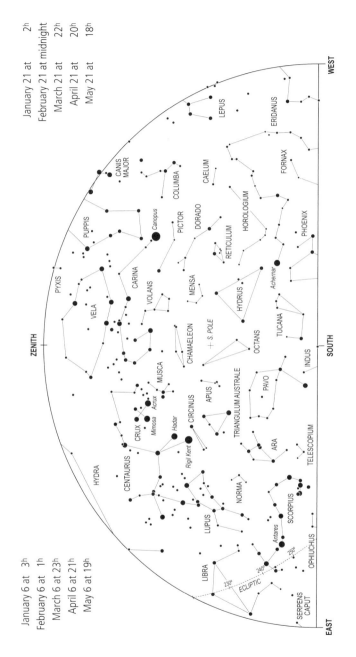

3S

WEST

SOUTH

EAST

ZENITH

January 6 at 3ʰ
February 6 at 1ʰ
March 6 at 23ʰ
April 6 at 21ʰ
May 6 at 19ʰ

LEPUS
ERIDANUS
CANIS MAJOR
COLUMBA
CAELUM
FORNAX
PUPPIS
Canopus
PICTOR
DORADO
RETICULUM
HOROLOGIUM
PHOENIX
PYXIS
CARINA
MENSA
Achernar
VELA
VOLANS
HYDRUS
TUCANA
CHAMAELEON
+ S. POLE
OCTANS
INDUS
MUSCA
Acrux
APUS
TRIANGULUM AUSTRALE
PAVO
CRUX
Mimosa
Hadar
CIRCINUS
ARA
Rigil Kent
TELESCOPIUM
CENTAURUS
HYDRA
NORMA
SCORPIUS
LUPUS
Antares
LIBRA
OPHIUCHUS
230°
240°
250°
ECLIPTIC
SERPENS CAPUT

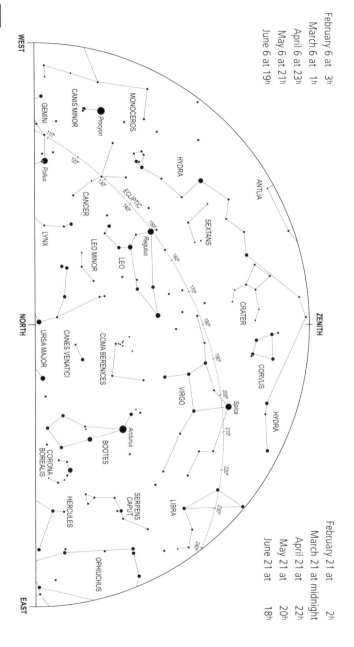

4N

4S

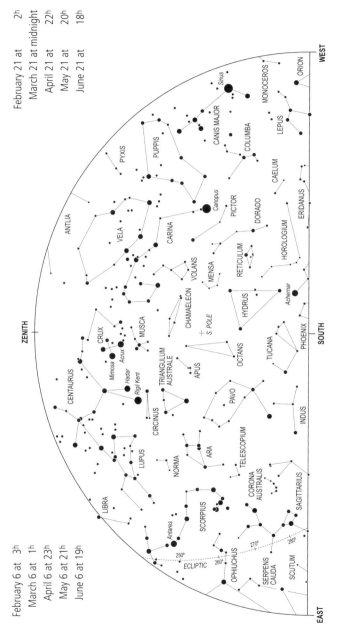

February 21 at   2ʰ
March 21 at midnight
April 21 at   22ʰ
May 21 at   20ʰ
June 21 at   18ʰ

WEST

ZENITH

SOUTH

EAST

ORION
MONOCEROS
Sirius
CANIS MAJOR
COLUMBA
LEPUS
PYXIS
PUPPIS
CAELUM
ERIDANUS
ANTLIA
Canopus
CARINA
PICTOR
DORADO
HOROLOGIUM
VELA
VOLANS
MENSA
RETICULUM
Achernar
CHAMAELEON
HYDRUS
CRUX
MUSCA
S. POLE
PHOENIX
Mimosa
Acrux
Hadar
OCTANS
TUCANA
CENTAURUS
Rigil Kent
TRIANGULUM
AUSTRALE
APUS
PAVO
INDUS
CIRCINUS
LUPUS
NORMA
ARA
TELESCOPIUM
LIBRA
SCORPIUS
CORONA
AUSTRALIS
SAGITTARIUS
Antares
250°
260°
270°
280°
ECLIPTIC
OPHIUCHUS
SERPENS
CAUDA
SCUTUM

February 6 at   3ʰ
March 6 at   1ʰ
April 6 at   23ʰ
May 6 at   21ʰ
June 6 at   19ʰ

5N

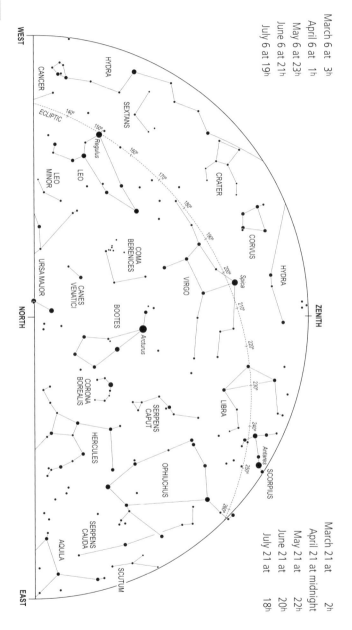

WEST

March 6 at 3h
April 6 at 1h
May 6 at 23h
June 6 at 21h
July 6 at 19h

HYDRA

CANCER

SEXTANS

ECLIPTIC 140°

150° Regulus

160°

170°

LEO MINOR

LEO

180°

COMA BERENICES

190°

CRATER

CORVUS

200° Spica

HYDRA

URSA MAJOR

CANES VENATICI

VIRGO

210°

ZENITH

NORTH

BOOTES

220°

Arcturus

230°

CORONA BOREALIS

SERPENS CAPUT

LIBRA

240° Antares

HERCULES

OPHIUCHUS

250° SCORPIUS

260°

AQUILA

SERPENS CAUDA

SCUTUM

EAST

March 21 at 2h
April 21 at midnight
May 21 at 22h
June 21 at 20h
July 21 at 18h

42

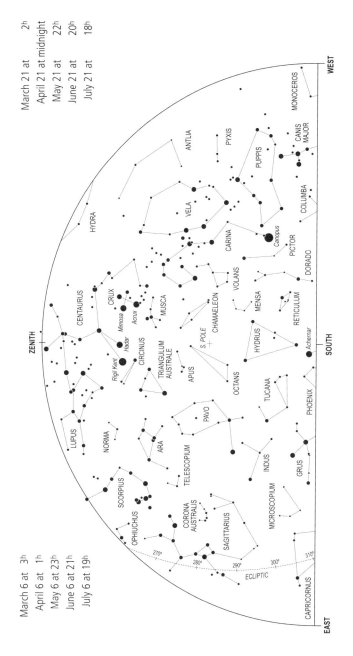

5S

March 21 at 2ʰ
April 21 at midnight
May 21 at 22ʰ
June 21 at 20ʰ
July 21 at 18ʰ

March 6 at 3ʰ
April 6 at 1ʰ
May 6 at 23ʰ
June 6 at 21ʰ
July 6 at 19ʰ

WEST

MONOCEROS
CANIS MAJOR
PUPPIS
ANTLIA
PYXIS
COLUMBA
HYDRA
VELA
CARINA
Canopus
PICTOR
DORADO
CENTAURUS
CRUX
Mimosa
Acrux
MUSCA
VOLANS
MENSA
RETICULUM
S. POLE
CHAMAELEON
Rigil Kent
Hadar
CIRCINUS
TRIANGULUM AUSTRALE
APUS
HYDRUS
Achernar
OCTANS
ZENITH
SOUTH
LUPUS
NORMA
ARA
TELESCOPIUM
PAVO
TUCANA
PHOENIX
SCORPIUS
OPHIUCHUS
CORONA AUSTRALIS
SAGITTARIUS
INDUS
GRUS
MICROSCOPIUM
270°
280°
290°
300°
310°
ECLIPTIC
CAPRICORNUS
EAST

6N

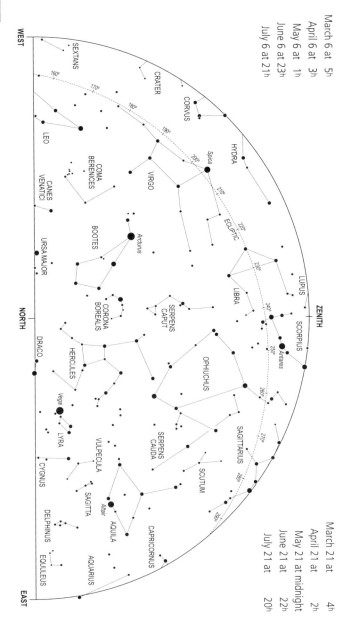

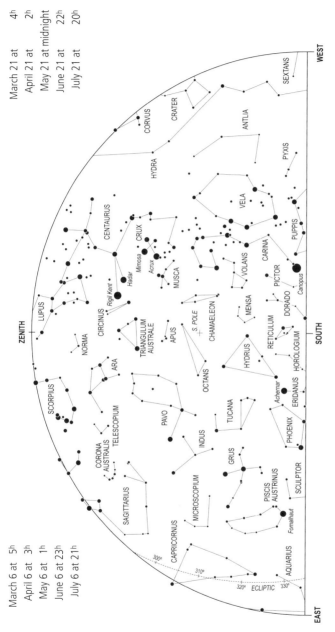

March 21 at 4h
April 21 at 2h
May 21 at midnight
June 21 at 22h
July 21 at 20h

March 6 at 5h
April 6 at 3h
May 6 at 1h
June 6 at 23h
July 6 at 21h

WEST

SEXTANS
CORVUS
CRATER
ANTLIA
HYDRA
PYXIS
CENTAURUS
VELA
PUPPIS
CRUX
Mimosa
Acrux
MUSCA
CARINA
PICTOR
VOLANS
Canopus
Rigil Kent
Hadar
DORADO
ZENITH
LUPUS
CIRCINUS
TRIANGULUM AUSTRALE
APUS
S. POLE
CHAMAELEON
MENSA
RETICULUM
HOROLOGIUM
NORMA
ARA
OCTANS
HYDRUS
Achernar
ERIDANUS
SOUTH
SCORPIUS
TELESCOPIUM
PAVO
TUCANA
PHOENIX
CORONA AUSTRALIS
INDUS
GRUS
SAGITTARIUS
MICROSCOPIUM
PISCIS AUSTRINUS
SCULPTOR
Fomalhaut
CAPRICORNUS
AQUARIUS
300°
310°
320°
ECLIPTIC
330°

EAST

6S

45

7N

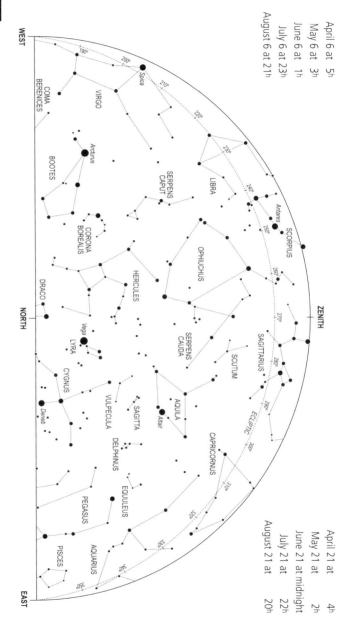

WEST

April 6 at 5h
May 6 at 3h
June 6 at 1h
July 6 at 23h
August 6 at 21h

COMA BERENICES
VIRGO
Spica
190°
200°
210°
220°
230°
BOOTES
Arcturus
SERPENS CAPUT
LIBRA
240°
CORONA BOREALIS
Antares
250°
SCORPIUS
DRACO
HERCULES
OPHIUCHUS
260°
NORTH
Vega
SERPENS CAUDA
270°
ZENITH
LYRA
SCUTUM
SAGITTARIUS
280°
CYGNUS
AQUILA
Altair
290°
Deneb
VULPECULA
SAGITTA
EQUULEUS
CAPRICORNUS
ECLIPTIC
300°
DELPHINUS
310°
PEGASUS
320°
AQUARIUS
330°
PISCES
340°
350°
EAST

April 21 at 4h
May 21 at 2h
June 21 at midnight
July 21 at 22h
August 21 at 20h

Southern Star Charts

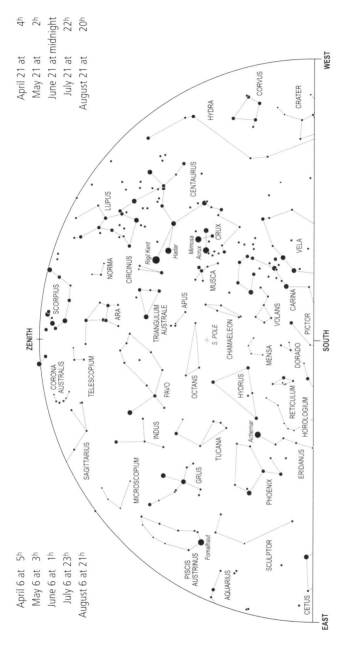

April 21 at   4ʰ
May 21 at   2ʰ
June 21 at midnight
July 21 at   22ʰ
August 21 at   20ʰ

WEST

CORVUS
CRATER
HYDRA
CENTAURUS
LUPUS
CRUX
Mimosa
Acrux
Hadar
Rigil Kent
NORMA
CIRCINUS
MUSCA
VELA
SCORPIUS
ARA
APUS
TRIANGULUM
AUSTRALE
CARINA
VOLANS
PICTOR
CHAMAELEON
S. POLE
ZENITH
CORONA
AUSTRALIS
TELESCOPIUM
PAVO
OCTANS
HYDRUS
MENSA
DORADO
SOUTH
RETICULUM
INDUS
HOROLOGIUM
SAGITTARIUS
TUCANA
Achernar
MICROSCOPIUM
GRUS
PHOENIX
ERIDANUS
Fomalhaut
PISCIS
AUSTRINUS
SCULPTOR
AQUARIUS
CETUS

EAST

April 6 at   5ʰ
May 6 at   3ʰ
June 6 at   1ʰ
July 6 at   23ʰ
August 6 at   21ʰ

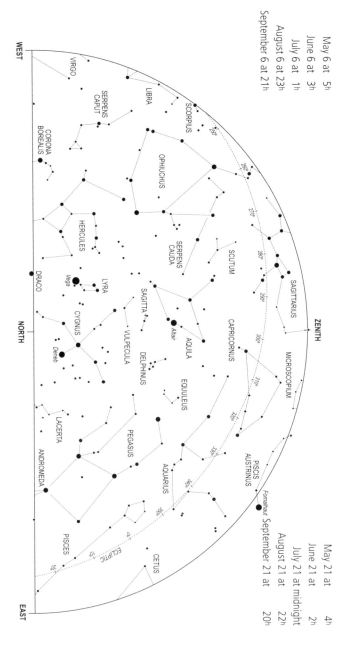

8N

Southern Star Charts

8S

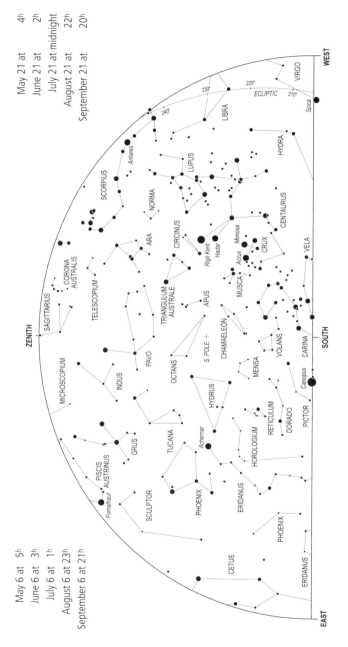

May 21 at 4ʰ
June 21 at 2ʰ
July 21 at midnight
August 21 at 22ʰ
September 21 at 20ʰ

May 6 at 5ʰ
June 6 at 3ʰ
July 6 at 1ʰ
August 6 at 23ʰ
September 6 at 21ʰ

49

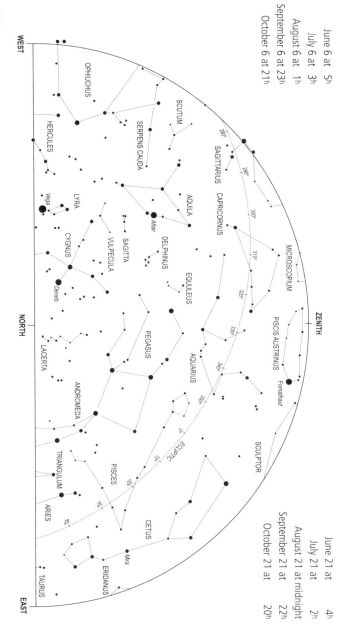

9N

June 6 at 5h
July 6 at 3h
August 6 at 1h
September 6 at 23h
October 6 at 21h

June 21 at 4h
July 21 at 2h
August 21 at midnight
September 21 at 22h
October 21 at 20h

WEST
NORTH
EAST
ZENITH

OPHIUCHUS
HERCULES
SCUTUM
SERPENS CAUDA
SAGITTARIUS
AQUILA
CAPRICORNUS
MICROSCOPIUM
LYRA
Vega
CYGNUS
Deneb
VULPECULA
SAGITTA
DELPHINUS
Altair
EQUULEUS
PISCIS AUSTRINUS
Fomalhaut
LACERTA
PEGASUS
AQUARIUS
SCULPTOR
ANDROMEDA
TRIANGULUM
PISCES
ARIES
CETUS
Mira
TAURUS
ERIDANUS
ECLIPTIC

9S

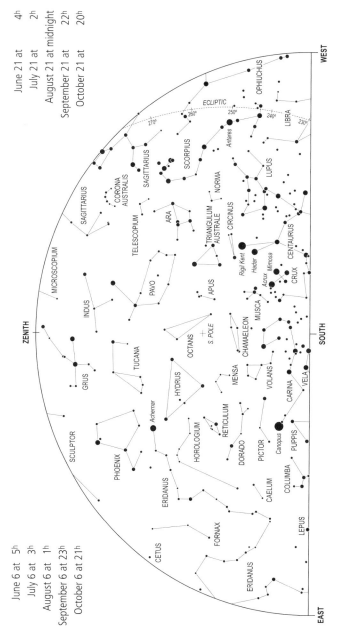

June 21 at 4ʰ
July 21 at 2ʰ
August 21 at midnight
September 21 at 22ʰ
October 21 at 20ʰ

June 6 at 5ʰ
July 6 at 3ʰ
August 6 at 1ʰ
September 6 at 23ʰ
October 6 at 21ʰ

WEST

OPHIUCHUS

ECLIPTIC

270° 260° 250° 240° 230°

LIBRA

Antares

SCORPIUS

SAGITTARIUS

LUPUS

CORONA
AUSTRALIS

NORMA

CENTAURUS

SAGITTARIUS

ARA

TRIANGULUM
AUSTRALE

CIRCINUS

TELESCOPIUM

Rigil Kent

Hadar

Mimosa

MICROSCOPIUM

PAVO

APUS

Acrux

CRUX

MUSCA

INDUS

OCTANS

CHAMAELEON

ZENITH

S. POLE

TUCANA

MENSA

VOLANS

VELA

GRUS

HYDRUS

CARINA

SOUTH

Achernar

RETICULUM

PICTOR

Canopus

PUPPIS

SCULPTOR

PHOENIX

HOROLOGIUM

DORADO

COLUMBA

ERIDANUS

CAELUM

LEPUS

CETUS

FORNAX

ERIDANUS

EAST

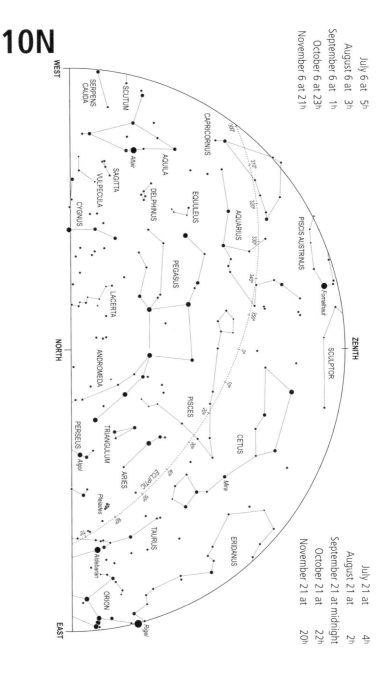

10S

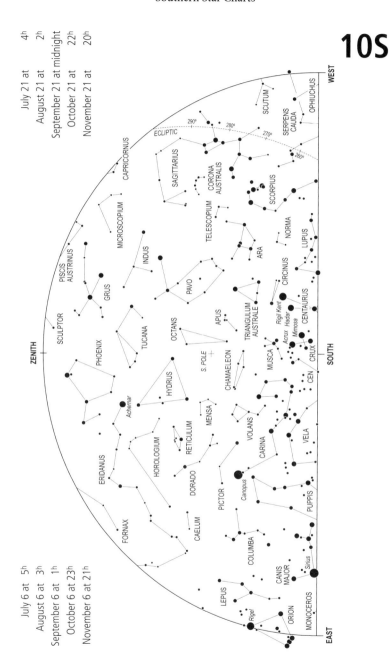

11N

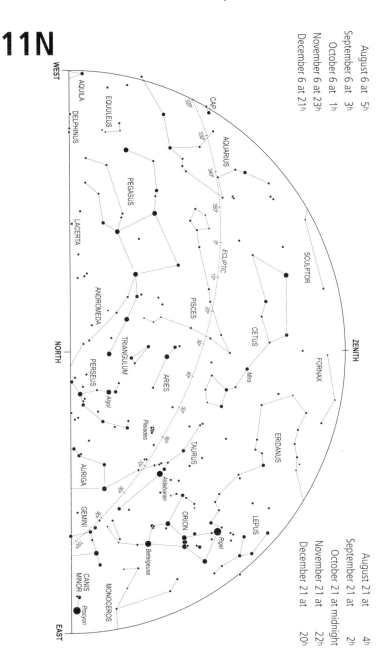

Southern Star Charts

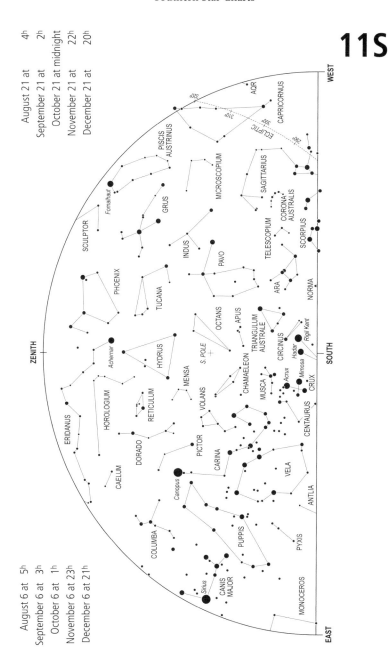

August 21 at 4h
September 21 at 2h
October 21 at midnight
November 21 at 22h
December 21 at 20h

August 6 at 5h
September 6 at 3h
October 6 at 1h
November 6 at 23h
December 6 at 21h

WEST

ZENITH

SOUTH

EAST

AQR
CAPRICORNUS
ECLIPTIC
320°
310°
300°
28°
PISCIS AUSTRINUS
SAGITTARIUS
Fomalhaut
MICROSCOPIUM
CORONA AUSTRALIS
GRUS
SCORPIUS
SCULPTOR
INDUS
TELESCOPIUM
PAVO
NORMA
PHOENIX
ARA
TUCANA
OCTANS
APUS
Achernar
HYDRUS
S. POLE
TRIANGULUM AUSTRALE
CIRCINUS
Rigil Kent
ERIDANUS
HOROLOGIUM
MENSA
CHAMAELEON
Hadar
HYDRUS
RETICULUM
VOLANS
MUSCA
Acrux
Mimosa
CENTAURUS
DORADO
PICTOR
CRUX
CAELUM
CARINA
VELA
COLUMBA
PUPPIS
ANTLIA
Canopus
PYXIS
Sirius
CANIS MAJOR
MONOCEROS

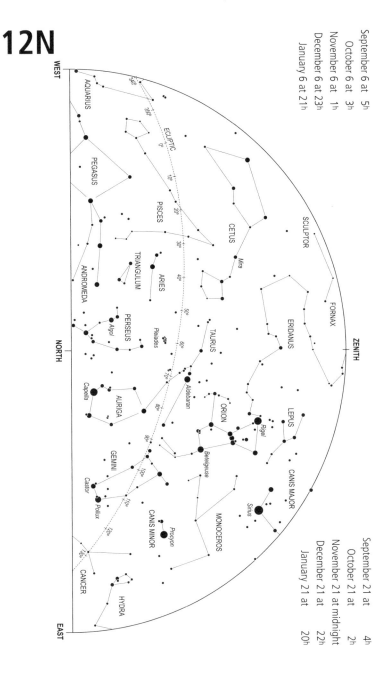

12N

September 6 at 5h
October 6 at 3h
November 6 at 1h
December 6 at 23h
January 6 at 21h

September 21 at 4h
October 21 at 2h
November 21 at midnight
December 21 at 22h
January 21 at 20h

WEST

AQUARIUS

PEGASUS

ANDROMEDA

TRIANGULUM

PISCES

ARIES

PERSEUS

Algol

Pleiades

TAURUS

AURIGA

Capella

GEMINI

Castor

Pollux

CANCER

HYDRA

CANIS MINOR

Procyon

MONOCEROS

Sirius

CANIS MAJOR

Betelgeuse

ORION

Rigel

LEPUS

Aldebaran

ERIDANUS

FORNAX

SCULPTOR

CETUS

Mira

ECLIPTIC

ZENITH

NORTH

EAST

Southern Star Charts

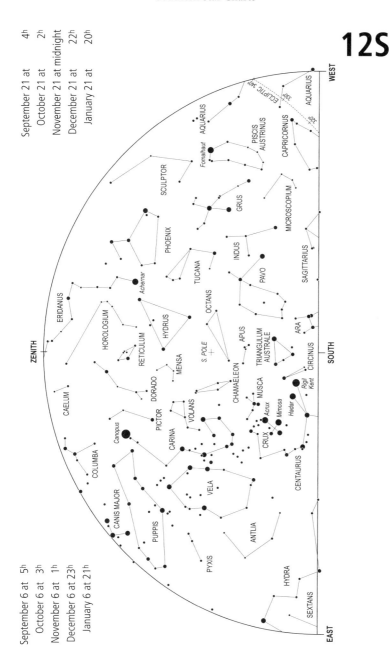

September 21 at 4h
October 21 at 2h
November 21 at midnight
December 21 at 22h
January 21 at 20h

September 6 at 5h
October 6 at 3h
November 6 at 1h
December 6 at 23h
January 6 at 21h

WEST

ZENITH

SOUTH

EAST

AQUARIUS
PISCIS AUSTRINUS
CAPRICORNUS
AQUARIUS
ECLIPTIC 340°
330°
320°
Fomalhaut
SCULPTOR
GRUS
MICROSCOPIUM
PHOENIX
INDUS
SAGITTARIUS
ERIDANUS
Achernar
TUCANA
PAVO
HOROLOGIUM
HYDRUS
OCTANS
RETICULUM
MENSA
S. POLE
APUS
ARA
DORADO
CHAMAELEON
TRIANGULUM AUSTRALE
CIRCINUS
CAELUM
Rigil Kent
Canopus
PICTOR
VOLANS
MUSCA
Acrux
Mimosa
Hadar
PUPPIS
CARINA
CRUX
COLUMBA
VELA
CENTAURUS
CANIS MAJOR
ANTLIA
PYXIS
HYDRA
SEXTANS

The Planets and the Ecliptic

The paths of the planets about the Sun all lie close to the plane of the ecliptic, which is marked for us in the sky by the apparent path of the Sun among the stars, and is shown on the star charts by a broken line. The Moon and naked-eye planets will always be found close to this line, never departing from it by more than about 7°. Thus the planets are most favourably placed for observation when the ecliptic is well displayed, and this means that it should be as high in the sky as possible. This avoids the difficulty of finding a clear horizon, and also overcomes the problem of atmospheric absorption, which greatly reduces the light of the stars. Thus a star at an altitude of 10° suffers a loss of 60 per cent of its light, which corresponds to a whole magnitude; at an altitude of only 4°, the loss may amount to two magnitudes.

The position of the ecliptic in the sky is therefore of great importance, and since it is tilted at about 23.5° to the Equator, it is only at certain times of the day or year that it is displayed to the best advantage. It will be realized that the Sun (and therefore the ecliptic) is at its highest in the sky at noon in midsummer, and at its lowest at noon in midwinter. Allowing for the daily motion of the sky, it follows that the ecliptic is highest at midnight in the winter, at sunset in the spring, at noon in the summer and at sunrise in the autumn. Hence these are the best times to see the planets. Thus, if Venus is an evening object in the western sky after sunset, it will be seen to best advantage if this occurs in the spring, when the ecliptic is high in the sky and slopes down steeply to the horizon. This means that the planet is not only higher in the sky, but also will remain for a much longer period above the horizon. For similar reasons, a morning object will be seen at its best on autumn mornings before sunrise, when the ecliptic is high in the east. The outer planets, which can come to opposition (i.e. opposite the Sun), are best seen when opposition occurs in the winter months, when the ecliptic is high in the sky at midnight.

The seasons are reversed in the Southern Hemisphere, spring beginning at the September equinox, when the Sun crosses the Equator on its way south, summer beginning at the December Solstice, when the Sun is highest in the southern sky, and so on. Thus, the times when the ecliptic is highest in the sky, and therefore best placed for observing the planets, may be summarized as follows:

	Midnight	Sunrise	Noon	Sunset
Northern latitudes	December	September	June	March
Southern latitudes	June	March	December	September

In addition to the daily rotation of the celestial sphere from east to west, the planets have a motion of their own among the stars. The apparent movement is generally *direct*, i.e. to the east, in the direction of increasing longitude, but for a certain period (which depends on the distance of the planet) this apparent motion is reversed. With the outer planets this *retrograde* motion occurs about the time of opposition. Owing to the different inclination of the orbits of these planets, the actual effect is to cause the apparent path to form a loop, or sometimes an S-shaped curve. The same effect is present in the motion of the inferior planets, Mercury and Venus, but it is not so obvious, since it always occurs at the time of inferior conjunction.

The *inferior planets*, Mercury and Venus, move in smaller orbits than that of the Earth, and so are always seen near the Sun. They are most obvious at the times of greatest angular distance from the Sun (greatest elongation), which may reach 28° for Mercury, and 47° for Venus. They are seen as evening objects in the western sky after sunset (at eastern elongations) or as morning objects in the eastern sky before sunrise (at western elongations). The succession of phenomena, conjunctions and elongations, always follows the same order, but the intervals between them are not equal. Thus, if either planet is moving round the far side of its orbit its motion will be to the east, in the same direction in which the Sun appears to be moving. It therefore takes much longer for the planet to overtake the Sun – that is, to come to superior conjunction – than it does when moving round to inferior conjunction, between Sun and Earth. The intervals given in the table at the top of p. 60 are average values; they remain fairly constant in the case of Venus, which travels in an almost circular orbit. In the case of Mercury, however, conditions vary widely because of the great eccentricity and inclination of the planet's orbit.

		Mercury	Venus
Inferior Conjunction	to Elongation West	22 days	72 days
Elongation West	to Superior Conjunction	36 days	220 days
Superior Conjunction	to Elongation East	35 days	220 days
Elongation East	to Inferior Conjunction	22 days	72 days

The greatest brilliancy of Venus always occurs about thirty-six days before or after inferior conjunction. This will be about a month after greatest eastern elongation (as an evening object), or a month before greatest western elongation (as a morning object). No such rule can be given for Mercury, because its distances from the Earth and the Sun can vary over a wide range.

Mercury is not likely to be seen unless a clear horizon is available. It is seldom as much as 10° above the horizon in the twilight sky in northern temperate latitudes, but this figure is often exceeded in the Southern Hemisphere. This favourable condition arises because the maximum elongation of 28° can occur only when the planet is at aphelion (furthest from the Sun), and it then lies well south of the Equator. Northern observers must be content with smaller elongations, which may be as little as 18° at perihelion. In general, it may be said that the most favourable times for seeing Mercury as an evening object will be in spring, some days before greatest eastern elongation; in autumn, it may be seen as a morning object some days after greatest western elongation.

Venus is the brightest of the planets and may be seen on occasions in broad daylight. Like Mercury, it is alternately a morning and an evening object, and it will be highest in the sky when it is a morning object in autumn, or an evening object in spring. Venus is to be seen at its best as an evening object in northern latitudes when eastern elongation occurs in June. The planet is then well north of the Sun in the preceding spring months, and is a brilliant object in the evening sky over a long period. In the Southern Hemisphere a November elongation is best. For similar reasons, Venus gives a prolonged display as a morning object in the months following western elongation in October (in northern latitudes) or in June (in the Southern Hemisphere).

The *superior planets*, which travel in orbits larger than that of the Earth, differ from Mercury and Venus in that they can be seen opposite the Sun in the sky. The superior planets are morning objects after conjunction with the Sun, rising earlier each day until they come to opposition. They will then be nearest to the Earth (and therefore at their brightest), and will be on the meridian at midnight, due south in northern latitudes, but due north in the Southern Hemisphere. After opposition they are evening objects, setting earlier each evening until they set in the west with the Sun at the next conjunction. The difference in brightness from one opposition to another is most noticeable in the case of Mars, whose distance from Earth can vary considerably and rapidly. The other superior planets are at such great distances that there is very little change in brightness from one opposition to the next. The effect of altitude is, however, of some importance, for at a December opposition in northern latitudes the planets will be among the stars of Taurus or Gemini, and can then be at an altitude of more than 60° in southern England. At a summer opposition, when a planet is in Sagittarius, it may only rise to about 15° above the southern horizon, and so makes a less impressive appearance. In the Southern Hemisphere the reverse conditions apply, a June opposition being the best, with the planet in Sagittarius at an altitude which can reach 80° above the northern horizon for observers in South Africa.

Mars, whose orbit is appreciably eccentric, comes nearest to the Earth at oppositions at the end of August. It may then be brighter even than Jupiter, but rather low in the sky in Aquarius for northern observers, though very well placed for those in southern latitudes. These favourable oppositions occur every fifteen or seventeen years (e.g. in 1988, 2003 and 2018). In the Northern Hemisphere the planet is probably better seen at oppositions in the autumn or winter months, when it is higher in the sky – such as in 2005 when opposition was in early November. Oppositions of Mars occur at an average interval of 780 days, and during this time the planet makes a complete circuit of the sky.

Jupiter is always a bright planet, and comes to opposition a month later each year, having moved, roughly speaking, from one Zodiacal constellation to the next.

Saturn moves much more slowly than Jupiter, and may remain in the same constellation for several years. The brightness of Saturn depends on the aspects of its rings, as well as on the distance from Earth and Sun. The Earth passed through the plane of Saturn's rings in 1995 and 1996, when they appeared edge-on; we saw them at maximum opening, and Saturn at its brightest, in 2002. The rings last appeared edge-on in 2009, and they are now opening nicely once again.

Uranus and *Neptune* are both visible with binoculars or a small telescope, but you will need a finder chart to help you to locate them (such as those reproduced in this *Yearbook* on pages 132 and 120). *Pluto* (now officially classified as a 'dwarf planet') is hardly likely to attract the attention of observers without adequate telescopes.

Phases of the Moon in 2014

NICK JAMES

New Moon				First Quarter				Full Moon				Last Quarter			
	d	h	m		d	h	m		d	h	m		d	h	m
Jan	1	11	14	Jan	8	03	39	Jan	16	04	52	Jan	24	05	19
Jan	30	21	39	Feb	6	19	22	Feb	14	23	53	Feb	22	17	15
Mar	1	08	00	Mar	8	13	27	Mar	16	17	08	Mar	24	01	46
Mar	30	18	45	Apr	7	08	31	Apr	15	07	42	Apr	22	07	52
Apr	29	06	14	May	7	03	15	May	14	19	16	May	21	12	59
May	28	18	40	June	5	20	39	June	13	04	12	June	19	18	39
June	27	08	09	July	5	11	59	July	12	11	25	July	19	02	08
July	26	22	42	Aug	4	00	50	Aug	10	18	09	Aug	17	12	26
Aug	25	14	13	Sept	2	11	11	Sept	9	01	38	Sept	16	02	05
Sept	24	06	14	Oct	1	19	33	Oct	8	10	51	Oct	15	19	12
Oct	23	21	57	Oct	31	02	48	Nov	6	22	23	Nov	14	15	16
Nov	22	12	32	Nov	29	10	06	Dec	6	12	27	Dec	14	12	51
Dec	22	01	36	Dec	28	18	31	Jan	5	04	53				

All times are UTC (GMT)

Longitudes of the Sun, Moon and Planets in 2014

NICK JAMES

Date		Sun	Moon	Venus	Mars	Jupiter	Saturn	Uranus	Neptune
		°	°	°	°	°	°	°	°
Jan	6	286	349	294	194	105	231	9	333
	21	301	173	286	200	103	232	9	334
Feb	6	317	38	284	204	102	233	10	334
	21	332	221	290	207	101	233	10	335
Mar	6	345	46	300	207	100	233	11	335
	21	0	231	314	205	101	233	12	336
Apr	6	16	91	330	200	102	232	13	337
	21	31	283	346	194	104	231	14	337
May	6	45	123	3	190	106	230	14	337
	21	60	323	21	189	108	229	15	337
June	6	75	167	39	191	111	228	16	338
	21	90	15	57	195	114	227	16	338
July	6	104	200	75	200	118	227	16	337
	21	118	51	93	207	121	227	17	337
Aug	6	133	248	112	216	125	227	16	337
	21	148	98	131	225	128	227	16	336
Sept	6	163	300	150	235	131	228	16	336
	21	178	142	169	245	134	230	15	336
Oct	6	193	339	188	255	137	231	15	335
	21	208	174	206	266	139	233	14	335
Nov	6	223	31	226	278	141	234	13	335
	21	239	220	245	289	142	236	13	335
Dec	6	254	67	264	301	143	238	13	335
	21	269	255	283	312	142	240	13	335

Moon: Longitude of the ascending node: Jan 1: 214°   Dec 31: 195°

Mercury moves so quickly among the stars that it is not possible to indicate its position on the star charts at convenient intervals. The monthly notes should be consulted for the best times at which the planet may be seen.

The positions of the Sun, Moon and planets other than Mercury are given in the table on p. 64. These objects move along paths which remain close to the ecliptic and this list shows the apparent ecliptic longitude for each object on dates which correspond to those of the star charts. This information can be used to plot the position of the desired object on the selected chart.

EXAMPLES

Two planets are visible in the south around midnight in mid-April. What are they?

The northern star chart 5S shows the southern sky on 21 April at midnight. The ecliptic longitude visible to the south ranges from 190° to 240°. With reference to the table on p. 64 it can be seen that two planets are in this range on 21 April: Mars is at longitude 194° and Saturn is at 231°. Therefore the two planets are Mars in Virgo (near the bright star Spica) and Saturn in Libra.

The positions of the Sun and Moon can be plotted on the star maps in the same way as the planets. This is straightforward for the Sun since it always lies on the ecliptic and it moves on average at only 1° per day. The Moon is more difficult since it moves rapidly at an average of 13° per day and it moves up to 5° north or south of the ecliptic during the month. A rough indication of the Moon's position relative to the ecliptic may be obtained by considering its longitude relative to that of the ascending node. The longitude of the ascending node decreases by around 1.7° per month, as will be seen from the values for the first and last day of the year given on p. 64. If d is the difference in longitude between the Moon and its ascending node, then the Moon is on the ecliptic when d = 0°, 180° or 360°. The Moon is 5° north of the ecliptic if d = 90°, and the Moon is 5° south of the ecliptic if d = 270°.

As an example, from the table on p. 63, it can be seen that the Moon is full on the evening of 14 February. The table on p. 64 shows that the Moon's longitude is 38° at 0h on 6 February. Extrapolating 9 days at 13° per day, the Moon's longitude at 24h on 14 February is around 155°. At this time the longitude of the ascending node is found by interpolation to be around 211°. (Now 211° – 155° = 56° and 360° – 56° = 304°.) Thus d = 304° and the Moon is south of the ecliptic moving north. Its position may be plotted on northern star chart 3S, where it is found to be in Leo, just south of the bright star Regulus.

Some Events in 2014

Jan	1	New Moon
	1	Moon at Perigee (closest to the Earth) (356,920 km)
	3	*Mars* at Aphelion (furthest from the Sun)
	4	*Earth* at Perihelion (closest to the Sun)
	5	*Jupiter* at Opposition in Gemini
	11	*Venus* in Inferior Conjunction
	16	Full Moon
	16	Moon at Apogee (furthest from the Earth) (406,535 km)
	30	New Moon
	30	Moon at Perigee (357,080 km)
	31	*Mercury* at Greatest Eastern Elongation (18°)
Feb	12	Moon at Apogee (406,230 km)
	14	Full Moon
	15	*Mercury* in Inferior Conjunction
	15	*Venus* attains greatest brilliancy (mag. –4.7)
	23	*Neptune* in Conjunction with Sun
	27	Moon at Perigee (360,440 km)
Mar	1	New Moon
	11	Moon at Apogee (405,365 km)
	14	*Mercury* at Greatest Western Elongation (28°)
	16	Full Moon
	20	Equinox (Spring Equinox in Northern Hemisphere)
	22	*Venus* at Greatest Western Elongation (47°)
	27	Moon at Perigee (365,705 km)
	30	New Moon
	30	Summer Time Begins in the UK
Apr	2	*Uranus* in Conjunction with Sun
	8	Moon at Apogee (404,500 km)
	8	*Mars* at Opposition in Virgo
	15	Full Moon
	15	Total Eclipse of the Moon

	23	Moon at Perigee (369,765 km)
	26	*Mercury* in Superior Conjunction
	29	New Moon
	29	Annular Eclipse of the Sun
May	6	Moon at Apogee (404,320 km)
	10	*Saturn* at Opposition in Libra
	14	Full Moon
	18	Moon at Perigee (367,100 km)
	25	*Mercury* at Greatest Eastern Elongation (23°)
	28	New Moon
June	3	Moon at Apogee (404,955 km)
	13	Full Moon
	15	Moon at Perigee (362,060 km)
	19	*Mercury* in Inferior Conjunction
	21	Solstice (Summer Solstice in Northern Hemisphere)
	27	New Moon
	30	Moon at Apogee (405,930 km)
July	4	*Pluto* at Opposition in Sagittarius
	4	*Earth* at Aphelion
	12	Full Moon
	12	*Mercury* at Greatest Western Elongation (21°)
	13	Moon at Perigee (358,260 km)
	24	*Jupiter* in Conjunction with Sun
	26	New Moon
	28	Moon at Apogee (406,570 km)
Aug	8	*Mercury* in Superior Conjunction
	10	Full Moon
	10	Moon at Perigee (356,895 km)
	24	Moon at Apogee (406,520 km)
	25	New Moon
	29	*Neptune* at Opposition in Aquarius
Sept	8	Moon at Perigee (358,385 km)
	9	Full Moon
	20	Moon at Apogee (405,845 km)

	21	*Mercury* at Greatest Eastern Elongation (26°)
	23	Equinox (Autumnal Equinox in Northern Hemisphere)
	24	New Moon
Oct	6	Moon at Perigee (362,480 km)
	7	*Uranus* at Opposition in Pisces
	8	Full Moon
	8	Total Eclipse of the Moon
	16	*Mercury* in Inferior Conjunction
	18	Moon at Apogee (404,895 km)
	23	New Moon
	23	Partial Eclipse of the Sun
	25	*Venus* in Superior Conjunction
	26	Summer Time Ends in the UK
Nov	1	*Mercury* at Greatest Western Elongation (19°)
	3	Moon at Perigee (367,870 km)
	6	Full Moon
	15	Moon at Apogee (404,335 km)
	18	*Saturn* in Conjunction with Sun
	22	New Moon
	27	Moon at Perigee (369,825 km)
Dec	6	Full Moon
	8	*Mercury* in Superior Conjunction
	12	Moon at Apogee (404,585 km)
	12	*Mars* at Perihelion
	21	Solstice (Winter Solstice in Northern Hemisphere)
	22	New Moon
	24	Moon at Perigee (364,790 km)

Monthly Notes 2014

January

New Moon: 1 and 31 January   *Full Moon:* 16 January

EARTH is at perihelion (nearest to the Sun) on 4 January at a distance of 147 million kilometres (91.3 million miles).

MERCURY passed through superior conjunction on the far side of the Sun at the end of December last, becoming an evening object in January, and reaching greatest eastern elongation (18°) on 31 January. For the last week of the month it is visible as an evening object to observers in the latitudes of the British Isles, rather low above the south-western horizon at the end of evening civil twilight, i.e., about thirty-five minutes after sunset. Observers near the Equator are best placed since they should be able to detect the planet after about the middle of January in the west-south-western twilight sky. The planet is brightest before elongation, fading from magnitude −1.0 to −0.5 during the second half of January. For observers in southern temperate latitudes, the planet is inconveniently low above the west-south-western horizon at the end of evening civil twilight and they are unlikely to glimpse it until the end of the month.

VENUS, magnitude −4.3, is a brilliant object low in the south-western sky in the early evenings just after sunset at the beginning of January. For observers in the latitudes of the British Isles this apparition will last for about a week, but in more southerly latitudes Venus will only be visible for the first few days of the month. The planet passes rapidly through inferior conjunction on 11 January when it is 5.2° north of the ecliptic and 39.8 million kilometres (24.7 million miles) from the Earth. On the following morning the planet becomes visible again to Northern Hemisphere observers, low in the south-eastern sky shortly before sunrise. For the last ten days of the month it is also visible in the mornings to those in the Southern Hemisphere.

Observers in northern temperate latitudes may be able to detect it telescopically just before and after inferior conjunction. On the evening of the 8th, just after sunset, optical aid should show Venus as an incredibly thin sliver of light (only 0.6 per cent illuminated) with an apparent diameter of 62.5 arc seconds. Again, on the morning of the 12th, just before sunrise, a similar phenomenon will occur with Venus only 0.4 per cent illuminated and with an apparent diameter of 62.6 arc seconds. Since the Earth is not far from perihelion and Venus's orbit is nearly circular, the planet must subtend almost the maximum apparent diameter that is possible.

The Mercury and Venus Section of the British Astronomical Association notes that: 'near inferior conjunction, given good observing conditions, the planet's cusps may be seen to extend beyond a half-circle. The cusps are the north and south parts of the disk – the horns of the crescent phase. Cusp extension is a twilight effect caused by diffused sunlight in the planet's atmosphere. When close to inferior conjunction observers sometimes see Venus completely encircled by this twilight arc.' WARNING – Inferior conjunction is for experienced observers only. Do not attempt these observations unless you use setting circles on the telescope to find Venus, because of the danger of accidentally getting the Sun in the field of view and of irreparably damaging your eyesight. In any event, you MUST exercise the very greatest care.

MARS is an early morning object, moving direct (i.e. towards the east) in Virgo and rising at about midnight. The planet is at aphelion (furthest from the Sun) on 3 January, but it grows rapidly brighter during January (its magnitude increasing from +0.8 to +0.2) as its distance from the Earth decreases from 204.1 million to 158.1 million kilometres (126.8 million to 98.2 million miles). The waning gibbous Moon passes about four degrees south of Mars early on 23 January.

JUPITER is at opposition on 5 January and is visible all night long. The planet is moving retrograde (i.e., towards the west) in Gemini, and is a brilliant object at magnitude −2.7. Figure 1 shows the path of Jupiter against the background stars during 2014. The planet's high northerly declination (+22° 40') makes this opposition the most favourable for observers in northern temperate latitudes since January 2002. At opposition the planet's apparent diameter is 44.8 arc seconds and it is 630 million kilometres (391 million miles) from the Earth. The dark evenings afford plenty of opportunities for observing the movements of

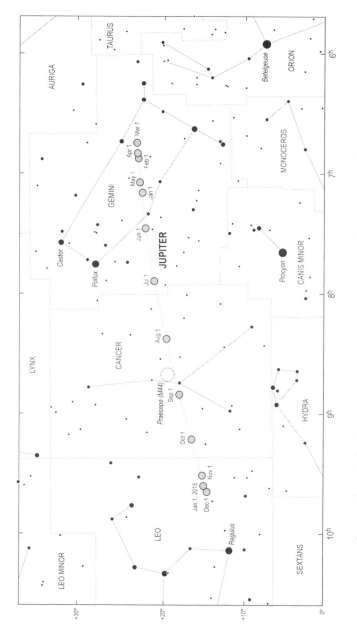

Figure 1. The path of Jupiter as it moves against the background stars of Gemini, Cancer and Leo during 2014.

the four Galilean satellites, Io, Europa, Ganymede and Callisto. The waxing gibbous Moon will make a striking configuration with Jupiter on the night of 14/15 January.

SATURN is an early morning object moving direct among the stars of Libra. By the end of January, it rises at about 02 hours for observers in northern temperate latitudes; a couple of hours earlier for those in the Southern Hemisphere. Its brightness increases very slightly from magnitude +0.6 to +0.5 during the month.

The Quadrantid Meteors and Quadrans Muralis. The first annual meteor shower of the year is active from 1–6 January. The Quadrantids generally reach maximum on the third of the month, and the peak is usually quite sharp with rates of about eighty meteors per hour, but this is under perfectly clear, dark sky conditions with the radiant – that is to say, the point in the sky from which the meteors appear to emanate – directly overhead. This year, with New Moon on 1 January, there will be no interference from moonlight and there is a good chance of seeing a reasonable number of Quadrantids, although peak activity is expected at about 18h on 3 January when the radiant will be rather low in the north from the UK. The best viewing is generally after midnight, when the radiant is higher in the sky, but this will be some hours after the peak this year. Even the faintest meteors should be visible from a dark site – weather permitting, of course.

The radiant of the Quadrantids is actually in the constellation of Boötes, the Herdsman, whose leading star is the brilliant Arcturus. However, this area was once separated out into another constellation, Quadrans Muralis (the Mural Quadrant), created by the German astronomer Johann Elert Bode in 1775 (Figure 2). There was indeed a time when every compiler of a star chart felt bound to introduce new groups of their own. Finally, in the 1930s, the International Astronomical Union – the controlling body of world astronomy – lost patience, and reduced the accepted number of constellations to eighty-eight. (Of these, forty-eight were included in the *Almagest*, the star catalogue compiled by Ptolemy in around AD 150.) Quadrans Muralis was one of the casualties of the IAU decision, but at least it is remembered by the name of the January meteor shower.

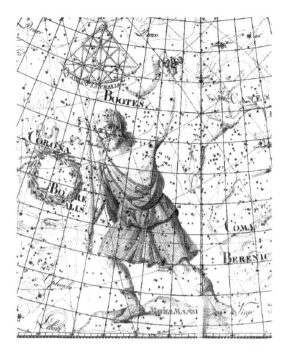

Figure 2. Johann Bode's celestial atlas Uranographica, published in 1801, contained the first accurately scaled star maps showing the positions of the stars overlaid with artistically presented constellations. Here we see the region occupied by Boötes, the Herdsman, with the now discarded pattern of Quadrans Muralis, the Mural Quadrant, top left. (Image courtesy of Wikimedia Commons.)

Among other rejected constellations are:

Original name	Anglicized version of name	Astronomer who named them & when	Modern constellation of which they are now part
Antinous	Antinous	Tycho Brahe, 1559	Aquila
Cerberus	Cerberus	Hevelius, 1687	Hercules
Felix	The Cat	Bode, 1775	Hydra
Globus Aerostaticus	The Air Balloon	Lalande, 1798	Piscis Austrinus
Honores Frederici	The Honours of Frederick	Bode, 1787	Andromeda

Lilium	The Lily	Royer, 1670	Aries
Machina Electrica	The Electrical Machine	Bode, 1787	Fornax
Musca Borealis	The Northern Fly	Hevelius, 1687	Aries
Noctua	The Night Owl	Burritt, 1833	Hydra
Officina Typographica	The Printing Press	Bode, 1787	Puppis
Sceptrum Brandenburgicum	The Sceptre of Brandenburg	Kirch, 1688	Lepus
Solarium	The Sundial	Burritt, 1833	Hydrus
Solitarius	The Solitaire	LeMonnier, 1776	Hydra
Taurus Poniatowski	Poniatowski's Bull	Poczobut, 1777	Ophiuchus
Tarandus	The Reindeer	LeMonnier, 1776	Cepheus
Triangulum Minor	The Little Triangle	Hevelius, 1677	Aries

Most of these small groups are unworthy of separate identity, but perhaps Quadrans may have been retained, and there may be a case for Noctua and Felix – the Owl and the Pussycat!

It is interesting to note that one of the most famous constellations, Crux Australis, the Southern Cross, is not a Ptolemy 'original'; it was created by Royer in 1679, and before that it was included as part of Centaurus. Moreover, Crux is actually the smallest constellation in the sky, covering a mere sixty-eight square degrees.

One 'original', Argo Navis – the ship Argo – was so large and unwieldy that it was split up into Carina (the keel), Vela (the sails) and Puppis (the poop deck). Thus Canopus, which had been Alpha Argus, became Alpha Carinae. The largest current constellation is Hydra, which covers 1,303 square degrees.

One southern constellation, Mensa, the Table – originally Mons Mensae, the Table Mountain – has no star above the fifth magnitude, although part of the Large Cloud of Magellan extends into it from neighbouring Dorado, the Swordfish. Mons Mensae was created by Lacaille in his maps of 1752.

The Tart-Like Moon. This month's full Moon on the 16th will be in Cancer, the Crab, south of the Twins of Gemini, Castor and Pollux, and more or less in line with them. It will appear high in the sky at midnight from the latitudes of the British Isles. It is often supposed that Galileo Galilei was the first man to look at the Moon through a telescope. This is not so. It was, in fact, an Englishman, Thomas Harriot, close friend of the luckless Sir Walter Raleigh and the equally luckless Earl of Northumberland, who was making telescopic lunar observations in July 1609, several months before Galileo; and, frankly, his map of the Moon is better than anything achieved by Galileo (see the feature article by Allan Chapman elsewhere in this yearbook). One of Harriot's ardent disciples was a Welshman, Sir William Lower, who corresponded extensively with him and was probably the second Englishman to observe the Moon. Apparently he received a 'cylinder' (telescope) from Harriot, and on 6 February 1610 wrote to him:

> I have received the perspective cylinder that you promised me and am sorrie that my man gave you not more warning … Accordingly as you wished, I have observed the moone in all his changes. In the new, I discover manifestlie the earthshine, a little before the dichotomie, that spot which represents unto me the man in the moone (but without a head) is first to be seene. A little after, neare the brimme of the gibbous parts, towards the upper corner appeare luminous parts like starres, much brighter than the rest; and the whole brimme along looke like unto the description of coasts in the Dutch bookes of voyages. In the full, she appeares like a tarte that my cooke made me the last weeke. Here a vaine of bright stuffe, and there of darke, and so confusedlie all over. I must confesse I can see none of this without my cylinder.

And in a letter dated 21 June 1610:

> In the moone I had formerlie observed a strange spottedness all over, but had no conceite that anie parte thereof might be shadowes; since I have observed three degrees in the darke partes, of which the lighter sorte hath some resemblance to shadinesse but that they grow shorter or longer I cannot yet perceive.

This is hardly scientific, and Lower himself is rather a shadowy figure. He was born at St Winnow in Cornwall in 1570, and entered Exeter College, Oxford, matriculating in 1586. He was admitted to the Middle Temple on 6 August 1589, but in February 1591, he was expelled for 'abusing the Master of the Bench following some rowdiness on the previous Candlemas night'. This does not seem to have affected his career. In 1601, he was elected Member of Parliament for

Bodmin, and from 1604 to 1611 sat as Member for Lostwithiel; he had been knighted in 1603. He married Penelope, the only daughter and heiress of Thomas Perrot of Treventy, a small mansion in the parish of St Clears in Carmarthenshire – about nine miles from Carmarthen itself. After his marriage he settled at Treventy, which his wife had inherited from her father, where he seems to have devoted a considerable part of his time to astronomy. He died on 12 April 1615, leaving one son, Thomas, who died in 1661. William Lower, the dramatist, was the astronomer's nephew, and on Thomas's death became Sir William's sole heir.

That, really, is about as much as we know, though his correspondence with Harriot ranged over many subjects. We can hardly regard him as a serious astronomer, but at least he deserves to be remembered for his graphic description of the tart-like Moon!

February

Full Moon: 14 February

MERCURY, for the first few days of February, is a difficult evening object for observers near the Equator and further north, and may be glimpsed low above the south-western horizon at the end of evening civil twilight. Mercury passes through inferior conjunction on 15 February and for the last few days of the month it becomes visible as a morning object, low above the south-eastern horizon, though its magnitude +1.0 makes it rather difficult to detect. It is not visible to observers in northern temperate latitudes. Observers nearer the Equator and in more southerly latitudes should consult Figure 5, accompanying the notes for March.

VENUS is a beautiful object in the early mornings, completely dominating the south-eastern sky before dawn. It attains its greatest brilliancy (magnitude −4.7) on 15 February. It is a lovely sight in a small telescope around this time as it exhibits a slender crescent phase. During the month the phase increases noticeably from 13 to 36 per cent as the planet's apparent diameter decreases. On the early morning of 26 February the waning crescent Moon will occult Venus as viewed from Central Africa, and the two objects will be in close proximity for a few hours, providing a good opportunity for Venus to be detected in the early morning daylight. Closest approach occurs around 0515 (GMT) on 26 February.

MARS now rises in the east before midnight and grows noticeably brighter during the month (its magnitude increasing from +0.2 to −0.5) as its distance from the Earth steadily decreases to 121.0 million kilometres (75.2 million miles). The planet is a conspicuous ruddy object still moving direct in Virgo, about four degrees north of the blue-white first-magnitude star Spica, or alpha Virginis (magnitude +1.2). The waning gibbous Moon passes about four degrees south of Mars on the night of 19/20 February.

JUPITER remains a brilliant evening object, setting about two hours before sunrise from northern temperate latitudes by the end of February, but somewhat earlier from locations further south. The planet is still moving retrograde in Gemini, its brightness decreasing slightly from −2.6 to −2.4 during the month. The waxing gibbous Moon will make an interesting pairing with Jupiter on the night of 10/11 February.

SATURN continues to move direct in Libra. By the end of the month it rises at about midnight for observers in northern temperate latitudes and a couple of hours earlier for those in the Southern Hemisphere. Its brightness increases very slightly from magnitude +0.5 to +0.4 during February.

The Twinkling of Sirius. On February evenings the brilliant star Sirius is well placed for observation. Observers in northern temperate latitudes should look for it in the south, rather low down. Though it is actually a whitish star of spectral class A, it seems to twinkle violently, flashing all the colours of the rainbow. Twinkling, or scintillation, has nothing to do with the stars themselves. It is due entirely to the unsteady atmosphere of the Earth. When a star is low, its light is coming to the observer after having passed through a deep layer of atmosphere, so that the twinkling is increased. The effect is more noticeable with Sirius than with any other star, simply because Sirius is so brilliant.

It is sometimes said that stars twinkle, while planets do not. This is not entirely true; when a bright planet is seen low in the sky, it will twinkle quite noticeably except when the air is exceptionally calm and steady. However, it is only right to add that a planet twinkles less than a star, because it appears as a small disk – whereas a star is effectively a point source of light.

The Shortest Month. The present calendar cannot be regarded as ideal; but it would be hard to devise a perfect calendar, since the true length of the Earth's sidereal period is about 365.25 days instead of exactly 365. However, the shortness of February is due to reasons which are not, strictly speaking, astronomical.

The 365-day calendar was adopted at an early stage, and was used by the Egyptians (replacing a still earlier 'year' of 360 days). The first

Roman calendars were imperfect, and in 44 BC, Julius Caesar decided to undertake a revision, carried out at his command by the astronomer Sosigenes. It was Sosigenes who adopted a 365-day year, but this was a quarter of a day too short, so that an extra day would have to be added every 4 years – a leap year, in fact. The number of months remained at 12, but since 12 will not divide exactly into 365, the months had to be unequal. On the Julian system, the first month became January instead of March, as previously; January, March, May, July, September and November had thirty-one days each and the rest thirty, apart from February, which had twenty-nine. The leap-year day was therefore tacked on to February. Incidentally, July was a new name, in honour of Julius Caesar; previously the month had been called Quintilis.

When Augustus attained supreme power, he clearly had to have a month of his own, and the old Sextilis was renamed August. Unfortunately, August had only thirty days, as against the thirty-one days for Caesar's month. This would not do, and so a day was taken away from February and added to August, with suitable readjustments elsewhere.

The Julian calendar was fairly accurate, but even when allowance was made for the leap year, the length was now eleven minutes and fourteen seconds too great. This adds up to a full day in 128 years. A new adjustment was made by Pope Gregory XIII, on the advice of the astronomer Clavius. Until then, every year which could be divided by four was a leap year, but Gregory ordered that the century years (1800, 1900, etc.) were to be regarded as leap years only if exactly divisible by 400. The error was thereby reduced to one day in 3,000 years, which is negligible. The Gregorian calendar was adopted in England in 1752, the days between 2 September and 14 September that year being dropped from the calendar altogether.

From time to time there have been suggestions for a more accurate and convenient World Calendar, but no alterations have been officially supported as yet, and certainly the Gregorian calendar is quite good enough for most purposes.

The Earliest Map of Venus. Before the Space Age we knew almost nothing about the surface of Venus. We can never see it, because it is always hidden by the dense, cloudy atmosphere; we did not even know the length of its rotation period, which was generally assumed to be of the order of a month (actually it is 243 days, and it spins in the opposite direction to the Earth). It is therefore rather surprising to find that the first map of Venus was drawn as long ago as 1726!

Its author was Francesco Bianchini, who lived from 1662 to 1729. He was born in Verona, becoming librarian to Pope Alexander VIII, and was an energetic observer, mainly from Rome. He made recognizable drawings of lunar formations, but is now remembered chiefly for his book *Hesperi et Phosphori Nova Phaenomena*, completed shortly before his death. Using one of the small-aperture, very long-focus refractors of the day (Figure 3) – it had a 2.5-inch (6.4-centimetre) object glass, and a focal length of 150 feet (45.7 metres) – he drew up a chart of the markings which he had observed on Venus, and even named them.

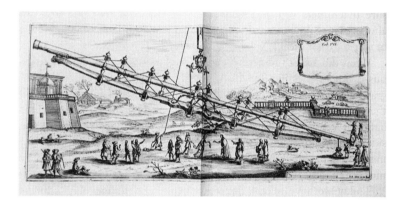

Figure 3. An impression of one of Francesco Bianchini's small-aperture, very long-focus refractors with which he drew up a chart of the markings he observed on Venus, taken from *Hesperi et Phosphori Nova Phaenomena, sive Observationes circa Planetam Veneris*, published by Romae, apud Joannem Mariam Salvioni, in 1728, a year before Bianchini's death. (Image courtesy of the late Sir Patrick Moore, who at one time owned a copy of the book.)

Naturally enough, he regarded the dark areas as seas and the bright regions as land. In all, he recorded seven seas, together with straits and promontories, and was quite confident that his chart was accurate. The names are fascinating – for example, his 'first sea' was named the Royal Sea of King John V of Algarvia and Lusitania, while the second was named after the Infante Henry, fifth son of King John I – better remembered today as Henry the Navigator, who never ventured far himself, but who dispatched expeditions to all known parts of the world and founded colleges of mathematics and science. The third sea was named after King Emmanuel; the fourth after Prince Constantine; the fifth after Christopher Columbus; the sixth after Amerigo Vespucci, who gave his name to America, and the seventh after Galileo, for whom Bianchini had the greatest admiration. Straits were named after Albuquerque (Alphonso de Albuquerque, who undertook the first Indian expedition under King Emmanuel in 1503); Francisco de Almeida; Nunni da Cunha; Vasco da Gama; Duartes Pacheco; John de Castro; Ferdinand Cortez; and Francisco Pizarro. Giovanni Cassini, undoubtedly the greatest of the early planetary observers, was also allotted a strait.

I am sure that you will recognize some of these names – and equally sure that others will be totally unfamiliar. In our own age it is not always easy to remember that Portugal and Spain were once the leaders of world exploration.

What did Bianchini actually see? That he was honest and industrious is not in question, but his unwieldy telescope with its poor light-grasp would have been inadequate to show markings on Venus even if they had existed. The problem is, and always has been, that the brilliance of Venus, plus the fact that when 'full' it is out of view on the far side of the Sun, makes visual work very difficult, even with modern instruments. Bianchini's 'seas', 'straits' and 'promontories' were no more than optical effects.

Today we have reliable maps of Venus (Figure 4), thanks to the radar equipment carried on spacecraft such as Magellan. There are no seas; instead we have volcanic plains, uplands and lowlands, valleys, a few craters and (possibly) active volcanoes. Bianchini had no means of knowing this – and so we must respect him as a pioneer observer, who did his best with the equipment at his disposal. Even if his map is of no scientific value, it is at least of historical interest, and it was a gallant first attempt.

Figure 4. One hemisphere of Venus, centred at 90°E longitude, as revealed by more than a decade of radar mapping, culminating in the 1990–94 Magellan mission, which imaged more than 98 per cent of Venus at a resolution of about a hundred metres. The effective resolution of this image is about three kilometres. A mosaic of the Magellan images (most with illumination from the west) forms the image base. Gaps in the Magellan coverage were filled with images from the Earth-based Arecibo radar in a region centred roughly on zero degrees latitude and longitude, and with a neutral tone elsewhere (primarily near the South Pole). The composite image was processed to improve contrast and to emphasize small features, and the original was colour-coded to represent elevation. Gaps in the elevation data from the Magellan radar altimeter were filled with altimetry from the Venera spacecraft and the US Pioneer Venus missions. An orthographic projection was used, simulating a distant view of one hemisphere of the planet. Data processed by NASA's Jet Propulsion Laboratory, Massachusetts Institute of Technology and the US Geological Survey. (Image courtesy of NASA/JPL/USGS.)

March

New Moon: 1 and 30 March *Full Moon:* 16 March

Equinox: 20 March

Summer Time in the United Kingdom begins on 30 March.

MERCURY is not visible from the latitudes of northern Europe or North America this month, but is an early morning object for observers in the tropics and more southerly latitudes. For Southern Hemisphere observers this is the most favourable morning apparition of the year. Figure 5 shows, for observers in latitude 35°S, the changes in azimuth

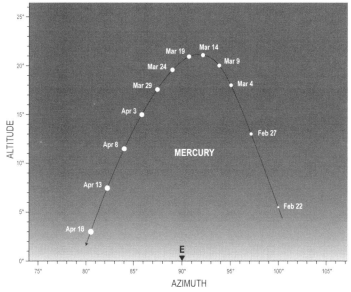

Figure 5. Morning apparition of Mercury from latitude 35°S. The planet reaches greatest western elongation on 14 March 2014. It will be at its brightest in mid-April, several weeks after elongation.

(true bearing from the north through east, south and west) and altitude of Mercury on successive mornings when the Sun is 6° below the horizon. This is at the beginning of morning civil twilight, which in this latitude and at this time of year occurs about twenty-five minutes before sunrise.

During its long period of visibility, which runs from the end of February until mid-April, Mercury brightens from magnitude +1.6 to −1.0. The changes in the brightness of the planet are indicated on the diagram by the relative sizes of the white circles marking Mercury's position at five-day intervals. It should be noted that Mercury is at its brightest some four weeks after it reaches greatest western elongation (28°) on 14 March. The diagram gives positions for a time at the beginning of morning civil twilight on the Greenwich meridian on the stated date. Observers in different longitudes should note that the actual positions of Mercury in azimuth and altitude will differ slightly from those given in the diagram due to the motion of the planet.

From latitude 35°S, before dawn on 28 March, the thin waning crescent Moon will appear below Venus and above and to the left of Mercury, about equidistant from the two planets.

VENUS is still a brilliant object in the early morning skies, although it fades from magnitude −4.6 to −4.3 during the month. It is south of the celestial equator, and observers in the latitudes of the British Isles will be able to see it for less than two hours before sunrise, low above the east-south-eastern horizon. Observers in the Southern Hemisphere are more fortunate, enjoying a visibility period of about three hours before dawn. The waning crescent Moon will be close to Venus on the morning of 27 March and the two will make a beautiful pairing in the dawn twilight sky. Venus reaches its greatest western elongation (47°) on 22 March. The phase of the planet continues to increase from 37 to 54 per cent during the month.

The observed and theoretical phases of Venus do not always agree. This is particularly evident during the time of dichotomy or half-phase (50 per cent). When the phase of Venus is waxing (increasing) in the morning sky – as it is this month – dichotomy is usually later than predicted. The discrepancy may amount to several days, although it is fair to say that timing the exact time of observed dichotomy is far from easy. The effect was first noticed by J. H. Schröter in 1793, and is now generally referred to as the Schröter Effect.

MARS reaches its first stationary point on 1 March in Virgo, slightly north and east of Spica, and thereafter the planet's motion is retrograde until the third week of May. As the planet retrogrades, its path actually forms a very small loop, the motion for a week or two after the stationary point being very slightly north of its path before that date. Figure 6 shows the path of Mars against the background stars for the first eight months of 2014. Mars grows rapidly brighter during March (increasing from magnitude −0.5 to −1.3) as it approaches opposition next month and rises less than an hour after sunset by the end of March. Its distance from Earth decreases to 95.2 million kilometres (59.2 million miles) by month end. The waning gibbous Moon passes about four degrees south of Mars on the night of 18/19 March.

JUPITER also reaches a stationary point this month (6 March) and then resumes its direct motion against the background stars of Gemini once more. The planet fades slightly from magnitude −2.4 to −2.2 during March. It is visible as soon as darkness falls and doesn't set until well into the early morning hours from northern temperate latitudes, but the period of visibility is markedly less for observers further south.

SATURN is the third planet to reach a stationary point this month (on 3 March) and from that date its motion is retrograde in Libra. The planet continues to brighten slowly from magnitude +0.4 to +0.3 during the month. By the end of March, Saturn is rising before midnight for observers in northern temperate latitudes and a couple of hours earlier for those further south.

Johann Schröter and the Schröter Effect. Have you ever heard of Johann Hieronymus Schröter? Unless you are astronomically minded, probably not. Born in Erfurt, Germany on 30 August 1745, he studied law at Göttingen University from 1762 until 1767 and later took up legal practice, but he is best known for his work as an amateur astronomer when he lived at Lilienthal, near Bremen. While serving as Secretary of the Royal Chamber of George III in Hanover from 1777, Schröter made the acquaintance of two of the brothers of William Herschel, the famous astronomer and telescope-maker. Although initially astronomy was just a hobby of Schröter's, it seems that Herschel's discovery of the planet Uranus in 1781 prompted Schröter to take up astronomy much more seriously, and he resigned his post and became

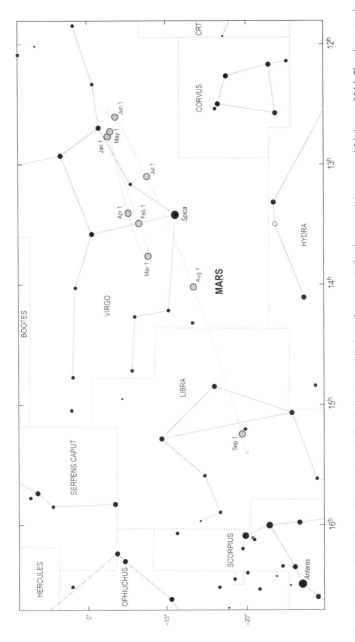

Figure 6. The path of Mars as it moves through the Zodiacal constellations of Virgo and Libra between 1 January and 31 August 2014. The planet reaches its first stationary point on 1 March; its motion is then retrograde before and after opposition on 8 April until it reaches its second stationary point on 20 May. Thereafter its motion is direct once more. The 'loop' in the planet's apparent motion during the first eight months of 2014 is clearly shown.

Chief Magistrate and District Governor of Lilienthal. He set up an observatory and equipped it with powerful telescopes. The largest of these was a 19-inch (48-centimetre) reflector by an instrument maker named Schrader, about whom not much is known except that he lived in Kiel and was deaf. The quality of the 19-inch is uncertain, but Schröter carried out most of his work with smaller telescopes, at least one of which (a reflector of 122-cm focal length and 12-cm aperture) was made by no less a person than William Herschel himself!

Schröter was concerned mainly with the Moon and planets. He made thousands of lunar drawings, and though he was not a skilful draughtsman he was certainly accurate, so that he ranks as the first really great selenographer or Moon-mapper. He made sketches of Mars which were better than any previously produced, and he also studied Venus, on which he could see few markings (well, who can?), but whose ever-changing phase was of considerable interest to him.

Venus, closer to the Sun than we are, shows phases similar to those of the Moon (Figure 7), because, obviously, the Sun can light up only

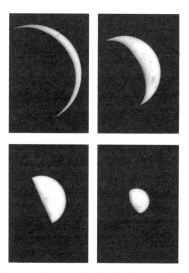

Figure 7. A series of telescopic drawings showing the changing phase of Venus. The view is inverted in an astronomical telescope. From a large, but very thin crescent (upper left), the phase steadily increases to a fatter crescent, then half-phase (dichotomy), and finally a small, gibbous disk, as the distance of Venus from Earth steadily increases. (Drawings courtesy of the late Sir Patrick Moore.)

half the planet at any one time, and it all depends upon how much of the sunlit half is turned in our direction. It should be easy to calculate just when Venus will be at exactly half-phase, or dichotomy. However, Schröter found that theory and observation did not agree. When Venus was an evening object, shrinking from half-phase to a crescent, dichotomy was always early. When Venus was a morning object, and changing from a crescent into a half, dichotomy was late. This phenomenon is now usually known as the 'Schröter Effect' in recognition of his discovery. The discrepancies do exist, and may amount to several days. Undoubtedly the thick atmosphere of Venus is responsible for them, since there is no chance that the calculations are wrong. The precise cause is not known even yet, and the phenomenon is interesting, even if it is not of tremendous importance.

Schröter made many other valuable observations. Sadly, his observatory was destroyed by the French during the wars of the early nineteenth century; all his unpublished manuscripts were burned, and even his brass telescopes were plundered, because the French soldiers believed them to be gold. Schröter died on 29 August 1816 and he will not easily be forgotten; luckily, enough of his work remains to show what a painstaking and honest observer he was. The lunar crater Schröter and the Martian crater Schroeter are named after him, as is Schröter's Valley (near the bright crater Aristarchus) on the Moon (see the notes for April).

The First Point of Aries. On 20 March, the Sun crosses the celestial equator, moving from south to north, after which date it will remain in the northern part of the sky until 23 September. Therefore, 20 March is the date of the spring or vernal equinox (in the Northern Hemisphere), and the Sun will lie at what is known as the First Point of Aries.

The positions of celestial bodies are given in terms of declination and right ascension. Declination is simply the angular distance north or south of the equator of the sky, so that it corresponds to latitude on the Earth's surface (though, rather confusingly, the term 'celestial latitude' has a rather different meaning). The declination of the north celestial pole is, of course, 90°N, and the current Pole Star, Polaris, is within one degree of this. Delta Orionis, the northernmost star in the Belt of Orion, the Hunter, is very close to the celestial equator.

Right ascension is measured eastwards from the First Point of Aries. This is simply the place in the sky where the ecliptic (which may be defined as the Sun's apparent yearly path against the background stars) cuts the celestial equator. The right ascension of a body is measured in hours, minutes and seconds of time, and is the interval which elapses between the meridian passage of the First Point of Aries and the meridian passage of the star. Thus Betelgeuse in Orion reaches the meridian 5 hours 55 minutes after the First Point of Aries has done so; and the right ascension of Betelgeuse is therefore 5h 55m.

The Sun, Moon and planets change their right ascensions and declinations comparatively quickly. The stars, which are to all intents and purposes fixed relative to each other, do not shift so rapidly. The only alterations are due to the effects of precession, or the movement of the direction of the Earth's axis of rotation. Because of precession, the polar point – and hence the Equator – shifts very gradually, and so the position of the First Point of Aries changes too. When the Egyptian Pyramids were built, the Pole Star was the comparatively obscure Thuban in the constellation of Draco, and in 12,000 years' time, the brilliant star Vega will be the north polar star.

The First Point of Aries is no longer in Aries. Precession over the centuries has shifted it into the neighbouring constellation of Pisces, the Fishes; and, strictly speaking, Pisces should now be regarded as the first constellation of the Zodiac instead of the last. There is no bright star close to the First Point; the position lies roughly between Iota Piscium (magnitude 4.1) and Iota Ceti (magnitude 3.6), rather closer to Iota Piscium. In the course of time, the First Point will move out of Pisces into the next Zodiacal constellation, Aquarius.

April

Full Moon: 15 April   **New Moon:** 29 April

MERCURY continues to be visible as a morning object before dawn, in the eastern twilight sky, for observers in the tropics and Southern Hemisphere during the first two weeks of April. Figure 5, given with the notes for March, shows, for observers in latitude 35°S, the changes in azimuth (true bearing from the north through east, south and west) and altitude of Mercury on successive mornings when the Sun is 6° below the horizon, about 25 minutes before sunrise in this latitude. The changes in the brightness of the planet are indicated on the diagram by the relative sizes of the white circles marking Mercury's position at five-day intervals. It will be noted that Mercury is at its brightest in mid-April some four weeks after greatest western elongation; the planet brightens from magnitude −0.2 to −1.0 during the first two weeks of April. From mid-month, Mercury will be lost from view as its elongation from the Sun rapidly decreases, the planet passing through superior conjunction on 26 April. For observers in the latitudes of the British Isles it remains unsuitably placed for observation throughout the month.

VENUS, fading slightly from magnitude −4.3 to −4.1 during April, continues to be visible as a brilliant object in the morning sky before dawn. However, it is visible to observers in northern temperate latitudes only for an hour or so before sunrise, low above the east-south-eastern horizon. Southern Hemisphere observers continue to enjoy more than three hours of visibility before dawn. Venus is close to the waning crescent Moon on the mornings of 25 and 26 April. The phase of Venus increases from 54 to 66 per cent during the month.

MARS is at opposition in Virgo on 8 April, when it will be at its brightest (magnitude −1.5) and visible from dusk to dawn, appearing due south at midnight. The apparent diameter of Mars at opposition is just over fifteen seconds of arc and the north pole of the planet is tilted towards the Earth. Owing to the eccentricity of the orbit of Mars, the planet is nearest to the Earth (92.4 million kilometres or 57.4 million miles) a few days after opposition this year, on 14 April. On the evening of the same day, Mars will lie quite close to the almost full Moon in the sky.

It has to be said that this is not a particularly favourable opposition of the Red Planet. At so-called perihelic oppositions (such as on 28 August 2003), the distance of Mars from the Earth is only 55.8 million kilometres (34.6 million miles), the magnitude is −2.9 (more brilliant than Jupiter), and the apparent diameter of the disk is 25 seconds of arc.

JUPITER will be easily recognized as darkness falls, a brilliant object among the stars of Gemini. Now well past opposition, the planet continues to fade slightly, from magnitude −2.2 to −2.0 during the month. From the latitudes of northern Europe and North America, the planet remains visible until well after midnight at the end of April, but from more southerly locations the period of visibility is much reduced on account of the planet's high northerly declination.

SATURN is now nearing opposition, so it rises soon after sunset and is visible until dawn. The planet brightens very slightly from magnitude +0.2 to +0.1 during April. It continues to move retrograde among the faint stars of Libra, the Scales.

The Brightest Crater on the Moon. The lunar crater Aristarchus, which is 40 kilometres in diameter and 3.7 kilometres deep, is by far the brightest crater on the entire Moon and can always be seen whenever it is in sunlight (Figure 8). It also shows up in Earthshine, and quite a few astronomers have mistaken it for a volcano in eruption. Even the great Sir William Herschel fell into this trap. It lies in the Oceanus Procellarum (Ocean of Storms) and it is not isolated by any means; it lies close to the crater Herodotus of much the same size but without the brightness of its neighbour.

Aristarchus is so bright simply because it is very young, formed at a late stage in the Moon's evolution. It is also one of the very youngest craters on the entire lunar surface. It is well formed, with high, terraced walls and a central peak. Its age is believed to be about 450 million years, which, indeed, is very young by lunar standards.

Figure 8. The lunar crater Aristarchus appears as a very bright spot (upper left) on the full Moon in this image mosaic obtained by the Galileo spacecraft on 7 December 1992, *en route* to the planet Jupiter. The distinct bright ray crater at the bottom of the image is Tycho. The dark areas are ancient lava-filled impact basins: Oceanus Procellarum (on the left) where Aristarchus is located, Mare Imbrium (centre left), Mare Serenitatis and Mare Tranquillitatis (centre) and Mare Crisium (near the right edge). (Image courtesy of NASA/JPL.)

The position of Aristarchus on the lunar disk means that it can be seen for a good part of every lunation, and it is fascinating to draw or image it from night to night and note the apparent alterations due to changes in solar illumination. Aristarchus is the centre of a small and not very prominent system of bright rays. However, a small telescope will show it easily under suitable conditions of illumination.

The adjacent crater Herodotus (named after the Greek historian Herodotus, c. 485–425 BC) is also well formed (Figure 9), but there is no marked central peak. In this area is the longest sinuous valley on the Moon, named in honour of the German astronomer Johann Schröter (see the notes for March), which, in a way, is misleading because the crater named after Schröter is a long way away in an entirely different part of the Moon. Aristarchus himself (c. 310–230 BC), the Greek astronomer from Samos, was the first to maintain that the Earth revolved around the Sun and rotates on its axis.

Figure 9. An oblique view of a portion of the lunar nearside located near the north-eastern edge of the Ocean of Storms (Oceanus Procellarum), photographed from the *Apollo 15* spacecraft in lunar orbit, showing the bright crater Aristarchus (23.6°N, 47.5°W) on the left, the crater Herodotus on the right, and Schröter's Valley lower right. This view is looking south. The head of Schröter's Valley, a sinuous rille in the Aristarchus Plateau, is called the Cobra's Head. (Image AS15-88-11980, 31 July–2 August 1971, courtesy of NASA/NSSDC.)

Inside crater Aristarchus are strange stripy lines up the walls, once believed to be low-type vegetation but, of course, this most certainly is not the case. However, a number of TLP (transient lunar phenomena) have been seen on or near the crater, and it is well worth keeping a look out. Phenomena reported in Aristarchus include periodical obscurations, and cloud-like features which do not persist for long. These have never been photographed or imaged, and their real existence has never been definitely proved. However, looking back at lists of reported TLP, Aristarchus heads the list by a very long way.

Schröter's valley begins twenty-five kilometres north of Herodotus and gives the impression of a dry river bed. Starting at a crater six kilometres in diameter, the valley widens to almost ten kilometres, forming a shape that some observers have nicknamed 'The Cobra's Head'. From this it narrows gradually to a width of fifty-five metres, finally terminating in a thousand-metre high bank on the edge of an uplifted area. The total length of the valley is 160 kilometres with a maximum depth of 1,000 metres. Nothing else quite like it can be seen on the Moon. Under good seeing conditions a powerful telescope will show a delicate rill on the floor of the valley.

Coma and Canes Venatici. South of the Plough, and well placed on April evenings, lies the constellation of Coma Berenices, or Berenice's Hair (Figure 10). An intriguing old legend is attached to it. It is said that when Ptolemy Euergetes, the warrior King of Egypt, set out on a dangerous campaign against the Assyrians, his wife Queen Berenice vowed to dedicate her beautiful hair to the gods if her husband came back safely. On his return, she kept her promise, and the gleaming tresses were placed in the sky! Yet Coma is not an ancient constellation in its own right; it was added to the sky by Tycho Brahe during the latter part of the sixteenth century.

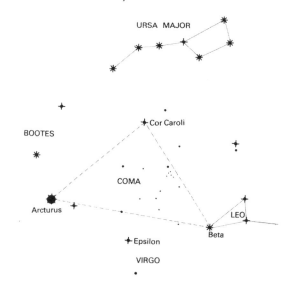

Figure 10. Map showing the location of the faint constellation of Coma Berenices, which lies roughly within a triangle marked by the brilliant Arcturus to the east, Cor Caroli in Canes Venatici to the north, and Beta Leonis (Denebola) to the south-west.

At first glance Coma gives the superficial impression of being a very large, dim open star cluster. Coma is easy to find when the sky is clear and dark, but the slightest haze or mist will hide it, so that the entire region will appear blank. Its principal stars (Beta, Alpha and Gamma) are only of the fourth magnitude, but although the pattern has no bright stars, there are many faint ones, and there are also numerous telescopic galaxies. Alpha Comae makes a triangle with Eta Boötis and Epsilon Virginis, and is not hard to locate as there are no other naked-eye stars close to it. The globular cluster M53 is in the same low-power field as Alpha. It is of magnitude 7.7, and is discernible in binoculars as a dim blur. Coma is also the region of the northern galactic pole, where we look perpendicular to and above the galactic plane, and many faint external galaxies are visible. The Black Eye galaxy, M64, magnitude 6.6, is within a degree of the star 35 Comae, not far from Alpha.

Between Coma and the Great Bear lies another small constellation, Canes Venatici (the Hunting Dogs), formed by Hevelius in 1690. Its only bright star is Cor Caroli, which is of the third magnitude. A line from Denebola (the tail of the Lion) to Alkaid (the last star in the tail of the Bear, or the handle of the Plough) may be seen as being divided into three roughly equal parts by Coma Berenices and Cor Caroli. It is a fine double star, and its name (Charles's Heart) is in remembrance of King Charles II. The story goes that on the evening before the return of Charles to London, the court physician, Scarborough, remarked that this star shone with a peculiar lustre, and suggested that it should be named in honour of the King. It is certainly true that many old star atlases (even those of a much later date) marked the star with a picture of a heart surmounted with a crown. The star actually had its place on the collar of Chara, one of the hunting dogs, but the incongruity of the crowned heart did not seem to matter! In later atlases and globes, the royal heart disappeared, but it is perhaps fitting that the king who founded the Royal Society and the Royal Observatory should be remembered in this simple way.

The globular cluster M3, magnitude 6.4, lies at the extreme edge of Canes Venatici, close to the border with Coma. M3 is almost midway between Cor Caroli and the brilliant Arcturus in Boötes. Canes Venatici is also crowded with galaxies. Probably the most celebrated of these is the Whirlpool Galaxy, M51 (Figure 11), magnitude 8.4, which lies quite close to Alkaid, the star at the end of the Great Bear's tail. M51 was the first galaxy to have its spiral structure recognized; it was in

1845 when the Third Earl of Rosse used his remarkable home-made 72-inch reflecting telescope at Birr Castle in Ireland to observe it. At the time, only the Birr telescope was capable of showing the forms of galaxies. It was a major breakthrough because they were recognized as star systems in their own right, lying well beyond our own Milky Way galaxy.

Figure 11. Full frame image of the Whirlpool Galaxy, M51, demonstrating the wide field of view of the One Degree Imager (ODI) on the 3.5-metre WIYN telescope at Kitt Peak National Observatory. Even though the galaxy is almost 30 million light years away, the image clearly shows clusters of hot, young stars that light up the spiral arms. Threaded through the arms are dark 'dust lanes', where very dark material left over from previous generations of stars has settled. More dust lanes can be seen in the bridge of luminous stars and gas that connects M51 to its companion, the peculiar galaxy NGC 5195, in the upper part of the image. (Image courtesy of K. Rhode, M. Young and WIYN/NOAO/AURA/NSF.)

May

Full Moon: 14 May   *New Moon:* 28 May

MERCURY is at greatest eastern elongation (23°) on 25 May. It does not become visible to observers in the Southern Hemisphere until almost the middle of the month, but further north it is visible much earlier. For observers in northern temperate latitudes this is the most favourable evening apparition of the year. Figure 12 shows, for observers in latitude 52°N, the changes in azimuth (true bearing from the north through east, south and west) and altitude of Mercury on successive evenings when the Sun is 6° below the horizon. This is at the end of evening civil twilight, which in this latitude and at this time of year occurs about thirty-five minutes after sunset.

The changes in the brightness of the planet are indicated on the diagram by the relative sizes of the white circles marking Mercury's posi-

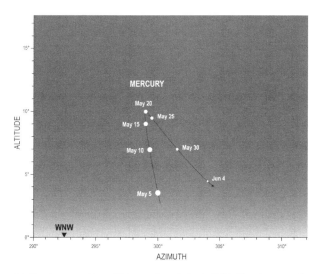

Figure 12. Evening apparition of Mercury from latitude 52°N. The planet reaches greatest eastern elongation on 25 May 2014. It is at its brightest in early May, before elongation.

tion at five-day intervals. It should be noted that Mercury is at its brightest before it reaches greatest eastern elongation, the planet fading from magnitude −1.7 to +1.3 during May. The diagram gives positions for a time at the beginning of morning civil twilight on the Greenwich meridian on the stated date. Observers in different longitudes should note that the actual positions of Mercury in azimuth and altitude will differ slightly from those given in the diagram due to the motion of the planet.

VENUS is still a splendid object in the early mornings before sunrise, at magnitude −4.1. Observers in northern temperate latitudes will find, however, that it is visible only for a short while before dawn, low above the eastern horizon. Southern Hemisphere observers continue to enjoy more than three hours of visibility before dawn. The phase of Venus increases from 67 to 77 per cent during the month.

MARS, just past opposition, is easily recognized as soon as darkness falls by its distinctive reddish hue among the much fainter stars of Virgo. The planet continues its retrograde motion until 20 May, when it reaches its second stationary point, resuming direct motion once again from that date. As its distance from Earth increases, the planet fades noticeably from magnitude −1.2 to −0.5 during the month.

JUPITER is an evening object setting at around midnight from the latitudes of the British Isles by month end, but much earlier for those located further south. The planet is moving direct amongst the stars of Gemini, fading very slightly from magnitude −2.0 to −1.9 during May. The waxing crescent Moon will make a nice pairing with Jupiter on the evening of 4 May.

SATURN, magnitude +0.1, is at opposition in Libra on 10 May. Figure 13 shows the path of Saturn against the background stars during the year. The planet becomes visible in the east-south-eastern sky as soon as darkness falls and is observable all night long. Saturn is a lovely sight in even a small telescope, with the rings beautifully displayed at an angle of 21.7° as viewed from the Earth. At opposition, the planet is 1,331 million kilometres (827 million miles) from the Earth. The full Moon will appear fairly close to Saturn on 14 May.

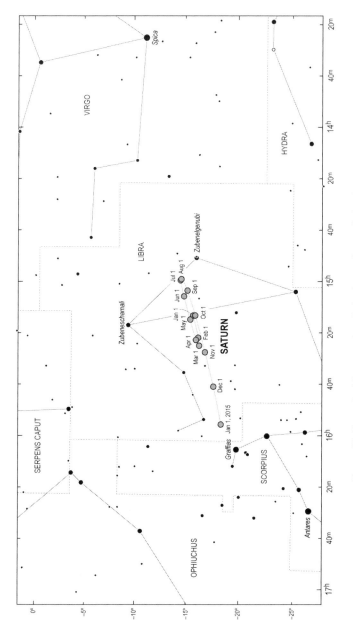

Figure 13. The path of Saturn against the background stars of Libra during 2014.

Green Stars. It is obvious to even a casual observer of the night sky that the stars are not all the same colour. In Orion, for example, Rigel is bluish-white while Betelgeuse is orange-red; Vega in Lyra, almost overhead from Britain during summer evenings, is decidedly bluish; Capella in Auriga, which occupies the overhead position during winter evenings, is yellow. In the Southern Hemisphere we have another excellent case of contrast. Three of the four main stars of the Southern Cross are hot and bluish-white, but the fourth, Gamma Crucis, is orange-red. The difference is quite marked.

Star colours are due to differences in surface temperature. Our yellow Sun has a temperature of below 6,000 degrees Centigrade, but Betelgeuse and Gamma Crucis are cooler, at between 3,000 and 3,500 degrees. On the other hand, Rigel measures over 12,000 degrees, and the hottest known stars have temperatures which are much higher still – over 50,000 degrees. Red stars, orange stars, yellow stars, blue stars, white stars – but what about green stars? Here we find something rather unexpected; green stars appear to be vanishingly rare except as binary companions to brighter stars which are red.

Double stars are common in the sky, and most of them are genuine binary pairs, moving through space together. One of these is Antares, leader of Scorpius, the Scorpion. Antares is a red supergiant star, much larger and more luminous than the Sun, but considerably cooler. Its redness is striking, and indeed its name means 'the rival of Ares' – Ares being the Greek name for the war-god better known to us as Mars.

Antares (magnitude 1.2) has a much fainter companion of magnitude 5.4. It was probably discovered on 13 April 1819 by Burg, in Vienna, who was watching an occultation of Antares by the Moon, and saw that the reappearance was not instantaneous. He stated that 'perhaps Antares is a double star, and the first observed small one is so near the principal star that both, even if viewed through a good telescope, do not appear separated'. In fact, the companion is not a really difficult object, and one has no problem in seeing it with a 12-inch reflector, since the current separation is 2.6 arc seconds, though it will become progressively more difficult in future years; it is a true companion, and the revolution period is 878 years, so that at the time of apparent closest approach (around the year 2110) it will be almost impossible to observe separately. It is often described as green, and certainly its surface is hot; the luminosity is about fifty times that of the Sun, and it is one of the very few 'normal' stars to be a definite source of detectable radio waves.

But is Antares B really green, or are we being tricked by contrast with the red primary? There are other similar cases; one is Rasalgethi or Alpha Herculis, also a red supergiant with a faint attendant which looks green. It is also sometimes said that both components of the bright binary Castor, in Gemini, the Twins, have greenish hues, but usually they appear pure white.

The most famous case of an allegedly green single star is that of Beta Librae, which has the barbarous proper name of Zubenelchemale – meaning, in Arabic, 'the Northern Claw'. Libra, the Scales or Balance, was once included in Scorpius as the Scorpion's Claws. It is 120 light-years away, and has a hot surface; the luminosity is over 100 times that of the Sun. The apparent magnitude is 2.6, so that it does not shine so brightly as the Pole Star, but there have been suggestions that it has faded over the past two thousand years. It has often been described as green. A well-known American observer, W. T. Olcott, said that it '… was the only naked-eye star to be green in colour', while the Revd T. W. Webb, author of the classic last-century book *Celestial Objects*, referred to its 'beautiful green hue'.

Have a look at it, with the naked eye, with binoculars and with tele-scopes, and see for yourself. Can you see a greenish tint?

Where Jules Verne Went Wrong. Probably the first great space travel story of near-modern times was *From the Earth to the Moon*, by the French science fiction writer Jules Verne, which was published in 1865 (its sequel, *Around the Moon*, came out a few years later). In it, Verne's three heroes – Barbicane, Captain Nicholl and Michel Ardan – were fired to the Moon from the barrel of a huge cannon. They went right round the Moon, but their orbit was perturbed by an encounter with an asteroid, so that they eventually fell back to Earth.

Verne himself was not a scientist (he had trained as a lawyer, then quit the profession early in life to become a writer), but he had plenty of scientific friends, and he believed in making his facts as accurate as possible. His speed of departure (seven miles per second or eleven kilo-metres per second) was correct; this is the Earth's escape velocity. His fictional telescope, on Long's Peak, was credible enough, though it was more like Lord Rosse's 72-inch 'Leviathan' than the 200-inch Hale tele-scope at Mount Palomar. His launching site on Stone's Hill in 'Tampa

Town', Florida was not far from Cape Canaveral (where NASA's main launch complex would later be sited), and his adventurers splashed down in the ocean much as the *Apollo* astronauts actually did a little more than a century later. We also now know that there are small asteroids which may pass through the region between the Earth and the Moon, as Verne had assumed. However, Verne did make some mistakes, even though they were not his fault.

In particular, the shock of being fired off from the cannon at escape velocity would be quite a jolt, to put it mildly. In fact, the occupants of the projectile would be turned into jelly and killed instantly. Moreover, the friction between the projectile and the thick lower layers of the atmosphere would have destroyed the craft before it had time to leave the Earth. But the most important of Verne's mistakes concerned weightlessness. In his novel, the travellers became weightless only when they reached a so-called 'zero point', where the Moon's gravity exactly balanced out that of the Earth. Actually, the travellers would have felt weightless as soon as they were in 'free fall' – a term used to describe the condition when the only forces acting on an object are gravitational, irrespective of which direction that object happens to be moving in. It isn't actually necessary to be 'falling' in the sense of moving towards the Earth's surface to be 'freely falling' in the physics sense. You can feel weightless in a roller coaster, elevator, aircraft or an orbiting spacecraft. It isn't that there's no gravity pulling; gravity is still present.

A body in free fall experiences weightlessness because that body's acceleration due to gravitational forces is independent of its mass. Consequently, all bodies that are locally in free fall experience the *same* acceleration. The *Apollo* spacecraft and the astronauts inside them (Figure 14) were in free fall, even when they were travelling from the Earth to the Moon. The Earth's gravity would pull the astronauts towards the back of the spacecraft, but it would also pull on the spacecraft itself. The astronauts and the spacecraft would experience the same acceleration, so there was no apparent pull. It would have been just the same for Jules Verne's travellers en route from the Earth to the Moon.

Despite all this, Verne's novels were fascinating, and even today, when the Moon has been reached, they have not lost their charm. If you have not read them, we strongly recommend you to do so.

Figure 14. Astronaut Buzz Aldrin on the way to the Moon inside the *Apollo 11* Command Module on 18 July 1969. (Image courtesy of NASA.)

June

Full Moon: 13 June   *New Moon:* 27 June

Solstice: 21 June

MERCURY begins the month as an evening object very low down in the north-western sky at the end of evening civil twilight from northern temperate latitudes, but inconveniently faint at magnitude +1.4. The planet passes through inferior conjunction on 19 June and remains too close to the Sun for observation for the remainder of the month, except for observers in the tropics who may be able to glimpse it low down above the north-eastern horizon at the beginning of morning civil twilight for the last few days of the month.

VENUS continues to be a splendid object in the early morning sky, with a magnitude of −4.0, visible above the eastern horizon before dawn. Observers in the latitudes of the British Isles will find that it becomes visible for a little longer each morning as the month progresses. This effect is the result of its northward movement in declination which more than offsets the fact that Venus is slowly moving in towards the Sun.

MARS is still an evening object in Virgo, but it is now fading more rapidly, declining in brightness from magnitude −0.5 to 0.0 during June as its distance from the Earth increases from 118.8 million to 147.8 million kilometres (73.8 million to 91.8 million miles). The planet sets around midnight from northern temperate latitudes by the end of the month; about an hour later from locations in the Southern Hemisphere. Mars is now moving direct, but is travelling well south of its previous path (see Figure 6, given with the notes for March). The curious shape of the planet's apparent path against the background stars is due to the fact that Mars passes through its descending node on 11 June, crossing the ecliptic from north to south.

JUPITER, magnitude −1.8, is visible from dusk but now sets before midnight. It is moving direct in Gemini, and by the end of June it will have moved south of the constellation's two principal stars, Castor and Pollux, but more or less in a line with them.

SATURN, just past opposition, is visible in the south-south-east from northern temperate latitudes as darkness falls and is observable for most of the night. From more southerly locations the planet is situated much higher in the sky. Saturn is moving retrograde in Libra. It fades slightly from magnitude +0.2 to +0.4 during the month.

Arcturus. Alpha Boötis, or Arcturus, the leader of Boötes, the Herdsman, is very prominent as darkness falls on evenings this month. Its declination is +19 degrees, so that it can be seen from every inhabited country, though from the southernmost part of New Zealand it is always low down in the north. It is the fourth brightest star in the sky (third, if you do not combine the two components of Alpha Centauri), and the brightest in the Northern Hemisphere of the sky. There are four stars which are almost equal: Arcturus (magnitude −0.04), Vega (+0.03), Capella (+0.08) and Rigel (+0.12). Vega is bluish, Rigel is pure white, Capella yellowish and Arcturus orange. The latest measurements indicate that Arcturus is 37 light years away, and is 115 times as luminous as the Sun. Admittedly, this does not seem much in comparison with a celestial 'searchlight' such as Rigel. In fact, Rigel is around five hundred times as luminous as Arcturus.

There are few definite mythological legends associated with Boötes. It has been said that the herdsman was honoured with a place in the heavens because he invented the plough drawn by two oxen. Arcturus is most easily found by extending the curve of the three stars in the tail of the Great Bear. Indeed, the star is said to take its name from its proximity to the stars of the Great Bear and Little Bear; its name in Greek means 'guardian of the bears' or 'bear watcher'. For some reason or other seamen of ancient times regarded Arcturus as unlucky, and the Roman writer Pliny even refers to it as 'horridum sidus' – which is indeed strange, because Arcturus is such a beautiful star.

The stars are so far away that their individual or proper motions are very slight, and the constellations look virtually the same today as they must have done to King Canute, Julius Caesar or the builders of the Pyramids. But the apparent positions of the stars do slowly change over time and Arcturus, which is one of our nearer neighbours, has a proper motion of 2.3 arc seconds per year. Stellar proper motion was discovered in 1718 by Edmond Halley. He realized that the stars Arcturus, Sirius and Aldebaran had shifted appreciably from the positions recorded by the famous Greek astronomer Hipparchus, around 1,800 years earlier. A large proper motion is usually an indication that a star lies relatively close to the Sun, and for this reason Arcturus was once thought to be the closest of the bright stars. This is quite wrong: of the first-magnitude stars, Alpha Centauri, Sirius, Vega, Procyon, Altair, Pollux and Fomalhaut are all closer. However, of the very brightest stars, only Alpha Centauri has a greater proper motion than Arcturus: 3.7 arc seconds per year.

Arcturus appears to be fast moving because probably it belongs to an older population of stars – known as Population II stars – located within the thick disc of our Galaxy, the Milky Way. The thick disc is generally formed of old stars that lie well above or below the galactic plane, unlike thin-disk stars, such as our Sun, which lie close to the plane. However, thick-disc stars tend to move in highly inclined and elliptical orbits around the galactic core. So Arcturus is travelling along a highly inclined orbit cutting through the galactic plane, which gives it a velocity relative to the Sun that is higher than the other bright stars. Compared with the other surrounding stars, which orbit the Galaxy in roughly circular orbits, Arcturus falls behind by around a hundred kilometres per second (about sixty miles per second).

Arcturus must have reached naked-eye visibility around half a million years ago, and since has brightened steadily; it is now just about at its nearest to the Sun. In the future it will draw away, until it drops below naked-eye visibility in about half a million years from now.

Basil Ringrose, Astronomer and Pirate. It may not be accurate to describe Basil Ringrose as an amateur astronomer, though he did record some observations. He was most certainly a professional pirate, which surely makes him unique!

He was first heard of in 1680 as a member of a pirate fleet which assembled in the West Indies and attacked the Spanish base of Porto Bello in Panama. He attached himself to a captured Spanish ship, *La Santissima Trinidad*, under the command of Captain Sharp, and acted as navigator as they burned and plundered their way down the coasts of Peru and Chile, arriving back in the Caribbean in February 1682.

During this voyage Ringrose observed the annular solar eclipse of 22 September 1680, and from it worked out the longitude of the ship. He described the Magellanic Clouds, and wrote: 'Last night we saw the Magellan Clouds, which are so famous among the mariners of these southern seas. The least of these clouds was about the bigness of a man's hat.'

Comets, too, came under his eye. One of these was the Great Comet of 1680 (Figure 15), also observed by Isaac Newton and Edmond Halley under rather more peaceful conditions. Ringrose described it:

> November 19th, 1680. This morning, about an hour before day, we observed a comet to appear a degree north from the bright star in Libra. The body thereof seemed dull, and its tail extended itself 18 or 20 degrees in length, being of a pale colour, and pointing directly NNW.

Figure 15. An artist's impression of the Great Comet of 1680 (also known as Kirch's Comet, and Newton's Comet) over Rotterdam, by the Dutch artist Lieve Verschuier. It was discovered by Gottfried Kirch on 14 November 1680 and was the first comet to be discovered by telescope. It became one of the brightest comets of the seventeenth century, sporting a spectacularly long tail, and was apparently visible even in daylight, reaching its peak brightness at the end of December 1680. Apart from its great brightness, the comet is notable for being used by Isaac Newton to test and verify Kepler's laws of motion. (Image courtesy of Wikimedia Commons.)

In fact, the 'bright star in Libra' was actually Spica, which is in the neighbouring constellation of Virgo, but at least Ringrose was not far wrong, and he followed the comet for some nights as it tracked past Spica. His descriptions agree well with those given by Newton and Halley.

In February 1682, Ringrose changed ships, and in March he arrived at the English port of Dartmouth. Not unnaturally, the authorities took action, and both Ringrose and Captain Sharp were arrested and brought to trial for piracy. One would have thought that the evidence against them was clear enough, but for some reason or other the court freed them, and left Ringrose time to write his journal. This was his last astronomical foray. In February 1686, he went off on another piratical voyage, but this time there was no happy ending: off the coast of Mexico the ship was attacked by the Spaniards, and Ringrose's career came to an untimely end.

Well, at least he had the satisfaction of seeing both the Magellanic Clouds and a brilliant comet!

July

EARTH is at aphelion (furthest from the Sun) on 4 July at a distance of 152 million kilometres (94.5 million miles).

MERCURY reaches greatest western elongation (21°) on 12 July, but the long morning twilight means that it will not be visible to observers in northern Europe or North America. It is a morning object for those living in the tropics for a three-week period extending from the end of the first week of July until a few days before the end of the month. From 14–18 July, Mercury may be found about six degrees below the far more brilliant Venus in the east-north-eastern sky at the beginning of morning civil twilight, about twenty-five minutes before sunrise. From the temperate latitudes of the Southern Hemisphere, Mercury is visible during the middle two weeks of the month, low above the east-north-eastern horizon around the beginning of morning civil twilight. Once again, Venus is a useful guide to locating the more elusive Mercury in the middle of the month. Observers should note that Mercury is at its brightest after elongation, the planet brightening from magnitude +1.2 on 7 July to magnitude −1.0 on the 25th.

VENUS, magnitude −4.0, continues to be visible as a brilliant object in the twilight sky before dawn. The planet is visible low in the east-north-east, rising about two hours before the Sun. Venus passes 4° north of the first-magnitude star Aldebaran (Alpha Tauri) on 1/2 July. The phase of the planet increases from 86 to 92 per cent during the month.

MARS will be seen in the south-western sky at sunset from northern temperate latitudes, and sets before midnight by the end of the month; about two hours later from the Southern Hemisphere. The planet is now moving more rapidly east and south, and continues to fade, from magnitude 0.0 to +0.4 during July as its distance from the Earth increases from 147.8 million to 177.8 million kilometres (91.8 million to 110.5 million miles). Mars passes about 1.5 degrees north of the first-magnitude star Spica (Alpha Virginis) on 12 July (magnitudes Mars +0.2, Spica +1.2), the two objects being of rather contrasting hues; Mars orange-red and Spica blue-white.

JUPITER is in conjunction with the Sun on 24 July. It may be glimpsed by observers in the tropics and southern temperate latitudes low above the west-north-western horizon at the end of evening civil twilight for the first few days of the month, but it will not be visible at all from the latitudes of the British Isles.

SATURN reaches its second stationary point on 20 July and resumes its direct motion once more. The planet is an evening object in Libra, magnitude +0.5, setting at around midnight from northern temperate latitudes by the end of the month, and a couple of hours later from locations much further south.

PLUTO, officially a dwarf planet, reaches opposition on 4 July, in the constellation of Sagittarius, at a distance of 4,737 million kilometres (2,944 million miles). It is visible only with a moderate-sized telescope since its magnitude is +14.

Zaniah. This month, Mars is in Virgo, the Virgin, and passes quite close to the first-magnitude star Spica, leader of that constellation, in mid-July. Virgo is one of the more conspicuous of the Zodiacal constellations, and contains some interesting telescopic objects, notably the fine binary Porrima or Gamma Virginis, and a wealth of faint galaxies.

Zaniah, or Eta Virginis, lies to the west of Porrima and makes up part of the familiar 'Y' bowl of Virgo, but it is not prominent; its apparent magnitude is 3.89, which means that it is a very easy naked-eye object on a dark night, but is apt to be swamped when close to the Moon. Zaniah is one of the closest naked-eye stars to the celestial equator, lying only 40 arc minutes to the south of it, and it is also only about 5 degrees to the east of the autumnal equinox, the point where the Sun crosses the Equator from north to south on or around 23 September.

Zaniah is white, its surface is hotter than that of the Sun, at about 9,000 degrees centigrade, and parallax measurements have shown it to be about 265 light years distant. It is approximately 130 times as luminous as the Sun. Although the star looks single, lunar occultations have shown Zaniah to be a close triple-star system consisting of a pair of stars only about 75 million kilometres (46.6 million miles) apart with a third star some 1,500 million kilometres (932 million miles) distant.

Zaniah has a somewhat unusual history. The first proper star catalogue which has come down to us was drawn up in the second century AD by Ptolemy of Alexandria. Ptolemy naturally included Zaniah, but he gave its magnitude as 3, and made it equal to Porrima, in the base of the 'Y' pattern. Porrima is still of the third magnitude, so that it is not only brighter than Zaniah, but also obviously brighter.

Around the year 903, an Arab astronomer named Al-Sufi produced another excellent star catalogue. He, too, made Zaniah of magnitude 3, and equal to Porrima. Much later – in the nineteenth century – the German astronomer Eduard Heis made it 3.5, and now, as we have noted, it is down to 3.9. It doesn't seem to have altered much for many years.

If Ptolemy and Al-Sufi were right, Zaniah used to be noticeably brighter than it is now. On the other hand, it is not the sort of star which would be expected to show steady fading. Its components should be completely stable, and unlikely to alter over periods of millions of years. So what is the answer? As with other stars which have allegedly faded or brightened up since ancient times, it seems most likely that the old astronomers were either mistaken or misreported.

The First Successful Ranger Probe. In the period from 1961 to 1965, the Americans launched their series of Ranger probes, their first attempt to obtain close-up images of the lunar surface. The Ranger spacecraft were designed to crash into the Moon and to send back valuable data and images until the moment of impact. It must be admitted that the early Ranger probes were not a success: the launch vehicle failed on Rangers 1 and 2; Ranger 3 missed the Moon by 37,000 kilometres (23,000 miles) and sent back no images; Ranger 4 landed on the night-side due to an instrument and guidance failure; and Ranger 5 missed the Moon by 630 kilometres (390 miles) and no data were received. Finally, in January 1964, Ranger 6 reached the Moon, coming down in the Mare Tranquillitatis, but the camera failed and no pictures were received.

Success was achieved at last, fifty years ago this month: on 31 July 1964, after 68.6 hours of flight, Ranger 7 crash-landed in an area between Mare Nubium and Oceanus Procellarum (subsequently named Mare Cognitum) at latitude 10.63°S, longitude 20.60°W. The first image was taken at an altitude of 2,110 kilometres about 17 minutes before impact, and 4,308 photographs of excellent quality were returned (Figure 16). Ranger 7 impacted in a region of lunar mare terrain modified by crater rays. The final image taken before impact has a resolution of 0.5 metres. Impact occurred at a velocity of 2.62 kilometres per second (5,860 miles per hour).

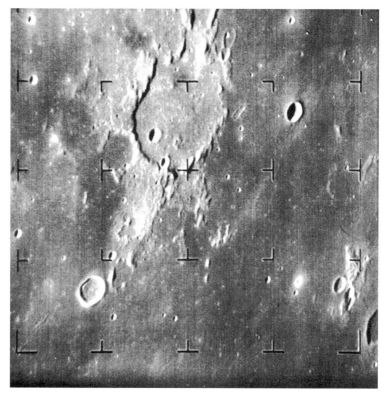

Figure 16a. Ranger 7 B-camera image of Guericke crater (11.5°S, 14.1°W, diameter 63 kilometres) taken from a distance of 1,335 kilometres. The dark flat floor of Mare Nubium dominates most of the image, which was taken 8.5 minutes before Ranger 7 impacted the Moon on 31 July 1964. The frame is about 230 kilometres across and north is up. The impact site is off the frame to the left. (Image courtesy of NASA/NSSDC.)

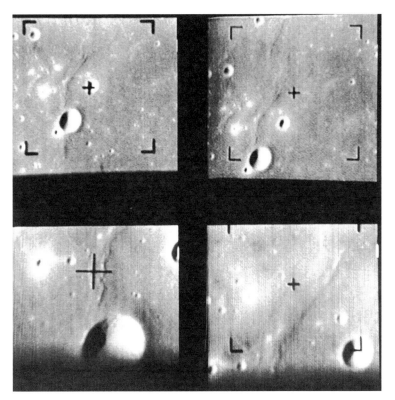

Figure 16b. Four Ranger 7 P-camera images showing part of the floor of Mare Nubium near the impact site. The images are ordered by camera (clockwise from upper left) P3, P4, P2 and P1. The images were taken from a distance of 250 kilometres about 90 seconds before impact. P3 and P4 overlap over most of the image, each one is about 15 kilometres across. Image P1 overlaps the lower left corner of P4, and the bottom of P2 overlaps the top of P1. Frames P1 and P2 are about 5.5 kilometres across. North is up. (Images courtesy of NASA/NSSDC.)

August

Full Moon: 10 August   *New Moon:* 25 August

MERCURY passes through superior conjunction on 8 August and remains unobservable from northern temperate latitudes throughout the month. From about 20 August, observers in equatorial and more southerly latitudes will be able to detect the planet as it moves slowly out from the glare of the Sun and becomes visible as an evening object, low in the western sky at the end of evening civil twilight about twenty-five minutes after sunset. Observers in these latitudes should consult Figure 20, given with the notes for September. The brightness of Mercury decreases from magnitude −0.8 to −0.2 during the last ten days of August.

VENUS continues to be visible as a splendid morning object, visible low above the east-north-east horizon before sunrise, but by the end of the month it is rising only about an hour before the Sun. On 18 August, Venus will appear extremely close to Jupiter, as it passes just to the north of it in the dawn twilight sky, and the two objects will make a lovely pairing for several mornings before and after this date. Venus (magnitude −3.9) will be about five times brighter than Jupiter (magnitude −1.8). Although the two planets appear close together in the sky – they will be only about one-fifth of a degree apart on the morning of the 18th – their distances from Earth are very different; Venus, 241 million kilometers (150 million miles) and Jupiter, 932 million kilometres (579 million miles). The thin, waning crescent Moon will appear above and to the right of Jupiter, with Venus below, on the morning of 23 August.

MARS continues to set about two hours after the Sun from northern temperate latitudes at the end of the month, but is visible for over two hours longer from the tropics and the Southern Hemisphere. It moves from Virgo into Libra on 10 August, passing about 3.5 degrees south of Saturn on 27 August; the two objects being of identical brightness at magnitude +0.6, but rather contrasting hues – Saturn yellowish and Mars orange-red. On 8 August, Mars will be twice as far from the Earth as it was at opposition in April, and is consequently much fainter.

JUPITER, magnitude −1.8, passed through conjunction with the Sun towards the end of July and it reappears in the early morning sky just before dawn after the middle of August. The close encounter between Jupiter and the more brilliant Venus for several days before and after 18 August has been mentioned above. By the end of the month Jupiter rises more than two-and-a-half hours before the Sun from the latitudes of the British Isles, but rather less from locations further south. The planet is in Cancer, the Crab.

SATURN is moving direct in Libra and is visible as an evening object in the south-western sky throughout August, but by the end of the month it sets only a little over two hours after the Sun from northern temperate latitudes; rather later from further south. Its brightness decreases slightly from magnitude +0.5 to +0.6 during the month. As mentioned above, Mars will pass a few degrees south of Saturn on 27 August. The first quarter Moon will lie roughly between Saturn and Mars on 3 August and the waxing crescent Moon will be just half a degree south of Saturn on the evening of 31 August.

NEPTUNE is at opposition on 29 August, in the constellation of Aquarius. It is not visible with the naked eye since its magnitude is +7.8. At opposition Neptune is 4,333 million kilometres (2,692 million miles) from the Earth. Figure 17 shows the path of Neptune against the background stars during the year.

The Perseid Meteors and Comet Swift-Tuttle. The annual Perseid meteor shower is among the most reliable of the year, producing an abundance of fast, bright meteors (Figure 18). Unfortunately, this August the shower will suffer considerable interference by moonlight, with first quarter Moon occurring on 4 August and full Moon on 10 August. Bright moonlight swamps all but the brighter meteors, reducing, quite considerably, the total number of meteors seen. This year, the Perseid peak occurs near 00h on 13 August, coinciding with a waning gibbous Moon in Pisces. Best observed rates are likely during the night of 12–13 August, particularly in the pre-dawn hours of 13 August.

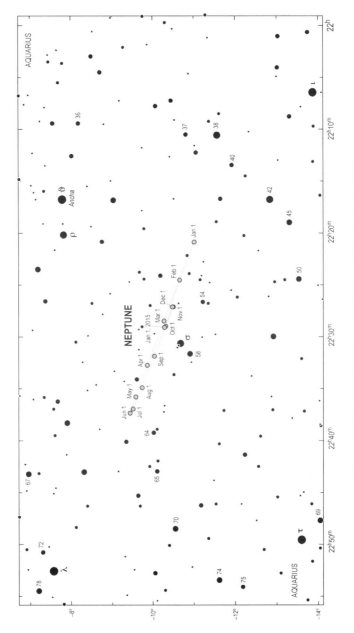

Figure 17. The path of Neptune against the stars of Aquarius during 2014.

Perseid meteors may be detected as early as late July/beginning of August and until about 21 August. The shower's activity displays a marked 'kick' around 8–9 August, with shower activity likely to be highest in the early morning hours on 11–12, 12–13 and 13–14 August. Best observed rates are generally found when the Perseid radiant (the region in the sky from which Perseid meteors appear to emanate), near the Double Cluster, on the Perseus-Cassiopeia border, is highest in the sky during the pre-dawn hours but, as stated earlier, moonlight will seriously affect observed rates this year.

The history of the Perseid stream goes back nearly two thousand years, the first recorded shower being noted by Chinese observers on 17 July AD 36. Between 1864 and 1866, the great Italian astronomer Giovanni Schiaparelli computed the orbit of the Perseid stream and showed that it was almost identical with that of the periodic comet 109P/Swift-Tuttle. This was the first time that any mathematical proof had been found to link meteors with comets.

Figure 18. A brilliant Perseid meteor with a terminal burst streaks from near Alpha Cephei, through the northern parts of Cygnus and into Lyra shortly after the peak of the shower on 12 August 2013. (Image courtesy of John Mason.)

Comet Swift-Tuttle itself was discovered on 16 July 1862 by Lewis Swift and three days afterwards, independently, by Horace Parnell Tuttle. The comet was a prominent naked-eye object for three weeks in August to September with a tail on 27 August as much as 25° long. The initial orbit was shown to be an ellipse by Theodor von Oppolzer, the comet being assigned a return period of 123 years, subsequently revised to 120 years. This being the case, one might have expected a return of comet Swift-Tuttle around 1981–82, but the comet never showed up. Because of this, there was speculation that the comet had disintegrated.

However, to some surprise, the comet was rediscovered in September 1992 by the Japanese astronomer Tsuruhiko Kiuchi and became visible with binoculars. From revised calculations made using the observations made in 1992 and those of 1862, it has been shown that the comet is identical with Comet Koegler observed from Beijing in 1737 by the Jesuit missionary Ignatius Koegler between 7 and 16 July of that year. Two of its previous returns prior to the telescopic period, in AD 188 and 69 BC, have now been identified in Chinese records. No other observations have been found AD 188 and 1737. These unobserved returns are easily explained, as the comet did not approach the Earth closely enough to reach naked-eye visibility. Calculations have shown that the comet's return period has varied between 127.4 and 136.5 years and it is not due back again until 2126.

Delphinus. One of the most prominent of the small constellations, and well placed during August evenings, is Delphinus, the Dolphin (Figure 19). It lies roughly between Altair and the Square of Pegasus. It has no star brighter than Beta, of magnitude 3.5, but it is a beautifully compact little group, and is quite unmistakable. According to an old legend, it represents the dolphin which rescued the famous singer, Arion, who had been thrown into the sea by a party of sailors who were anxious to lay hands upon his riches. The dolphin brought Arion safely to shore, and was rewarded by being placed in the sky!

The stars Alpha and Beta Delphini have the curious names Sualocin and Rotanev, respectively. These were allotted to the stars by one Nicolaus Venator, for reasons which should be obvious! Alpha is sixty times more luminous than our Sun, and lies at a distance of 170 light years, while Beta is 46 times as luminous and is 108 light years distant.

One of the stars in Delphinus, Gamma, is double; the components are of magnitudes 4.5 and 5.5, and 9.0 seconds of arc apart. Both the

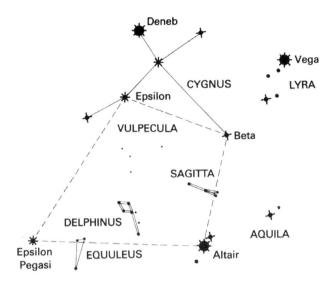

Figure 19. Map showing the location of the little constellation of Delphinus, the Dolphin, which lies slightly north of a line connecting the first-magnitude star Altair (in Aquila, the Eagle) to the west and the second-magnitude star Enif (Epsilon Pegasi) to the east.

primary and its companion are yellowish. Gamma Delphini is a beautiful object in a moderate telescope.

Delphinus is not the only small constellation in the region, but the others – Equuleus (the Little Horse), Sagitta (the Arrow) and Vulpecula (the Fox) – are much less conspicuous. Vulpecula does, however, include the Dumb-bell Nebula (Messier 27), which is a fine example of a planetary nebula – too faint to be well seen in small telescopes, but showing considerable detail when imaged with large instruments.

September

Full Moon: 9 September   **New Moon:** 24 September

Equinox: 23 September

MERCURY remains unsuitably placed for observation for those in northern Europe and North America throughout September. However, for observers in equatorial and more southerly latitudes, this will be the most favourable evening apparition of the year. Figure 20 shows, for observers in latitude 35°S, the changes in azimuth and altitude of Mercury on successive evenings at the end of evening civil twilight, about twenty-five minutes after sunset. The variations in the brightness of the planet are indicated by the relative sizes of the white circles marking Mercury's position at five-day intervals: Mercury is at its

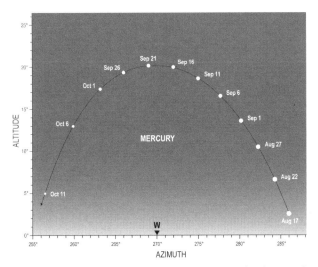

Figure 20. Evening apparition of Mercury from latitude 35°S. The planet reaches greatest eastern elongation on 21 September 2014. It was at its brightest in mid-August, several weeks before elongation.

brightest before it reaches greatest eastern elongation (26°) on 21 September, with the planet fading gradually from magnitude −0.2 to +0.4 during the month. The diagram gives positions for a time at the end of evening civil twilight on the Greenwich meridian on the stated date. Observers in different longitudes should note that the actual positions of Mercury in azimuth and altitude will differ slightly from those given in the diagram due to the motion of the planet. The thin waxing crescent Moon will appear fairly close to Mercury on the evening of 26 September.

VENUS, magnitude −3.9, remains a brilliant object low above the eastern horizon before dawn. However, it is getting noticeably closer to the Sun and for those in southern latitudes the planet will not be visible after the first week of the month. By the third week of September, observers in the latitudes of the British Isles are unlikely to be able to see it for more than about ten minutes or so before it disappears in the brightening dawn sky, while those in the tropics may be able to glimpse it for a few days longer. By the end of September the planet is becoming lost in the glare of the rising Sun.

MARS is an evening object visible low in the south-west after sunset. It begins the month in Libra, moves into Scorpius on 13 September and into Ophiuchus on the 26th. It fades from magnitude +0.6 to +0.8 during the month. Figure 21 shows the path of Mars against the background stars during the last four months of the year. On 27 September, Mars will be three degrees north of the reddish star Antares, the 'Rival of Mars', and the brightest star in Scorpius. This will afford an opportunity to compare their colours: Mars (magnitude +0.8) will be slightly brighter than Antares (magnitude +1.2). At this time, Mars is actually in the constellation of Ophiuchus, which intrudes into the Zodiac between Scorpius and Sagittarius. On the evening of 29 September, the waxing crescent Moon passes just under five degrees north of Mars.

JUPITER, magnitude −1.9, is a morning object, rising shortly after 02h by the end of the month for observers in northern temperate latitudes, but over two hours later from locations further south. It is moving direct in Cancer and completely dominates an otherwise rather barren part of the sky.

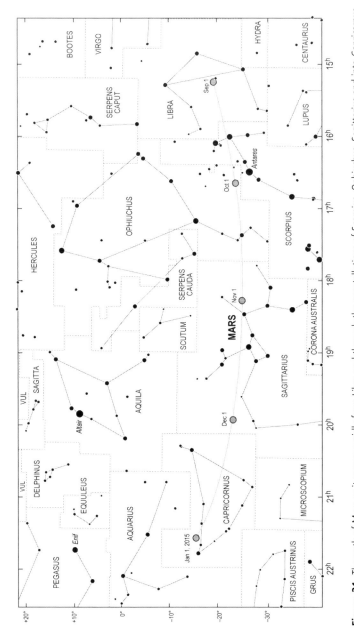

Figure 21. The path of Mars as it moves rapidly from Libra and through the constellations of Scorpius, Ophiuchus, Sagittarius and into Capricornus during the last four months of 2014. The motion of the planet is direct throughout this period.

SATURN, magnitude +0.6, is visible in the south-western sky as darkness falls. From northern temperate latitudes, Saturn will be rather low in the twilight at dusk by month end, although somewhat easier for observers further south. The waxing crescent Moon will be slightly west of Saturn on the evening of 27 September, and the following night will be positioned between Saturn and Mars, which is in the same part of the sky, but about twenty degrees to the east of Saturn.

Crosses in the Sky. Almost everyone must have heard about the constellation of the Southern Cross, even though it is never visible from Europe or the main part of the United States; it is as familiar to Australians and South Africans as the Great Bear is to Britons. Yet it is not the only cross in the sky. There are two more, and it may be of interest to compare them.

Crux Australis, the Southern Cross itself (now known simply as Crux), is actually the smallest constellation in the whole of the sky; there are eighty-eight accepted constellations altogether, and in its dimensions the Cross comes eighty-eighth. (The No.1 position used to be occupied by Argo Navis, the Ship Argo, but it was so unwieldy that finally the International Astronomical Union lost patience with it and chopped it up into a keel, sails and a poop deck.) Crux was not even recognized as a separate constellation until 1679, when it was formed by an astronomer named Royer. Before that it had been included in Centaurus, the Centaur, which surrounds it on three sides. The brilliant leaders of Centaurus, Alpha and Beta, are known as the Pointers to the Cross.

The four leading stars of Crux are Alpha or Acrux (magnitude 0.8), Beta (1.3), Gamma (1.6) and Delta (2.8). These four are arranged in a shape which resembles a box or a kite. There is a fifth star, Epsilon Crucis (magnitude 3.6), roughly between Alpha and Delta. It does not really spoil the main pattern, but it is nowhere near the middle of the 'box'. There is no central star at all and, impressive though it may be, Crux is not in the least like a cross.

Two of the four main members are notable: Alpha Crucis and Gamma Crucis. Alpha Crucis is a lovely double, separable with a small telescope, with a third star in the same field. Gamma Crucis, third in order of brilliancy, is a red giant, whereas the other leading stars are hot and bluish-white. This is obvious even with the naked eye, and binoculars bring out the contrast splendidly.

Many unwary observers have been deceived by the False Cross, which lies approximately between Crux to one side and the brilliant star Canopus (Alpha Carinae) to the other (though admittedly it is some way off the line joining the two). The False Cross lies partly in Carina, the Keel of the old Ship, and Vela, the Argo's sails. Its shape is very like that of Crux. The four principal stars are Epsilon Carinae (Avior), Iota Carinae (Tureis), Kappa Velorum (Markeb) and Delta Velorum (which has no accepted Arabic name; in any case, proper names of stars are hardly ever used nowadays, except for stars of the first magnitude and a few special cases such as Polaris and Mira). All four are between magnitudes 1.8 and 2.5, so that the overall aspect is more symmetrical than that of Crux, and the whole group is larger as well as being less brilliant. As with Crux, one of the main stars is orange-red – in this case, Epsilon Carinae – while the other three are white.

Both Crux and the False Cross are immersed in the Milky Way, and the same is true of our third candidate – Cygnus, the Swan. This is a northern constellation, and indeed part of it is circumpolar from Britain – that is to say, it never sets. The stars of Cygnus are well placed from northern temperate latitudes during September evenings.

This time we really do have a cross-like pattern. The leading star, Deneb, is of the first magnitude, and is an extremely luminous star. The centre of the cross is marked by Sadr or Gamma Cygni (magnitude 2.2); to the left and right are Delta (2.9) and Epsilon Cygni (2.5). The remaining member of the pattern, Albireo or Beta Cygni, is fainter (3.1) and further away from the centre than the rest, and so slightly upsets the symmetry, but to make up for this Albireo is a lovely double star, with a golden yellow primary and a blue-green companion.

Cygnus is often nicknamed the Northern Cross, for reasons which are obvious as soon as you look at it. Deneb makes up a large triangle with Vega in Lyra and Altair in Aquila; often nicknamed 'the Summer Triangle', even though the term is completely unofficial and the three stars of the Triangle belong to three separate constellations.

Sir James Jeans. There have been many popularizers of astronomy. Undoubtedly one of the best was Sir James Hopwood Jeans (Figure 22), who was born on 11 September 1877, in Ormskirk, Lancashire, and was educated at Merchant Taylors' School, Northwood, Wilson's Grammar School, Camberwell and Trinity College, Cambridge. He first taught at

Cambridge, but in 1904 went to Princeton University as professor of applied mathematics, returning to Cambridge in 1910. Jeans first became known because of his researches into the origin of the Solar System; he believed that the Earth and the other planets condensed from material pulled off the Sun by the gravitational action of a passing star, and this so-called Tidal Theory was widely accepted for many years, even though it is now known to be wrong. Today, it seems certain that the planets condensed out of a rotating disc of dust and gas which surrounded the youthful Sun.

Figure 22. Portrait of Sir James Hopwood Jeans, the English physicist, astronomer and mathematician who made many innovations in astronomical and physical theory, but is perhaps most widely known as the writer of several best-selling popular astronomy books. (Image courtesy of University of St Andrews.)

Jeans paid great attention to problems of the internal constitution of the stars, and his name is often coupled with that of another famous astrophysicist, Sir Arthur Eddington, though actually their points of view as to how stars produce their energy were rather different. Jeans wrote several technical books and many papers, and he was responsible for major advances in our understanding of how the stars evolve. Later in his career, he concentrated more and more upon popular writing, and some of his books, such as *The Stars in Their Courses*, *The Universe Around Us* and *The Mysterious Universe*, were classics of their time. He had a delightfully fluent style, and a knack of making difficult problems sound easy, though as a true scientist he was always wary of over-simplification.

Jeans was also the first famous radio broadcaster on astronomy. During the 1930s his voice became very familiar to listeners to the BBC; he continued to broadcast regularly during the Second World War, and, indeed, until a very short time before his death on 16 September 1946. It is a great pity that he died before television became an integral part of modern living; he would have been so good at it.

Astronomy did not occupy his whole time. He was a man of varied interests, and in particular he was a good musician. Unquestionably, Jeans was responsible for encouraging many beginners to take up astronomy as a serious hobby, and even as a profession. He was always ready to give a helping hand. Many professional scientists of the day owed much to him, and his death left a gap which could not easily be filled. A reporter once asked him how he would describe himself. Jeans thought for a moment, and then gave a perfect answer: 'I am', he said, 'a publicity man for the planets.' How true that was!

October

Full Moon: 8 October   *New Moon:* 23 October

Summer Time in the United Kingdom ends on 26 October.

MERCURY passes through inferior conjunction on 16 October and then moves rapidly out from the Sun. Although it is unsuitably placed for observation from southern temperate latitudes throughout the month, observers in equatorial and northern temperate latitudes will be able to see the planet low in the eastern sky at the beginning of morning civil twilight about half an hour before sunrise during the last week of October. Observers in these latitudes should consult Figure 24, given with the notes for November. The brightness of Mercury increases noticeably from magnitude +1.1 on 24 October to −0.4 by the end of the month.

VENUS, although theoretically a morning object, is now lost in the brightening dawn twilight sky before sunrise and is unlikely to be seen this month. The planet passes through superior conjunction on 25 October.

MARS, magnitude +0.9, is still an evening object and setting about two and a half hours after the Sun from northern temperate latitudes, but this visibility period is over four hours from locations in the Southern Hemisphere. The planet moves from Ophiuchus into Sagittarius on 21 October and reaches its most southerly point four days later. It is because of the planet's far southerly declination that it is visible for so much longer to Southern Hemisphere observers than to those in northern Europe and North America.

JUPITER, magnitude −2.0, is a morning object, rising around midnight by month end from northern temperate latitudes, but a couple of hours later from locations further south. The planet moves from Cancer into Leo on 14 October.

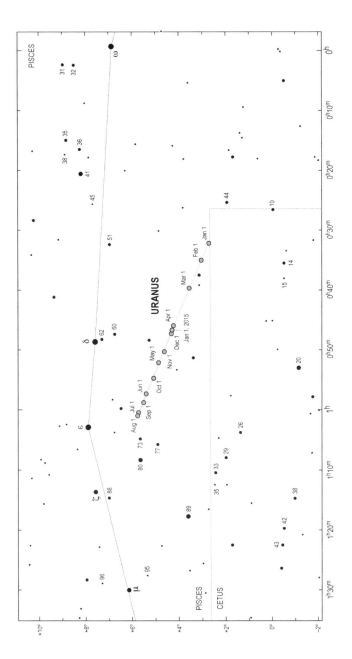

Figure 23. The path of Uranus against the background stars of Pisces during 2014.

SATURN, magnitude +0.6, is visible in the south-western sky as darkness falls. From northern temperate latitudes, Saturn will be inconveniently low in the twilight at dusk by month end, although somewhat easier for observers further south. The planet continues to move direct in Libra.

URANUS is at opposition on 7 October in the constellation of Pisces. Uranus is barely visible to the naked eye as its magnitude is +5.7, but it is easily located in binoculars. Figure 23 shows the path of Uranus against the background stars during the year. At opposition Uranus is 2,845 million kilometres (1,768 million miles) from the Earth.

Pehr Wargentin and the Vanishing Moon. Unless you are interested in the history of science, it is not likely that you will have heard of Pehr Wilhelm Wargentin. Nevertheless, he was an eighteenth-century Swedish astronomer of considerable eminence, and he was associated with several interesting events. Wargentin was born on 11 September 1717. After taking his degree at the University of Uppsala, he went to Stockholm, to become director of the observatory there. At an early age he had been attracted to astronomy by an eclipse of the Moon, and it was this which launched him upon his career.

There is a total eclipse of the Moon this month, on 8 October. Sadly, no part of this eclipse will be observable from Europe, although it will be visible in its entirety from Alaska and the westernmost states of the US, northern Japan, eastern Siberia, eastern Australia and New Zealand. From South America and the eastern US seaboard the Moon will be setting before or just after totality starts. From Western Australia, India, China and much of Asia, the Moon will be rising while in totality. A lunar eclipse occurs when the Moon passes into the cone of shadow cast by the Earth. The direct supply of sunlight is temporarily cut off, and the Moon turns a dim, often coppery-red colour until it emerges from the shadow. Generally, it does not vanish completely, because some of the Sun's rays are refracted onto the lunar surface by way of the blanket of atmosphere surrounding the Earth. But on 18 May 1761, things were quite different. Wargentin wrote:

> The Moon's body disappeared so completely that not the slightest trace of the lunar disk could be seen either with the naked eye or

with the telescope, although the sky was clear, and stars in the vicinity of the Moon were distinctly visible in the telescope.

Since any sunlight reaching the eclipsed Moon must first pass through the atmosphere of the Earth, conditions in our upper air are all-important. Two years earlier, in 1759, the Mexican volcano El Jorullo had erupted violently and hurled large quantities of volcanic ash and dust into the upper part of the atmosphere. This took a long time to settle, which no doubt accounts for Wargentin's observation.

Other very dark eclipses have been those of 15 June 1620 and 4 October 1884, but the last occasion upon which the Moon vanished completely was that of the eclipse of 10 June 1816. Once again a major volcanic eruption was responsible. In April 1815, the volcano Tambora, on the Indonesian island of Sumbawa, exploded so catastrophically that over ninety thousand people were killed, either directly or by subsequent starvation as the crops failed. Indeed, 1816 has been termed 'the year without a summer'; it was even worse than that of 1815 when the actual eruption occurred. It has been estimated that around a hundred cubic kilometres of rock was blasted into the atmosphere by the Tambora eruption. By contrast, the lunar eclipse of 19 March 1848 was so bright that the Moon turned blood-red, and many people doubted whether an eclipse was in progress at all.

Pehr Wargentin himself carried out much valuable work; he published excellent tables of the movements of Jupiter's four bright satellites, and did much to organize astronomy in Sweden. He died on 13 December 1783. It is fitting that his name should have been attached to a formation on the Moon – a ninety-kilometre (fifty-five-mile) plateau or lava-filled crater, unlike anything else on the lunar surface. Certainly Wargentin deserves to be remembered.

The Strange Fate of Eduard Vogel. One of the most unusual careers in the history of astronomy is that of Eduard Vogel. It led him to an early death – at least, so we assume – but just what caused him to act in the way he did remains a complete mystery.

Vogel's early life was conventional enough. He was born in 1829 at Krefeld, son of the headmaster of the local school. He turned his attention to astronomy, and went first to Leipzig University where he studied under Heinrich D'Arrest (later to become famous as Johann Galle's assistant on the night of the discovery of Neptune). Vogel then went on to Berlin, where the Observatory director was Johann Encke. Vogel received his doctorate, and began serious work in computing the orbits of comets and minor planets. Then, in 1851, he went to England as an assistant to John Russell Hind at George Bishop's private observatory in Regent's Park. From here, Vogel was the first to detect Encke's Comet at its return in 1852.

He seemed set for a successful career as an astronomer, but then came a diversion. In 1852, the British Government became alarmed at the fate of an expedition which had been sent in 1849 to a then-unexplored region of the Sahara Desert to find a new trade route. One member of that expedition was the famous explorer, Heinrich Barth. Vogel was asked to go and find Barth and replace a member of the expedition who had died two years earlier. (It subsequently transpired that both of Barth's companions had died.) It seemed strange to select a young astronomer for such a task, and even stranger for Vogel to accept; but he did, and, on 20 February 1853, he sailed for Africa. He never returned.

In October 1853 he wrote a letter from southern Libya, addressed to the German explorer Alexander von Humboldt, in which he described some observations made in the desert; these were actually printed in a leading German astronomical periodical in the following year. And certainly he found Barth; he met him in December 1854 on the shores of Lake Chad. By that time Vogel had joined with two young English soldiers, the expedition's engineers, named MacGuire and Church. The party had dinner together, and it is said that Barth even reproached Vogel for not having brought along some good German wine!

They stayed in the native village for a week, and then split up. Barth returned to England, accompanied by Church; later he published a book, *Travels and Discoveries in North and Central Africa*. MacGuire went off on his own, and is believed to have been murdered by tribesmen in the Sahara. What, then, of Vogel? There seemed no reason why he should not return to his home and to astronomy; instead, he continued his travels alone, later becoming the first European to cross the Muri mountains. The last record of Vogel shows him in the Upper Congo; his expedition notes cease on 1 December 1855 – after that there is silence. Several search expeditions were organized to ascertain Vogel's fate and to recover his papers, and it seems that he was killed by local people in Wara, the capital of Wadai, in February 1856.

Astronomy was the poorer for his loss; had he returned with Barth, he could so easily have made his mark in the scientific world.

November

Full Moon: 6 November   *New Moon:* 22 November

MERCURY is at greatest western elongation (19°) on 1 November. Consequently, the planet is visible from the tropics and northern temperate latitudes as an early morning object until the third week of November. It is inconveniently low from the Southern Hemisphere. For observers in the latitudes of the British Isles this will be the most favourable morning apparition of the year, with the planet being visible in the south-eastern twilight sky before dawn. Figure 24 shows the changes in azimuth and altitude of Mercury on successive mornings at the start of morning civil twilight, about 40 minutes before sunrise, for observers in latitude 52°N. The changes in the brightness of the planet are indicated by the relative sizes of the white circles marking

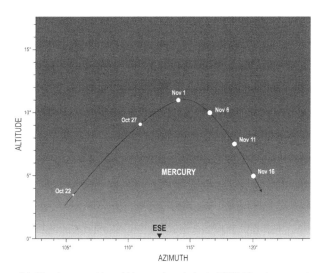

Figure 24. Morning apparition of Mercury from latitude 52°N. The planet reaches greatest western elongation on 1 November 2014. It will be at its brightest in late November, after elongation.

Mercury's position at five-day intervals: Mercury is at its brightest after it reaches greatest western elongation, with the planet brightening gradually from magnitude −0.5 to −0.8 between 1 and 18 November. The diagram gives positions for a time at the end of evening civil twilight on the Greenwich meridian on the stated date. Observers in different longitudes should note that the actual positions of Mercury in azimuth and altitude will differ slightly from those given in the diagram due to the motion of the planet.

VENUS remains too close to the Sun for observation throughout November, except for observers in the tropics. They should be able to glimpse the planet for a short while, low above the south-western horizon immediately after sunset, at the very end of the month. Its magnitude is −3.9.

MARS may be seen as a rather inconspicuous first-magnitude object in Sagittarius. It is now beginning to move northwards once again and sets about the same time each evening, around two and a half hours after the Sun from northern temperate latitudes, but an hour or so later from further south.

JUPITER rises shortly before midnight by the end of November and is visible until dawn. It continues to move direct in Leo, the planet brightening slightly from magnitude −2.0 to −2.2 during the month. The last quarter Moon will appear quite close to Jupiter in the early morning sky on 14 and 15 November.

SATURN is in conjunction with the Sun on 18 November and consequently will not be visible at all this month.

The Great Square of Pegasus. In northern temperate latitudes, the Square of Pegasus dominates the southern part of the evening sky during the autumn months of October and November. On star maps, Pegasus (the Flying Horse) looks quite conspicuous, since its four main stars make up an obvious square (Figure 25), and you might think that it would stand out clearly in the night sky. Certainly, once you have found Pegasus, it will be easily located again, but to begin with you must look for it carefully. This is partly because its stars are not remarkably brilliant – all four are between the second and third magnitudes –

and partly because the Square is very large. The 'W' of Cassiopeia, which lies almost overhead during autumn evenings, makes a useful pointer; an imaginary line passing through its stars Gamma and Alpha will lead you straight to the Great Square.

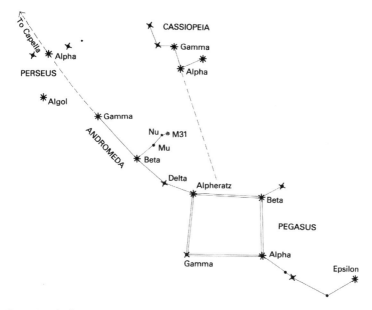

Figure 25. The four main stars comprising the Great Square of Pegasus are well placed during November evenings, but they are not especially bright and the Square is larger than many people expect it to be: once located it is easy enough. The 'W' of Cassiopeia makes a useful pointer; an imaginary line passing through its stars Gamma and Alpha leads directly to the Great Square. The line of three main stars comprising Andromeda, the beautiful daughter of Queen Cassiopeia in mythology, is also well shown, running north-eastwards from the Great Square.

The upper left-hand star of the Square used to be known as Delta Pegasi, but it has now been officially – and, frankly, illogically – transferred by the IAU (International Astronomical Union) to the neighbouring constellation of Andromeda, as Alpha Andromedae; its proper name, still often used, is Alpheratz. The upper right-hand star of the Square, Beta Pegasi or Scheat, is a red giant. Like many of its kind, it is variable; the magnitude range is from 2.3 to 2.8, and there is a very rough period of from 35 to 40 days. Alpha Pegasi or Markab (2.5) at the bottom right of the Square, and Gamma Pegasi or Algenib (2.8) at the bottom left, act as good comparison stars, and the light variations may be followed with the naked eye. The only other important star is Epsilon Pegasi or Enif (2.4), which lies well to the west of the Square, in a relatively isolated position roughly between Alpha Pegasi and Altair in Aquila, the Eagle.

It is interesting to count the number of faint stars visible inside the Square without optical aid. There are not a great many of them, though the area covered is considerable; anyone who counts a dozen will be doing rather well.

Well below the Square, fairly close to the horizon from Britain, is Fomalhaut in Piscis Austrinus (the Southern Fish), the southern-most of the first-magnitude stars visible from Europe or the main United States. It is never well seen from these locations, but fortu-nately a line extended downwards from Scheat through Markab points almost directly to it. The best time to look for Fomalhaut is around 1900 to 2000 hours in mid-November; by midnight it will be too low to be seen, although from the latitude of New York it is visi-ble for longer.

The Craters of Mars. Fifty years ago – on 28 November 1964 – the first successful Mars probe was launched. Mariner 4 flew past Mars on 14 July 1965 at a range of 9,846 kilometres (6,118 miles) and sent back the first pictures which showed unmistakeable craters on Mars.

It was not the first attempt. Russia's Mars 1, launched on 1 November 1962, had undoubtedly encountered Mars, but all contact with it had been lost much earlier, and no scientific data were obtained. The American probe Mariner 3 (launched 5 November 1964) was a total failure, and all contact was lost soon after launch. However, Mariner 4 more than made up for these earlier setbacks, becoming the first spacecraft to get a close look at Mars. In addition to carrying vari-ous field and particle sensors and detectors, the spacecraft confirmed the thinness of the Martian atmosphere, and took twenty-two pictures covering about one per cent of the planet with its television camera. Initially stored on a four-track tape recorder, these pictures took four days to transmit to Earth. Mariner 4 remained in contact until 21 December 1967.

Up to that time, it had been thought that Mars was a world without major mountains or valleys, although, many years earlier, it had been claimed that craters had been seen from Earth by E. E. Barnard, using the Lick Observatory 36-inch refractor (1892) and J. Mellish, using the Yerkes 40-inch refractor (1917). Unfortunately, their observations were never published. Craters had been predicted in 1944 by D. L. Cyr; his reasoning was completely wrong, but Mariner 4 showed that craters did exist, and that some were very large indeed.

By sheer bad luck, Mariner 4 and the next two successful Mars probes, Mariners 6 and 7 (1969) surveyed the least interesting parts of Mars. It was only when Mariner 9 was put into a closed path around the planet, in November 1971, that we had our first views of the valleys and the mountains. Moreover, excellent images were obtained of the polar caps – then widely believed to be composed mainly of carbon dioxide ice. Not until 2003 was it finally shown that the caps consist almost entirely of water ice with only a thin coating of carbon dioxide ice.

The Mariner 4 pictures (Figure 26) seem very poor by today's

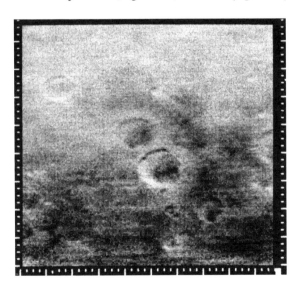

Figure 26a. This image, the eighth taken by Mariner 4, confirmed the existence of craters south of Amazonis Planitia on Mars. The image was taken from a range of 13,400 kilometres and covers 255 kilometres by 296 kilometres. The two craters at the centre of the image are about 32 kilometres in diameter. North is up. (Image courtesy of NASA/NSSDC.)

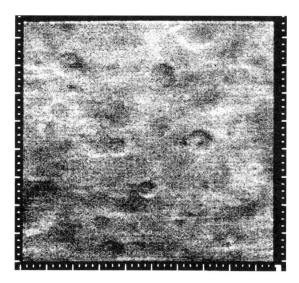

Figure 26b. Mariner 4 image showing at least twenty craters of various sizes in the western Memnonia Fossae region of Mars, resembling parts of the lunar surface. The image was taken from a range of 13,000 kilometres and measures 253 by 225 kilometres. The Sun angle is 39 degrees from the zenith, allowing some detail to be seen, including a central peak in the crater right of the centre. North is up. (Image courtesy of NASA/NSSDC.)

standards, but at the time they represented a tremendous technical triumph, and paved the way for all that followed. We have learned a great deal about Mars in the past fifty years.

December

Full Moon: 6 December   *New Moon:* 22 December

Solstice: 21 December

MERCURY passes through superior conjunction on 8 December and consequently is too close to the Sun for observation for most of the month. However, those living in the tropics and the Southern Hemisphere should be able to locate it low in the west-south-western sky at the end of evening civil twilight during the last week of December; its magnitude is −0.8. By the very end of December, Mercury will have moved so that it is only three degrees below Venus, the brilliant planet being a useful guide to locating the more elusive Mercury in the bright twilight sky.

VENUS, magnitude −3.9, is an evening object visible with increasing ease by observers in the tropics and Southern Hemisphere as the month progresses, low above the west-south-western horizon at dusk. However, observers in the latitudes of the British Isles will have to wait until the last few days of the month before they are able to glimpse the planet, because it is so far south of the celestial equator. It will then be seen low above the south-western horizon for a short while immediately after sunset.

MARS, magnitude +1.1, continues to be visible as an evening object, passing from Sagittarius into neighbouring Capricornus early in the month. It sets about three and a half hours after the Sun at the end of December from the latitudes of the British Isles, now slightly less from locations further south. Although the planet is at perihelion on 12 December, when its distance from the Sun will be 207 million kilometres (128 million miles), it is a long way from the Earth and consequently is rather inconspicuous. There is no opposition of Mars in 2015, the planet being in conjunction with the Sun on 14 June.

JUPITER now rises before midnight and reaches a stationary point on 8 December in Leo; thereafter its motion is retrograde. The planet continues to increase in brightness, from magnitude −2.2 to −2.4 during the month, as it approaches opposition in early February next year.

SATURN was in conjunction with the Sun in mid-November and is visible in the south-eastern sky before dawn during December from northern temperate latitudes. By the end of the month from such locations, the planet will be rising more than three hours before the Sun, and only slightly less for those situated further south. The planet is in Libra, magnitude +0.6.

The Fading of Mars. Having approached the Earth to within 92.4 million kilometres (57.4 million miles) in April last, when it was a bright object of magnitude −1.5 in Virgo, Mars has now drawn away from us, and is receding all the time. By the end of December it will have faded to below first magnitude (slightly inferior to Aldebaran), whereas in April it was the fifth brightest object in the entire sky after the Sun, Moon, Venus and Jupiter.

Because it is a small body, and its distance from the Earth is so variable, Mars undergoes changes in apparent brightness which are more noticeable than with any other planet. Venus and Jupiter are always strikingly brilliant when they are visible at all, and Saturn remains between magnitudes 0 and 1 almost all the time. Mars, however, can be either very bright or else relatively obscure; at its dimmest it is only of second magnitude, and unwary observers can all too easily mistake it for an ordinary red star. For most of 2015, Mars will not be particularly prominent, becoming steadily less and less evident until it reaches conjunction in June. It will then reappear as a morning object, but even by the end of next year it will still be well below the first magnitude.

Of course, adequate telescopes will show markings on the small Martian disk; but modest instruments will not show very much, and for most amateurs Mars may be to all intents and purposes disregarded throughout most of 2015.

Mars next comes to opposition on 22 May 2016, when it will be only 76.2 million kilometres (47.4 million miles) distant – rather closer than it was in April of this year – and even brighter at magnitude −2.0. Unfortunately, for observers in northern Europe and North America, this will be a somewhat disappointing opposition since Mars will be rather low in the southern sky among the stars of Scorpius.

The Return of the Hunter. By December evenings, the brilliant winter constellations have again come into view. Of these, Orion, the Hunter, is pre-eminent; with its characteristic outline, its prominent stars and its surrounding retinue, it dominates the southern aspect of the sky (Figure 27).

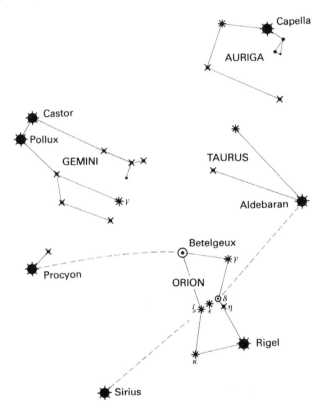

Figure 27. During December evenings, the brilliant winter constellations have again come into view. Of these, Orion, the Hunter, dominates the southern aspect of the sky, surrounded by its retinue of Aldebaran in Taurus (the Bull), Capella in Auriga (the Charioteer), Castor and Pollux in Gemini (the Twins), Procyon in Canis Minor (the Little Dog), and the brilliant Sirius in Canis Major (the Great Dog).

Betelgeuse, the red M-type supergiant in the upper left-hand part of the constellation, is a semi-regular variable which varies between magnitudes 0.1 and 0.9. Its distance is uncertain, but somewhere between 500 and 640 light years. Betelgeuse – whose name can also be spelled Betelgeux – is different from the other main stars of Orion, which generally are hot, white and of early spectral type (O or B). Rigel, in the Hunter's foot, which is of spectral type B8, is one such star. Rigel is actually variable over a very small range, but it has a mean apparent magnitude of +0.12, so it is less than one tenth of a magnitude fainter than Capella and Vega. When seen from northern Europe or North America it does not appear their equal, simply because it never rises particularly high. Yet Rigel is vastly more luminous than either of these two stars; a blue supergiant which, according to recent estimates, is 85,000 times as luminous as the Sun, and lies at a distance of some 860 light years.

Luminous though Rigel is, some of the other stars of Orion are comparable. Kappa or Saiph, in the lower left-hand region, has an apparent magnitude of 2.1, so that it is slightly fainter than the Pole Star, but its distance from us is thought to be about 720 light years, so that it – like Rigel – is a true 'celestial searchlight' with a luminosity 65,000 times that of the Sun. Gamma, or Bellatrix, and the three stars of the Belt are also highly luminous. Below the Belt may be seen the Hunter's Sword, containing the gaseous nebula Messier 42, visible with the naked eye and a superb sight in a moderate telescope. Altogether, Orion lays claim to being the most spectacular constellation in the entire sky.

Eclipses in 2014

MARTIN MOBBERLEY

During 2014 there will be four eclipses: two total lunar eclipses, an annular eclipse of the Sun and a partial eclipse of the Sun. All four eclipses occur in two specific months, namely April and October. Sadly, no total solar eclipse will occur in 2014.

1. *A total eclipse of the Moon* on 15 April will be visible in its entirety from the western and central US, Canada, western South America and the eastern Pacific Ocean. From the eastern US and eastern South American countries the Moon completes totality just before it sets. From the extreme western tip of Africa the Moon almost enters totality before it sets, but unfortunately, from the UK, it will barely have entered the penumbra before British moonset occurs. California, Mexico and neighbouring regions will be optimally placed to see the entire eclipse with the Moon peaking in altitude during totality.

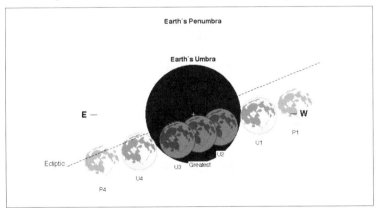

Figure 1. The path of the Moon through the penumbra and umbra (darkest area) of the Earth's shadow on 15 April. The corresponding P1, U1, U2, Greatest, U3, U4 and P4 times are as follows in UT (Universal Time): 04:54, 05:58, 07:07, 07:46, 08:25, 09:33 and 10:38. (Diagram based on the eclipse prediction by Fred Espenak, NASA/GSFC.)

The edge of the Moon first enters the umbral shadow at 05h 58m UT (Universal Time), with the whole lunar disc being immersed by 07h 7m UT. Mid-totality occurs at 07h 46m UT. The Moon starts to emerge from the umbra at 08h 25m UT and is completely free of the umbra by 09h 33m UT. Totality will last for 1 hour 18 minutes.

2. *An annular eclipse of the Sun* on 29 April will be visible as a partial solar eclipse in the far Southern Hemisphere. The partial phase will first be visible at sunrise, around 03h 52m UT, from the Southern Ocean, south of South Africa, from the southern Indian Ocean, from Australia, and also in the Southern Ocean below Australia (including Tasmania). From the eastern coast of Australia the partial eclipse will occur at sunset, close to 08h 14m UT. The region experiencing a full annular eclipse, with the Moon surrounded by a ring of fire, will be tiny and

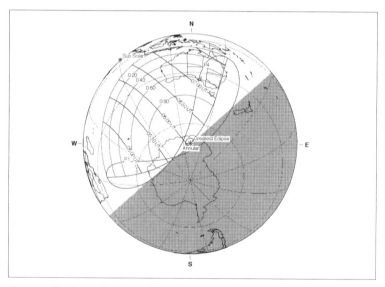

Figure 2. The view looking towards the Earth's South Pole on 29 April 2014 at the time of greatest eclipse, with the partial eclipse magnitude contours drawn on the illuminated region. Most of the Pacific Ocean hemisphere is experiencing night-time darkness and the curved lines on the sunlit hemisphere indicate the degree by which the Sun is eclipsed, namely 80, 60, 40, 20 and 0 per cent contours. The area within the tiny circle near the Antarctic day/night boundary will see an annular eclipse with the Sun literally on the horizon. (Diagram courtesy of Fred Espenak, NASA/GSFC.)

restricted to a small area of Antarctica, centred on latitude 70° 38.7' S and 131° 18.3' E, exceptionally close to the terminator and therefore with the Sun being almost on the Antarctic horizon. The time of greatest eclipse at this point will occur at 06h 03m UT. From the south coast of Australia the solar disk will be 60 per cent covered by the Moon. From the northernmost coastal regions of Australia less than 10 per cent of the solar disk will be covered.

3. *A total eclipse of the Moon* on 8 October will be visible in its entirety from the centre of the Pacific Ocean, Alaska, the westernmost states of the US, northern Japan, eastern Siberia, Eastern Australia and New Zealand. From South America and the eastern US seaboard the Moon will be setting before or just after totality starts. From Western Australia, India, China and much of Asia the Moon will be rising while in totality. Sadly, no part of the eclipse will be visible from Europe or Africa.

The edge of the Moon first enters the umbral shadow at 09h 15m UT, with the whole lunar disc being immersed by 10h 25m UT. Mid-totality occurs at 10h 55m UT. The Moon starts to emerge from the umbra at 11h 24m UT and is completely free of the umbra by 12h 34m UT. Totality will last for fifty-nine minutes.

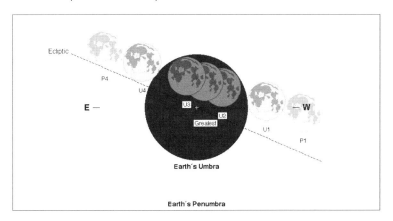

Figure 3. The path of the Moon through the umbra (darkest) and penumbra of the Earth's shadow on 8 October. The corresponding P1, U1, U2, Greatest, U3, U4 and P4 times are as follows in UT: 08:16, 09:15, 10:25, 10:55, 11:24, 12:34 and 13:34. (Diagram based on the eclipse prediction by Fred Espenak, NASA/GSFC.)

4. *A partial eclipse of the Sun* on 23 October will start at sunrise, around 19h 38m UT, in the eastern tip of Siberia, travel across the northern Pacific Ocean, and be visible across all of western Canada and the western states of the US before ending, close to sunset in the eastern states of the US, around 23h 52m UT. Slightly more than 80 per cent of the Sun will be eclipsed as seen from northern Canada, compared to 60 or 70 per cent from Alaska, slightly more than 40 per cent from California and roughly 20 per cent in Mexico. Residents of Hawaii just miss out on seeing any part of the solar disk eclipsed by the Moon.

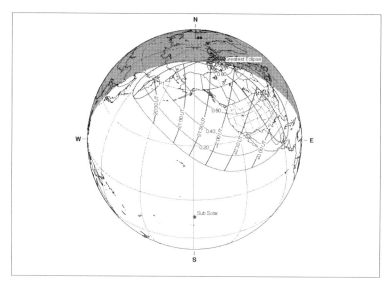

Figure 4. The view looking towards the Pacific Ocean and western US seaboard states on 23 October 2014 at the time of greatest eclipse, with the partial solar eclipse magnitude contours drawn on the illuminated region. Most of the non-Pacific hemisphere is experiencing night-time darkness and the curved lines on the sunlit hemisphere indicate the degree by which the Sun is eclipsed, namely 80, 60, 40, 20 and 0 per cent contours. (Diagram by Fred Espenak, NASA/GSFC.)

Occultations in 2014

NICK JAMES

The Moon makes one circuit around the Earth in just over twenty-seven days and as it moves across the sky it can temporarily hide, or occult, objects that are further away, such as planets or stars. The Moon's orbit is inclined to the ecliptic by around 5.1° and its path with respect to the background stars is defined by the longitude at which it crosses the ecliptic passing from south to north. This is known as the longitude of the ascending node. After passing the node, the Moon moves eastwards relative to the stars reaching 5.1° north of the ecliptic after a week. Two weeks after passing the ascending node it crosses the ecliptic moving south, and then it reaches 5.1° south of the ecliptic after three weeks. Finally it arrives back at the ascending node a week later, and the cycle begins again.

The apparent diameter of the Moon depends on its distance from the Earth but at its closest it appears almost 0.6° across. In addition, the apparent position of the Moon on the sky at any given time shifts depending on where you are on the surface of the Earth. This effect, called parallax, can move the apparent position of the Moon by just over 1°. The combined effect of parallax and the apparent diameter of the Moon means that if an object passes within 1.3° of the apparent centre of the Moon as seen from the centre of the Earth, it will be occulted from somewhere on the surface of our planet. For the occultation to be visible the Moon would have to be some distance from the Sun in the sky and, depending on the object being occulted, it would have to be twilight or dark.

For various reasons, mainly the Earth's equatorial bulge, the nodes of the Moon's orbit move westwards at a rate of around 19° per year, taking 18.6 years to do a full circuit. This means that, whilst the Moon follows approximately the same path from month to month, this path gradually shifts with time. Over the full 18.6-year period all of the stars that lie within 6.4° of the ecliptic will be occulted.

Only four first-magnitude stars lie within 6.4° of the ecliptic. These are Aldebaran (5.4°), Regulus (0.5°), Spica (2.1°) and Antares (4.6°). As the nodes precess through the 18.6-year cycle there will be a monthly series of occultations of each star followed by a period when the star is not occulted. In 2014 there will be no occultations of first-magnitude stars.

In 2014 there will be twenty-two occultations of bright planets. One of Mars, two each of Mercury and Venus, six of Uranus and eleven of Saturn. Eighteen of these events take place at a solar elongation of greater than 30°. The table below lists occultations of the brighter planets which are potentially visible from somewhere on the Earth and where the solar elongation exceeds 30°. More detailed predictions for your location can often be found in magazines or in the *Handbook of the British Astronomical Association.*

Object	Time of Minimum Distance (UT)			Minimum Distance °	Elongation °	Best Visibility
Saturn	25 Jan	2014	13:54	0.6	−73	South Pacific
Saturn	21 Feb	2014	22:18	0.3	−100	Western Australia
Venus	26 Feb	2014	05:15	0.3	−44	Central Africa
Saturn	21 Mar	2014	03:20	0.3	−127	South Africa
Saturn	17 Apr	2014	07:10	0.4	−155	South Pacific
Saturn	14 May	2014	12:13	0.6	176	Australia
Saturn	10 June	2014	18:42	0.6	148	South Africa
Mars	6 July	2014	01:25	0.2	96	South America
Saturn	8 July	2014	02:08	0.4	121	South Pacific
Saturn	4 Aug	2014	10:32	0.1	95	Australia
Saturn	31 Aug	2014	19:10	0.4	70	North Africa
Saturn	28 Sept	2014	04:46	0.7	45	Alaska

Comets in 2014

MARTIN MOBBERLEY

Dozens of short-period comets should be observed approaching perihelion in 2014, although three of these, 25D/Neujmin, 72D/Denning-Fujikawa and 75D/Kohoutek have been declared defunct and so have a D/ prefix. Essentially, a D/ prefix means that these comets have either run out of volatile material or disintegrated, but with so many deep surveys now scouring the night sky they may yet be rediscovered. All of the comets expected to return in 2014 orbit the Sun with periods of between four and sixteen years and many are too faint for amateur visual observation, even with a large telescope. Bright or spectacular comets have much longer orbital periods and, apart from a few notable exceptions like 1P/Halley, 109P/Swift-Tuttle and 153P/Ikeya-Zhang, the best performers usually have orbital periods of many thousands of years and are often discovered less than a year before they come within amateur range. For this reason it is important to regularly check the best comet websites for news of bright comets that may be discovered well after this yearbook is finalized. Some recommended sites are:

British Astronomical Association Comet Section: www.ast.cam.ac.uk/~jds/

Seiichi Yoshida's bright comet page: www.aerith.net/comet/weekly/current.html

CBAT/MPC comets site: www.minorplanetcenter.net/iau/Ephemerides/Comets/

Yahoo Comet Images group: http://tech.groups.yahoo.com/group/Comet-Images/

Yahoo Comet Mailing list: http://tech.groups.yahoo.com/group/comets-ml/

The CBAT/MPC web page above also gives accurate ephemerides of comet positions in right ascension and declination.

Less than twenty periodic comets are expected to reach a magnitude of thirteen or brighter during 2014 but they should all be observable visually with large amateur telescopes, or with amateur CCD imaging systems, in a reasonably dark sky. Just after the 2013 yearbook was committed to press (in late September 2012) an exciting new cometary prospect was discovered, named C/2012 S1 (ISON). The prospects for this comet looked very good, with a very close perihelion distance of 0.12 AU (Astronomical Units) on 28 November 2013 and a potential for a zero-magnitude 'Great Comet' display in late November and early December of 2013. If the best predictions come true, then December 2013 could be a very memorable one indeed! By January 2014, the current estimate is that C/2012 S1 (ISON) will have faded from fifth to eighth magnitude. However, at the time of writing, there is considerable uncertainty as this comet may be a new arrival from the Oort cloud and so its discovery magnitude could be very misleading. In addition, the long-period comet C/2012 K1 (PanSTARRS) reaches perihelion on 27 August 2014 at 1.05 AU from the Sun and this retrograde orbit object looks like the most promising mid-year comet. Apart from those celestial visitors perhaps the best of the rest in 2014 may turn out to be the returning comets P/1998 U3 (Jäger) and 154P/Brewington. The long-period comet C/2011 J2 (LINEAR) should also be within visual range of large amateur telescopes at the start of 2014. As well as these, the tiny comet 209P/LINEAR is predicted to make a very close pass of the Earth on 29 May.

The infamous comet 29P/Schwassmann-Wachmann, now two years past aphelion and well south of the celestial equator, will usually be too faint for visual observation even in large amateur telescopes but is renowned for going into outburst several times per year when it can reach magnitude 11. It should perhaps be explained that the distances of comets from the Sun and the Earth are often quoted in Astronomical Units (AU), where 1 AU is the average Earth–Sun distance of 149.6 million km or 93 million miles.

The brightest cometary prospects for 2014 are listed below in the order they reach perihelion. The dual-status asteroid/comet (596) Scheila and the comet 29P/Schwassmann-Wachmann are nowhere near perihelion during the year but are best placed in December and May respectively.

Comet	Period (years)	Perihelion	Peak Magnitude
(596) Scheila	5.0	19 May 2012	13 in outburst
C/2012 S1 (ISON)	Long	28 Nov 2013	5 in Jan 2014
154P/Brewington	10.8	12 Dec 2013	10 in Jan 2014
C/2011 J2 (LINEAR)	Long	25 Dec 2013	13 in Jan 2014
169P/NEAT	4.2	15 Feb 2014	12 in Feb 2014
P/1998 U3 (Jäger)	15.2	14 Mar 2014	10 in Feb 2014
25D/Neujmin	5.4	March 2014	Defunct!
117P/Helin-Roman-Alu	8.3	27 Mar 2014	13 in July 2014
209P/LINEAR	5.1	4 May 2014	11 in May 2014
134P/Kowal-Vavrova	15.6	21 May 2014	13 in May 2014
4P/Faye	7.5	29 May 2014	12 in Aug 2014
16P/Brooks	6.2	7 June 2014	13 in July 2014
181P/Shoemaker-Levy	7.5	10 June 2014	13 in July 2014
72D/Denning-Fujikawa	9.0	July 2014	Defunct!
75D/Kohoutek	6.7	July 2014	Defunct!
210P/Christensen	5.7	17 Aug 2014	12 in July 2014
C/2012 K1 (PanSTARRS)	Long	27 Aug 2014	5 in Oct 2014
P/2007 H1 (McNaught)	7.0	2 Sept 2014	13 in Sep 2014
32P/Comas Sola	9.6	17 Oct 2014	13 in Dec 2014
C/2013 A1 (Siding Spring)	Long	25 Oct 2014	8 in Sept 2014
110P/Hartley	6.9	17 Dec 2014	13 in Dec 2014
15P/Finlay	6.5	26 Dec 2014	12 in Dec 2014
29P/Schwassmann-Wachmann 1	14.7	12 April 2019	11 in outburst

WHAT TO EXPECT

As already mentioned, the comet C/2012 S1 (ISON) was due to reach perihelion on 28 November 2013 and, if the best predictions held true, the comet may have been a negative-magnitude spectacle, visible in twilight, around the time of publication of this yearbook. However, as David Levy once said, 'Comets are like cats: they have tails and they do what they want!' Similar things were expected of the comets Kohoutek and Austin in 1973/74 and 1990 respectively, but they failed to live up to the hype, despite being splendid objects for experienced amateur astronomers. Also, when any comet passes very close to the solar surface it may disintegrate during or after perihelion. So, at the start of 2014, we may have a bright fifth-magnitude comet, fading rapidly, to study, or we may have nothing. The good news for UK observers is that C/2012 S1 (ISON) will be very well placed in the far north of the sky in the early months of 2014. From 23 December 2013 onwards the fourth-magnitude comet will be circumpolar (it never sets) from UK latitudes and, although better placed in the pre-dawn morning skies, will still be twenty degrees above the horizon at 18h GMT. The comet will move rapidly through north-western Hercules and cross into Draco on 26 December 2013. The current orbit predicts that it will pass closest to the Earth on 27/28 December 2013, just 64 million kilometres distant. At

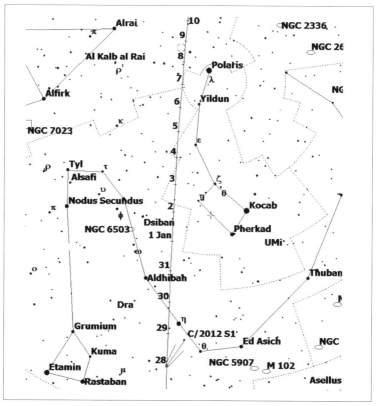

Figure 1. The track of C/2012 S1 (ISON) from 28 December 2013 to 10 January 2014 as it travels along the Draco/Ursa Minor border, and passes Polaris.

the start of January 2014, C/2012 S1 (ISON) will be at a lofty +73 degrees in declination, travelling along the border between Draco and Ursa Minor and, between 6 January and 8 January, will travel within a few degrees of Polaris itself. By this time the comet may have faded to sixth magnitude. The comet then moves steadily south through Cepheus and Camelopardalis and, on 9 February 2014, enters Perseus, by which time it will probably have faded to ninth magnitude. On 4 March, by now faded to magnitude 11, the comet enters Auriga, just a few degrees west of the brilliant star Capella.

As the year 2014 starts, four other comets are likely to be within visual range of the largest amateur telescopes (0.4 m aperture class) or maybe CCD targets for those using more modest telescopes. These comets are 154P/Brewington, P/1998 U3 (Jäger), C/2011 J2 (LINEAR) and C/2012 K1 (PanSTARRS). Amateur astronomer Howard J. Brewington of Cloudcroft, New Mexico, discovered the first of these comets with a 0.4 m Newtonian on 28 August 1992 and, ten years later, it returned on time to the inner solar system in 2002. This apparition is therefore the comet's second return since discovery and it will, hopefully, reach tenth magnitude as it travels through Pegasus and Andromeda in the January evening sky. The second comet, P/1998 U3, was also found by an amateur astronomer during the 1990s, namely by the Austrian comet-photography maestro Michael Jäger, who discovered it on 23 October 1998. Comet Jäger is therefore on its first return to the inner solar system since discovery and is expected to reach perihelion (closest approach to the Sun) on 14 March. During the period from January to March, as the comet approaches the Sun to within 2.2 AU, comet P/1998 U3 (Jäger) should reach tenth magnitude in the evening sky as it tracks south-west through Auriga and into Gemini. In contrast, C/2011 J2 (LINEAR) was a routine discovery by the robotic LINEAR patrol and although faint, at magnitude 13, it will be very high up in Cepheus for northern European and North American observers in January 2014, crossing the border into Cassiopeia in February.

A fifth comet, 169P/NEAT, is a tiny object which may be lost in the twilight glare until the start of March. It arrives at a small perihelion distance of 0.61 AU on 15 February, which could mean a short tail will develop in the following weeks, when it will be a CCD target, very low in the dusk twilight, near the Cetus/Pisces/Aries border region.

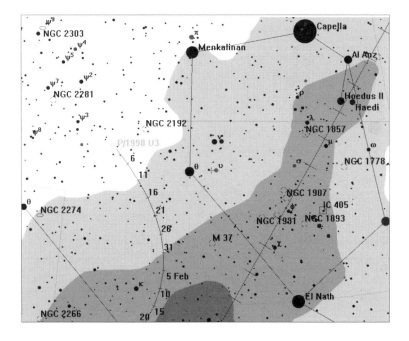

Figure 2. The curved track of P/1998 U3 (Jäger) can be seen in the left of the graphic as it passes through Auriga and into Gemini in January and February.

C/2012 K1 (PanSTARRS)

One of the aforementioned comets visible in early 2014 is, at the time of writing, by far the best mid-year prospect for 2014 and while C/2012 K1 (PanSTARRS) will only start the year as a morning object in Hercules at magnitude 12, it steadily brightens to magnitude 10 as it enters Corona Borealis in late March and magnitude 9 as it crosses northern Boötes in late April. By this time the comet will be circumpolar from UK latitudes, that is, it never sets, because it will be within fifty degrees of the northern celestial pole. By 26 April C/2012 K1 (PanSTARRS) is crossing from Boötes to Ursa Major (The Plough) and Canes Venatici, transiting at local midnight and it will be at a declination of +48 degrees, so the eighth-magnitude comet will be almost at the zenith for UK observers, an ideal situation. On 29 April the comet

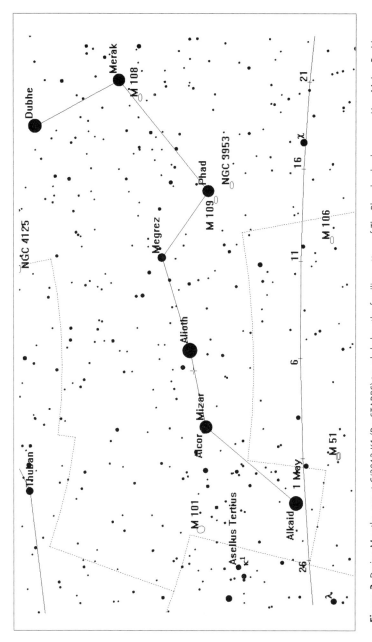

Figure 3. During May the comet C/2012 K1 (PanSTARRS) travels below the familiar pattern of The Plough, also known as Ursa Major. Positions are indicated, in five-day intervals, from 26 April to 21 May.

will lie just half a degree to the south of Alkaid, the tail star of Ursa Major, and it will also be slightly more than two degrees to the northeast of the famous Whirlpool galaxy Messier 51. The galaxy and the comet may have a very similar brightness around this time, so comparing them through the eyepiece could be interesting. Of course, the two objects are actually mind-bogglingly different distances away. The reflected sunlight from the comet has taken a mere twelve minutes to arrive at Earth, whereas the light from the stars in M51 has taken thirty-one million years!

Sadly, after May, the brightening comet starts to plunge rapidly south (and west) as it approaches perihelion on 27 August, when it closes to within 1.06 AU of the Sun. From mid-May to 6 June the

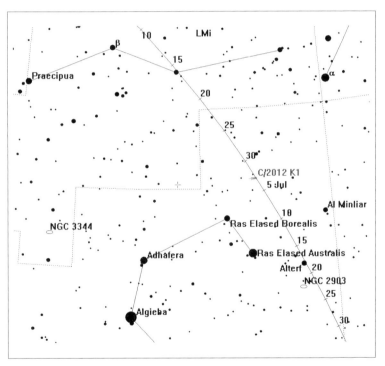

Figure 4. During June and, possibly, the first few days of July, observers from UK latitudes should be able to follow C/2012 K1 (PanSTARRS) as it plunges into the evening twilight near the head of Leo's 'sickle'. However, much will depend on the clarity of the sky, your local horizon, and the brightness of the comet.

comet crosses through south-western Ursa Major and, viewed from the southern UK, despite summer twilight, it should still be observable. C/2012 K1 will be a seventh-magnitude object in Leo Minor up to mid-June, although it will be very low and in the north-western evening twilight by then. Admittedly, the Moon, at half-phase (first quarter) on the fifth, and waxing up to full on the thirteenth, does us no favours at this point, but by mid-month it will be the permanent UK summer twilight that is the bigger problem. As the comet enters northern Leo in late June, just above the famous 'Sickle', it will surely be lost to most observers in the UK.

However, the show will eventually resume in the Southern Hemisphere because, after perihelion, the comet should be a fifth- or sixth-magnitude object, travelling south-west through Hydra in the morning twilight during September and entering Puppis on 2 October.

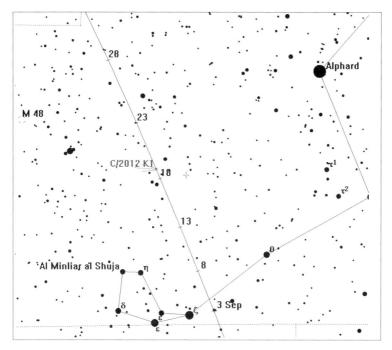

Figure 5. During September, C/2012 K1 (PanSTARRS) emerges from the morning twilight and travels through Hydra, passing some twelve degrees west of the bright star Alphard on 27 September.

It may have a tail one degree long at this time, stretching due west. Up to mid-October its magnitude should increase slightly because, although it has passed its closest approach to the Sun, its closest approach to the Earth occurs on 1 November, when it will be 0.95 AU from our planet and moving south-west at more than two degrees per day. C/2012 K1 will end the year travelling through the southern constellations of Pictor, Doradus, Reticulum, Horologium, Eridanus and Phoenix and by the end of December will probably have faded to ninth magnitude. It will not be a spectacular comet, but, apart from C/2012 S1 (ISON) in January, it is the next brightest prospect for 2014 at the time of writing.

MID-YEAR COMETS

Apart from C/2012 K1, a few other faint comets of magnitude 12 or 13 should be visible in large amateur telescopes during the middle of the year. These include 134P/Kowal-Vavrova (moving slowly in eastern Virgo in May), 16P/Brooks (best seen from the Southern Hemisphere in June), 210P/Christensen (a small comet, close to the Sun, best seen from the Southern Hemisphere in July) and 117P/Helin-Roman-Alu (moving slowly through Capricornus and Microscopium from May to August). That old favourite, the regularly outbursting comet 29P/Schwassmann-Wachmann, is at opposition in mid-May but does not actually return to perihelion until April 2019. However, perihelion is rather academic for a comet that is so far from the Sun. This May comet 29P will lie a distant 5.1 AU from the Earth and 6.1 AU from the Sun, but this will not prevent it from outbursting to, perhaps, magnitude 11, if previous years are anything to go by. Unfortunately for UK observers it is now firmly in the Southern Hemisphere, close to a declination of −30 and on the border between northern Lupus, southern Libra and western Scorpius, so it is virtually unobservable from even the southern UK.

Comet 4P/Faye flirts with the twilight after its May perihelion date, but the keenest observers may be able to image it by August in Gemini, where 181P/Shoemaker-Levy will also spend the month. Sadly, none of these comets are exciting targets as they are faint, often hug the twilight close to perihelion, and, due to summer twilight, UK prospects for observing them are, frankly, a bit grim!

TWO VERY CLOSE APPROACHES!

A more interesting target is, perhaps, the periodic comet 209P/ LINEAR. This comet (originally given the asteroidal designation 2004 CB) is tiny, having an absolute magnitude (its brightness if it were one AU from the Earth and one AU from the Sun) of 18. However, it makes up for this by passing within 0.055 AU of the Earth on May 29.33. This close pass will make it one of the closest cometary encounters with Earth in recorded history. Excluding the alleged approach of C/1491 B1, which may have passed within 0.0094 AU on 1491 February 20.0, there are only eight other comets which have come closer to the Earth than 209P/LINEAR will this May. Of course, when a comet whizzes just eight million kilometres from the Earth, a mere twenty times further than the Moon, it crosses the sky quickly; 209P will be moving at twenty-five arc seconds per minute at its fastest and that's ten degrees per day! Also, where you are observing from on the Earth will affect the position of such a nearby comet by several arc minutes. 209P/LINEAR should be brighter than magnitude 14.0 from mid-May to the end of June. At first the comet will be well placed for UK observers, being high up in western Ursa Major in mid-May and moving slowly south-east at magnitude 13. The comet enters Leo Minor on 22 May and Leo on 25 May. It will then be moving south at a quarter of a degree every hour and will have reached magnitude 12. The comet will then be just 0.07 AU from the Earth. It is likely that 209P will not be observable from the UK's summer twilight skies after the night of 27/28 May as it will then be in Sextans, eleventh magnitude, and plummeting southward at (as mentioned) ten degrees per day. However, Southern Hemisphere observers will be able to observe the comet as it speeds through Crater, Hydra, Centaurus, Crux and Musca. A few words of caution are needed here, though. When a comet is passing this close to the Earth even tiny refinements to the orbital elements will affect its position in the sky greatly. It is therefore highly advisable to check the latest MPC ephemeris in May to ensure that you will be looking in the right place.

Martians will also enjoy an extraordinary close approach on 19 October when C/2013 A1 (Siding Spring) passes within 0.0008 AU of the Red Planet and could reach magnitude −8 from there. From Earth the situation is very different as the comet may reach magnitude +8 in September, but only in the far southern sky, being invisible from Europe.

AUTUMN AND WINTER COMETS

Again, apart from C/2012 K1, which should be a very pleasing Southern Hemisphere object in October and November and has already been described in detail, a few other cometary morsels await the patient observer in the final months of 2014. The first of these is P/2007 H1 (McNaught), discovered by the indefatigable Robert McNaught. This comet has a period of seven years and arrives at perihelion on 2 September. Although it will then be 2.3 AU from the Sun it will also be at opposition, so just 1.3 AU from the Earth, and travelling south-south-west through Aquarius. The comet may just achieve thirteenth magnitude in the weeks after perihelion so large apertures are needed to see the comet visually, or a CCD imaging system. Between 12 and 13 September, C/2012 K1 will track through the field of the tenth-magnitude galaxy NGC 7727, which should make a splendid photo opportunity.

The periodic comet 32P/Comas Solá also returns to perihelion in 2014, on 17 October. This comet was discovered by Josep Comas Solá from the Fabra Observatory in Barcelona on 5 November 1926 and this will be its tenth return to perihelion since that discovery year. 32P/Comas Sola has the distinction of being part of the title of a track on the Tangerine Dream album *Alpha Centauri*, for no obvious reason! The faint comet will be in the pre-dawn northern sky crossing Leo from west to east from mid-October until the end of the year. It will be just fifty arc minutes due north of the splendid galaxy NGC 2903 on the night of 17/18 October, although probably only fourteenth magnitude at that time, so strictly a CCD target. It should peak in brightness around 20 December when still a morning object and travelling through the hind quarters of Leo within the Denebola/Chort/Zosma bright triangle.

The minor planet (596) Scheila was, up to 2010, classified as an asteroidal object. However, on 11 December 2010, Steve Larson of the Catalina Survey noted it was displaying a faint coma and it was subsequently imaged by many amateur astronomers at around magnitude

13. Although (596) Scheila will not reach perihelion until 2017, it will be very well placed, moving through Taurus during November and December. Regular monitoring by amateurs this year could result in another cometary outburst being detected.

The periodic comet 110P/Hartley should also achieve thirteenth magnitude in December and will be favourably placed from UK latitudes as it spends the whole month in northern Gemini, drifting slowly south-west and ending the year just one degree north of the third-magnitude star Mebsuta (epsilon Geminorum).

Finally, the periodic comet 15P/Finlay will be a very challenging target as evening twilight deepens in the final week of 2014. It will be very low above the south-west horizon (less than twenty degrees) in north-eastern Capricornus and it reaches perihelion on 27 December. For those with CCD equipment and a flat south-west horizon it could be worth a try on a crystal clear December evening at about 17h 30m UT from the UK. The bright planet Mars will be just four degrees to the comet's south-west on the last day of the year.

THE DEFUNCT COMETS

Although three of the comets listed in the table at the start of this section are prefixed by a D, meaning that they are thought to be defunct, having presumably disintegrated or run out of volatile material, this does not mean that they will not be recovered this year. We are living in an era when ever more powerful robotic telescopes are scouring the skies every night, and each year, comets that were once thought to have been lost for ever seem to be tracked down. So it may be worth spending a small amount of time considering three D-prefixed comets that, who knows, may reappear this time around after all! 25D/Neujmin was discovered as long ago as February 1916, by Grigory N. Neujmin. However, since its second subsequent return to perihelion, in 1927, it has not been seen, despite having had a 5.4-year orbit. Such a long absence probably means it really has totally disintegrated, but if its orbit is still accurate, its remnants might return to perihelion around March this year.

72D/Denning-Fujikawa was originally discovered by the great British observer W. F. Denning in 1881 and has a nine-year orbit. However, the comet was subsequently lost, until accidentally rediscovered by Fujikawa in 1978, hence its double-barrelled name. Bizarrely, it was then not seen in 1987, 1996 or 2005. As this comet spent a staggering ninety-seven years and ten returns lost in the wilderness before Fujikawa's recovery, I feel that there is a reasonable chance of recovery in 2014, given the number of robotic machines now scouring the sky.

Finally, what about 75D/Kohoutek? This, of course, is not the famous over-hyped comet of the same name from the 1970s, but it was discovered by that same astronomer, Lubos Kohoutek, from Hamburg Observatory, in February 1975. The comet was recovered in 1980, well before its first return, and it was seen again in 1987, when it reached thirteenth magnitude. However, it was not seen in 1994, 2001 or 2007. Will it be seen in 2014? Only time will tell.

The tables below list the right ascension and declination of, arguably, the six most promising comets in 2014, at their peak, as well as the distances, in AU, from the Earth and the Sun. The elongation, in degrees from the Sun, is also tabulated along with the estimated visual magnitude, which can only ever be a rough guess as comets are, without doubt, a law unto themselves!

C/2012 S1 (ISON)

Date	RA (2000)			Dec.			Distance from Earth	Distance from Sun	Elong- ation from Sun	Mag.
	h	m	s	°	'	''	AU	AU	°	
Jan 1	16	42	39.5	+70	28	38	0.449	1.122	96.0	4.8
Jan 6	18	33	45.5	+85	01	46	0.505	1.234	107.6	5.4
Jan 11	02	54	15.9	+81	43	21	0.589	1.341	114.7	6.1
Jan 16	03	40	08.6	+73	11	49	0.692	1.443	117.9	6.8
Jan 21	03	55	19.9	+66	42	57	0.808	1.542	118.5	7.4
Jan 26	04	04	40.5	+61	47	05	0.933	1.638	117.4	8.0
Jan 31	04	12	03.8	+57	57	47	1.065	1.732	115.2	8.5
Feb 5	04	18	38.6	+54	56	38	1.202	1.823	112.4	9.0
Feb 10	04	24	51.2	+52	30	57	1.344	1.911	109.3	9.5
Feb 15	04	30	53.0	+50	31	56	1.488	1.998	105.9	9.9
Feb 20	04	36	49.8	+48	53	18	1.634	2.083	102.3	10.3
Feb 25	04	42	45.1	+47	30	31	1.783	2.166	98.7	10.6
Mar 2	04	48	40.8	+46	20	19	1.932	2.248	95.1	10.9
Mar 7	04	54	38.0	+45	20 1	2	2.082	2.328	91.4	11.3

154P/Brewington

Date	RA (2000)			Dec.			Distance from Earth	Distance from Sun	Elong- ation from Sun	Mag.
	h	m	s	°	'	"	AU	AU	°	
Jan 1	23	47	20.8	+18	43	10	1.383	1.623	84.8	9.5
Jan 11	00	12	30.0	+21	33	32	1.464	1.641	81.7	9.8
Jan 21	01	07	13.4	+26	45	36	1.645	1.699	75.9	10.5
Feb 10	01	36	19.2	+29	00	51	1.747	1.737	73.0	10.9
Feb 20	02	06	11.8	+30	58	33	1.856	1.780	70.0	11.4
Mar 2	02	36	34.1	+32	36	47	1.972	1.828	67.0	11.8

169P/NEAT

Date	RA (2000)			Dec.			Distance from Earth	Distance from Sun	Elong- ation from Sun	Mag.
	h	m	s	°	'	"	AU	AU	°	
Feb 25	00	32	18.7	−02	11	14	1.233	0.636	30.9	12.8
Mar 02	01	04	36.3	+00	12	54	1.188	0.670	34.3	13.0
Mar 07	01	37	19.4	+02	40	10	1.153	0.714	37.9	13.1
Mar 12	02	10	16.7	+05	06	23	1.131	0.765	41.6	13.2
Mar 17	02	43	12.3	+07	26	48	1.122	0.821	45.2	13.3
Mar 22	03	15	45.9	+09	36	40	1.126	0.881	48.6	13.5
Mar 27	03	47	34.6	+11	32	00	1.143	0.943	51.7	13.6

P/1998 U3 (Jäger)

Date	RA (2000)			Dec.			Distance from Earth	Distance from Sun	Elong- ation from Sun	Mag.
	h	m	s	°	'	"	AU	AU	°	
Jan 1	06	25	22.2	+38	26	32	1.299	2.261	164.1	10.6
Jan 11	06	16	59.2	+36	29	53	1.290	2.235	158.7	10.5
Jan 21	06	10	47.2	+34	15	35	1.305	2.212	149.8	10.5
Jan 31	06	07	46.1	+31	53	39	1.344	2.193	140.1	10.6

P/1998 U3 (Jäger) *continued*

Date	RA (2000)			Dec.			Distance from Earth	Distance from Sun	Elong-ation from Sun	Mag.
	h	m	s	°	'	''	AU	AU	°	
Feb 10	06	08	22.9	+29	33	05	1.403	2.178	130.6	10.6
Feb 20	06	12	32.4	+27	19	49	1.478	2.167	121.6	10.7
Mar 2	06	19	52.1	+25	16	12	1.566	2.159	113.4	10.8
Mar 12	06	29	55.2	+23	21	58	1.663	2.156	105.7	10.9
Mar 22	06	42	11.1	+21	35	22	1.769	2.157	98.7	11.1
Apr 1	06	56	12.3	+19	54	00	1.880	2.163	92.2	11.2

C/2012 K1 (PanSTARRS)

Date	RA (2000)			Dec.			Distance from Earth	Distance from Sun	Elong-ation from Sun	Mag.
	h	m	s	°	'	''	AU	AU	°	
Mar 2	16	34	59.7	+20	40	27	2.526	2.811	96.2	11.0
Mar 12	16	29	17.0	+24	22	07	2.267	2.696	104.7	10.6
Mar 22	16	18	07.9	+28	54	18	2.026	2.580	112.7	10.1
Apr 1	15	58	54.8	+34	15	58	1.813	2.463	119.4	9.7
Apr 11	15	27	53.7	+40	06	56	1.643	2.345	123.1	9.3
Apr 21	14	41	11.0	+45	32	00	1.528	2.227	121.8	8.9
May 1	13	38	54.1	+49	00	22	1.475	2.109	115.0	8.6
May 11	12	31	16.2	+49	19	58	1.485	1.991	104.2	8.3
May 21	11	33	01.5	+46	48	48	1.547	1.873	91.7	8.2
May 31	10	50	26.0	+42	45	42	1.643	1.756	78.9	8.0
June 10	10	21	25.0	+38	17	45	1.756	1.641	66.5	7.9
June 20	10	01	47.7	+33	57	51	1.871	1.529	54.7	7.7
June 30	09	48	13.0	+29	55	49	1.976	1.422	43.5	7.5
July 10	09	38	22.4	+26	11	15	2.060	1.323	32.6	7.3

Comet in N. Hemisphere dusk and S. Hemisphere dawn twilight

Date	RA (2000)			Dec.			Distance from Earth	Distance from Sun	Elong-ation from Sun	Mag.
Sept 8	08	58	26.9	+03	46	10	1.790	1.071	31.6	6.1
Sept 18	08	49	15.5	−01	40	24	1.610	1.113	43.1	6.0

C/2012 K1 (PanSTARRS) *continued*

Date	RA (2000)			Dec.			Distance from Earth	Distance from Sun	Elong- ation from Sun	Mag.
	h	m	s	°	'	"	AU	AU	°	
Sept 28	08	36	37.1	−08	36	03	1.412	1.176	55.2	6.0
Oct 8	08	17	09.9	−17	46	59	1.215	1.255	68.3	5.9
Oct 18	07	43	49.6	−29	56	09	1.050	1.348	82.4	5.9
Oct 28	06	41	24.9	−44	07	30	0.959	1.450	95.9	6.0
Nov 7	04	50	37.5	−54	44	00	0.980	1.558	104.4	6.4
Nov 17	02	43	56.2	−55	36	27	1.116	1.671	105.0	7.0
Nov 27	01	23	12.2	−50	25	35	1.333	1.786	99.6	7.6
Dec 7	00	42	21.4	−44	32	20	1.597	1.904	91.9	8.3
Dec 17	00	21	56.5	−39	30	23	1.882	2.022	83.4	8.9
Dec 27	00	11	59.2	−35	24	34	2.174	2.140	74.9	9.5

209P/LINEAR

NB: The positions for this very-close-approach comet may change significantly if the orbital elements are adjusted. Checking at www.minorplanetcenter.net/iau/MPEph/MPEph.html is advised in May.

Date	RA (2000)			Dec.			Distance from Earth	Distance from Sun	Elong- ation from Sun	Mag.
	h	m	s	°	'	"	AU	AU	°	
May 25	10	15	44.4	+29	22	36	0.070	1.005	81.9	11.9
May 26	10	22	50.1	+22	35	27	0.064	1.009	84.8	11.6
May 27	10	30	15.6	+14	40	23	0.060	1.013	88.4	11.3
May 28	10	38	02.3	+05	42	57	0.057	1.017	92.5	11.1
May 29	10	46	11.7	−03	57	41	0.056	1.022	97.0	10.9
May 30	10	54	45.0	−13	49	46	0.056	1.026	101.5	10.7
May 31	11	03	43.6	−23	17	32	0.058	1.031	105.7	10.7
June 1	11	13	08.6	−31	52	44	0.061	1.036	109.3	10.7
June 2	11	23	00.6	−39	20	58	0.066	1.041	112.1	10.8
June 3	11	33	20.2	−45	40	20	0.072	1.046	114.4	11.0

209P/LINEAR *continued*

Date	RA (2000)			Dec.			Distance from Earth	Distance from Sun	Elong-ation from Sun	Mag.
	h	m	s	°	'	"	AU	AU	°	
June 4	11	44	07.4	−50	56	31	0.078	1.051	116.1	11.1
June 5	11	55	21.6	−55	18	16	0.086	1.057	117.4	11.3
June 6	12	07	01.8	−58	54	34	0.093	1.062	118.4	11.4
June 7	12	19	06.1	−61	53	32	0.101	1.068	119.3	11.6
June 8	12	31	31.9	−64	21 5	5	0.110	1.074	119.9	11.8
June 9	12	44	16.0	−66	25	11	0.118	1.080	120.5	11.9

Minor Planets in 2014

MARTIN MOBBERLEY

Some 600,000 minor planets (also referred to as asteroids) are known. They range in size from small planetoids hundreds of kilometres in diameter to boulders tens of metres across. More than 350,000 of these now have such good orbits that they possess a numbered designation and almost 18,000 have been named after mythological gods, famous people, scientists, astronomers and institutions. Most of these objects live between Mars and Jupiter, but some 8,000 have been discovered between the Sun and Mars, and more than 1,300 of these are classed as potentially hazardous asteroids (PHAs) due to their ability to pass within eight million kilometres of the Earth while also having a diameter greater than 200 metres. The first four asteroids to be discovered were (1) Ceres, now regarded as a dwarf planet, (2) Pallas, (3) Juno and (4) Vesta which are all easy binocular objects when at their peak, due to them having diameters of hundreds of kilometres.

In 2014, most of the first ten numbered asteroids reach opposition during the year. However, with orbital periods of, typically, four or five years, it is often the case that the Earth cannot 'overtake' an asteroid on the inside track, so to speak, in a specific twelve-month period. This is the case when opposition has occurred late in the previous year. In these instances the asteroid will not be transiting the meridian at midnight during any month in 2014 and so will not be seen at its brightest and closest during the year. So, this year the asteroid (3) Juno will not quite achieve opposition and neither will (7) Iris or (8) Flora. Asteroid (10) Hygiea will just achieve opposition on the final night of the year. As far as the remaining top ten asteroids are concerned, (2) Pallas will be the first to reach opposition, in late February, at magnitude 7.0. It will be near the Hydra/Sextans border, not far from the bright star Alphard. On the evening of 1 March, star hopping almost four degrees due east of Alphard should place (2) Pallas in the middle of a low-power field of view.

The dwarf planet (1) Ceres and (4) Vesta are the next minor planets to reach opposition, in late April, and both can be found in Virgo, roughly midway between the bright stars Spica and Arcturus. Confusingly, the even brighter planet Mars will be less than five degrees north-east of Spica during this time. Ceres and Vesta stay within a few degrees of each other during March, April and May and so both can be

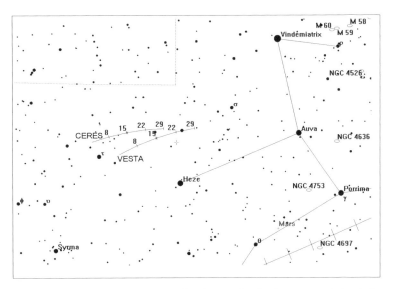

Figure 1a. Ceres and Vesta stay within a few degrees of each other, in Virgo, during April.

Figure 1b. Vesta imaged by NASA's Dawn space probe. (Image courtesy of NASA.)

squeezed into the same field of view with binoculars or a small-aperture telescope. The observer of these two asteroids might like to ponder the position of the NASA Dawn spacecraft, which left Vesta on 5 September 2012 and will arrive at Ceres in February 2015, and will be roughly halfway between the two at opposition this year.

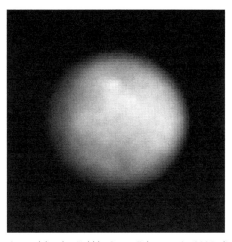

Figure 1c. Ceres imaged by the Hubble Space Telescope in 2004. (Image courtesy of NASA/STScl.)

In mid-May, (9) Metis transits at midnight in Libra at around magnitude 9.6. There will then be a gap of around four months before (5) Astraea reaches opposition on 29 September, near the Cetus/Pisces border, at around magnitude 10.7. In mid-November, (6) Hebe will be at its best at a healthy magnitude 8.1 in the constellation of Eridanus. On 5 December, Hebe will appear to drift just a degree and a half to the north of one of the closest stars to our solar system, magnitude 3.7 epsilon Eridani, a mere ten and a half light years distant. Of course, in reality, it is purely a line-of-sight proximity; Hebe is only nine and a half *light minutes* from Earth, so is actually more than half a million times closer than epsilon Eridani.

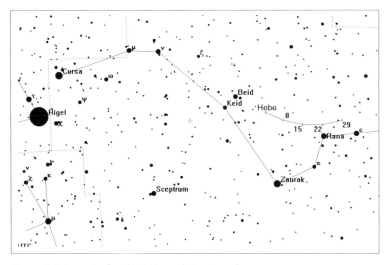

Figure 2. Hebe can be found in Eridanus during November.

Then, as already mentioned, (10) Hygiea reaches opposition on the last day of 2014, where it can be found, transiting at midnight, in Gemini.

Although (3) Juno will not reach opposition until January 2015 it

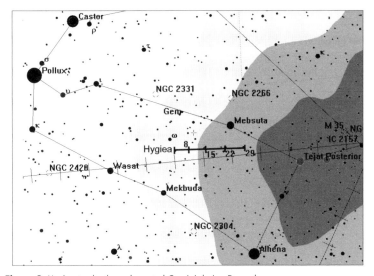

Figure 3. Hygiea tracks through central Gemini during December.

will be reasonably placed in Hydra, after midnight, during the previous month of December, and so it should be easy to track down with large binoculars at magnitude 8.7.

Ephemerides for the best-placed bright minor planets at, or approaching, opposition in 2014, listed in calendar order, appear in the following tables.

(2) Pallas

Date	RA (2000)			Dec.			Distance from Earth	Distance from Sun	Elong- ation from Sun	Mag.
	h	m	s	°	'	"	AU	AU	°	
Feb 10	09	56	09.5	−16	28	50	1.257	2.161	148.5	7.1
Feb 15	09	52	34.9	−14	45	43	1.242	2.166	152.4	7.0
Feb 20	09	48	59.7	−12	51	31	1.233	2.171	155.4	7.0
Feb 25	09	45	33.6	−10	48	24	1.231	2.177	156.9	7.0
Mar 2	09	42	25.7	−08	39	03	1.237	2.182	156.7	7.0
Mar 7	09	39	44.7	−06	26	26	1.250	2.188	154.7	7.0
Mar 12	09	37	37.6	−04	13	38	1.270	2.195	151.5	7.1

Dwarf planet (1) Ceres

Date	RA (2000)			Dec.			Distance from Earth	Distance from Sun	Elong- ation from Sun	Mag.
	h	m	s	°	'	"	AU	AU	°	
Mar 31	14	05	28.9	+02	34	43	1.671	2.619	156.9	7.2
Apr 5	14	01	41.0	+02	54	10	1.655	2.622	161.2	7.1
Apr 10	13	57	33.0	+03	11	38	1.646	2.625	164.5	7.0
Apr 15	13	53	12.4	+03	26	24	1.643	2.628	165.9	7.0
Apr 20	13	48	46.6	+03	37	50	1.648	2.631	165.0	7.0
Apr 25	13	44	23.2	+03	45	24	1.659	2.634	162.1	7.1
Apr 30	13	40	09.9	+03	48	41	1.676	2.637	158.1	7.2

(4) Vesta

Date	RA (2000)			Dec.			Distance from Earth	Distance from Sun	Elong- ation from Sun	Mag.
	h	m	s	°	'	''	AU	AU	°	
Mar 31	13	56	22.4	+01	31	05	1.269	2.232	159.4	5.9
Apr 5	13	52	26.8	+02	02	15	1.250	2.228	163.6	5.8
Apr 10	13	48	06.9	+02	31	34	1.238	2.224	166.5	5.8
Apr 15	13	43	31.9	+02	57	58	1.231	2.220	167.1	5.7
Apr 20	13	38	51.3	+03	20	24	1.231	2.216	165.0	5.8
Apr 25	13	34	14.9	+03	38	01	1.236	2.213	161.2	5.8
Apr 30	13	29	52.7	+03	50	06	1.248	2.209	156.6	5.9

(9) Metis

Date	RA (2000)			Dec.			Distance from Earth	Distance from Sun	Elong- ation from Sun	Mag.
	h	m	s	°	'	''	AU	AU	°	
May 1	15	45	13.6	−17	05	12	1.670	2.648	162.2	10.0
May 6	15	40	26.4	−16	57	35	1.655	2.650	168.1	9.9
May 11	15	35	23.4	−16	49	21	1.646	2.653	174.0	9.7
May 16	15	30	13.0	−16	40	52	1.645	2.655	177.7	9.6
May 21	15	25	03.7	−16	32	29	1.650	2.658	173.1	9.8
May 26	15	20	03.6	−16	24	37	1.662	2.660	167.3	9.9
May 31	15	15	21.1	−16	17	41	1.681	2.662	161.4	10.0

(5) Astrae

Date	RA (2000)			Dec.			Distance from Earth	Distance from Sun	Elong- ation from Sun	Mag.
	h	m	s	°	'	''	AU	AU	°	
Sept 16	00	43	48.1	−01	13	50	1.905	2.880	162.4	11.0
Sept 21	00	40	01.7	−01	47	45	1.883	2.872	167.9	10.9
Sept 26	00	35	59.7	−02	22	07	1.868	2.865	172.6	10.8

Oct 01	00	31	48.5	−02	56	05	1.860	2.858	174.0	10.7
Oct 06	00	27	35.2	−03	28	47	1.859	2.850	170.4	10.8
Oct 11	00	23	26.8	−03	59	25	1.866	2.842	165.2	10.9
Oct 16	00	19	29.6	−04	27	14	1.879	2.834	159.5	11.0

(6) Hebe

Date	RA (2000)			Dec.			Distance from Earth	Distance from Sun	Elong- ation from Sun	Mag.
	h	m	s	°	'	''	AU	AU	°	
Oct 31	04	03	34.5	−07	47	39	1.074	1.978	146.3	8.1
Nov 05	03	59	53.9	−08	17	56	1.067	1.984	148.9	8.1
Nov 10	03	55	42.9	−08	39	57	1.065	1.989	150.8	8.1
Nov 15	03	51	11.8	−08	52	40	1.069	1.996	151.7	8.1
Nov 20	03	46	32.0	−08	55	24	1.078	2.002	151.5	8.1
Nov 25	03	41	55.8	−08	47	49	1.092	2.009	150.2	8.1
Nov 30	03	37	35.2	−08	30	04	1.111	2.016	148.0	8.2

(10) Hygiea

Date	RA (2000)			Dec.			Distance from Earth	Distance from Sun	Elong- ation from Sun	Mag.
	h	m	s	°	'	''	AU	AU	°	
Dec 01	07	01	32.0	+23	29	49	2.554	3.405	144.4	10.8
Dec 06	06	58	37.4	+23	30	42	2.511	3.401	150.1	10.7
Dec 11	06	55	15.0	+23	31	46	2.475	3.398	156.0	10.6
Dec 16	06	51	28.5	+23	32	50	2.445	3.394	161.9	10.5
Dec 21	06	47	22.4	+23	33	44	2.422	3.391	168.0	10.3
Dec 26	06	43	02.6	+23	34	18	2.407	3.387	174.0	10.2
Dec 31	06	38	35.8	+23	34	24	2.400	3.383	179.5	10.0

(3) Juno

Date	RA (2000)			Dec.			Distance from Earth	Distance from Sun	Elong- ation from Sun	Mag.
	h	m	s	°	'	''	AU	AU	°	
Dec 01	08	56	06.1	+01	21	55	1.587	2.155	111.6	8.9
Dec 06	08	57	51.4	+01	00	04	1.546	2.166	115.9	8.9
Dec 11	08	58	51.2	+00	42	54	1.506	2.177	120.4	8.8
Dec 16	08	59	04.0	+00	31	03	1.470	2.188	125.0	8.7
Dec 21	08	58	29.4	+00	25	05	1.436	2.200	129.9	8.6
Dec 26	08	57	08.0	+00	25	35	1.405	2.212	134.9	8.5
Dec 31	08	55	02.4	+00	32	54	1.379	2.224	140.0	8.5

NEAR-EARTH ASTEROID APPROACHES

A list of some of the most interesting numbered, named and provisionally designated close-asteroid approaches during 2014 is presented in the following table. It should be borne in mind that the visibility of close-approach asteroids is highly dependent on whether they are close to the solar glare and from which hemisphere the observer is based, but by the very nature of their proximity they move rapidly across the sky. The table gives the closest separation between the Earth and the asteroid in AU (1 AU = 149.6 million km) and the date of that closest approach and also the constellation in which the object can be found when closest. The brightest magnitude achieved and the corresponding date and constellation for that condition are also given. The reader might wonder why the dates when the Near-Earth asteroid is closest and when it is brightest are not the same. Well, sometimes they are, but if an object is not behind the Earth, it may have a poor phase (like the crescent Moon) with most of it in shadow, regardless of its proximity to the Earth. Some of the objects listed are as faint as magnitude 17 at their best and so present a real challenge, even to advanced amateur astronomers using CCDs. Scores of other tiny asteroids, with provisional designations, will come within advanced amateur CCD range during 2014, many of them undiscovered as this yearbook goes to press.

Some interesting numbered, named and provisional designation close-asteroid approaches during 2014.

Asteroid (number)/ designation/name	Closest (AU)	2014 Date when closest	Constell. closest	Peak mag.	Peak date	Const. brightest
(251346) 2007 SJ	0.04863	Jan 21.65	Aquila	15.3	3 Jan	Pegasus
2005 AY28	0.03939	Feb 7.30	Camel.	16.6	5 Feb	Ursa Maj.
2006 DP14	0.01603	Feb 10.80	Doradus	12.8	12 Feb	Canis Maj.
(85953) 1999 FK21	0.19096	Feb 18.36	Fornax	17.0	1 Jan	Sagittarius
2000 RS11	0.03525	Mar 11.39	Sagittarius	15.0	15 Mar	Ophiuchus
(143649) 2003 QQ47	0.12832	Mar 26.50	Auriga	15.9	28 Mar	Auriga
(86878) 2000 HD24	0.10840	Apr 4.95	Puppis	15.3	10 Apr	Vela
2006 SX 217	0.03156	Apr 23.72	Aries	17.2	16 Apr	Cassiopeia
(21374) 1997 WS22	0.12094	May 21.79	Scorpius	14.1	21 May	Scorpius
2010 NY65	0.03000	June 23.41	Leo	17.8	29 June	Boötes
(177049) 2003 EE16	0.09665	July 1.91	Pisces	17.4	27 June	Pisces
(154229) 2002 JN97	0.15786	Aug 2.40	Volans	15.1	27 July	Hydrus
2010 LE15	0.03993	Aug 12.40	Fornax	15.1	10 Aug	Cetus
(277475) 2005 WK4	0.07204	Aug 12.48	Virgo	17.3	19 Aug	Scorpius
(281375) 2008 JV19	0.13868	Aug 16.29	Sagittarius	17.7	3 Aug	Aquila
(285944) 2001 RZ11	0.08791	Aug 17.14	Pisc. Aust.	12.0	18 Aug	Capricorn.
(163132) 2002 CU11	0.03468	Aug 30.13	Taurus	13.9	31 Aug	Eridanus
2007 DL41	0.04741	Sep 27.16	Lynx	16.7	2 Oct	Eridanus
(68267) 2001 EA16	0.09128	Oct 7.02	Scorpius	15.7	13 Oct	Hercules
(2340) Hathor	0.04824	Oct 21.89	Taurus	15.0	28 Oct	Aries
(36017) 1999 ND43	0.15260	Oct 29.93	Delphinus	17.4	11 Nov	Androm.
(138852) 2000 WN10	0.12614	Nov 11.43	Eridanus	17.2	17 Nov	Eridanus

Accurate minor-planet ephemerides can be computed for your location on Earth using the MPC ephemeris service at: www.minorplanet-center.org/iau/MPEph/MPEph.html.

Meteors in 2014

JOHN MASON

Meteors (popularly known as 'shooting stars') may be seen on any clear moonless night, but on certain nights of the year their number increases noticeably. This occurs when the Earth chances to intersect a concentration of meteoric dust moving in an orbit around the Sun. If the dust is well spread out in space, the resulting shower of meteors may last for several days. The word 'shower' must not be misinterpreted – only on very rare occasions have the meteors been so numerous as to resemble snowflakes falling.

If the meteor tracks are marked on a star map and traced backwards, a number of them will be found to intersect in a point (or within a small area of the sky) which marks the radiant of the shower. This gives the direction from which the meteors have come.

Bright moonlight has an adverse effect on visual meteor observing, and within about five days to either side of Full Moon, lunar glare swamps all but the brighter meteors, reducing, quite considerably, the total number of meteors seen. Of the major showers in 2014, only the maximum of the Perseids will suffer interference by moonlight. The Perseid peak occurs near 00h on 13 August, coinciding with a waning gibbous Moon in Pisces. Best observed rates are likely during the night of 12/13 August, particularly in the pre-dawn hours of 13 August. Observations of the April Lyrids may be hampered by a last quarter Moon in the early morning hours. The Taurids will suffer considerable interference by moonlight in 2014, with the two peaks occurring either side of the full Moon on 6/7 November. Visual observers can often minimize the effects of moonlight by positioning themselves so that the Moon is behind them and hidden behind a wall or other suitable obstruction.

There are many excellent observing opportunities in 2014, beginning with the Quadrantids in early January. Maximum occurs just after New Moon, but peak activity is expected at about 18h on 3 January, when the radiant will be rather low in the north from the UK. The

Delta Aquarids, Piscis Australids, Alpha Capricornids and Iota Aquarids are all favourably placed with respect to the Moon this year and watches carried out any time in late July or early August should yield good observed rates. The autumn of 2014 also looks good for meteor observers with both the Orionids in October and the Leonids in November being observable in dark skies. In December it is hoped that observers will take advantage of the very favourable conditions for the Ursids, a minor but important shower much in need of observation.

The Geminids are now the richest of the annual meteor showers and this year's peak coincides with a last quarter Moon in Virgo, so there should be comparatively little interference by moonlight even during the early morning hours. The highest observed rates are most likely during the night of 13/14 December, particularly in the pre-dawn hours of 14 December. Geminid maximum is expected at around 07h, but past observations show that bright Geminids become more numerous some hours after the rates have peaked, a consequence of particle-sorting in the meteoroid stream.

The following table gives some of the more easily observed showers with their radiants; interference by moonlight is shown by the letter M:

Limiting Dates	Shower	Maximum	Radiant		
			RA		Dec.
			h	m	°
1–6 Jan	Quadrantids	3 Jan, 18h	15	28	+50	
19–25 Apr	Lyrids	22 Apr, 17h	18	08	+32	
24 Ap–20 May	Eta Aquarids	5–6 May	22	20	−01	
17–26 June	Ophiuchids	20 June	17	20	−20	
July–Aug	Capricornids	8,15,26 July	20	44	−15	
			21	00	−15	
15 July–20 Aug	Delta Aquarids	29 July, 6 Aug	22	36	−17	
			23	04	+02	
15 July–20 Aug	Piscis Australids	31 July	22	40	−30	
15 July–20 Aug	Alpha Capricornids	2–3 Aug	20	36	−10	
July–Aug	Iota Aquarids	6–7 Aug	22	10	−15	
			22	04	−06	
23 July–20 Aug	Perseids	13 Aug, 00h	3	13	+58	M
16–30 Oct	Orionids	21–24 Oct	6	24	+15	
20 Oct–30 Nov	Taurids	5,12 Nov	3	44	+22	M
			3	44	+14	

Meteors in 2014

15–20 Nov	Leonids	18 Nov, 01h	10	08	+22
Nov–Jan	Puppid-Velids	early Dec	9	00	−48
7–16 Dec	Geminids	14 Dec, 07h	7	32	+33
17–25 Dec	Ursids	22–23 Dec	14	28	+78

Some Events in 2014

ECLIPSES

There will be four eclipses, two of the Sun and two of the Moon.

20 March: Total eclipse of the Sun – Southern Greenland, North Atlantic, Faroe Islands and Svalbard.

4 April: Total eclipse of the Moon – North and South America, Hawaii, Pacific Ocean, New Zealand, Australia and Central and Eastern Asia.

13 September: Partial eclipse of the Sun – Southern Africa and Antarctica.

28 September: Total eclipse of the Moon – North and South America, Europe, Africa and Central and Western Asia.

THE PLANETS

Mercury may be seen more easily from northern latitudes in the evenings about the time of greatest eastern elongation (7 May) and in the mornings about the time of greatest western elongation (16 October). In the Southern Hemisphere the corresponding most favourable dates are 4 September and 29 December (evenings) and 24 February and 24 June (mornings). The planet may also be spotted from both hemispheres in the evenings around the time of greatest eastern elongation on 14 January.

Venus is visible in the evenings from January until July. It reaches greatest eastern elongation (45°) on 6 June and attains its greatest brilliancy on 12 July. Venus passes through inferior conjunction on 15 August and will then become visible in the mornings until the end of the year. It attains its greatest brilliancy on 20 September and reaches greatest western elongation (46°) on 26 October.

Mars does not come to opposition in 2015. The planet is in conjunction with the Sun on 14 June, and becomes visible in the morning sky later in the year. It will next be at opposition on 22 May 2016, when the planet will be in Scorpius.

Jupiter is at opposition on 6 February in Cancer.

Saturn is at opposition on 23 May in Libra.

Uranus is at opposition on 12 October in Pisces.

Neptune is at opposition on 1 September in Aquarius.

Pluto is at opposition on 6 July in Sagittarius.

Part Two

Article Section

The Spring Comet of 2013

NICK JAMES

A bright comet can be one of the most beautiful objects in the sky. Figure 1 shows a comet that was very spectacular back in 1997. This comet was discovered in 1995 by two observers (Alan Hale and Thomas Bopp) and it has the official name C/1995 O1 (Hale-Bopp). This comet displayed all of the usual features of a very bright comet. It had a bright head, multiple tails and lots of interesting detail to see visually or to photograph.

Figure 1. Comet C/1995 O1 (Hale-Bopp). 8 March 1997. (Image courtesy of Denis Buczynski.)

In the spring and summer of 2013 we had another beautiful comet in the sky. This was nowhere near as bright or as spectacular as Hale-Bopp but it was an interesting object which almost broke a long-standing cometary record and which was well recorded by visual and imaging observers around the globe. In this article I will review observations of this comet, C/2011 L4 (PanSTARRS), and some of the interesting aspects of its behaviour, but first I'll give a quick summary of what comets are and why they appear as they do in our skies.

THE LIFE OF COMETS

Comets started their lives in the frozen depths of our Solar System and they are thought to consist of remnants of the interstellar dust cloud that collapsed under gravity to form the Sun and planets. The solid object at the centre of a comet is called the comet nucleus, believed to consist of a frozen sample of the constituents of the original cloud. As a result there is a great scientific interest in understanding what comets are made of.

From observations we know that the nucleus consists of very fine carbonaceous and silicate dust grains (finer than talcum powder) embedded in a deep-frozen mix of water ice and frozen gases such as carbon dioxide. Spacecraft have shown that bare cometary nuclei are very dark. Technically, they are said to have low albedo and they reflect less than 5 per cent of the sunlight landing on their surface. It is thought that there is a 'crust' of dark material on their surface. This dark crust means that the nucleus is very efficient at absorbing heat from the Sun if the comet falls into the inner Solar System.

You can think of a comet nucleus as a dirty snowball made up of a mixture of snow and soot with a thin layer of carbon crust on the surface. In the far depths of the Solar System where temperatures are low, this nucleus is thought to be completely inactive. The nucleus that generated Hale-Bopp's spectacular display was probably 40–70 km in diameter. This is the largest comet nucleus known and most comet nuclei are much smaller than this. Spacecraft showed that the famous comet 1P/Halley has a peanut-shaped nucleus around 15 km long and 8 km wide. Other comet nuclei visited by spacecraft are smaller but just as irregular (Figure 2).

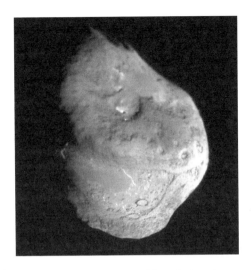

Figure 2. The nucleus of Comet Tempel-1 imaged from the Deep Impact spacecraft in July 2005. The nucleus is around 5 × 7 km across. (Image courtesy of NASA/JPL-Caltech/UMD.)

Since comet nuclei are so dark they are difficult to see when they are in deep freeze since small nuclei far away are very faint. There are, however, some objects that we see in the distant Solar System which could be very large versions of cometary nuclei. These are the Trans Neptunian Objects, or TNOs, and one of the largest of these objects is the ex-planet Pluto. At present Pluto is officially called a dwarf planet, but perhaps it should really be a giant comet. We will know more when the *New Horizons* spacecraft passes by Pluto in July 2015.

COMET ORBITS AND BRIGHTNESS

The Earth travels around the Sun in a roughly circular orbit with a radius of around 150 million km. We call this distance one Astronomical Unit (1 AU). We believe that most of the objects that become comets with long orbital periods are held in cold storage in a vast spherical shell called the Oort Cloud, which is gravitationally bound to the Sun, perhaps 50,000 AU from the inner Solar System. Every now and again an inactive comet nucleus will be perturbed from this cloud (perhaps by the gravity of nearby stars) and it will start to fall in towards the Sun. The Oort Cloud has never been observed directly but it fits in well with the observed orbital behaviour of comets and current theories for the origin of the Solar System.

Since they come from very far away, incoming long-period comets move in long, thin orbits. They spend most of their time far from the Sun then rush around it, reaching their closest point at perihelion, and climb back outwards. The shape of the orbit is defined by a parameter called the eccentricity, 'e'. A perfectly circular orbit has e = 0. Ellipses get longer and thinner as e increases until we get to e = 1. At this point the ellipse is not closed and we have what is called a parabolic orbit. A parabolic orbit is what you would expect if a comet fell from the Oort Cloud with very little initial velocity.

Another parameter defining the orbit is the inclination, 'i' (Figure 3). All of the planets move around the sun in the same direction and almost in the same plane. The plane of the Earth's orbit is called the ecliptic plane and this defines i = 0°. The most highly inclined planet is Mercury with i = 7°. Long-period comets can have any inclination up to and beyond 90°. Inclinations beyond 90° mean that the comet is going around the sun in the opposite direction to the planets. Comet 1P/Halley, for instance has i = 162°, so its orbit is actually inclined to the ecliptic by 18° but it is going around the 'wrong' way.

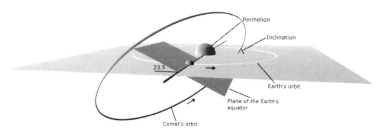

Figure 3. Comet orbits are defined by their eccentricity and size and by their orientation with respect to the Earth's roughly circular orbit. Most comets move in very elongated orbits and they come closest to the Sun at perihelion.

As the comet nucleus moves into the inner Solar System it absorbs energy from the Sun, and the ices heat up and turn directly into gases in a process called sublimation. These gases then escape through fissures in the surface, taking a lot of dust with them. This forms a temporary atmosphere around the nucleus which we observe as the coma (Figure 4). The dust is very fine and sunlight is able to push it away from the nucleus to form a dust tail. In images the dust tail is usually white or yellow, since it shines by reflected sunlight, and it is often curved into a fan, since the relatively heavy dust grains tend to follow the nucleus along its orbit. Ultraviolet radiation from the Sun is absorbed by the escaping gas molecules to produce ionized molecular forms which then interact with the gusty solar wind. The solar wind is a stream of particles moving outwards from the Sun at several hundred kilometres. This wind blows the gas out into what is called the gas, ion or plasma tail. This tail is usually straight and radial to the Sun and often has a blue colour on images, since its light comes mainly from fluorescing carbon monoxide.

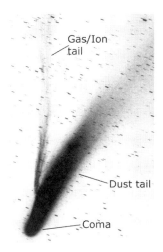

Figure 4. The comet nucleus first generates an almost spherical coma. Dust and gas are then pushed away from the nucleus to form the dust and gas/ion tails.

When a comet is discovered, the first objective is to compute its orbit. We do this by measuring positions of the comet relative to the background stars using a process called *astrometry*. This is something that amateur astronomers with fairly small telescopes and CCD (charge-coupled device) cameras can do effectively. For most comets, astrometry carried out over a period of several weeks can define the orbit very accurately. The orbit can then be used to predict where the comet will be in the future. Many things about comets are difficult to predict but usually the orbit, and hence the comet's position on the sky and its distance from the Earth and Sun, can be predicted with incredible accuracy very shortly after discovery.

We can use the known orbit to predict where the comet will be seen, but we would also like to predict how bright it will be. This is much more difficult. The basic principle is straightforward. We measure the absolute brightness (magnitude) of the comet over a period of several weeks or months and we plot this against the comet's distance from the Sun. We then use this graph to estimate a simple magnitude 'law' and we extrapolate this forward to our selected future observation time. This is all very well, but success is critically dependent on how we expect the comet's activity to change as it approaches the Sun.

DISCOVERING COMETS

Often in the past, comets would be discovered by amateurs when they were already quite active and close to the Sun. More recently, professional surveys have been set up to discover potentially dangerous near-Earth asteroids. These are so powerful that they frequently discover comets when they are still a long way away. This makes brightness predictions even more difficult since we are trying to predict how the nucleus will behave when it is close to the Sun based on observations made when it is far away and only just coming out of deep freeze. Another problem is that a comet behaves differently depending on whether it is a first-time visitor to the Sun (known as a *dynamically new* comet) or has been in the inner Solar System before (*dynamically old*). This can be quite difficult to determine from the orbit since even the 'old' comets can have very long orbital periods. New comets can be quite active when they are far from the Sun but they rarely maintain this activity as they come in. Older comets tend to become active closer to the Sun, but then they have a consistent increase as they approach perihelion.

One of the very successful professional sky surveys is the Panoramic Survey Telescope and Rapid Response System (PanSTARRS). This telescope is situated at a 3,000 metre altitude near the summit of Haleakalā on Maui, Hawaii (Figure 5). It has a 1.8-metre-diameter primary mirror and optics which are corrected to provide a very large field of view of over 3° (roughly six Moon diameters). The focal-plane camera is the largest CCD detector currently in operation in astronomy. Called GPC-1, it consists of a 1.4-Gigapixel imager made up of 60 tiles, each of which is a 4800 × 4800 pixel detector. Each image from GPC-1 is 1.8 GB in size and the telescope takes images at a rate of around one per minute throughout the night.

Figure 5. The PanSTARRS-1 telescope on Haleakalā, Maui. (Image courtesy of PS1 Science Consortium.)

COMET C/2011 L4 (PANSTARRS)

On the night of 6 June 2011 this survey system detected a nineteenth-magnitude moving object in the constellation of Scorpius on four image frames. The images showed that the object was fuzzy (Figure 6), and so it was likely to be a comet rather than an asteroid. Further images the next night using a telescope on Mauna Kea confirmed the cometary nature and showed a hint of a faint tail. The discovery was reported and archive searches then revealed pre-discovery images from a number of other observatories on frames dating back to 24 May. Initial orbital computations made by Gareth Williams at the Minor Planet Center showed that the object was around 8 AU from the Sun at discovery and it was named Comet C/2011 L4 (PanSTARRS). For brevity in the rest of this article I'll refer to this object as Comet PanSTARRS, but you should be aware that there are many comets discovered by the PanSTARRS telescope, so the full designation is important.

An accurate orbit was quickly determined and this showed that the comet would come to perihelion on 10 March 2013 at a distance of 0.3 AU from the Sun. The comet was in an orbit with an inclination of 84° and so it was travelling at almost right angles to the Earth's orbit. Southern Hemisphere observers had the best view prior to perihelion but the steep orbital inclination meant that the comet moved rapidly north in the sky following perihelion (Figure 7).

Figure 6. Discovery image of C/2011 L4 (PanSTARRS), 6 June 2011, 10h 02m UTC. (Image courtesy of Henry Hsieh, PS1 Science Consortium.)

We knew where it was going, but how bright was it likely to be? This was a difficult question to answer. Immediately following the discovery announcement there was considerable discussion about the comet's prospects. Initial estimates suggested that the comet could become very bright. Others cautioned that, since the orbital eccentricity indicated a dynamically new comet, the comet could actually turn out much fainter. The media got hold of the predictions and printed some 'Comet of the Century' stories. They didn't point out that, even if the comet were to be bright, it would be seen in a very bright twilight sky and would be very low on the horizon.

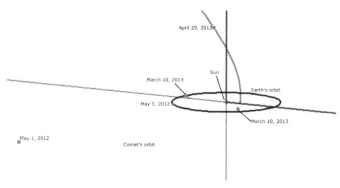

Figure 7. The orbit and position of Comet PanSTARRS and the Earth through 2012 and early 2013. (Based on a diagram from JPL Horizons.)

The best guess in late 2011 was that the comet could become a relatively bright object, possibly visible to the naked eye, in the Northern Hemisphere evening sky during March 2013. It would then move through Pisces and Andromeda and pass close to the Andromeda Galaxy (M31) on 4 April (Figure 8). The viewing geometry was interesting in that, for several weeks after perihelion, any dust tail would be presented nearly face-on to the Earth. This meant that, potentially, the dust tail could cover a large area of sky.

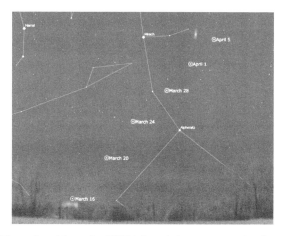

Figure 8. The motion of Comet PanSTARRS through the western evening sky as seen from the UK in spring 2013.

EARLY OBSERVATIONS

Visual observations of the comet began in March 2012, when it appeared as a stellar fourteenth-magnitude object in Ophiuchus. By the summer of 2012 visual observers with large telescopes could see the coma and the comet had brightened to around twelfth magnitude. The comet was brightening quickly and by September it was reported as tenth magnitude. All this time the comet was around 25° south of the celestial equator and so it was difficult to see and image from the UK.

Based on visual observations up to the end of October 2012 the peak brightness at perihelion was expected to be anything from −12 (very bright indeed) to +2 (quite faint). One of the problems with predicting the brightness at perihelion was that the comet would be lost behind the Sun for the last few months of 2012 and then it would only be visible in twilight skies. Rob Kaufman in Victoria, Australia picked up the comet on images taken on 18 December as it reappeared from behind the Sun. The first visual observations were made at the end of December 2012 when it was reported to be at magnitude 8. It appeared that the rate of brightening had slowed significantly and, in January 2013, predictions for the peak visual magnitude were reduced to −2 with an uncertainty of ±3 magnitudes.

Southern observers continued to image the comet through the first few months of 2013 and images in bright twilight with wide-angle lenses showed that the comet had a short, stubby dust tail.

THE COMET AT ITS BRIGHTEST

The day of perihelion finally arrived and Northern Hemisphere observers started to look for the comet in the evening twilight sky. Observers in the US and the Canary Islands saw it on 11 March, but the first UK observations were on 12 March when the comet was only a few degrees above the western horizon at civil twilight. The weather was patchy on that day, but James Abott in Witham, Essex saw the comet using 15 × 70 binoculars and he estimated the coma as magnitude +1 with a ¾° tail. Ian Sharp and Denis Boon also managed to obtain images on that day which showed the comet faintly against the bright twilight sky.

Up in space, on the same date but unencumbered by cloud or twilight, the STEREO-B spacecraft imaged the comet using its Heliospheric Imager payload. This showed a spectacular and highly structured dust tail and it also showed the distant Earth as the brightest object in the frame (Figure 9).

Figure 9. Comet PanSTARRS from space at 23h 29m UT on 12 March 2013. The bright star-like object is the Earth. (Image courtesy of STEREO-B HI and NASA.)

The next day, 13 March, was much clearer and many observers across the UK reported good views of the comet. Jamie Cooper obtained a good image of the comet below the two-day-old crescent Moon (Figure 10). My image in clear skies showed a short dust tail and one background star (Figure 11). The bright twilight meant that the comet was not visible to the naked eye, despite being around first magnitude.

Figure 10. Comet PanSTARRS and the two-day-old crescent Moon, 13 March 2013. (Image courtesy of Jamie Cooper.)

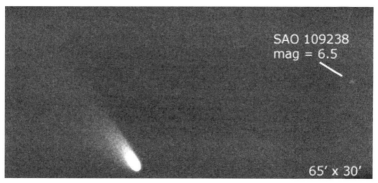

Figure 11. The dust tail of Comet PanSTARRS in the twilight sky. 19h 06m UT, 13 March 2013. 19 × 2.5s exposures. Canon EOS550D + 100mm, f/2 lens. (Image courtesy of Nick James.)

Over the following few days and weeks the comet moved further from the Sun and, although it was fading, it became visible with the naked eye in a darker sky. By 17 March the tail was visible more clearly. Denis Buczynski in northern Scotland had a good view (Figure 12) and

Damian Peach obtained a photogenic view from Selsey (Figure 13). On 19 March, Michael Jäger was obtaining images from Austria which showed similar tail structure to that seen a week earlier in the STEREO images (Figure 14). The tail was essentially dominated by dust with only a very faint gas tail visible.

Figure 12. High-resolution view of Comet PanSTARRS using a C14 telescope. 19h 45m on 17 March 2013. 10 × 1s exposures. (Image courtesy of Denis Buczynski.)

Figure 13. Wide-angle view of Comet PanSTARRS from Selsey, 19h 05m UT, 17 March 2013. (Image courtesy of Damian Peach.)

Figure 14. View of Comet PanSTARRS from Austria tracked on the comet's motion 100 mm aperture, f/2.9 astrographic Newtonian. Processed with a rotational gradient filter. 18h 14m UT, 19 March 2013. (Image courtesy of Michael Jäger.)

AN INTERESTING DUST TAIL

As March turned into April the comet had moved high enough in a dark sky for observers to record a very broad dust fan. This is particularly well shown in Richard Miles's image of 1 April (Figure 15). On that date he estimated that the tail was at least 3° long. Another feature of the fan was a bright spike which would become more prominent over the next few weeks. Richard obtained a set of accurately calibrated images which showed that the comet's brightness was very well behaved with no sign of any outbursts and that it was probably around magnitude zero at perihelion.

By 5 April the comet was approaching M31 (the Andromeda Galaxy) and many observers captured images of this conjunction. I was at the annual Winchester meeting of the British Astronomical Association and the college football field had a low, dark horizon to the west. This allowed us to show the comet to a large group of people through various binoculars and telescopes. The comet was still an easy

Figure 15. Processed image of Comet PanSTARRS to show the extent of the dust tail. 105 mm aperture, f/2.8 lens. 66 × 15s exposures. Field of view 2° × 1°. 20h 20m UT, 1 April 2013. (Image courtesy of Richard Miles.)

binocular object and the inner coma was considerably brighter than the core of M31 (Figure 16).The comet continued to be visible throughout April as a circumpolar object moving from the evening to the morning sky. As the orbital geometry changed, the dust tail fan got wider and wider (Figure 17).

Figure 16. Comet PanSTARRS and M31. Canon EOS550D +135 mm, f/2.8 lens. 20h 43m UT, 5 April 2013. (Image courtesy of Nick James.)

Figure 17. Deep image of Comet PanSTARRS obtained remotely from New Mexico. 08h 38m UT 14 May 2013. (Image courtesy of Damian Peach.)

The bright spike to the east also became more and more prominent until, by May 20, it dominated the view (Figure 18).

Figure 18. Deep image of Comet PanSTARRS obtained remotely from New Mexico. 106 mm aperture, f/5 FSQ refractor. 300s exposure. 10h 30m UT, 20 May 2013. (Image courtesy of Martin Mobberley.)

The reason for this spike was that the Earth was approaching the point where it would pass through the plane of the comet's orbit. Since most of the dust emitted from the nucleus was still in the orbital plane this meant that we would see the dust tail edge-on and this comet had been a very dusty comet indeed. Fifty-six years earlier, at the very dawn of Sir Patrick Moore's *Sky at Night* programme, observers had witnessed a similar spike in a comet called C/1956 R1 (Arend-Roland). The Earth passed through this comet's orbital plane in late April 1957, shortly after perihelion, and around that time the comet produced a forward-pointing spike around 13° long. The comet was photographed by Reggie Waterfield, from his observatory at Ascot, on 24 April (Figure 19) and the spike is obvious. Arend-Roland also had a very long 'normal' dust tail at the time and so was a spectacular view in the sky.

Figure 19. Comet C/1956 R1 (Arend-Roland), 24 April 1957. This photograph was taken near the orbital plane crossing and shows the long forward spike or anti-tail. (Image courtesy of Dr Reginald Waterfield.)

The plane crossing for Comet PanSTARRS was predicted for 26 May and on this date the comet produced a spectacular anomalous tail spike. It was clear over much of the UK on that night and the comet was near Polaris. Unfortunately, there was also a nearly full Moon to drown out faint detail, but my image (Figure 20) shows a spike that is nearly 8° long. PanSTARRS didn't quite break the long-standing record

Figure 20. Mosaic image of Comet PanSTARRS taken during the orbital plane crossing at 23h 00m UT on 26 May 2013. Each tile of the mosaic has a field of view of 71 × 53 arc minutes. (Image courtesy of Nick James.)

of Arend-Roland, but it was a close-run thing, and it may have been different if there had been no Moon around.

Following the plane crossing, the dust tail fan reappeared as we were viewing it from the other side and the spike diminished in intensity. The comet then faded as it continued its journey back to the outer Solar System. It will be in the range of amateur telescopes for many years, but once it is gone we won't see it again.

The light curve (Figure 21) shows that the comet was well behaved

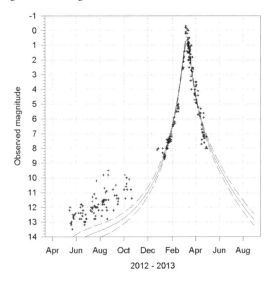

Figure 21. The visual light curve of Comet PanSTARRS. (Courtesy of Jonathan Shanklin/ BAA/TA.)

from December 2012, when it came out from behind the Sun, through to May 2013, when it faded back below eighth magnitude. It probably reached around magnitude zero at perihelion. The only anomalous measurements were those made in 2012 before solar conjunction, when the comet was faint and far from the Sun. This is another reminder of why trying to predict performance from early magnitude estimates is prone to error.

Comet PanSTARRS has been one of the dustiest comets observed and it has shown a very high ratio of dust to gas. It did have a gas tail but this was hardly visible. It certainly hasn't been a 'Great' comet and it hasn't lived up to some of the early hype, but it has been a very good comet with much to interest amateur astronomers. It may not have been easy for the general public to find, but we can all help by showing objects such as this to family, friends and the public and then explaining how a small, dirty snowball, frozen 4.6 billion years ago, can put on such an impressive show in our skies.

A Memory of Patrick

Stephen Webb
Physicist and science writer

I first met Patrick on Friday, 3 July 1987. At that time I was engaged in the painful process of writing up my PhD thesis and, as is often the case with students coming to the end of their studies, I was grateful for any opportunity to procrastinate with a clean conscience. When I received an invitation to a party at the Jodrell Bank Observatory, therefore, I accepted immediately. The venue was 'scientific' enough for me not to suffer too many pangs of guilt. Besides, I was promised that there would be free food and drink.

The party turned out to be in celebration of the thirtieth anniversary of the completion of the famous MkIA radio telescope at Jodrell Bank. That day the telescope was to be renamed in honour of Professor Sir Bernard Lovell, the driving force behind its construction. Dozens of VIPs had been invited, of course, but Jodrell Bank PhD students were also there in force. (It was only because I played football with these students that I wangled a ticket: I was studying physics at Manchester rather than astronomy at Jodrell.)

It was a swelteringly hot day, and after several drinks my footballing friends and I started to explore the grounds. Two of us wandered off and experimented with the whispering dishes. And then Patrick appeared. He asked what we were doing before launching into a fascinating, impromptu lecture on Bernard Lovell – a 'Newton of radio astronomy'; the newly renamed Lovell telescope, the building of which had proven so difficult that the project had been close to bankruptcy, and how it was Sputnik that probably saved it since, in the Cold War, Western governments needed just such a device to track Soviet satellites and detect ballistic missiles; sound mirrors – how in the First World War Britain built an acoustic 'early warning system' based on concave mirrored surfaces of concrete, which brought the sound waves from Zeppelins to a focus and allowed an operator using a stethoscope to determine the direction of approach of the enemy aircraft; and radar – how it had been vital in the

208

Second World War, and how it could be used in astronomy … all this stream-of-consciousness science delivered in his signature machine-gun delivery and seemingly without pause for breath.

I thought about that encounter a lot as I was writing up my thesis. I was impressed, of course, by Patrick's vast-ranging knowledge and unbounded enthusiasm – but what impressed me even more was how readily he had given his time to students he'd never met before. There were many more important people there he could have been talking to. My childhood interest in astronomy had been dulled somewhat by a succession of lecturers who'd made it clear that they had better things to do than teach students. My encounter with Patrick rekindled that interest. And for that I remain grateful.

It was Patrick's success as a teacher – through the clarity of his writing, the professionalism of his broadcasting, and simply the enthusiasm with which he talked to people who wanted to learn – that will, I believe, be his greatest legacy.

Planck's New View
of the Universe

STEPHEN WEBB

INTRODUCTION

Readers of a certain age might recall how cosmologists once argued about the basic numbers underpinning their science. For example, the age of the universe was uncertain to a factor of two while the curvature of the universe – whether open, flat or closed – was unknown. That's all changed. The various parameters that characterize the so-called standard model of cosmology have been determined with an exactness that is astonishing to those of us who can remember heated debates about the size of the Hubble constant and the shape of the universe. We have entered the era of precision cosmology.

The key to precision cosmology is the in-depth study of the cosmic microwave background (CMB), since a detailed analysis of the CMB allows cosmologists to determine what combination of model parameters best fits observation. It becomes possible to say how much dark energy must be in the mix, how much dark matter, how long these elements have been interacting, and much else besides. The European Space Agency (ESA) Planck mission has recently completed the most accurate observations ever made of the CMB, and in March 2013 scientists announced their initial analysis of the data: the results are simply stunning.

This article gives a brief account of the Planck mission, presents some of the highlights from the first analyses of the 2013 Planck data, and discusses the significance of the results for cosmology. Before getting to Planck, however, it makes sense first to discuss the CMB in more detail and then to describe how Planck's two satellite predecessors – COBE and WMAP – led scientists to the standard model of cosmology.

THE OLDEST PHOTONS IN THE UNIVERSE

In 1964, Arno Penzias and Robert Wilson, researchers at Bell Telephone Labs, were experimenting with antennae intended for use in the testing of communication satellites. In doing this work they discovered an interesting fact about the universe: there's a faint background hum spread evenly over the sky, a hum that is present day and night, summer and winter. Penzias and Wilson heard it at a wavelength of 7.35 cm, which is in the microwave region of the spectrum. Their discovery was important because any cosmological model had to account for the presence of this microwave background radiation.

In the early 1960s, there were two competing cosmological models: the steady state model and the Big Bang model. In the steady state model the universe is essentially unchanging. In the Big Bang model the universe started out in a small, hot, opaque, dense state that subsequently expanded, cooled and evolved into the universe we see today. In the steady state model it's not easy to come up with a simple, compelling reason for the existence of a microwave background. In the Big Bang model the microwave background arises quite naturally. Let's see why.

For the first 380,000 years or so after the Big Bang the universe was too hot for neutral atoms to exist and so all the 'normal' matter would have taken the form of a soup of freely moving electrons, protons and neutrons. Photons could not travel far before scattering off the electrons in this hot, dense soup, with the result that the early universe was opaque. Thus the universe was filled with blackbody radiation. (A blackbody emits a particular type of continuous spectrum that depends only upon temperature.) As the universe expanded it cooled. When it was about 380,000 years old, the temperature of the universe dropped to 3,000 K – cool enough for neutral atoms to form. Suddenly the photons were no longer scattering off free electrons: the universe became transparent and photons began to move unimpeded – which they have been doing ever since until, roughly 13 billion years later, astronomers catch them in their telescopes. This picture explains the existence of background radiation, but why should the photons we detect be *microwave* photons?

When the temperature of the universe was 3,000 K, the peak in the blackbody radiation spectrum would have been at around 1 micron, which is in the infrared. (There would also have been significant amounts of visible light, and if you'd been there to see it, you'd have perceived the universe as possessing a uniform, dull orange colour.) However, since the time when matter and photons first separated, the universe has expanded by a factor of about 1,000 and thus the wavelength of those photons has increased by a factor of about 1,000. In other words, according to the Big Bang model the peak in the blackbody spectrum has shifted from about 1 micron when the universe was 380,000 years old to about 1 millimetre today – and that present-day peak lies in the microwave region of the electromagnetic spectrum. In terms of temperature we can say that the universe has cooled from about 3,000 K at the time when photons separated from matter to about 3 K today.

Whereas explanations of the CMB in the steady state model are rather contrived, the Big Bang model *predicts* that microwave background radiation should fill the present universe. It was mainly thanks to Penzias's and Wilson's discovery that the Big Bang model won out over the rival steady state theory, and it is fitting that they received the 1978 Nobel Prize for their work.

The Big Bang predicts more than just the *existence* of microwave background radiation: it predicts the *form* of the radiation – namely, that it should be a blackbody. Astronomers in the 1960s assumed that the background radiation was blackbody in form, but Penzias and Wilson had observed the radiation only at 7.35 cm, and that was many times longer than the peak wavelength. Subsequent observations suggested that the radiation was indeed that of a blackbody, but astronomers couldn't *prove* it was blackbody radiation without observing at a variety of wavelengths and from a variety of locations. Astronomers thus began to lobby for a mission to observe the CMB in detail, and they pointed out that there would be much more to gain from such a mission: it would give us the deepest view of the universe. Since no photons exist from before the decoupling of matter and energy, the CMB photons are the oldest photons in the universe and it's thus impossible to 'see' further back in time using electromagnetic radiation. The trouble is, observing the CMB is difficult because water molecules in Earth's atmosphere tend to absorb microwaves with a wavelength less than about 3 cm. In order to study the cosmic microwave background in detail, and prove beyond doubt that the Big Bang occurred, astronomers would need to get their instruments above the atmosphere. They would need a satellite mission.

THE DAWN OF PRECISION COSMOLOGY

In 1989, NASA launched a four-year mission to measure the intensity of the cosmic microwave background at a variety of infrared and microwave wavelengths. The Cosmic Background Explorer (COBE) satellite carried three instruments and one of them, the Far Infrared Absolute Spectrophotometer, spent ten months measuring the difference in spectra between the CMB and an internal blackbody over the wavelength range 0.1–10 mm. It found that the CMB spectrum is astonishingly close to an ideal blackbody, and possesses a temperature corresponding to 2.725 ± 0.002 K. Figure 1 shows how the CMB appeared to COBE in 1990.

Figure 1. A map of the cosmic microwave background as it appeared in measurements made up to and including 1990: the lack of variation represents the fact that the microwave background is an astonishingly good blackbody. Note the elliptical shape of the map: all-sky maps of the microwave background typically use the Mollweide equal-area projection, which favours accurate proportions in area over accuracy of angle and shape. (Image courtesy of NASA.)

If the CMB is a *perfect* blackbody, however, then the Big Bang model runs into difficulties. The problem is that the universe we observe today is 'lumpy'. We see lots of structure – stars, galaxies, clusters of galaxies, superclusters of galaxies, and even larger formations. Such structure must have been present in the early universe as tiny density fluctuations, and those regions of under- and over-density would leave their mark as fluctuations in the microwave background: hot spots in the CMB would correspond to regions of higher-than-average density, cold spots to regions of lower-than-average density. Therefore, in order to explain the development of structures in the present-day universe there must be variations, or anisotropies, in the CMB.

A second instrument on COBE, the Differential Microwave Radiometer, used a pair of horn antennae to measure the difference in power received from two directions in the sky separated by 60°. By measuring temperature *differences* it was able to map the CMB with exquisite sensitivity and it succeeded in finding anisotropies, small ripples at the level of 1 part in 100,000. The anisotropies were on a large angular scale; COBE had insufficient resolution to see the small-angular-scale anisotropies that would lead to the structure we see today. Nevertheless, the detection of anisotropies, even if they were on a large angular scale, constituted a major advance. Figure 2 shows how the CMB appeared to COBE in 1992 after the Differential Microwave Radiometer results.

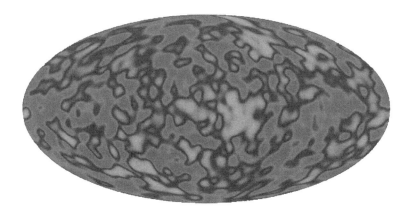

Figure 2. A map of the cosmic microwave background as it appeared in 1992: temperature variations appear at the level of one part in one hundred thousand. At the time these observations were made, only variations on large angular scales could be made out. A high-definition picture would require improved technology. (Image courtesy of NASA.)

These COBE observations firmly cemented the Big Bang as the preferred model for the origin of the universe: no competing theory can easily explain both the blackbody nature of the microwave background and the existence of tiny fluctuations. Even more important than this, though, was how COBE demonstrated that precision cosmology was possible. It's perhaps for this reason, as much as the results themselves, that John Mather and George Smoot from the COBE team were awarded the 2006 Nobel prize.

The COBE team put the Big Bang picture on a firm footing, but cosmologists still had to grapple with a number of serious problems with the traditional model. Let's briefly consider just three of the problems.

First, there is the horizon problem: the CMB is just too smooth. To understand what this means, face due north and look at the sky; then turn your head a few degrees and look at the sky again. Those two patches of sky you have observed were not in causal contact 380,000 years after the Big Bang. In other words, those two regions of sky were so far apart that there was insufficient time for any signal, even one travelling at light speed, to pass between them. However, those patches of sky – indeed, all patches of sky – have essentially the same temperature: 2.7 K in today's universe. When photons decoupled from matter, some 380,000 years after the Big Bang, there were many thousands of causally disconnected regions; none of them could possibly 'know' what the other regions were doing. So how could they possess the same temperature?

Second, there is the flatness problem: the geometry of the universe seems to be Euclidean, or flat. The issue here is that in a Big Bang cosmology, curvature grows with time. For a universe to be as flat as we see it today, it would require conditions in the early universe to have been fine-tuned to an unbelievable degree.

Third, there is the problem of present-day structure: how does gravitational attraction work on those primordial density fluctuations in order to generate the structures we see today? There's simply not enough visible matter in the universe to generate the clustering we observe.

The cure for the first two problems, and for various other problems in cosmology which I won't discuss here, is inflation. The basic idea is simple: in the period between about 10^{-36} s and 10^{-33} s after the Big Bang, the universe increased in volume by an incredible factor, at least 10^{78}. In a sense, during the inflationary epoch, space itself was expanding very much faster than the speed of light. This may sound bizarre, but the phenomenon is allowed in general relativity. Matter, on the other hand, must obey the 'local' speed limit imposed by special relativity – the light speed limit. Inflation solves the horizon problem because, prior to that brief phase of exponential growth, distant regions of the universe were much closer than the traditional Big Bang model assumes. Widely separated parts of the sky were in causal connection after all, and so different regions *could* have attained a uniform temperature. Inflation solves the flatness problem because any curvature that might have been present would have been stretched to effective flatness by that exponential increase in the size of the universe. It's like blowing up a party balloon to be the size of the Earth. The balloon starts out highly curved, but if you could stand on the inflated balloon you would say it was flat – just as the Earth appears flat to us. Well, the difference in volume between the pre-inflationary universe and the post-inflationary universe is *much* greater than the difference in volume between a party balloon and Earth. Inflation thus demands that the universe is flat.

The cure for the third problem is straightforward: there must be more matter in the universe than we can see. In other words, the universe must contain some form of dark matter. The dark matter paradigm did not, in fact, originate in cosmology: several independent observations caused astronomers to posit the existence of large quantities of non-luminous material in galaxies and galaxy clusters. The relevant point in this context, however, is that when dark matter is added to the mix it turns out that gravity can indeed generate the clustering we observe in the present-day universe. Computer models of structure formation in a Big Bang model indicate that the dark matter must be slow-moving – 'cold', in other words – since if it were 'hot' dark matter the structures would be washed away.

So COBE results not only supported the Big Bang paradigm, they suggested that a successful cosmological model had to incorporate two elements new to physics: cold dark matter (CDM) and inflation. Both of these elements are essentially unknown quantities: in the absence of an underlying theory, physicists have proposed over a hundred different mechanisms to implement inflation, while, so far, they have searched in vain for dark matter. (Various experiments are currently trying to detect dark matter particles directly; in a couple of years from now there may be some interesting news to report.) The success of COBE, combined with the way it hinted at the existence of new physics, made it inevitable that scientists would demand a follow-up mission to study the CMB with even greater precision and sensitivity.

In 1995, the American astrophysicist Charles Bennett pitched a mission to NASA called the Microwave Anisotropy Probe (MAP): the spacecraft would measure temperature differences in the CMB from opposite directions on the sky and, month-on-month and year-on-year, it would construct an increasingly precise all-sky map of the microwave background. MAP would carry instruments that were forty-five times more sensitive than those on COBE and possess thirty-three times the angular resolution. Bennett argued that by making such an all-sky study of the minuscule CMB temperature differences at angular scales down to about a quarter of a degree, MAP would be able to determine much about the age, contents and structure of the universe. Bennett's proposal was accepted. A rocket carrying the MAP mission was launched in 2001 and placed at the L_2 point of the Earth–Sun system, where it observed the CMB in five radio frequency bands. In 2003, following the death of David Wilkinson, one of the MAP team's leading scientists, the mission was renamed the Wilkinson Microwave Anisotropy Probe (WMAP). The satellite ceased observing in 2010; the nine years of data from WMAP have transformed cosmology so that the subject is now, without question, a precision science.

Figure 3 shows the WMAP map of the CMB fluctuations. Notice the increase in definition over previous maps.

Figure 3. A map of the CMB as seen in 2012. The map shows temperature variations in the CMB as determined by nine years of WMAP data; dark patches represent 'cold' spots, bright patches represent 'hot' spots. The small variations seen here later evolved into the very large-scale structures that are present in the universe today. (Image courtesy of NASA.)

The WMAP team analyzed the temperature fluctuations in the CMB at different angular scales. At large scales, corresponding to regions that stretch about 30° or more across the sky, the fluctuations are not particularly noticeable; similarly, at very small scales, corresponding to regions that stretch only about 0.1° or less across the sky, the fluctuations are tiny. For regions that stretch about 1° across the sky, however, the temperature fluctuations are quite obvious. A plot of the CMB temperature deviations versus angular scale is known as the CMB power spectrum. According to WMAP, then, the power spectrum has a definite peak at about 1° and several smaller peaks as shorter angular scales. (Figure 7 later in the chapter illustrates the power spectrum as measured by the Planck mission; this is essentially a more precise version of the spectrum measured by WMAP.)

The CMB power spectrum is important because its form is determined by the distribution and behaviour of matter in the early universe. For example, the spectrum at angular scales from about 1° down to about 0.2° arises because of oscillations – in essence, sound waves – in the plasma that filled the universe. The first peak in the spectrum at about 1° corresponds to a fundamental wave which, at the time when photons and matter decoupled, caused some regions to be at maximum compression (hot regions in the CMB) and others to be at maximum rarefaction (cold regions). The second peak corresponds to the first overtone of that fundamental wave, the third peak to the second overtone, and so on. Crucially, certain key features of the universe determine the position and structure of those peaks, and so by studying the peaks we learn about those key features. For example, the density of cold dark matter in the universe affects the relative amplitudes of the first three peaks while the ratio of the heights of the first two peaks is determined by the relative energy densities of 'normal' matter and photons. Furthermore, different models of inflation make slightly different predictions for the structure of the peaks – so the power spectrum contains information about inflation too. In addition to all this, cosmologists can use the data to determine whether the universe is flat. They do this by calculating the actual size of the regions of most intense temperature fluctuations; since they know how far those CMB photons have travelled to reach us, the system forms a vast cosmic triangle. Cosmologists can measure the angles in those triangles, and if they see that the angles add up to 180°, then they know the universe is flat. In short, WMAP data allowed cosmologists to place tight constraints on the content, age and geometry of the universe.

According to WMAP the universe is, to within 0.5 per cent, 13.77 billion years old; the geometry of the universe is, to within 0.4 per cent, flat; and baryonic matter accounts for only 4.6 per cent of the mass–energy content of the universe, with dark matter accounting for a further 24 per cent.

From the above figures it follows that, if the universe is flat, about 71.4 per cent of its mass–energy content must be in some unknown form. Readers will be aware that one of the most surprising results in modern science has been the discovery that the universal expansion is accelerating, a finding that is best understood if the universe is filled with so-called dark energy (the form of which is uncertain, but it is currently best described as being a non-zero cosmological constant Λ). The WMAP data agree with the notion that dark energy, in the form of a non-zero Λ, currently is the largest component of the universe.

The WMAP measurements also provide evidence for inflation. In particular, WMAP found that the temperature variations on large scales is slightly bigger than the variations on small scales. This is precisely what inflationary scenarios predict.

The exquisite precision of the WMAP measurements has led to the consolidation of a self-consistent, standard model of cosmology: 'inflation-plus-Λ CDM'. This so-called 'concordance model' may seem rather bizarre, in that its most important ingredients – inflation, dark matter, dark energy – are not well understood! However, the model is a fundamentally simple one and it is consistent with all observations. It is surely a tremendous achievement of cosmology that a simple theoretical model can account for the myriad of observations made by astronomers.

Although WMAP exceeded the sensitivity of COBE in all respects it did not possess enough sensitivity to extract all the information encoded within the CMB. The European Space Agency (ESA) therefore planned its own space mission to study the CMB temperature fluctuations, a mission that would improve upon WMAP just as WMAP had improved upon COBE. Indeed, the planned ESA mission would measure the CMB temperature fluctuations with an accuracy determined by fundamental astrophysical limits.

PLANCK: THE COLDEST OBJECT IN SPACE

In 2009, after a sixteen-year gestation period, Planck was launched on an Ariane 5 rocket and then made the journey to the L_2 point of the Earth–Sun system. (The same rocket also carried the Herschel infrared space telescope. WMAP was, of course, already at L_2, and in future years the James Webb Space Telescope and the Gaia probe will also travel to the Lagrange point. This is a preferred location for astronomical satellites.) In fact, Planck does not sit precisely at L_2; rather, it orbits the point at an average distance of 400,000 km. This means that Planck is never in Earth's shadow and so its solar panels, which power the spacecraft, always see the Sun. (See Figure 5.)

Planck spins continuously on an axis that points towards the Sun and completes one revolution per minute. Its instruments point at right angles to the rotation axis and so, as Planck spins, it observes a ring of the sky; and, as the L_2 point orbits the Sun at the same rate as Earth, Planck makes a map of the entire sky in about six months.

Figure 4. The Planck mission is named in honour of the German physicist Max Planck, who was the first to offer a successful theory of blackbody radiation. (Photo taken in 1930.)

Figure 5. An artist's conception of Planck, with Earth in the background. Solar panels power the satellite; a telescope focuses radiation onto two detectors. (Image courtesy of ESA.)

The mission team always intended that Planck should be a major advance on WMAP as an instrument for studying the cosmic microwave background: it would observe in nine frequency bands rather than five; it would possess ten times the sensitivity; and its higher resolving power would allow it to probe the CMB to much smaller scales. In order to deliver these advances, the Planck team decided to employ two different instruments.

Planck's low-frequency instrument (LFI) built on COBE and WMAP technology by using microwave radiometers to map the sky at 30, 44 and 70 GHz. The high-frequency instrument (HFI) employed a quite different technique. The HFI had fifty-two bolometers that captured photons from the cosmic microwave background – each thimbleful of space contains about four hundred such photons – and then measured the tiny amount of heat released when the photons interacted with electrons in the device. The HFI approach was quite different to that taken by WMAP, and allowed the detection of temperature variations in the CMB at the level of about a millionth of a degree. However, for the HFI approach to work, the bolometers had to be cooled to extremely low temperatures: without cooling, the bolometers would be overwhelmed by thermal radiation from the satellite itself. Fifty days after launch, the HFI reached its operating temperature: a frigid 0.1 K. During its operating period, the HFI was the coldest thing in space – the background temperature, after all, is a comparatively balmy 2.7 K. It is worth noting that it took a tremendous feat of engineering to bring the instrument down to its operating temperature. The cooling happened in stages. A passive cooling system brought the heart of Planck down to 43 K, then three active cooling systems brought the temperature down first to 20 K, then 4 K, and then finally 0.1 K. Such cooling systems inevitably have a relatively short lifetime: the coolants for the HFI were exhausted in January 2012, after which time observations became impossible. The LFI did not need to be quite so cool as the HFI and so it was able to observe for almost 600 additional days. Planck ceased its operations on 14 August 2013 and was boosted away from its orbit at L_2. On 23 October 2013, Planck was turned off.

The first all-sky image from Planck was released in 2010; Planck continued to spin, however, observing the sky strip by strip and continuously adding to the information contained in that first image. The first analysis of Planck data was of about a thousand measurements made on about a billion points of sky: that's a trillion observations the team had to analyze. The analysis was complicated by the need to remove all the foreground emissions that lie between the satellite and the CMB and the need to account in detail for how the bolometers reacted when they detected a CMB photon. It will come as no surprise to learn, then, that the satellite was not the only critical element in the Planck mission: without the availability of supercomputing resources it would have been impossible to extract the CMB signal from the masses of data. Fortunately, the Planck mission had access to Hopper, a Cray supercomputer that in late 2010 was ranked fifth in a list of the world's most powerful supercomputers.

In March 2013, the Planck team released their first analysis of the HFI and LFI data. The results were as exciting as one would expect from such a groundbreaking experiment.

FIRST RESULTS FROM PLANCK

The fact that Planck observed the CMB with more precision than WMAP is evident from Figure 6. Indeed, if you compare the level of detail contained in Figures 1, 2, 3 and 6, you will appreciate the increasing definition in the CMB all-sky maps as time has passed.

Figure 6. A map of the universe in high definition, as seen by Planck in 2013. The map shows tiny temperature fluctuations in the cosmic microwave background, which correspond to regions of space having slightly different densities. These density fluctuations grew into the structure we see today. A greyscale image such as this inevitably loses some of the information in the original; visit the ESA website to see a colour version. (Image courtesy of ESA and the Planck Collaboration.)

The superb sensitivity of Planck allowed the CMB power spectrum to be drawn with astonishing precision. The result is shown in Figure 7. The dots in Figure 7 are the Planck data, with error bars; the curve is the best fit to the data using the standard concordance model. This graph is destined to be one of the defining elements of modern cosmology: the curve sums up our universe.

It is immediately apparent from only a brief glance at Figure 7 that the concordance model of cosmology, which is defined by just six numbers (fewer numbers than the digits in your phone number), is in remarkable agreement with observation – particularly at smaller angular scales. With its increased sensitivity Planck might have taken

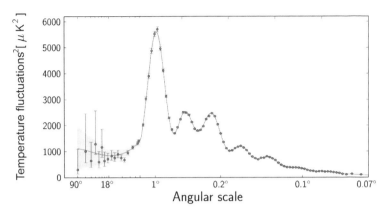

Figure 7. The CMB power spectrum – temperature fluctuations in the microwave background at different angular scales on the sky – as seen by Planck. The left part of the diagram shows the largest angular scales, with progressively smaller angular scales to the right. The dots are the Planck data, with error bars shown; the curve is the best fit to these data from the concordance model of the universe. (Image courtesy of the Planck Collaboration.)

measurements that contradicted the findings of WMAP, but instead it confirmed those measurements and the validity of the standard model. There can be little doubt, then, that the standard model of cosmology contains at least some element of 'truth'.

Although Planck confirms the concordance model, it refines some of the elements of the model. Below, from the more than two dozen papers published by the Planck team, I present a few of the highlights.

First, the age of the universe is 13.798 billion years, give or take 37 million years. This is a touch older than previously thought. (Note that you may see slightly different ages given in other sources. There is no inconsistency. The figure given depends on whether extra information is combined with the raw Planck data.)

Second, Planck confirms the WMAP result that the universe is flat. The amount of dark energy in the universe is slightly less than previously thought (69.2 per cent, down from 71.4 per cent). On the other hand, there's slightly more dark matter (26.8 per cent) and baryonic matter (4.9 per cent) than in previous estimates. See Figure 8 for the new cosmic recipe.

Third, the Planck observations determine the Hubble constant to be 67.80 ± 0.77 km s^{-1} Mpc^{-1}. This is interesting because, although it is in

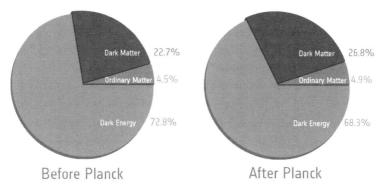

Before Planck   After Planck

Figure 8. The contents of the universe. (Image courtesy of the Planck Collaboration.)

good agreement with the value determined by WMAP, it does not quite agree with the value derived from 'local' standard-candle distance measurements, which is 73.8 ± 2.4 km s^{-1} Mpc^{-1}. A tension appears to exist between scientists investigating the early stages of cosmic history and those investigating recent stages: they fail to meet up in the middle. Resolving this discrepancy will surely be high on cosmologists' 'to-do' lists.

Fourth, according to the Standard Model of particle physics, there are three flavours of neutrino and they have all been discovered: the electron-neutrino, the muon-neutrino and the tau-neutrino. Some theoreticians, searching for signs of physics beyond the Standard Model, have postulated the existence of other types of neutrino; Planck, however, confirms that there are only three types. (The Planck results also place an upper bound on the sum of all three neutrino masses: taken together, they can have no more than 0.0002 per cent of the electron mass.)

Fifth, almost all theoretical models make a prediction regarding the end of the inflationary period: they predict that quantum fluctuations were marginally stronger on larger scales than smaller scales. This prediction is encapsulated in a number called the spectral index: inflation says the spectral index should be slightly less than 1. Well, cosmologists can obtain the spectral index from the CMB power spectrum and the Planck team finds it to be 0.96; furthermore, the error bars are so small that the team can say with certainty that the spectral index is less than 1. This isn't an absolute proof of inflation, but it is an extremely strong indication that inflation occurred. In addition, Planck had enough sensitivity to disentangle two spectral parameters that WMAP could not distinguish; these parameters rule out many complicated models of inflation. The simplest models of inflation pass all the constraints placed by Planck.

If we ended the discussion here we would undoubtedly conclude that Planck has shown the concordance model of cosmology to be in excellent health. Indeed, the model *is* in excellent health. Nevertheless, as can be seen from Figure 7, the agreement between theory and observation at large angular scales is less good than at small angular scales; indeed, there is one data point that lies outside the range of allowed cosmological models. The Planck data thus contain tantalizing hints of something beyond the standard picture. One item of interest is the existence of an anomalous cool spot in the CMB. Of even more interest is the fact that the Northern and Southern Hemispheres of the sky are, statistically, not quite the same: when cosmologists fit the six fundamental parameters of the concordance model to each half of the sky separately, they get slightly different values. The anomalies might be just the result of a fluke – but they could also hint at structure that originated before the Big Bang! Cosmologists will pore over the Planck data for years to come, investigating what it all means for the concordance model and trying to make sense of the anomalies.

WHAT NEXT?

As with all the best science missions, Planck has answered some questions while raising many more. Answering those new questions, however, will require a new approach. The line from COBE to WMAP to Planck ends with Planck: the mission observed with such sensitivity that it makes little point to aim for even more sensitivity. Planck has 'squeezed the juice' out of temperature variations in the CMB. Nevertheless, the Planck observations might contain information of a kind even more exciting than that outlined above.

The standard cosmological model predicts that, at the time radiation decoupled from matter, tiny density fluctuations would polarize the photons: in other words, we should be able to observe polarization around hot and cold spots in the CMB. The polarization would be of a particular type, called E-mode polarization, which possesses a high degree of symmetry. Measuring the polarization of the CMB is even more difficult than measuring the temperature variations, but it is possible and it has been done (by ground-based observatories as well as by WMAP and Planck). Polarization measurements are important because they enable cosmologists to determine not only the location of density variations but also how matter was moving at the time when radiation decoupled from matter. Even more interesting is the fact that something else could have polarized the background radiation: primordial gravitational waves.

A gravitational wave is a disturbance of space itself. When a gravitational wave passes a particular point, space gets stretched in one direction and squeezed in the perpendicular direction. Theory suggests that this squeezing and stretching would have been extreme in the very early universe, and inflation would have expanded those early gravitational waves. Now any light waves moving through a distorted space – a space that is stretched in one direction and squeezed in another – would be forced to vibrate in particular directions: they would be polarized, in other words. Two different polarization patterns would be generated: an E-mode pattern, similar to that produced by density variations, and a B-mode pattern, which has a swirling sort of aspect. In July 2013, the South Pole Telescope made the first detection of a B-mode signal in the CMB – but this effect was caused by gravitational lensing. If scientists find the B-mode from primordial gravitational waves in the CMB, then they will have proved beyond any reasonable doubt that a period of inflation took place in the early universe and they will have made the first direct detection of gravitational waves. It will be a discovery worthy of a Nobel Prize or two. If a primordial B-mode polarization pattern exists in the CMB, then it will be an incredibly tiny effect (the signal found by the South Pole Telescope was at the level of one part in ten million), but Planck scientists are currently scouring the data and hunting for the signal. It's possible they will find it. The team will announce the results of their analysis in 2014, some time after this book is published. Keep an eye out for news!

If Planck fails to detect the primordial B-mode polarization pattern, then there is no shortage of other experiments hoping to make the crucial discovery, mainly from Earth-based and balloon-borne observatories. Some current experiments include the Atacama B-mode Search (ABS), the E&B Experiment (EBEX), Polarization of Background Microwave Radiation (POLARBEAR) and the Q&U Bolometric

Interferometer for Cosmology (QUBIC). If Planck or one of these other experiments glimpses the primordial B-mode in the cosmic microwave background, then we will be seeing the effects of something generated when the universe was only a trillionth of a trillionth of a trillionth of a second old. Back in 1964, Penzias and Wilson could hardly have dreamed that the microwaves they detected in their horn antenna, radiation they initially tried hard to remove, would give us so much interesting information about the universe.

FURTHER READING

Amedeo Balbi, *The Music of the Big Bang: The Cosmic Microwave Background and the New Cosmos* (Springer, Berlin, 2008).

John Boslough and John Mather, *The Very First Light* (Basic Books, New York, 2008).

Alan Guth, *The Inflationary Universe* (Basic Books, New York, 1998).

Martin Rees, *Just Six Numbers* (Basic Books, New York, 2001).

George Smoot and Keay Davidson, *Wrinkles in Time* (William Morrow, New York, 1994).

A Drink with Sir Patrick

David A. Rothery
Planetary scientist, lecturer and author

I grew up reading Patrick's books and watching his *Apollo* coverage, and I learned my way around the sky with his *Observer's Book of Astronomy*. I was rarely allowed to stay up late enough to watch *The Sky at Night*, but, like many schoolboys, I once wrote to Patrick and received a reply. I met him years later in 1996, when we were speakers in Birmingham on the 150th anniversary of the discovery of Neptune. Patrick spoke about Neptune itself, and I about its main satellite, Triton. Afterwards he was kind enough to remark that he had read my book *Satellites of the Outer Planets*.

Our first joint TV appearance was *Live from Mars*, an Open University TV programme on a Saturday morning in 1997 when NASA's Mars Pathfinder landed, allowing us to broadcast the first new pictures from the surface of Mars for nearly twenty years. Patrick began to invite me onto *The Sky at Night*, and this led to a friendship, as with so many of his guests. The programme was usually recorded at Farthings, Patrick's home in Selsey, and Patrick delighted in putting his guests up overnight. That was a cue for an impressively laden supper table, copious quantities of lubricant, and entertaining – if sometimes outrageous – conversation.

I witnessed Patrick's mobility decline from walking sticks to Zimmer frame, to wheelchair – and he spoke to me of his regret at no longer being able to play cricket. His once famously rapid speech became slurry, but his mind and monocle-assisted eyesight stayed sharp. Co-presenters assumed ever greater roles on *The Sky at Night*, but Patrick remained the pivotal host. I last saw him less than three weeks before his death, when guesting for the December 2012 *Sky at Night* episode, entitled 'The Moon and Mercury'. I think this was the last day of filming that Patrick was able to do. He was drowsy at first, but his intellect soon kicked in. He steered our discussion ably, and we were treated to a vintage Patrick moment of scepticism about ice in

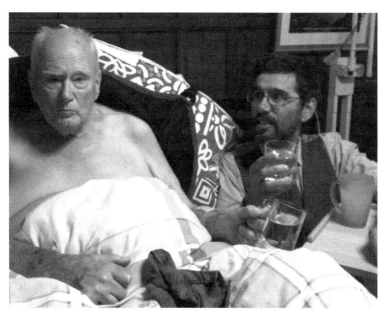

Patrick and David enjoy a gin and tonic together, 19 November 2012. (Image courtesy of David Rothery.)

permanently shadowed lunar craters: 'When someone gives me a cupful of lunar water, then I'll admit I was wrong.'

Afterwards Patrick retired to bed, and when he'd had a nap I went in for a chat – inevitably partly about cats. Patrick confirmed my commission to write the Mercury chapter that you will find in this yearbook, and encouraged me to write a complete book about Mercury, kindly agreeing to write the foreword if I did. Noticing the time, he rang for his carer to mix a gin and tonic for each of us, posed with me while she took a photo of us, and was soon involved in good-natured banter with her about why she would not let him have a top-up of gin.

It would be disingenuous to pretend that Patrick was not sometimes regarded as a figure of fun, but nor was he above self-parody. He was widely respected, and showed enormous kindness and patience. Patrick inspired two or three generations of astronomers and planetary scientists – professionals as well as amateurs – to seek to understand what's out there. I wish I'd got round to asking him whether 'Farthings' was a deliberate pun on 'Far things'.

Mercury – More Than Just a Pale Pink Dot

DAVID A. ROTHERY

Mercury is the smallest of our Solar System's four terrestrial (rocky) planets, and is the closest to the Sun. Only a few years ago, it was an unregarded little world that scarcely impinged on most astronomers' consciousness. Being three times nearer the Sun than we are, it is hard to see, even if you pick the right moment to look. Until recently it had been visited by only one space probe, Mariner 10, which made three flybys in 1973–4.

Every astronomer should see Mercury at least once in their life, if only to tick it off their mental 'bucket list'. Mercury is often easiest to locate with binoculars by scanning above the horizon in the correct direction, after which you should then be able to make it out with the naked eye. It looks like a first-magnitude star with a pinkish tinge. Mercury's surface is genuinely slightly red, though less so than the Moon, and its visually pink appearance at twilight is because we see it through such a thickness of our own atmosphere.

To see Mercury in the post-sunset or pre-dawn twilight sky you need to choose your date and time well, and have a good, clear horizon. If you are in the Northern Hemisphere, your best chances to see Mercury in 2014 will be shortly after sunset in evenings a few days either side of greatest eastern elongation on 31 January and 25 May or, for early risers, before dawn a few days either side of greatest western elongation on 1 November. Those in the Southern Hemisphere will have their best chances in the evenings around Mercury's 25 May and 21 September eastern elongations and in the mornings around the 14 March and 12 July western elongations. For more detailed information on viewing Mercury, see the Monthly Notes elsewhere in this yearbook.

It was once thought that Mercury's rotation is synchronous with its orbit (a not-unlikely consequence of tidal drag on a planet so close to its star) so that the same side would face permanently towards the Sun.

Radar measurements in 1965 showed that in fact it rotates exactly three times for every two orbits about the Sun. This 3:2 spin:orbit coupling probably results from the combined effects of tidal drag and the eccentricity of Mercury's orbit, which is greater than that of any other planet. Three rotations per two orbits results in opposite points on Mercury's equator having the Sun directly overhead at alternate perihelia (the closest orbital point to the Sun). It also means that Mercury's day length (defined, for example, as sunrise to sunrise) is twice as long as its year. If you find one day lasting two years hard to reconcile with a 3:2 spin:orbit ratio, then consider that a planet would have to rotate once per orbit for its spin to keep pace with its orbital motion – in which case, the Sun would never rise or set (so the day would be infinitely long). To have a day length equal to its year, a planet would need to spin twice per orbit. Three spins per two orbits results in a day twice as long as a year.[1] By the way, what I have just described applies only to a planet rotating in the same direction as its orbital motion (so called 'prograde' rotation); the numbers are different for a planet whose spin is opposite to its orbital motion. I've also simplified things by assuming a circular orbit. In fact, Mercury has a more strongly elliptical orbit than any other planet, and for about four Earth-days either side of perihelion (when Mercury is travelling fastest), Mercury's angular orbital velocity is slightly faster than its angular rotational velocity. Then, as seen from Mercury's surface, the Sun briefly backtracks in its sky, so that at certain longitudes it rises about halfway, then sets again only to rise again shortly after!

Mercury passes exactly between the Sun and the Earth about a dozen times per century, when a transit of Mercury across the Sun's disc can be observed. The next transit is ideally timed for visibility in the UK. It will happen on 9 May 2016, beginning at 11.12 and ending at 18.42 GMT (12.12–19.42 BST). Mercury's angular size will be 12 arc seconds, which is $1/_{150}$th the diameter of the Sun's disc. This is too small to see without optical aid, but it should be easy to spot by using a small telescope (or one side of a pair of binoculars) to focus an image onto a shaded card. Do not try to look directly at the Sun through a telescope unless fitted with an approved solar filter.

---

[1] If you still can't visualize it, then I hope that a sixty-second animation that I prepared on the topic will do the trick: www.open.edu/openlearn/mercuryday

MARINER 10

Even the best telescopes show little surface detail on Mercury, but Mariner 10 revealed a heavily cratered globe, whose main surprises were numerous 'lobate scarps' showing where thrust-faults cut up to the surface (Figure 1), and a magnetic field like a miniature version of the Earth's but only about 1 per cent as strong. The lobate scarps were swiftly accepted as consequences of thermal contraction as Mercury's interior cooled. The magnetic field was a surprise, and showed that part of Mercury's iron-rich core, already deduced to be relatively large on account of the planet's high density, must contain a fluid shell where internal motion causes electric currents and an associated magnetic field that extends into space. The same processes occur in the Earth's outer core, but not in Venus and Mars. Their cores, despite being reasonably large, must be entirely solid.

The sharp outline displayed by Mercury when it transits the Sun had long made it apparent that Mercury has effectively no atmosphere.

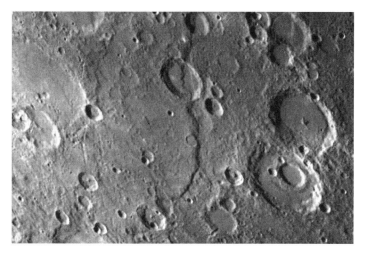

Figure 1. A fairly representative Mariner 10 image of part of Mercury, about 500 km across. Solar illumination is from the left. There are many impact craters, demonstrating that the surface is probably about three billion years old. Running from top to bottom is a lobate scarp, visible thanks to its shadow. This is named Discovery Rupes, and is clearly younger than the two largest craters that it crosses. (Image courtesy of NASA.)

Mariner 10 found atoms of hydrogen, helium and oxygen accompanying the planet, forming an 'exosphere', which is the term used to describe an atmosphere so tenuous that an atom has more chance of completing an unimpeded ballistic trajectory than it has of colliding with another atmospheric atom. The outer layer of every planet's atmosphere is an exosphere, but Mercury's exosphere extends right down to its surface, because even at its base it is far too tenuous to behave in any other way. It was soon realized that the hydrogen and helium in Mercury's exosphere are likely to be supplied from the solar wind, whereas the oxygen atoms probably escape from the surface, being released when ultraviolet radiation or micrometeorite bombardment breaks the bonds attaching oxygen to silicon and other metallic elements in the rocky (silicate) minerals that make up its surface.

POST-MARINER 10

The late 1970s view of Mercury could probably be summed up as 'interesting, but not sufficient to qualify Mercury as a priority for further exploration', and so Mercury generally languished for three decades. Ground-based spectroscopic studies revealed sodium and potassium in Mercury's exosphere in the 1980s and calcium in 1998 – all of these being expected in surface minerals and being susceptible to release when oxygen–metal bonds are broken. It also became apparent from spectroscopic study of sunlight reflected by Mercury that its surface minerals are deficient in iron, or at least in chemical bonds between iron and oxygen that should cause characteristic absorption of sunlight in the 900–1,000 nm wavelength range.

You may be surprised to learn that it was by means of radar, transmitted and received by the giant antennae at Arecibo and Goldstone, that most was learned about Mercury prior to the next spacecraft visit. The radar reflectivity of most of Mercury's surface is similar to that of rock powder (less than half that of solid rock), demonstrating that, like the Moon, Mercury is blanketed in regolith. Because Mercury is airless, its surface is unprotected from meteorite bombardment, so that any billion-year-old surface must have become fragmented into a regolith several metres deep, like the lunar soil, but probably even more finely powdered as a consequence of greater impact energy resulting from faster orbital speeds closer to the Sun.

More surprisingly, in the early 1990s, radar imaging revealed craters near the poles containing areas that reflect radar much more strongly than rocky regolith. The strong signal from these 'radar-bright' deposits, together with its polarization characteristics, requires a substance of special composition. The only plausible candidates suggested were water-ice and sulphur, either of which feasibly could collect in permanently shadowed, high-latitude, craters. In 2007, another type of radar study capable of measuring slight oscillations in Mercury's rotation period as it progresses round its orbit demonstrated that its surface must be detached from its inner solid core, confirming the molten outer core already strongly suspected because of the presence of the magnetic field.

BEPICOLOMBO AND MESSENGER

Mariner 10 could image only about half the globe, because the same hemisphere was in darkness during each of its flybys. Apart from the obvious frustration of the unseen hemisphere, big questions remained concerning why Mercury is so dense, how it is able to sustain its fluid outer core when Mars and Venus have lost theirs, whether the smoother parts of its surface are volcanic lava plains or blankets of impact ejecta, and how Mercury formed in the first place. Eventually, Mercury's turn for another visitor came round. The European Space Agency was the first to begin planning. A proposal for a Mercury orbiter was submitted to ESA by a team of scientists in 1993, and I myself was recruited to help to make the geological case for renewed exploration of Mercury at a mission selection meeting held at ESA headquarters in Paris in 1994. Finally (in 2000!), ESA gave approval for an ambitious 'Cornerstone' mission named BepiColombo consisting of two orbiters and a 44 kg lander. The lander was cancelled for budgetary reasons in 2003, by which time NASA had overtaken ESA and prepared a less ambitious single-orbiter mission called MESSENGER that was launched in 2004. This flew past Mercury three times in 2008–9 and went into orbit in March 2011, carrying a fifty-kilogram payload of scientific instruments. It was placed in an eccentric eleven-and-a-half-hour polar orbit around Mercury, about two hundred kilometres above the surface near the north pole, but fifteen thousand kilometres above the south pole. In April 2012, MESSENGER used most of

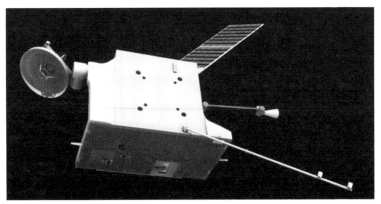

Figure 2. Top: BepiColombo's Mercury Polar Orbiter as it will appear in orbit about Mercury; its high-gain antenna for communication back to Earth is on the left, its solar panel (for power) is at the upper right, and the long boom at the lower right carries magnetometers. Bottom: MPO after building at Astrium Ltd, Stevenage, in November 2012, prior to shipping to Italy for testing and installation of the instruments. The large panel at the base in both views is the radiator designed to remove as much heat as possible from the craft's interior. (Images courtesy ESA.)

its remaining fuel to lower its apoherm (maximum distance from Mercury) to 10,314 km, decreasing the orbital period to 8 hours.

BepiColombo, now a joint project with the Japan Aerospace Exploration Agency (JAXA), is due for launch in 2016. It will arrive in orbit in 2023/4 and deploy two orbiters: ESA's Mercury Planetary Orbiter (MPO) with eighty kilograms of instruments (Figure 2) and JAXA's Mercury Magnetospheric Orbiter (MMO) with forty-five kilograms of instruments. MPO will be placed in a less eccentric polar orbit than MESSENGER, ranging between 400 and 1500 km above the surface, which is more suitable than MESSENGER's orbit to achieve detailed surface coverage of both hemispheres. MMO will have a more eccentric orbit, ranging between 400 and nearly 12,000 km above the surface, optimized for exploring the magnetosphere and exosphere. BepiColombo's heavier payload allows it to carry a fuller complement of more sophisticated instruments than could be fitted into MESSENGER. For example, BepiColombo has a thermal infrared imaging system that MESSENGER lacks entirely, a much more capable X-ray mapping experiment (designed at the University of Leicester), more instruments to measure particles and fields in the space around Mercury, and a laser altimeter that will map topography and the global shape of the whole of Mercury, whereas MESSENGER's can do this only for the Northern Hemisphere.

If BepiColombo functions as intended, it will provide a feast of information about Mercury. In the meantime, MESSENGER has provided an extremely tasty hors d'oeuvre. That is the subject of the rest of this chapter, which is an illustrated commentary on MESSENGER's main findings.

THE MAGNETIC FIELD

Data collected by MESSENGER's magnetometer during the flybys showed a magnetic field around Mercury that was indistinguishable from what Mariner 10 had found more than forty years previously. Once MESSENGER got into orbit, the structure of the field could be mapped in more detail. It then became apparent that although the field is lined up to within a fraction of a degree of Mercury's rotational axis (whereas Earth's is inclined by 11°), it is not symmetric. Mercury's 'magnetic equator' is offset by about 480 km (nearly 20 per cent of the

Figure 3. Mercury's present-day asymmetric magnetic field, seen from above its north and south poles. The Sun is to the right in each view, and Mercury's magnetic field is displaced away from the Sun by the Sun's own field. When the Sun is particularly active, the sunward part of Mercury's field could be forced down below the planet's surface. (Image courtesy of NASA/Johns Hopkins University Applied Physics Laboratory/Carnegie Institution of Washington.)

planet's radius) northwards of the true equator (Figure 3). We have no idea whether this asymmetry is a long-term state of affairs, or whether it oscillates north and south over thousands or even millions of years. Of course, the field could also reverse from time to time, as is known from the geological record in the case of the Earth.

Mercury's magnetic field shields much of its surface from direct impact by solar wind particles, which are mostly electrons and protons. These carry an electric charge, which means that they cannot cross magnetic field lines, and so can reach the surface only where magnetic field lines do. Except during a major solar storm, which could push the Sun-facing part of the field right back to ground-level, only the polar regions are exposed to solar wind particles. As illustrated in Figure 3, the field's asymmetry means that the vulnerable region is larger around the south pole than around the north pole. Solar wind particles hitting the surface are a major cause of 'space weathering', which causes rocky material to become darker and redder with exposure age, and it will be interesting to find out if there is any difference in the amount and distribution of space weathering at opposite poles, because this would be evidence for long-term magnetic asymmetry.

SURFACE COMPOSITION

If you want to find out the composition of an airless planet's surface, there are several ways to do it from orbit: you can look for spectral features in the reflected sunlight, which can tell you about some of the chemical bonds in the minerals that make up the rock; you can look for spectral features in radiated infrared, which gives other information about mineral composition; you can measure X-rays fluoresced from the surface in response to illumination by solar X-rays, and deduce the abundance of elements by means of the flux at the specific energies characteristic of each chemical element; you can look for gamma-rays of characteristic energies that were either emitted by atomic nuclei that have been struck by cosmic rays or were emitted because of natural radioactivity, and this, too, can tell you about the abundances of some elements; and you can measure the speeds of neutrons emitted in response to cosmic ray impacts, because if they have been slowed down this indicates collision between the neutron and a low-mass nucleus that almost certainly has to be hydrogen. MESSENGER is equipped for all of these, except infrared spectroscopy, for which we will have to wait for BepiColombo.

MESSENGER found that Mercury's surface is dominated by magnesium-rich (as opposed to iron-rich) minerals, such as the variety of pyroxene known as enstatite, and plagioclase feldspar. In terms of its elemental abundances, it is richer in magnesium and poorer in iron and calcium than lunar crust and terrestrial ocean floor. It does vary from place to place, but differences are far less extreme than the contrast between the lunar highlands and the lunar maria. It is probably mostly volcanic in origin, a conclusion that is supported by the detailed images returned by MESSENGER, including those used in Figures 4–10.

The surface deficiency in iron had been suspected previously, but could be confirmed only when MESSENGER began to operate its X-ray spectrometer in orbit. This showed that iron makes up at most about 4 per cent of the surface, whereas silicon, aluminium, magnesium and calcium are 25 per cent, 5–7 per cent, 8–15 per cent and 4–5 per cent respectively. Totally unexpected was a high sulphur content, which varies between about 2 and 4 per cent in different regions. Sulphur is a volatile element, easily lost to space, and such a high abundance is hard to explain in a planet that formed so close to the Sun as Mercury's present orbit. It is even harder to explain if the large relative size of

Mercury's core is a result of much of its original rocky mantle having been stripped away by a giant impact (until recently the most credible theory), because that should have further depleted the volatile content of its surviving rocky fraction.

The chemical state of Mercury's surface sulphur is unknown, but its abundance rises and falls from area to area in step with the abundances of calcium and magnesium (but not with iron), so it may be in the form of calcium sulphide and magnesium sulphide. Sulphur is not the only volatile element to be found in unexpectedly high abundance on Mercury. MESSENGER's gamma-ray spectrometer was able to measure the ratio of potassium to thorium, because both have naturally radioactive isotopes. Potassium is a moderately volatile element whereas thorium is the opposite (refractory). Mercury's potassium/thorium ratio is similar to that of Mars, the most distant terrestrial planet from the Sun. It is higher than for the Earth and Venus, and especially much higher than the Moon, which is believed to have been depleted in volatile elements during the Moon-forming giant impact. Did Mercury form much further from the Sun than its present orbit? That would make Mercury's high potassium/thorium ratio and high sulphur abundance easier to explain, but would make its large core even harder to account for!

MESSENGER's neutron spectrometer settled the water-versus-sulphur ambiguity in permanently shadowed polar craters, by demonstrating that a hydrogen-rich phase occurs in the local regolith. This can hardly be anything other than frozen H_2O. It is likely to have found its way into these 'cold traps' as a result of cometary impacts onto Mercury's surface. Most of the vaporized cometary water would escape to space, but any H_2O molecules that found their way into a permanent shadow would stick there rather than bounce out, and so became trapped there. Similar water-ice deposits are known on the Moon. If this is correct, Mercury's polar ice is a late veneer, and is unrelated to other indicators of Mercury's volatile richness that seem to reflect volatiles from the planet's interior.

SURFACE TERRAIN

For me as a geologist, it is its high-resolution images that are MESSENGER's most fascinating legacy. I am looking forward to even clearer images from BepiColombo, as well as the insights sure to come from its thermal infrared imager and its superior X-ray mapper. In the meantime, there is plenty still to digest from MESSENGER.

Lava Plains and Ghost Craters. Even the flyby images were sufficient to remove any doubts about the volcanic nature of Mercury's so-called 'smooth plains'. The 'smooth' description arises because they have fewer impact craters than other areas, and must therefore be younger. MESSENGER images reveal classic lava plains features including 'wrinkle ridges' that form when lava surfaces subside during thermal contraction as the lava cools. There are identifiable flow fronts, where you can see that something behaving exactly like lava has flooded over the pre-existing terrain (Figure 4). There are also places where lava has completely flooded a pre-existing impact crater, but where the crater can now be discerned as a result of the lava that buried it having contracted (Figure 5). Such 'ghost craters', as they are called, are known on the Moon and Mars, but they are especially common on Mercury.

Figure 4. 290 km-wide MESSENGER view of a region near 27°N, 58°E. Part of the large peak-ring basin Rachmaninoff occupies the upper left. Lava has flooded the region within the peak-ring, and over-topped the lowest part of the peak-ring to flood the part of the southern region of the basin. (Image courtesy of NASA/Johns Hopkins University Applied Physics Laboratory/Carnegie Institution of Washington.)

Figure 5. 80 km-wide MESSENGER view of a region near 79°N, 36°E. The 30 km-impact crater in the upper right post-dates flooding of this region by lava. In the lower left is the trace of an older similar-sized crater that was already there when the lava was emplaced. It became completely flooded, and is visible now as a 'ghost crater'. (Image courtesy of NASA/Johns Hopkins University Applied Physics Laboratory/Carnegie Institution of Washington.)

As with the lunar maria, the vents from which the lava was erupted can rarely be seen. This could be because in the later stages of eruption the lava field grew by 'inflation', being pumped up below its flexible skin rather than spilling out across the surface. However, there are places where surface flow of lava is evidenced, notably around the fringes of Mercury's northern volcanic plains where broad channels appear to have been scoured by lava that was either thermally or mechanically erosive (Figure 6).

The ages of the youngest lava plains on Mercury are uncertain, but judging from the low density of the impact craters superimposed on them, the youngest may be only about a billion years old. As for the oldest lava terrains, the more I look at Mercury the more convinced I become that the older, more cratered regions are just older, more battered lava plains. There is some evidence that rock chemistry differs with age (or maybe just with location), but it could all be lava. This is a contrast with the Moon, whose ancient highlands were probably

Figure 6. 280 km-wide MESSENGER view of a region near 57°N, 115°E. Lava has spilled from upper left to lower right, scouring out a broad valley, and largely flooding the peak-ring basin Kofi at lower right. Some particularly prominent wrinkle ridges can be seen in the eastern part of the basin. (Image courtesy of NASA/Johns Hopkins University Applied Physics Laboratory/Carnegie Institution of Washington.)

formed by masses of low-density crystals rising to the top of its primordial magma ocean.

Explosive Volcanic Vents. The youngest volcanic activity on Mercury was probably not eruption of lava flows at all. Instead, it appears to have been explosive. Various depressions have been identified that have complex outlines, in contrast to the smooth, almost always circular, outlines of impact craters. They also lack the raised rim that characterizes an impact crater. Some of them (perhaps the most recently active) are surrounded by a thin but spectrally distinct deposit that fades away with distance. This is interpreted as material blasted out of a volcanic vent by the force of expanding gas. In Earth's atmosphere a high, convecting column would develop, but on airless Mercury the eruption would take an umbrella-like form shaped by the ballistic trajectories of the erupted particles (as exemplified by active explosive volcanism imaged on Jupiter's satellite Io). An example of the volcano at the source of one of these deposits is shown in Figure 7. Here it can be seen that the complex outline of the depression is because it contains several volcanic vents of different ages.

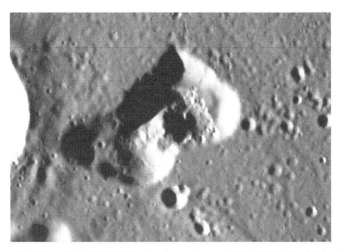

Figure 7. 50-km-wide MESSENGER view of a region near 22°N, 146°E. The 30 km-long irregular-shaped depression contains several volcanic vents of various ages. It is the source of a surrounding explosive volcanic deposit, and lies at the summit of a very gently sloping volcano. (Image courtesy of NASA/Johns Hopkins University Applied Physics Laboratory/ Carnegie Institution of Washington.)

When a volcanic eruption has been explosive, it tells you that the magma rising from depth originally contained something in solution that 'exsolved', forming gas bubbles, in response to the pressure-drop as it neared the surface. The expansion of the gas bubbles was powerful enough to disrupt the magma into fragments, and blast them skywards. Volcanic gases on Earth include water vapour, carbon dioxide and sulphur dioxide. We don't know which were involved in Mercury's explosive eruptions, but the important point is that the degree of explosivity is a further demonstration of Mercury being internally rich in volatiles. The dimensions of Mercury's explosive eruption deposits are considerably greater than their equivalents on the Moon, especially after allowing for Mercury's stronger gravity, which should result in a more tightly constrained deposit for an eruption of equal explosive force.

Impact Basin Tectonics. Mercury has many impact basins, all of them flooded to a greater or lesser extent by lava. The largest of these, the Caloris basin, was discovered by Mariner 10. It straddled the terminator during each Mariner 10 flyby, and so about half of it was in darkness and unseen. MESSENGER has given us a complete view, and under a variety of illumination conditions. The whole floor has been flooded by lava, and it can be seen that the central part of the basin floor is marked by a pattern of radial fractures, which have been given the official name of Pantheon Fossae (Figure 8). Each of these is probably a graben (a valley whose floor has dropped down between two parallel faults), in which case the pattern was caused by radial extension. However, in the outer 50 per cent of the Caloris basin the radial fracture pattern is lost, and the surface is scarred by a pattern of fractures and ridges that varies from seemingly random to circumferential.

The fracturing of the Caloris basin floor can be explained as a result of Mercury's outer shell (its lithosphere) responding to the changing

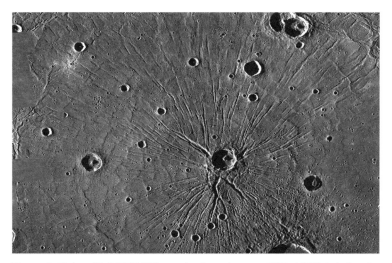

Figure 8. 70 km-wide MESSENGER mosaic of a region near 30°N, 161°E, including the centre of the Caloris basin. The Pantheon Fossae system of radial grabens is clearly seen. The crater (Apollodorus) at the centre of the pattern is probably caused by an impactor that scored a flukey 'bull's eye' after the fractures had been initiated. (Image courtesy of NASA/Johns Hopkins University Applied Physics Laboratory/Carnegie Institution of Washington.)

load at its surface. Excavation of the basin removed a large mass of material, and for hundreds of millions of years afterwards the weaker mantle underlying the lithosphere could have been flowing inwards below Caloris to compensate for the mass deficit, causing the basin floor to bow upwards. This would lead to radial fractures of the kind seen near the centre. Whatever the cause of the lava eruptions, eventually the weight of the lava flows pressing down on the basin floor would cause it to sag, and this could explain the fracture pattern nearer to the edge. It sounds like a simple story, but many large basins on Mercury have a fracture pattern, and it is different in every case; for example, Rachmaninoff basin (Figure 4) has mainly circumferential grabens within its inner peak-ring.

Global Contraction. Although the patterns of deformation in basin interiors often reflect local extension, tectonic features almost everywhere else on Mercury demonstrate compression. MESSENGER images have revealed a great many more lobate scarps than were seen

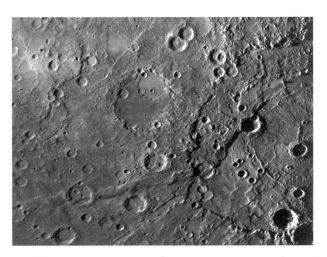

Figure 9. 930 km-wide MESSENGER mosaic of a region near 32°S, 77°E. In the east is part of the 720 km-diameter Rembrandt basin. Various tectonic ridges and scarps deform the cratered plains to its west, and one of these continues across Rembrandt's floor. The broad valley heading south-west away from Rembrandt is probably a chain of coalesced secondary craters, formed by ejecta flung out during the impact that created the basin. (Image courtesy of NASA/Johns Hopkins University Applied Physics Laboratory/Carnegie Institution of Washington.)

by Mariner 10 (Figures 9 and 10), as well as smaller-scale related features. Adding up the displacements represented by all the lobate scarps on Mercury suggests that the planetary radius may need to have decreased by as much as five kilometres to account for them. Lobate scarps cross lava plains, including those flooding the interiors of some basins, and relatively few impact craters are superimposed across lobate scarps. It is therefore accepted that the most recent significant contraction on Mercury is probably younger than about three billion years.

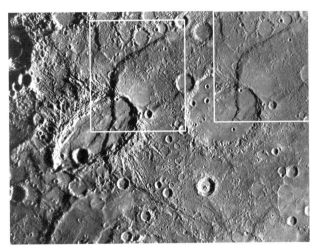

Figure 10. 650 km-wide MESSENGER flyby mosaic of a region near 2°S, 103°E, showing Beagle Rupes, a strongly curved lobate scarp. The outlined area is shown again at the top right in a mosaic obtained from orbit, at higher resolution and with the Sun higher in the sky. (Image courtesy of NASA/Johns Hopkins University Applied Physics Laboratory/Carnegie Institution of Washington.)

In some places, the location of contractional thrust faults has been controlled by the presence of a pre-existing, lava-filled basin. A prime example of this is shown in Figure 11. This is worth describing in detail, because this single picture demonstrates a long and complex sequence of events, deduced by simple common-sense detective work.

First, somewhat more than three billion years ago, in a terrain that was already old enough to have accumulated a fairly dense cover of impact craters, a 470-km impact basin was formed. The basin floor became cratered in turn (which could have taken several hundred

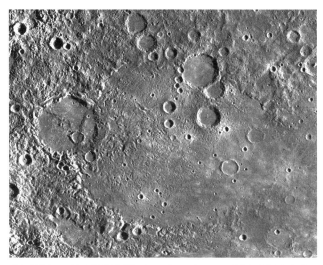

Figure 11. 550-km-wide MESSENGER view of a region near 27°S, 3°W, including a 440-km-diameter unnamed basin that has been flooded by lavas. The interface between the basin-filling lavas and the basement was later mobilized as a thrust fault, that cuts younger craters overlying the original basin rim in the west. (Image courtesy of NASA/Johns Hopkins University Applied Physics Laboratory/Carnegie Institution of Washington.)

million years), before both the basin interior and much of the terrain to the south and east was flooded by lavas. Some of the pre-lava craters can be discerned as ghost craters, but most of the visible craters inside the basin post-date the lavas. Then a 135-km-diameter impact crater was formed, straddling the western rim of the lava-filled basin. Its floor, in turn, became lava-flooded, giving it a flat bottom with no trace of a central peak. A 25-km-impact crater was then imposed on the floor of the 135-km lava-flooded crater, also probably lava-flooded as no central peak is visible. After all this, a curved thrust fault was created, just inside the original rim of the large basin, and cutting across both the 135-km and the 25-km craters. Presumably, the mechanical contrast between the basement and the basin-filling lava acted to concentrate contractional stresses, so that the thrust fault occurred at the interface between them.

Hollows. Perhaps the most intriguing mystery on Mercury concerns features that have come to be known as 'hollows'. On Mercury, this term is reserved for steep-sided flat-bottomed depressions that are a few tens of metres deep and hundreds of metres to a few kilometres across (Figure 12). These hollows occur in clusters distributed widely across the globe, mostly on the floors of impact craters. Often they are surrounded by, and sometimes floored by, patches of high albedo, spectrally slightly blue material. Hollows could not be discerned at the resolution available on flyby images, but the high-albedo material manifested itself as irregular bright patches, giving rise to the term 'bright crater floor deposits'. Patrick Moore and I puzzled over these on *The Sky at Night* in 2008, and I gave some suggestions as to what they might be in my Mercury chapter in the 2010 *Yearbook of Astronomy* (page

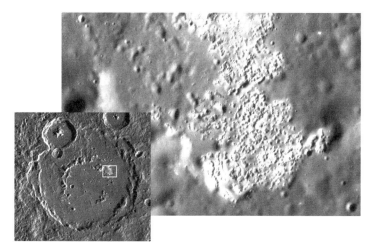

Figure 12. Hollows on the floor of a 150-km-diameter impact basin in the Northern Hemisphere, seen in a high-resolution MESSENGER image, 17 km across, centred near 44°N, 292°E. Inset: 200 km-wide MESSENGER mosaic, with the area of the main figure shown by the outline. (Image courtesy of NASA/Johns Hopkins University Applied Physics Laboratory/Carnegie Institution of Washington.)

209). One of my suggestions was that they are 'sites where some kind of volatile material has exhaled through the crust and condensed at the surface'. This seems to have been along the right lines, because the hollows fit quite neatly into the picture: volatile material has been removed to form the hollows. The hollows can't have formed by being scooped-out wind (there's no air!), and the hollows show no sign of being formed by collapse inward into caves (they would not have such wide, flat floors), so whatever was formerly occupying the hollows must have gone upwards. Hollows are not explosive volcanic vents (too shallow-floored, too closely spaced), so the material has not been blasted away; rather, it has been removed, molecule by molecule, into space. Essentially, it has been turned to vapour – either by sublimation (because it is thermally unstable, like dry ice at room temperature on Earth) or because solar radiation or charged particles (when the magnetic field allows) have broken chemical bonds and liberated atoms.

The closest analogue to Mercury's hollows known on any other planet occurs on Mars, round the fringes of its polar caps, where layers of carbon dioxide ice sublime to leave flat-bottomed rounded hollows in the so-called 'Swiss cheese terrain'. On Mars this is an ongoing process, and changes can be made out from one year to the next. No changes have yet been detected on Mercury, but we can tell that the hollows are in general very young because impact craters have not had time to occur on their floors. As to how the hollow-forming volatile substance got there, the fact that it occurs predominantly on crater floors is surely significant. A suggestion that it is something that segregated out from impact melt seems unlikely to be correct, because patches of hollows tend to be concentrated near central peaks, peak-rings and basin walls. Maybe the hollow-forming material was brought close to the surface during the crater-forming process, and then migrated upwards along fractures.

Another contrast with Mars is that in the case of Mercury we have no idea of the composition of the volatile substance that is dissipating to leave the hollows behind. It is even unclear whether the high-albedo stuff is the volatile substance itself, or what is left behind after the volatile substance has gone! Someone may come up with convincing answers to these questions using MESSENGER data, but I suspect that we will have to wait for elemental and mineralogical determinations by BepiColombo's X-ray and thermal infrared cameras to settle the issue.

Patrick Moore:
A Personal Reflection

Richard Baum
Astronomer and historian

On the evening of 21 July 1956, following our arrival in London after our wedding that afternoon, we had a phone call from Patrick Moore. Within the hour he had visited and informed us of his audition as possible presenter for a projected series of six television programmes the BBC planned to show in 1957 that would eventually become *The Sky at Night*.

Even then it was apparent that Patrick's future beckoned like a bright star. Indeed, he had already translated from the French Gérard de Vaucouleurs' small book on Mars, published in the UK as *The Planet Mars* (Faber and Faber, London, 1950), and had published his *Guide to the Moon* (1953) and *Guide to the Planets* (1955).

Patrick, a self-made man, was endowed with astonishing abilities and limitless enthusiasm and energy. He imparted his knowledge with envious ease and fluency, transforming him, the amateur astronomer, into a skilled disseminator of popular astronomy, not just of local but global significance, one who was rated by many alongside the great popularizers of yesterday such as Richard Anthony Proctor and Camille Nicholas Flammarion.

Many will have fond memories of his inspiring presence, recalling his dynamism and, above all, his infectious enthusiasm. He had his faults and failings, but then, why look at a sun without spots?

I first corresponded with him in 1946, long before he became a public figure. He had been demobbed after war service with the RAF, taken up a teaching position, and become Secretary of the Lunar Section of the British Astronomical Association (BAA), under its new Director, Hugh Percival Wilkins. Patrick was very keen about the topography of what was then the east limb of the Moon (now the west limb) and offered to extract pertinent material from the classic selenographical texts. It was a very generous gesture, for the photocopier had yet to come into common usage. Nevertheless, he kindly supplied what was requested. Eventually Patrick and I collaborated on a study of the profiles of the D'Alemberts Mountains and published our results. (Mem. Brit. Astron. Assoc. **36** (3), 1950, 7–9).

By then we had met on numerous occasions, first at a meeting of the BAA in November 1946, and again in January 1947, and subsequently on numerous occasions in Chester. Our last personal meeting was in London at a BAA Exhibition meeting in the 1990s.

Some time later, Ewen Whitaker, a world authority on lunar nomenclature, and I challenged Patrick's oft-repeated claim that he discovered the Mare Orientale, the giant impact basin on the Moon, and published our paper in 2007 (Journal of the British Astronomical Association, **117** (3), 129–135). We laid out the case against Patrick's claim in detail and explained exactly how he came to believe what he did. It was a shock to him, but he admitted his error in a short note (J. Brit. Astron. Assoc., **117** (5), 277) and accepted that a German astronomer, Julius Franz, had discovered and named the feature as early as 1906. Some months later during one of his *Sky at Night* programmes, Patrick apologized for his mistake. Somehow I knew he would, for beneath his public persona he was that rarity of today, a man of honour.

What Star is That?

RICHARD BAUM

Where there is light so there is shadow. The biblical implications of this saying were dramatically exemplified on the morning of 15 February 2013, when a superbolide trailing fire and smoke exploded over the Russian city of Chelyabinsk. The consequent shock wave caused an estimated $33 million in property damage, chiefly in shattered windows and weakened walls. It also injured about 1,200 people, most of them hurt by flying glass. Now the orbital path of the meteor has been calculated, and it appears that the meteoroid behind the blast had crossed Earth's orbit regularly for thousands of years.

Other than providing a fascinating spectacle, however, the event served to illustrate the unpredictable and hazardous nature of the interplanetary environment: more significantly, perhaps, it emphasized the place of surprise in our understanding of the physical world, reminding us of unannounced events like the Tunguska incident of June 1908, and the Sikhote-Alin bolide that enlivened Siberian skies in February 1947. To a somewhat lesser extent it also revived a memory of less spectacular but no less cautionary events, whose history and circumstances will never be known.

One such incident concerns 'The Mysterious Visitor' of August 1921, so called by the eminent director of the Princeton Observatory, Henry Norris Russell (1877–1957). Reminiscing about his recent trip to the Pacific coast where he visited four great observatories, Lowell, Mount Wilson, Dominion and, notably, Lick, in his monthly column in the *Scientific American* of September 1921, Russell described Mount Hamilton, on which the last-named observatory is located, as a narrow ridge with several peaks of similar height. The observatory crowns one of the central peaks, and the associated buildings, including dwelling houses, are strung out either side of the crest (Figure 1). 'Very little can

Figure 1. The Lick Observatory, Mount Hamilton, California as it appeared at the close of the nineteenth century. (Image courtesy of George F. Chambers, *A Handbook of Descriptive and Practical Astronomy* (3 vols.), Vol. 2, p. 238 (Oxford, 1890).)

be seen of the ocean,' Russell said, 'for it is hidden by the westernmost of the coast ranges; but the view across the foothills to San Francisco Bay and the valley which runs southward from it is of great beauty, especially at sunset, when the air fills with a ruddy violet light of extraordinary tone.' But what have the aesthetics of landscape to do with astronomy? Quite simply he added, 'if it had not been for views and sunsets a remarkable observation … might not have been made.'

Here he refers to the puzzling object he and others at the observatory saw on 7 August 1921. Later that evening, the telegraph clicked, and within forty-eight hours observatories across the world were on alert. News agencies picked up on the story and newspapers informed their readers of a strange apparition in the heavens. Meanwhile, the vigil continued, but now an extraordinary story began to unfold; for although the Lick observers were the first to make an announcement, they were, in fact, the last to sight the apparition. Yet it is at that point the story really begins.

A MYSTERIOUS VISITOR

At sunset on Sunday, 7 August 1921, a small group of people relaxed on the veranda of the director's residence on Mount Hamilton. High up in the west, fleecy clouds glowed rose-pink in the light of the low Sun, overarching a broad expanse of clear sky that extended down to a narrow band of smoke, haze and thin cloud adjoining the apparent horizon. As the Sun came in contact with this stratum, the two astronomers in the group, Professor Russell, whose name is immortalized in the Hertzsprung-Russell (H-R) diagram which plots the relationship between spectral type and the luminosity of stars, and William Wallace Campbell (1862–1938), director of the Lick Observatory, watched closely the effects of atmospheric refraction on its figure as it dropped towards the band of haze and cloud. 'Starting with the ellipse,' Campbell later wrote, 'the succeeding figures resembled the old-fashioned Rochester lamp shade, the straw hat now in vogue with men, an extremely elongated ellipse, the cigar form, and finally, at disappearance, the knitting needle form.' The latter endured for at least a minute of time.

Just before the Sun disappeared, a member of the group, Major Reed Chambers (1894–1972), a World War I air ace, casually asked, 'What star is that to the left of the Sun?' At the query his colleague, the legendary racecar driver, aviation pioneer and fellow World War I air ace Captain Edward Vernon Rickenbacher (1890–1973), said that he, too, had been watching it for several minutes but thought it well known. Chambers said that he hadn't remarked on it earlier for the same reason.

Distracted from their pursuit, the two astronomers quickly looked up and, along with Mrs Chambers, easily saw the object, and all agreed it was star-like. Campbell caught it briefly with binoculars before it disappeared from view. Russell offered a plausible excuse for his failure to comment earlier on the object, saying that the 'very life of the military aviator depends continually upon his ability to see, at a glance, all that may be in the sky above him, or the air beneath'. In the circumstances it was perhaps inevitable that the two airmen would preempt the astronomers who were narrowly focused on the fascinating series of optical effects displayed by the Sun.

Soon after, notes were compared. Campbell thought it was probably

Mercury. No, corrected Russell, its brightness negated that possibility. Rickenbacher said he first saw the object at a distance of about 3° from the Sun, then entirely above the horizon. He estimated a line joining that body and the object made an angle of 45° with a vertical line through the Sun's centre.

Campbell thought the object more yellow than a star in that position would be. He estimated that at its disappearance the Sun had a true zenith distance of approximately 93° and that the true zenith distance of the object must have been between 91° and 92°. 'Venus has frequently been observed to set below the western mountains as a bright object not distinctly orange or red at approximately that zenith distance.' Russell and Campbell agreed that this seemed to suggest the stranger was a great deal brighter than Venus would have been 'if seen in the same position and circumstances'. Having consulted the *Nautical Almanac*, Russell confirmed that it could not have been Mercury; Mercury was below and to the right of the Sun. All the other planets were likewise accounted for.

What could it have been? It retained its stellar aspect in the binoculars, and partook of the diurnal motion of the stars. Its brightness on the sunset sky, its sudden appearance and position close to the Sun, all hinted at its celestial nature. Was it a comet that had approached the Sun from such a direction as to escape detection? Could it have been a nova like the one that suddenly appeared in the constellation Aquila in June 1918? Campbell thought its position, about 40° from the galactic plane, opposed that idea.

At 11 p.m., after further discussion, Russell and Campbell telegraphed the following message to Harvard College Observatory:

> *Star-like object certainly brighter than Venus three degrees east, one degree south of Sun seen several minutes before and at sunset by naked eye. Five observers. Set behind low clouds. Unquestionably celestial object. Chances favor nucleus bright comet, less probably a nova.*

Searches at dawn and dusk the next day were unsuccessful. It seemed that the object had vanished. After another fruitless search at sunrise on the ninth, Campbell drew up a report for the *Publications of the Astronomical Society of the Pacific*. Even as he put pen to paper the observation was announced in *Harvard College Observatory Bulletin* No. 757. In addition, news was telegraphed to the *Centralstelle* in

Copenhagen, the clearing house for astronomical discoveries, and published in the next issue of the *Astronomische Nachrichten*.

REACTION

Within days the object was common gossip in the daily and scientific press. 'Bright Object Near the Sun,' proclaimed a headline in *Nature*, while correspondents to the *English Mechanic and World of Science* asked if it was a 'New Star, Or Comet, or What?' Others were more assured and referred to 'Campbell's Comet', 'The Surprise Comet', 'The Mysterious Comet', or simply 'The Coy Comet'. Leader writers enlarged on the topic and speculation was rife. Here and there people ransacked their memory, and inevitably a few vaguely remembered how, on or around the day in question, they too had seen something strange at sunset.

Writing to the *English Mechanic and World of Science* a week after the event, S. Fellows of Wolverhampton, England described what he had seen just before sunset on 7 August:

A few days ago the statement appeared in our newspapers that an observer at the Lick Observatory had seen, on the evening of 7 August, a bright star near the Sun, and that it was visible without optical aid. My experience on that evening may be worth recording. About 8.30 on that Sunday evening, I noticed a bit of very clean sky over the place of the recently set Sun, and, thinking I might pick up Jupiter and Saturn, I took my binoculars (power about 3) and commenced to search. I soon alighted upon a bright object, which I at the moment thought was Jupiter, but the next moment I saw was not the planet at all; neither did I think it was a star. It was elongated in the direction of the Sun, and was of a distinct reddish tinge. I judged it to be about 6° from the Sun and a very little south of him. It was unfortunate that I was not able to get the telescope on the object, as it was too low, I only held it for about three minutes, as clouds came and hid it. If the object which I saw was the same as that seen by the American observer, and if our estimates of its position were fairly accurate, then the object must have passed inwards towards the Sun some 3° in five or six hours. It must also have greatly increased in brightness in that time, as the object which I saw could not be compared to Venus.

Here the object is described as elongated. Campbell reported it as star-like, but he held it for lesser time.

From West Moors, Dorset, England, Ernest Elliot Markwick (1853–1925), former president of the British Astronomical Association (1912–1914), congratulated Fellows on his wonderfully interesting and lucky observation. 'Taking his observation in conjunction with that made at the Lick Observatory,' he said, 'there is, to my mind, no reasonable doubt but that it was a brilliant comet that was seen.'

It must be remembered that the Great Comet of 1882 [II][1] was easily seen in full daylight, close to the Sun, and was also observed in telescopes at the Royal Observatory, Cape of Good Hope, until it disappeared at the Sun's limb. Hence its intrinsic brightness must have been enormous, and if it could have been seen with its perihelion brilliancy projected on a dark, starlight sky, it would probably have been like a miniature Sun, throwing distinct shadows from objects interposed in its rays. I merely mention this to show that from practical experience there is nothing to prevent a brilliant comet being seen in daylight close to the Sun.

On 2 September, Markwick again wrote to the *English Mechanic*, this time to say he had found another observation. In the course of a conversation with a neighbour much interested in astronomy, he was informed that she had seen the new star on the evening of 7 August from the residence of her daughter at Ferndown, Dorset, England, while in the company of her daughter and son-in-law, F. C. Nelson Day, a lieutenant in the Royal Naval Reserve. It was a striking object, to the left of, and a little below, the Sun, she said.

Markwick promptly visited Day and asked if he would draw up a short account of what he remembered of the observation. 'On 7 August,' Day reported, 'when the Sun was at an altitude of about 8°, and setting, an unknown bright star was observed bearing approximately S 45°W of the Sun, and at an angular distance of about 4° from it. The magnitude of this body was about −2.0. I was in the garden at the above address (Sparrow's Wick, Ferndown, Dorset) at the time, and it was seen by others besides myself.'

Day gave no time, but Markwick deduced that it was about 8 p.m.

[1] This form of comet designation, comprising a year followed by a Roman numeral, indicates the comet's order of coming to perihelion in that year, so 1882 [II] would be the second comet to pass perihelion in 1882.

summer time (7h GMAT–Greenwich Mean Astronomical Time), beginning at noon, a system discontinued on 1 January 1925). That an object of such brilliance could escape general notice seemed inconceivable to Day, who believed navigators at sea would have seen it when preparing to make twilight observations with the sextant. Apparently no one did.

Although it had been compiled from memory three weeks after the event, Markwick believed the report reliable, even if it added nothing significant to Mr Fellows's surmise, 'as to the rate at which the object was travelling towards the Sun; yet it is valuable as serving to corroborate that gentleman's observation'.

As the observation predated the Mount Hamilton sighting by four to five hours, one correspondent to the *English Mechanic* proposed that the object ought to be called Comet Fellows. Markwick agreed but noted that '[a]lthough Mr Fellows was, in point of time, before the Lick observers in detecting the object in question, yet the latter were the first – so far as I am aware – in making public the news of the discovery.'

CONFUSION

All question of priority disappeared on 22 September, when Max Wolf (1863–1932), director of the Königstuhl Observatory, Heidelberg, mailed Mount Hamilton:

> Your bright object at sunset August 7th has been observed too at Plauen (lat. +50° 30' , long. 12° 7' E.) Germany: August 7th, 7h 35m.0. Gr.M.T., in R.A. 11h 6.7m and Decl. +7° 9' .

The Sun was then still above the horizon and the object referred to must have been very bright to be visible.

Wolf's attention had been directed to a report in the 16 August edition of the *Neuen Vogtländer Zeitung*. The object, which appeared like Venus at greatest brilliancy, was low in the west shortly after sunset on 7 August, reported the daughter of Professor E. Kaiser and other inhabitants of Plauen (latitude 50° 29' 45" N and longitude 12° 7' 11" E), Vogtländ, Saxony in Germany. The time was 7h 35m GMT, and Miss Kaiser accurately noted its position relative to terrestrial landmarks which allowed Wolf to deduce the object was in RA 11h 6.7m. and Dec. 7° 9' N.

Commenting on the observation in the *Journal of the Royal Astronomical Society of Canada*, Canadian astronomer J. A. Pearce underlined a discrepancy between the position given by Wolf and the observations made in England:

> Miss Kaiser's observation was made one hour after sunset. According to the position given by Professor Wolf, its azimuth and altitude at sunset were 87° and 11°, respectively, which differs considerably from the observation made in England half an hour earlier, the azimuth of the Sun when setting being 116°. It would be interesting to know more details concerning Miss Kaiser's observation as the position of the body is so accurately stated. It should be pointed out that Jupiter at the time of the observation had an altitude of 3°, and an azimuth of 93°, which is indeed very near the position assigned by her. It is therefore not unlikely that she observed Jupiter otherwise it is difficult to account for the great difference between the position of her object and the position as stated by the English and Californian observers.

Matters were further confused when the British amateur astronomer and historian Sidney Bertram Gaythorpe (1880–1964) of Barrow-in-Furness, England, introduced an observation made in the early morning of the day prior to the Lick sighting. He described this at the monthly meeting of the British Astronomical Association in London on 30 November. The object, he said, was seen by two young students of astronomy, John L. and Gilbert Kershaw, at about 1921 on 5 August at 16h 5m GMT, when looking for Mercury, and was described by Gilbert Kershaw, who saw it only with the naked eye, as being very similar to the appearance of that planet during its evening apparition in the first week of June. Soon after it was first noticed, the body was lost to sight behind a cloud. Just before it finally disappeared, it was seen for a few seconds by J. L. Kershaw through a small telescope, x20, in which, however, it did not present any sensible disc. Owing to clouds and the strong twilight its position with respect to the stars could not readily be determined, but it was seen to be a little to the left of a vertical line through Capella, which Gaythorpe computed was at that time in azimuth 106° 30' E of S, at an altitude of 48° 40', the longitude and latitude of the place of observation being 12m 51sW and 54° 6'.6N.

Having carried out a thorough examination of the observing site and checked the position of the object in relation to distant landmarks, Gaythorpe concluded from theodolite measures that the object could not have been Mercury.

The well-known comet expert A. C. de la C. Crommelin (1865–1939), director of the Comet Section of the British Astronomical Association, said that 'the observation … added to the mystery surrounding the bright apparition in August'. But it seemed clear to him 'that if all the observations related to real celestial bodies, then at least two were present; for the Plauen observation was nearly simultaneous with the two made in England on 7 August, yet some 20° distant from them. If the body described by Mr Gaythorpe was identical with any of the others its motion must have been eastward, whereas the other indications were in favour of westward motion.'

Significantly, the much-respected American astronomer Joseph Ashbrook (1918–1980) pointed out in 1971 that Mercury was about 8° from where the object was seen. Given the unfavourable circumstances under which the observation was made, and that the alignments used by Gaythorpe were less reliable than he imagined, it is quite possible that the object seen by the Kershaws was indeed the planet Mercury and not the Mount Hamilton object.

Moreover, the Kershaws were interviewed in a climate of expectation; a fact reflected by Gaythorpe's opening statement: 'Four observations of an unknown star-like object, seen near the Sun on the evening of 7 August 1921, are recorded by Dr A. C. D. Crommelin in the Annual Report of the Comet Section. A similar phenomenon, observed here in the early morning of the day before, has lately been brought to my notice.' It takes very little to arouse the sleeping images of subliminal chaos to convert the ordinary into enigma.

Two further observations subsequently came to light. The 6 October 1921 issue of *Nature* reported Dr W. Bell Dawson, of Ottawa, Canada, had seen, 'a bright object low in the west in unusually clear air just after sunset on September 4, which he assumes to be the same as that observed at Mount Hamilton on August 7'. This is improbable; most likely it was either Mercury or Jupiter, the Sun then being in RA 10 h. 53m., Dec. 7° 6' N.

Little more than a week later, on 14 October 1921, *Harvard College Observatory Bulletin* No. 759 announced a letter received at the observatory from Dr H. C. Emmert of Detroit, Michigan, claimed a further sighting. The object was in the western sky on 6 August at 5h 50m p.m., Eastern Standard Time. Its altitude was 14.5° to 15°, its azimuth 85°; the Sun's altitude and azimuth were 15° and 90° respectively. The object was fully as bright as Venus in twilight at her greatest brilliancy, and its light was perfectly steady. Was this the Lick object? J. A. Pearce expressed doubts after he checked the given positions; he was certain of discrepancy in Emmert's report.

Such is the strange affair of the mystery light of 1921. It began with Chambers's query and was substantiated by Rickenbacher, both of whom were unconnected with the astronomical profession. Until then the two astronomers Campbell and Russell had been narrowly absorbed in the changing geometry of the setting Sun, unaware of the minor drama unfolding around them. Thus, had it not been for Chambers, the object might well have passed from sight unremarked upon.

The accounts by S. Fellows and Nelson Day may be reconciled with the Mount Hamilton observation. The former described an elongated object of reddish tint 6° east of the Sun, whereas Campbell called his object star-like, but he only saw it for little more than a couple of seconds. The Sun was still above the horizon and the object 4° east of it when Nelson Day looked, so his estimate of brightness is not entirely revelatory. Setting aside the differences, there is nothing to suggest that these were other than bona fide sightings, although the process of trying to reconstruct something from memory is notoriously unreliable. Discrepancies over orientation and date characterize Emmert's report, as Pearce pointed out, and there was also confusion with Venus. It is just possible that Emmert did see something, i.e., the enigmatic object, but his report is flawed by inconsistency and offers nothing new. Date alone excludes the Bell Dawson observation. He probably saw either Mercury or Jupiter, both of which set soon after the Sun on that date. As Mercury was about 8° from the Kershaw object, it is possible that they did indeed observe that body; furthermore, as Ashbrook pointed out, the alignments employed by Gaythorpe may have been less reliable than he supposed.

The report in *Nature* of 15 September 1921 gave credence to the Plauen observation because it was made 'in a much more exact manner'. But Jupiter was close by the position derived by Wolf. So is this the body that was mistaken for the Lick object? If the Plauen and the Lick objects are assumed to be identical, Pearce observed, 'to account for the great motion along the ecliptic of 27° in eight hours, the distance of the body from the earth on 7 August, was, according to Professor Wolf, 0.005 astronomical units, or about twice the moon's distance'. This was unlikely, Pearce thought, because surely a comet at that distance would not have had such a well-defined *stellar* appearance.

As Russell noted, if the object was a nova, it should have been observable on Monday evening, 8 August, unless its brightness had greatly diminished, in which case there would have been little chance of observing the object in the bright sky around the Sun for several weeks to come. Moreover, the position of the object (about 40° from the galactic plane) militated against the idea. If the object was indeed a comet, 'its position could not be predicted because the orbit is totally unknown. It might be too near the Sun, either between Sun and Earth, or on the far side of the Sun.' The possibility of a near-Earth asteroid was never considered.

THE MYSTERY DEEPENS

Nature itself now added to the confusion. Reports of unusual events in the night skies of Europe began to circulate. A cablegram, supposedly from Heidelberg, Germany, widely reported in the American press around 10 August, alleged that observers had evidence that the Earth had passed through the tail of a comet on the night of 8–9 August. As summarized by the *English Mechanic and World of Science* of 19 August 1921, the Baden State Observatory at Königstuhl, Heidelberg, reported that the Earth passed through the tail of a comet during the night of Monday–Tuesday (8–9 August). Seemingly a number of luminous bands in the form of a wreath were seen to extend from WNW to ESE across a clear sky. The bands moved slowly in a NNE direction, growing paler at dawn. The head of the comet passed southwards between Earth and the Sun. The phenomenon, it was said, had not previously been reported, and was caused by the same body as that reported from the United States near sunset on 7 August.

Nature had reported on the Lick observation in its issue of 11 August. The following week it carried a brief account of the Königstuhl phenomenon. Again it was conjectured this might have been due to the Earth passing through the presumed tail of the Lick object, a possibility that induced the writer to recall the passage of the Earth through the tail of the great comet of 1861 on 30 June of that year. Nevertheless, although the report was garbled, it did contain an element of truth.

Nature of 8 September stated that on 5 August, Max Wolf at Königstuhl had seen 'a long, very bright cloud west of the Pleiades, brightest near δ (Delta) Arietis'. First noticed at 11h 15m GMT, 'it faded rapidly only a trace visible at 11h 36m'. Similar observations at midnight on the eighth were given additional credence by including the name of the leading German meteor authority C. Hoffmeister (1892–1968) at Sonneberg, and no doubt this played a role in what subsequently transpired. Nevertheless, the news was confused. The cablegram did not come from Max Wolf. Campbell suspected its source was the Wolff News Agency.

Wolf and Hoffmeister collated reports from their respective stations and published them in the *Astronomische Nachrichten*. They were also summarized in *Nature*; and auroral streamers were postulated as the most likely explanation of the excitement. Support for this hypothesis came from a French amateur astronomer, J. L. Herzog in La Ferrière (Jura Bernois, France), who published a sketch of the phenomenon as it appeared to him during the early hours of 9 August 1921 (Figure 2).

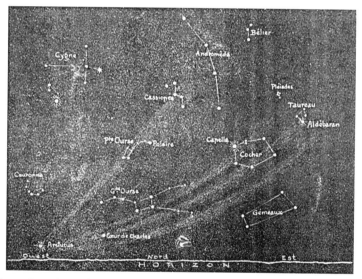

Figure 2. Luminous phenomenon observed by J. L. Herzog at La Ferrière (Jura Bernois), France, 8–9 August 1921, 01.30 a.m. to 03.00 a.m. Initially thought to indicate the passage of the earth through the tail of the supposed comet seen from the Lick Observatory, California, at sunset on 7 August. (Image courtesy of *Bulletin de la Société Astronomique de France*, Vol. 35 (1921), p. 435.)

A well-known British meteor watcher, Miss A. Grace Cook, writing in the 8 August issue of the *English Mechanic and World of Science*, added to the tension by her request to 'hear from anyone who saw the luminous night sky on 4 August':

> I went out to observe meteors at 9.30 [p.m.] GMT, and at once noticed a bright patch about 2 degrees square, 10 degrees preceding beta Pegasi. I mapped its course, as I thought it might be the after-streak of a bright fireball I had missed. I found it was moving very slowly towards the north, therefore not in the prevailing wind, which was west and strong. Dark clouds were passing over from the west at the time. The little patch was visible two minutes. At 10.34 I altered my mind as to the appearance I had seen earlier, for I saw a long streak of very thin white cloud, not so bright as the Milky Way, but more like the Zodiacal Light, and the stars shone through it. The outer edge of the streak was touching alpha Pegasi at 10.34, and had reached alpha Andromedae by 11 h., by that time the cloud appeared thinner and more difficult to see. I then saw other streaks stretching across the south and coming up gradually, lengthwise on, with dark gaps between. This continued till 13 h., when I came in. I have often seen these luminous clouds or mist, but seldom so well.

CONCLUSIONS

Was it all circumstantial, an extraordinary coincidence? A comet with retrograde motion near the plane of the ecliptic and a small perihelion distance, approaching the Sun from behind might remain in close proximity to it the whole time that it was bright; in this case, the nucleus observed in bright twilight might well have been the only part visible. Markwick, a very experienced observer, was confident a brilliant comet had been seen. Crommelin was of the same persuasion, and ventured to designate the object comet 1921e.[2]

Such confidence triggered a lively correspondence in the columns of the *English Mechanic and World of Science*. 'By the way,' wrote

---

[2] This form of comet designation, comprising a year followed by a lowercase letter, indicates the comet's order of discovery in that year, so 1921e would be the fifth comet to be discovered in 1921, 'e' being the fifth letter of the alphabet.

'Busybody', in the issue of 18 November, 'I noticed that the great "surprise comet" of August last was recently referred to in these columns as Campbell's Comet. This is an error. It should be Fellowes's [sic] Comet. It was seen by Mr Fellowes five hours before Mr Campbell.' Markwick corrected the spelling of Fellows in the succeeding issue, gave credit to the Lick observers as being the first to report on the object, then as 'a graceful compliment to the Americans' suggested a compromise to the appellation 'Campbell-Fellows' and querulously asked: 'Are the experts going to produce a definite, satisfactory orbit for this object? What has become of it?'

Oil merchant Scriven Bolton (c.1888–1929) of Leeds, a leading British amateur astronomer of the time, expressed his opinion succinctly in the opening sentence of a letter to the *English Mechanic*: 'It does not yet appear to be quite clear as to who was the first to see the [surprise comet].'

The episode reminded the eminent American astronomer Edward Emerson Barnard (1857–1923) of the 'sungrazing' comet registered on plates exposed during the total solar eclipse of 1882 (Figure 3). It was

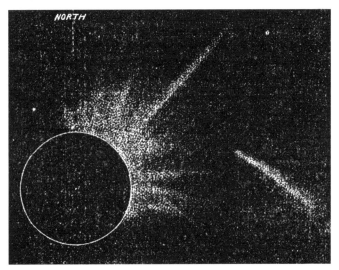

Figure 3. Eclipse comet (Comet Tewfik) discovered amid coronal streamers during totality at the solar eclipse of 17 May 1882. The sketch shows the orientation of the comet in relation to the sun as shown on photographs taken by the well-known British astronomer Arthur C. Ranyard. (Image courtesy of *Knowledge*, Vol. 2 (37) 14 July 1882, p. 105.)

discovered about half a solar diameter from the Sun during the total eclipse of 17 May by parties stationed at Sohag, Egypt, and named Tewfik after the then Khedive of Egypt. The comet was never seen again. It seemingly came close to hitting the Sun and had a tail half a degree in length; it identified so well with the coronal plumes that several authorities were inclined to look upon it as a detached fragment of the solar corona. Along with others, Barnard said that he 'hunted faithfully for that comet morning and night for a long time. Of course, if the present comet was a sungrazer,' he added, 'it would move in a very narrow orbit, the whole of which might lie in daylight. It may be discovered yet in the Southern Hemisphere.'

Russell, writing in the *Scientific American*, was also hopeful: '[W]e may yet receive news from some southern point which may enable us to say more than is at present known concerning this strange visitor to our skies.' However, eight days later, no further news of the suspected comet had come in. But, Russell continued, this did 'not mean that there was any illusion about the original observation. There are a number of instances on record in which comets, at perihelion, close to the Sun, have been visible in broad daylight … It is entirely possible for a comet's orbit to be so situated that it may approach the Sun from behind, for a terrestrial observer, in such a way that there may be no chance of seeing it upon a dark sky, and so detecting it by the ordinary methods of search. If the comet came from the southern part of the celestial sphere, and had a small perihelion distance, it might never be visible to northern observers at all, except in daylight, when close to the Sun. It may be recalled that the great comet of 1882 [II] was first seen at Rio de Janeiro, but owing to defective cable communication news did not reach the Northern Hemisphere until after it had passed perihelion, and been discovered by numerous observers in broad daylight.'

Again, the great Daylight Comet 1910 I was first seen by diamond mine and rail workers just after sunrise on 13 January as they walked home after completing a night shift. Seeing the strange-looking object in the eastern sky, they supposed it was Halley's Comet; it was a paragraph in a local newspaper that alerted astronomers at the Transvaal Observatory. The comet was later observed in daylight about 4° away from the Sun; towards the end of January the tail, which by then had taken on a distinctive yellowish tint, had grown to 40° in length.

But could 1921e, to use Crommelin's presumption, belong to the sungrazer group of comets? Since all known members of the group follow very similar orbits, have small perihelion distances, and brighten considerably during the brief interval they are near the Sun, Joseph Ashbrook decided to put the idea to the test 'calculating the coordinates that an object tracing the orbit of 1882 II would have had at the time of the Lick observation, assuming this object's perihelion occurred in early August, 1921'. Brian G. Marsden of the Smithsonian Astrophysical Observatory provided ephemerides for 1882 II with perihelion times ranging from 6 August to 9 August. None agreed with the Lick position, and Ashbrook concluded that if the object was a comet, it did not belong to the famous sungrazing family.

The problem here, as with the bright objects seen near the Sun from Broughty Ferry, Dundee, Scotland in December 1882; Echo Mountain in the Sierra Madre range, California in September 1896; and the unidentified lights seen near the Sun during the total eclipses of 1869, 1878, 1883, 1898 and 1973, is what the observer unconsciously grafts onto the observation. As a correspondent to the *English Mechanic and World of Science* wisely said:

> It is hardly possible to admit that a very brilliant comet could pass its perihelion without being seen in its gradual approach and recedence. I do not impugn the veracity of the observers or call in[to] question their ability, but it seems to me that the whole incident is surrounded with doubt … [We] must remember … that if one observer announces an object or a discovery, no matter how extraordinary or mysterious it may be, there will be sure to be another observer, or several others, who will confirm the statement.

The implication is inescapable. The only reliable evidence of something unusual near the Sun at its setting on 7 August 1921 is what was reported to Harvard from the Lick observatory later that evening. That something noteworthy inscribed the night sky about the same time is also beyond doubt, but whether the two events were connected will never be known.

FURTHER READING

W. W. Campbell, 'Observations of an Unidentified Object Seen Near the Sun on Sunday, August 7, 1921', *Publications of the Astronomical Society of the Pacific*, Vol. 32 (1921), pp. 258–62.

J. A. Pearce, 'The Unidentified Bright Object Seen Near the Sun', *Journal of the Royal Astronomical Society of Canada*, Vol. 15 (1921), pp. 364–7.

The English Mechanic and World of Science.

The Journal of the British Astronomical Association.

Forty-Four Years as a Patrick Moore Fan

Martin Mobberley
Astronomer, author and biographer

My very first encounter with the name Patrick Moore occurred in January 1968. A school friend had been given a copy of the 1967 edition of Patrick's *Observer's Book of Astronomy* and I was mesmerized by this pocket-sized book, with its superb colour plates by Leslie Ball. I just had to have one myself. My parents quickly obliged and I was soon hooked on astronomy and space travel. Patrick, of course, became a major part of the BBC coverage of the Moon landings in subsequent years, so the man who had written my favourite book was suddenly appearing on TV more and more during my most formative period. In the back of all Patrick's books you would invariably find the address of The British Astronomical Association, which I joined in 1969, aged eleven. From late 1970 my father started taking me to many of the BAA's Lunar Section meetings and it was at one of these, in September 1970, that I first met Patrick.

From the 1970s onward, the arrival of any BAA publication became an important part of my life. I was always keen to work alongside the 'observing greats' I had looked up to in my youth and none were more influential than Patrick. So many anecdotes about the great man spring to mind from literally hundreds of astronomy meetings I attended. His arrival in a beat-up wreck of a car was always entertaining, as was his reaction to anyone mentioning politics during the pre-Thatcher era. 'Harold Wilson – worst thing to happen to this country,' he would bellow. After any Out-of-Town residential BAA meeting had concluded for the day he would invariably shout, 'Where's the bar?'

From 1980 to 1991, I was a regular contributor to Patrick and Peter Foley's BAA Lunar Section 'TLP Network', on call to photograph any suspicious appearances of lunar craters. These days I am a TLP sceptic, but that era, with Patrick regularly phoning me up to take a lunar

Martin with Patrick at the BAA Centenary meeting in October 1990. (Image courtesy of Martin Mobberley.)

photograph, was one of my most enjoyable. You were simply driven along by Patrick's boundless enthusiasm, eccentricities and praise.

From the 1990s Patrick asked me to write some technical chapters in books he was writing for Springer and then I was asked to write entire books, too. As with so many of his BAA friends he eventually asked me to join him as an occasional guest on *The Sky at Night*, then broadcast from the BBC TV Centre, in the happy days when he was still totally in charge of proceedings.

Patrick's legacy is massive. He wrote hundreds of books, inspired a generation, and fronted a monthly TV programme on astronomy for almost fifty-six years. Surely there will never again be such a prolific author, broadcaster and publicity machine for astronomy.

Imaging Jupiter

MARTIN MOBBERLEY

This year sees the giant planet Jupiter reach opposition on 5 January, at a very healthy northerly declination of almost +23°. The giant planet will be well placed in the evening sky right through the January to March period and will also ride high in the dawn sky from October onwards. In recent years, some turbulent atmospheric upheavals have taken place in the Jovian weather system so the planet is always worth observing and imaging. The giant planet has been high in Northern Hemisphere skies for a while now, but make the most of these times; by the end of this year, it will still be at +15°N, but during 2015 it will slide from +15° to +4° and in the years following we will be back to the dismal situation of the planet being below the celestial equator and sinking fast. For those observers based nearer to the equator, or intrepid amateurs, such as Damian Peach, who choose to travel abroad to view the planets at a high altitude, this is not a problem. However, for most readers of this yearbook, based in the UK, the times when the giant planet is at a high declination need to be savoured, as only when a planet is high in the sky can space-probe views be glimpsed visually, or captured digitally. In the past decade a few dozen dedicated amateurs worldwide have astounded professional astronomers with the resolutions they have achieved when imaging the planets. Many of the top Jupiter observers contribute to the British Astronomical Association's Jupiter Section (www.britastro.org/jupiter/) and many discuss imaging methods on the ALPO (Association of Lunar and Planetary Observers) Yahoo! Forum at http://tech.groups.yahoo.com/group/ALPO_Jupiter/.

The planetary images secured by the best back-garden observers like Damian, Dave Tyler, Anthony Wesley, Chris Go and others, have only been surpassed by NASA space probes or by the Hubble Space Telescope, yet the majority of amateur astronomers find it hard to approach the levels set by these pioneering observers. So, what, precisely, are these top planetary imagers doing that sets them apart? Over the past decade, my own planetary efforts have been improving steadily; on a good night I can compare one of my own shots with those of Damian without being too embarrassed! Looking back, I've come a long way, but it has been a hard slog. However, it has taught me that none of these planetary imagers are using any magical 'tricks' but simply using sheer hard work. From the point of view of someone starting out from scratch in lunar and planetary imaging, the mountain must seem a very hard one to climb. Hopefully, I may be able to soften the pain of the learning curve just a bit! There are no instant fixes, just a slow process of getting better and eliminating the weaknesses in your techniques.

To me, advanced planetary imaging is a competitive pursuit. Amateurs are always trying to raise the bar and, as in any competitive activity, your best strategy is simply to copy the best imagers' methods as a first step and then try to eliminate any flaws in your system. I have studied closely the techniques of a number of top planetary observers over recent years, and it is clear that the best ones are great problem solvers. Whatever hurdles are placed in their way in the form of lack of spare time, weather, finances, poor health, or sheer bad luck, they simply find a way out of the situation, whereas others just give up. So, when all's said and done, sheer bloody-mindedness, bordering on manic obsessiveness, helps a lot! Nevertheless, there are a few crucial areas where many amateurs fall down in their quest to take great images and I have narrowed these down to a number of key areas in which the best excel, but the others fall by the wayside. These areas are:

1. Having a very user-friendly observing station and telescope, ready to go in minutes, just outside your back door.
2. Being 100 per cent sure that you have collimated your telescope to perfection.
3. Keeping a close eye on the weather and the jet stream.
4. Using a telescope that is at the same temperature as the night air.
5. Taking focussing very seriously indeed!
6. Waiting very patiently for the moments of better seeing on as many nights as possible.
7. Using a high-speed (typically, 60 frames per second) monochrome camera with colour filters.

8. Spending a lot of time processing the images in a calm and patient manner.

I will now deal with each of these points in a bit more detail.

A USER-FRIENDLY OBSERVING STATION

It is no surprise to me that the 14-inch Schmidt-Cassegrain, specifically, Celestron's C14, is the telescope of choice for so many advanced planetary imagers worldwide. The Schmidt-Cassegrain design is certainly not optimum for observing planets; for starters, it does not hold collimation that well, and the closed tube takes a long time to cool down. However, the system has a large aperture, is rugged, lightweight for its size, and is sealed against the damp night air. The position of the eyepiece also means that the observer never has to climb ladders to check if a planet is in the field. All these points may seem trivial, but, I can assure you, they are not. If a system can be kept outside, under a tarpaulin, and can be brought to bear on a planet in a few minutes at 3 a.m. in sub-zero temperatures, it will make the difference between you

Figure 1. The author's 12-inch (300 mm) f/5.3 Newtonian is on wheels and glides out from a shelter for a quick operation and cool-down.

getting out of bed or just not bothering. Of course, your budget may not permit the purchase of a Celestron 14. However, with the newer 'Edge HD' models now being very popular, the older basic Schmidt-Cassegrains can be purchased at a decent price on the second-hand market. Failing that I have seen excellent lunar and planetary images taken with basic Celestron 11 and Celestron 9.25 SCTs. But the bottom line is that aperture and user-friendliness are everything in astronomy and despite the fact that they may seem to be mutually exclusive parameters (when a huge brute of a telescope is involved), with a 14-inch SCT you can have both.

However, a big Schmidt-Cassegrain is not essential. My own planetary observing reflector is shown in Figure 1. Although I own a Celestron 14 and have used it for planetary imaging, I have devised my own user-friendly system that works with a more unwieldy 12-inch f/5.3 Newtonian, freeing the C14 for dedicated long-exposure work. My Orion Optics reflector is mounted on a Skywatcher EQ6 Pro mounting with cut-down legs; a heavily weighted triangular structure with wheels is attached to the base. The extra weight lowers the centre of gravity to prevent the system from ever tipping over on its short tripod. The telescope lives in a wooden shelter, bolted to the east-south-east facing wall of my house. Once the double doors of the shelter are opened, an old and thick carpet rolls out from the shelter and the telescope can easily be pulled the six feet to its rest position. As far as polar alignment is concerned, well, this is not a critical issue for planetary observing. Purely from experience, and noting how the base ends up oriented with respect to marks on the paving slabs, I can roll this telescope out to within a couple of degrees of being polar aligned, which is good enough for planetary imaging runs of a few minutes' duration. Power points and a pull-out shelf on the doors of the shelter, as well as a comfy stool and a wheeled desk, mean that, within minutes, I can be comfortably seated watching the laptop image. I never bother with the tedious keypad star-alignment menu, I just jab through the menu until I get to sidereal rate (or lunar rate) and hit enter. The 12-inch Newtonian is just outside the back door of the house and so is less hassle than using my Celestron 14, which is one hundred feet away and dedicated to remote deep-sky and comet imaging. By having the telescope in the open air it cools down rapidly to the night air.

One issue that seems to cause endless frustration for many planetary imaging beginners is how to position the planet on the imaging chip.

To stand any chance of resolving the smallest detail at the theoretical diffraction limit of your telescope the planet needs to be enlarged to a point where at least two pixels cover that tiny angle. For example, the theoretical resolution of a Celestron 14 (35 cm aperture) is roughly a third of a second of arc. As there are 3,600 seconds of arc in one degree, this translates to one-10,800th of a degree. We need each pixel to cover half this angle, a sixth of a second of arc, to be sure of capturing the finest details. As Jupiter spans some 47 arc seconds at opposition in 2014, this means it will need to span 282 pixels on our imaging chip. Many imagers use even finer image scales, as high as one tenth of an arc second per pixel, resulting in Jupiter being 470 pixels across. The actual sampling formula is: arc seconds per pixel = 206 x CCD pixel size in microns/focal length in millimetres, so, for my 300-mm reflector at f/30 the formula is 206 x 7.4 microns/(300 mm x 30), which gives 0.169 arc seconds per pixel.

Now, as typical high-speed imaging cameras (like the Lumenera SKYnyx 2-0, or the smaller Imaging Source units, or the Point Grey Flea) only have 640 x 480 pixels, it can easily be seen that Jupiter can almost fill the field of view. So, you need to devise a system where you can point the telescope at an area of sky not much bigger than Jupiter and be sure that it will be there when you view the live laptop image. I have known amateur astronomers give up at this hurdle alone! Various tricks can help ease the pain of this alignment problem. In my own case, I position Jupiter on the crosshairs of the finder telescope first. I then look through the main telescope and put Jupiter *almost* in the centre of a medium-power eyepiece with the sidereal drive running. Why 'almost'? Well, experience and instinct have told me that when I replace the eyepiece with the heavier-imaging camera, and its 5x Powermate, the telescope will drop by a couple of Jupiter diameters, so I allow for this. I have the laptop software running already, show-ing the image from the camera, as I slide it into the drawtube, and so I can quickly see if Jupiter is in the field. If I have missed the planet by an arc minute or so, some very delicate hand jiggles will soon tell me where Jupiter is lurking and then I can use the hand controller to fine-position the planet into the imaging field. If you are a complete beginner at this imaging malarkey, then I would seriously recommend that you practise by imaging the Moon first; it covers an area of the sky some 1500 x that of Jupiter, and so is much harder to miss!

The only items I bring outdoors to each planetary observing session are my laptop and a small equipment case. This contains the Lumenera SKYnyx 2-0 imager attached to a 5x Powermate lens, some planetary filters, and a few eyepieces. Laptop hard discs and LCD screens do not like cold weather and so I try to minimize the time the laptop is outside. I also attach a thin, transparent plastic sheet over the screen to stop it getting dirty. In cold and damp conditions telescope optics can quickly dew over, and invariably do, even if dew heaters and dew shields are employed. To combat this I have a mains-powered hairdryer on a very long lead plugged into the power socket inside the 12-inch reflector's storage shelter. Mains voltages and damp conditions can be dangerous and so the whole system is on a sensitive Earth leakage trip switch to avoid me being electrocuted! This may all sound unrelated to imaging planets, but all these little tricks help keep the observing system going. A user-friendly workstation is worth its weight in gold: trust me on this one!

One of the biggest enthusiasm killers for all UK-based planetary imagers is the typical sub-zero winter temperatures. The British media seem to have the bizarre idea that amateur astronomers just love freezing cold winter weather and long winter nights, as if we were all polar bears! I can assure any media people reading this that we all hate bone-chilling winter weather. The most blissful UK observing sessions are those experienced in the evenings of August and September, when nights are dark, but still well above freezing. To have a workable planetary observing system you need a good set of suitable clothing, one that would look at home in the wardrobe of an Arctic explorer. On the coldest nights I wear two sets of trousers, thermal underwear, insulated boots, many layers of upper-body clothing, a balaclava, mittens and a hefty winter anorak. When you are sitting around watching a laptop screen in sub-zero conditions you can get very cold very quickly, so if you are new to astronomy invest, in some serious winter clothing NOW! It makes all the difference.

COLLIMATION

If there is one issue that stops the average planetary observer taking images of the quality of Damian Peach, it is telescope collimation. While it may seem, at least on Internet astronomy forums, that every 'expert' can collimate a telescope, in practice few people really collimate them precisely. For deep-sky observing a rough collimation is good enough, but for planetary observing it needs to be absolutely perfect. Modern commercial telescopes, of virtually every type, are unfit for purpose from this aspect unless they are a long-focus reflector of f/7 or longer. The so-called 'sweet spot' of a telescope, the area at the focal plane in which you can resolve to the limit of the telescope aperture, is tiny in modern systems and it varies inversely with the cube of the f-ratio in a Newtonian. So, at f/8, the sweet spot diameter at the focus is a healthy 11 mm in diameter, whereas at f/5 it is less than 3 mm in diameter and at f/4 it is a tiny 1.4 mm in diameter. In the early 1900s, it was rare for a Newtonian to be faster than f/8, so reflectors stayed in collimation, but in the modern era this is not the case. The commercial pressure to make systems more portable has made collimation a tedious chore. Every drawtube I have ever seen is capable of a millimetre of rattle and flexure with respect to the eyepiece or lens inserted into it, which is enough to wreck collimation.

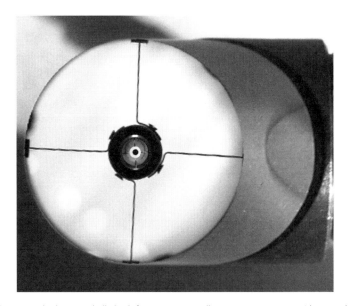

Figure 2. The basic eyeball check for Newtonian collimation is to ensure, with a peephole eyepiece, that the circular primary mirror reflection is concentric with the secondary mirror outline and that the reflection of the peephole, and the observer's eye, coincide with the centre of the ring, placed by the manufacturer, in the primary mirror's centre.

The situation is no better with Schmidt-Cassegrains either, as the f/2 primary mirror tends to tilt as the telescope is moved around the sky. There is certainly plenty of information on the Internet (and in telescope manuals) about how to collimate the different systems, and various pricey gadgets are often suggested as the solution. Laser collimators can be used to quickly rough-collimate a Newtonian (with only one person involved) but they are far less useful for planetary-level collimation due to the aforementioned drawtube rattle issues; they are also useless for Schmidt-Cassegrain collimation. If you have a very long back lawn, an artificial star device, placed a hundred feet or so from your instrument, can be used to tweak the mirrors until the star appears textbook-perfect through the eyepiece. This can be done on a cloudy night, but only with the telescope horizontal; and things can change when you swing the telescope to a completely different position.

When all is said and done, what do the top planetary imagers actually do, as surely this is one thing that they must have nailed? Well, in practice, they use their exact same imaging cameras and planetary-imaging systems to image a bright star near to the planet in question. Then, with the laptop screen in view, they can gently tweak the relevant adjustment screws until a textbook-perfect star image appears. Of course, as the screws are adjusted, the star will move and so the hand controller will be needed to re-centre the star. Nevertheless, this is the ultimate collimation method, as if you get a perfect star image, you are perfectly collimated.

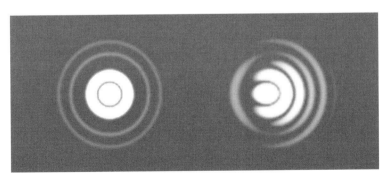

Figure 3. In perfect seeing, a focussed star at high power will look like the image on the left, whereas a primary-mirror misalignment will look like the image on the right.

Of course, on nights of bad seeing it is often very difficult to glimpse textbook-perfect stars; however, in those conditions all you can do is try your best and collimate as well as possible. At least if you use a high-speed imaging camera, you can analyse individual 1/60th-second frames where the seeing is briefly good. Beyond all this, once collimation has been nailed, these same amateurs tend not to move their telescopes wildly about the sky. Some even leave the tube in the same position when the drive is switched off, the tarpaulin put back over the telescope, or the observatory roof closed. This usually means that they will not have to repeat this tedious chore each night. It may sound paranoid, but it is the price that often needs to be paid with modern telescopes that lose collimation so easily.

In my own case, the mirror cell of my Orion Optics Newtonian retains collimation well and I collimate the system by initially eye-balling the mirrors with a peephole eyepiece (sometimes called a Cheshire eyepiece) in daytime and then fine-tuning on a star if required. By rolling my telescope out of its shelter along a smooth carpet, I avoid the jolts that might alter the collimation if it were running over concrete. I generally find that after every three or four sessions I have to tweak the collimation slightly.

The only way to totally avoid this collimation chore would be to pay for a Newtonian of f/7 or slower to be made for you, along with acquiring a stepladder to reach the eyepiece!

WEATHER

In recent years, the British weather has seemed to come in extreme ruts. These ruts are usually month-long cloudy and wet ruts, but are sometimes followed by clear-sky ruts lasting a week or two in length. So, the UK amateur astronomer is either totally frustrated or in desperate need of some sleep! To make things worse, the ability of forecasters to predict night-time cloud seems to be getting worse, with the TV weather simulations being nothing more than works of total fiction on many nights. Satellite images are of great help, though, as they enable you to spot a clear gap coming. However, for planetary imagers the situation is far more complicated. In general the best weather for high-resolution work is very calm, stable weather, such as develops under a long-lived High Pressure system anchored over the UK. Sadly, many of these High Pressure systems, especially in winter, are cloudy ones, but some are clear. Those crystal-clear nights, experienced after a cold front and a heavy rain shower have passed through, from north to south, are not the best for the planetary imager, as they are invariably unstable at high magnifications. However, rather murky nights, with some cloud about, and with mist or even a light fog, are often perfect for stable planetary views. The rate the temperature is falling is critical too. After a sunny day the temperature drops sharply and an hour or two after sunset the air temperature is dropping at two degrees per hour, or faster, whereas your telescope mirror is cooling much more slowly. This means that a layer of turbulence will reside just above the mirror surface and the planet will appear to wobble and ripple wildly. Even powerful fans attempting to cool the mirror will struggle to cool a large slab of warm glass in less than a few hours. Conditions are sometimes better at precise sunset and, if you can locate a bright planet like Jupiter at this time, some good images can be captured only minutes after local sunset with the sky still bright blue! The best conditions occur late in the night, though. If the day has been cloudy, and the cloud has broken after sunset, a very good thermal equilibrium can exist between the telescope and the atmosphere after midnight. Sometimes, in the predawn skies, the air can be so tranquil that Jupiter can look just like the view from a space probe, rather than the more typical jelly on top of a spin dryer.

There is another factor too and this is called the jet stream. This is the fast-flowing river of high-altitude air which meanders around various latitudes and tends to be a near-permanent winter feature over the UK. If light from a planet passes through the jet stream, the fine detail can just fuzz out; in these situations the planetary surface can appear almost featureless. However, when the jet stream is absent, and winds at all altitudes are close to zero, the view can be very crisp with Jupiter's moons even appearing as tiny discs! Fortunately, as airline pilots need to know where the jet stream is, and how fast it is flowing, various Internet sites can be consulted to tell you if you would be better off lying in bed or going out to observe. Two of the best web pages are the Unisys and Netweather sites:

http://weather.unisys.com/gfs/gfs.php?inv=0&plot=300&region=eu&t=4p

http://www.netweather.tv/index.cgi?action=jetstream;sess=

FOCUSSING AND WAITING

Anyone who has looked at Jupiter 'live' on a laptop monitor will be well aware that focussing such a ghostly rippling gas ball is far from easy. With the Moon things are simple, especially near the terminator. Contrast is high and tiny craters at the telescope limit snap into view when you hit the focus precisely, despite all the wobble and jitter. If only things were that easy with Jupiter! A lot of the focussing problem is tied up with catching the good seeing. When seeing is poor and variable, it is hard to tell if the low-contrast planet suddenly looks blurred simply because you have missed the focus, or because conditions have deteriorated. When you are tired and it is 3 a.m., you can easily get into a situation where you start believing that your own focussing can alter the seeing! The mind plays funny tricks when you need sleep and are cold. I should stress here that it is absolutely 100 per cent essential that you have a high-quality electric focuser for planetary imaging work. A planetary imager's telescope, without a hands-free electric focuser, is as useful as the proverbial ashtray on a motorbike. Every time you touch a manual focuser, the telescope shakes by tens of arc seconds. I have even seen some old Schmidt-Cassegrains where the manual focus knob not only shakes the telescope but also de-collimates it! There needs to be a cerebral closed feedback loop between the observer's brain, focuser hand-controller finger and the observer's eye watching the laptop screen. Trying to focus and then looking back at the screen doesn't work: you need to study the screen intently as you focus in and out, back and forth, around the focus point, studying the planetary features, the limb and the moons, shimmering and distorting, until you are happy. You also need to check if the image of the planet is saturating (whiting out) the equatorial zone of Jupiter as you hit the perfect focus. This is easy to forget and means that you will burn out the brightest region in the final image.

One of the things I have learned in recent years is that some of the poorest planetary images are secured simply because the imager has a total lack of patience, both when imaging and when processing and when learning new techniques. Frustration with the seeing can make you think that you are cursed and that the best imagers simply have secret tricks they will never divulge! This simply is not the case. Patience and hard work are the keys to success. I have, on occasion, seen impatient planetary imagers at work. The equipment is assembled in a rush, and, regardless of seeing, some quick images are taken. The equipment is then dis-assembled, often in a bad-tempered and stressed rush, with a few choice swear words being uttered, and only a few minutes of imaging time are actually acquired. I have also watched some of the UK's finest planetary imagers in action too. Collimation is checked in a calm manner with these guys and then a few early images are secured through various coloured filters. A long waiting game ensues, with various imaging runs being made in slightly better seeing and, all the time, a long and patient wait for really good seeing takes place. If the good seeing comes along, after an hour or two, more intense imaging runs take place, with a sequence of many filtered videos being secured. At the end of the night these top imagers have tens of gigabytes of videos (sometimes more) on their hard discs: the result of serious work during the best seeing. After many days, or even weeks, a masterpiece will emerge. By contrast, a horrendously over-processed extremely poor image will be churned out by the impatient observer within minutes of getting the laptop indoors and the image will be posted with a comment such as: 'I just never seem to get good seeing'. My own early efforts were somewhere between these two extremes! The bottom line is, the more nights you observe and the longer you observe each night, and the more patient you are, the more chance you have of catching the good seeing.

COLOUR ISSUES

Unlike the Moon and Venus, the planets Mars, Jupiter and Saturn show distinct colours and so it is understandable that the beginner will consider acquiring a high-speed colour-imaging camera to capture the details on view. Low-cost colour planetary imagers include the Celestron NexImage and the Meade LPI. However, using a monochrome camera with colour filters is a far better approach. There are a number of reasons for this. First, although Jupiter is nice and high in the UK sky this year, reaching sixty degrees altitude when it transits from the southernmost counties, it is often much lower than this. When a planet drops in altitude the light is dispersed through the atmosphere and this dispersion rapidly exceeds the theoretical resolution of amateur telescopes. By using colour filters, dispersion is minimized so that when a planet is as high up as 60 degrees, a very sharp image can result. As you drop lower in altitude a colour camera will rapidly start exhibiting unsightly red and blue fringes around the planetary edges and resolution will be lost, but the monochrome camera, using filters, will fare much better. In recent years, the most advanced amateurs have started using anti-dispersion prisms, such as those made by ASH (Astro Systemes Holland). For planets as low in the murk as Saturn currently is from the UK, these can save the day, although they do add a significant level of complexity to the process. Another factor with colour cameras is that they capture colour by a grid of filters placed over the CCD pixels in what is called a Bayer matrix. This usually consists of a four-pixel 2 x 2 matrix in which one pixel is covered by a red filter, one by a blue filter and two by green filters. Thus, every pixel is filtered in some way and so the signal-to-noise ratio of all pixels is only about a quarter as good as for an unfiltered system and the resolution is halved. Finally, one trick used by many amateurs when imaging Jupiter is to not use a green filter at all, just a red filter and a blue filter. The green result can be synthesized remarkably well by simply averaging the final red and blue filter results. The only downside of this method is that Jupiter's dark brown 'barges' appear slightly less dark and the moons can appear rather brighter than is accurate. However, only having to use two filters is sheer bliss as Jupiter rotates very rapidly. I might add that if you are imaging the Moon, a single red filter (or even a green filter if it is higher than fifty degrees altitude) will give a sharper result than using no filters at all. In really poor seeing and at low altitudes a deep red or near infra-red filter can dramatically sharpen the view.

THE OUTDOOR PROCEDURE

In this section I am going to list precisely what I do when imaging Jupiter. Other observers' methods vary slightly, but at least I know exactly what I do each night. The equipment I use is a Lumenera SKYnyx 2-0 attached to a 5x Powermate. I purchased the camera second-hand from a friend for £400 (the full price would have been £750). The lens transforms my f/5.3 system into an f/30 system, which means the 5x Powermate is actually magnifying the image by more like 5.7x. It also gives me an image scale of approximately six pixels per arc second which is close to the optimum for a telescope with a theoretical resolution of roughly 0.4 arc seconds. Schmidt-Cassegrain users will prefer to use a 3x Barlow lens to give approximately f/30.

I rarely observe planets in the one-to-three-hour window after sunset, simply because of those aforementioned cool-down issues. I vastly prefer to image at least five hours after sunset, or at sunset itself, but when Jupiter is in the early evening sky this is often not practical. So, I just have to hope the thermal issues of atmosphere (and telescope) cooling down are not too severe. I do have fans on the telescope but they have little instant effect on such a large slab of glass as a 300 mm mirror.

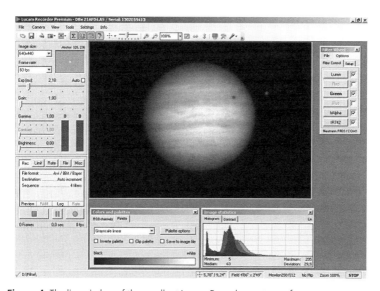

Figure 4. The live window of the excellent Lucam Recorder capture software.

The capture software I use is the excellent Lucam Recorder by the amateur astronomer Heiko Wilkens. This is, by far, the best capture software around, and, bizarrely, Lumenera do not make any software that is anything like as good for amateur astronomers using their cameras! Some other manufacturers' cameras do come with software supplied, but, in my view, those packages are not quite as good and intuitive as Lucam Recorder. When you have parted with a modest sum of money for the software, Heiko gives you a licence code which matches the serial number of your camera and you are then in business. Heiko moderates a useful Lucam Recorder discussion group at: http://tech.dir.groups.yahoo.com/group/LucamRecorder/.

The software enables you to run the camera at various frame rates, typically 7.5, 15, 30 and 60 frames per second. By downloading a smaller part of the chip than the full 640 x 480 pixels, you can run at even higher rates with a USB 2.0 laptop (some competing systems use the Firewire interface system). High frame rates help to freeze the endless jitter and distortion caused by the light from the planet passing through twenty miles of our turbulent atmosphere. However, I find that beyond 40 or so frames per second Jupiter needs quite a high gain at f/30, and I often use 30 frames per second. After carefully centring the planet as already described, I place it near the middle of the chip. If conditions are breezy, Jupiter can jiggle around quite a bit and, above fifteen miles per hour, gusts can even cause it to temporarily leave the frame! Jupiter can have a diameter of almost fifty arc seconds at a perihelic opposition and it rotates rapidly, in nine hours and fifty minutes. At the equator, on the meridian, this translates into a motion of sixteen arc seconds per hour, or roughly a quarter of an arc second per minute with respect to the limb. So, with a telescope capable of resolving 0.4 arc seconds it is clear that the imaging video limit will be perilously close after only one minute of imaging time. Fortunately, a number of factors reduce this problem. First, I am using red and blue filters, and so even though Jupiter has rotated slightly, between the two runs, I can simply allow for this when I align the final image colours on planetary details. Also, the software I use to stack the video frames can lock onto features near the planetary centre and so any subsequent smearing will occur at the foreshortened limb regions. Finally, away from the centre of the planet, features on Jupiter will appear to move more slowly than in the middle, due to their higher latitude or foreshortening. All these factors combined mean that, in practice, I tend to image Jupiter for up to ninety seconds in the red filter, then change the filter, refocus, and image for another ninety seconds in the blue filter. The total imaging time is thus almost three minutes, with maybe thirty seconds to change the filters and refocus.

I actually do not use a custom filter wheel, but a home-made system as shown in Figure 5. This enables me to drop filters into the telescope drawtube before the Powermate and takes up none of the precious back-focus travel on my Newtonian. It is also very light in weight and so less strain on the drawtube and the electric focuser.

Figure 5. The author's home-made filter holder allows filters to be inserted into a slot in the drawtube without any Newtonian back focus or weight issues.

In general, because Spode's law means that clouds will appear as soon as I am set up, I always take a quick red and blue filter run as soon as Jupiter is centred and focussed. At least this means that I will have something to show for my efforts outdoors! If it stays clear, I just sit and wait to see if the seeing is improving, or getting worse. Poor seeing initially caused by residual telescope heat is easy to spot as it manifests itself as ripple and wobble once the telescope is uncapped, and should slowly improve. Atmospheric seeing is often identifiable as an overall fuzz, or a river of turbulence streaming across the image in the direction of the jet stream flow. Depending on conditions, I either pack up after the first few video runs (if seeing is truly appalling), wait for maybe an hour or so (if seeing is just mediocre), or, if seeing is good, persevere for much longer. If seeing is excellent, I have sometimes gone back indoors to warm up a bit, and then resumed outside after an hour or two to see if a different area of interest has rotated into view, under similar conditions. Grabbing as many photons as possible is crucially important in all astronomical endeavours and so if you are imaging at, say, 60 frames per second, it is a good plan to expose for a full 1/60th of a second too, so you are capturing as many photons as possible. With

some early systems this maximum exposure strategy produced artefacts, but it seems to be the best one to use now.

It almost goes without saying that the most popular feature to image
on the Jovian disk is the Great Red Spot (GRS), that enormous whirling
storm that has survived for hundreds of years, even if its size and redness have changed quite a bit over the years. Most keen Jupiter watchers will make a special effort to observe the planet if they know that the
GRS is near the centre of the disc and this can easily be determined if
you know its System II longitude and have an astronomical handbook,
such as the one produced by the British Astronomical Association, or a
software package that enables you to enter the GRS longitude (such as
Guide 9.0). Other features that amateurs like to observe and image are
the four main moons and their shadows crossing the planet. The
moons are large enough for details to be recorded on their disks during
good seeing, although their motions relative to the face of Jupiter can
mean that their tiny images need to be aligned and processed separately
when the videos are stacked and when the different colours are combined. Io moves slightly faster across the planet than the surface features, but Europa has a very similar motion, which is very convenient.
Ganymede and Callisto move more slowly, but, being further out, they
rarely cross the disk anyway, especially when the Jovian orbital plane is
tilted well away from our viewpoint. Again, satellite phenomena can be
obtained by consulting the *Handbook of The British Astronomical
Association* or using software such as Guide 9.0.

PROCESSING THE IMAGES

Well away from the cold, dark and damp battle outdoors, the next stage
of the procedure is the image processing. This can be a relatively
leisurely pursuit, although if you find yourself in the middle of a clear
week with good seeing you can soon end up with an imaging backlog
and life getting a bit fraught. Most people have busy lives and do not
find it easy to suddenly fit a couple of hours of imaging into their
night-time schedule along with several hours of image processing.
Having studied the techniques of the most diehard amateurs, I find it
quite amazing to see how they cope with such a situation. Sometimes
image backlogs a month deep can develop with hard disks filling up
and external Terabyte storage drives being used to hold the videos

awaiting processing. For the dedicated observers it is hard to ignore a week of good seeing when months of cloud and poor seeing have passed by, but lives (and relationships) can be pushed to the limit with sleep being caught in small chunks of a few hours each night. In extreme cases I have seen the top observers fake a couple of days off sick from the day job so that some sleep recovery and image processing can take place in the working week. It can be a tough and ruthless life being a dedicated planetary astronomer! Nevertheless, in the more normal sequence of events, a somewhat more leisurely procedure can take place with the best AVI videos from a good night being examined on the next cloudy night and gradually coaxed into a really nice colour image.

The first step is to use software to run through your videos, frame by frame, assessing the quality and then stacking the best frames to give a clean image in each colour. The raw video frames, which are snapshots of maybe ⅓₀th or ⅟₆₀th of a second, are not a pretty sight as they are very noisy indeed. The beginner may find it hard to believe that anything decent can come from such noisy frames, but it is amazing what stacking thousands of the better frames can achieve.

Figure 6. The raw frames of each imaging video (a red Jupiter frame is shown here) will always look very noisy and uninspiring!

I have used two image sorting and stacking systems in recent years. From 2002 to 2012, I used Cor Berrevoets' excellent RegiStax software in its various incarnations. Cor's pioneering work helped hundreds of amateurs worldwide to produce images they could only have dreamed of before the 'webcam' era. RegiStax also includes some magical wavelet sharpening methods to enhance the details once the raw images have been stacked. While I still use RegiStax for lunar and solar image stacking I have, in the last year or two, gradually migrated to Emil Kraaikamp's software called AutoStakkert! This seems to produce marginally better planetary stacking alignment, especially in poor seeing. Essentially, both software packages are grading the quality of each frame and using the best frames to align and stack into a clean image. Because the CCD noise is pretty random in nature, stacking the frames with respect to common features on the disc will average out and drastically reduce the grainy background. Also, because Jupiter slowly jiggles around due to the seeing (and the telescope drive idiosyncrasies), this actually helps erase tiny imperfections (like specks of dust) on the CCD cover-glass surface, so they magically vanish in the final stack. More violent movements (due to a wind gust) can be detrimental to the final image, though. Clearly Cor Berrevoets and Emil Kraaikamp have written some pretty powerful software here as getting the algorithms to lock onto vague and distorting features on a low-contrast object is a formidable challenge. The web pages for these two freeware programs can be found at: http://www.astronomie.be/registax/ and http://www.autostakkert.com/.

After opening AutoStakkert!, two windows appear, one eventually showing the progress of the processing and the other showing frames from the video. The video can be loaded simply by clicking 'Open'. For Jupiter I tend to set Image Stabilization to Planet (COG) and Quality Estimation to Gradient. In the Video Frames window I simply click through the frame incrementer, looking for a nice, sharp frame and then, with Alignment Points set to Multiple (Map) and AP size set to 50 (minimum brightness 30 and Replace box ticked), I click about 15 sample box points along areas of nice details, such as the NEB and SEB on the Jupiter image. I then set the Analyse tick box to Auto size and hit Analyse. The progress of the analysis is then displayed. In decent seeing, I might choose 70 per cent of the frames to be stacked into a TIF file with the HQ refine box also ticked. Hitting the stack button then stacks all the best image frames (typically two thousand or more) and deposits the TIF result into a folder of my choice. It can be tempting to be more fussy with the percentage of frames stacking number, but if seeing is poor, setting the software to reject more than half the frames that are of low quality just makes the final image noisier. Everything always boils down to atmospheric seeing in the end.

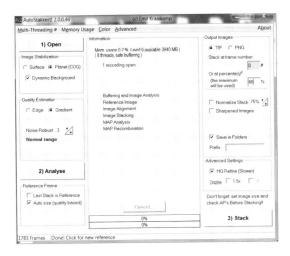

Figure 7. The main processing window of AutoStakkert!

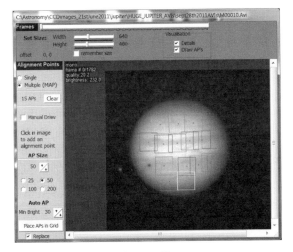

Figure 8. The frame viewing window of AutoStakkert!

Figure 9. A smooth stack of thousands of Jupiter frames. Compare this with the raw single frame in Figure 6.

I then load the stacked AutoStakkert! TIF image into RegiStax and the wavelet page comes up ready to sharpen the TIF image. Everyone has their own personal preference with the RegiStax wavelet sharpening sliders and the settings will need to vary to suit the quality of the stacked image. I prefer to stretch the image intensity levels on loading and then set the system to Default Dyadic. I then typically move wavelet slider number 1 to at least 50 per cent, sometimes more, and the wavelet slider number 2 a fraction, say, maybe 10 per cent. I also choose to resize the image by 200 per cent, using the B Spline resampling system and also reducing the image brightness by 15 per cent to prevent Jupiter's Equatorial Zone whiting out. I then save the image as a BMP.

I then repeat this AutoStakkert!/RegiStax processing for my blue filter AVI and so I end up with a sharpened red frame and a sharpened blue frame as two different bitmaps. A mistake many beginners make is to use wavelet sliders 2 or even 3 far too aggressively, which gives a high contrast but over-processed view. The wavelet 1 slider sharpens the finest details the best, but it also enhances the noise, so to use it perfectly you need a very smooth stacked image to work on. There is a

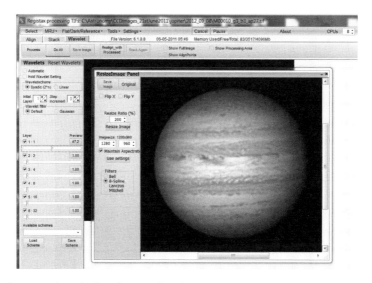

Figure 10. The author's preferences when sharpening images using wavelets in RegiStax.

veritable infinity of combinations that can be used, so trial and error experimentation is the key. However, subtle sharpening is best and will give a more natural end result.

To create the colour image, I then load both the red and blue sharpened bitmap images, created by RegiStax, into Maxim DL, align them, and combine them into an average synthetic green image. Many other imagers prefer to use the Layers commands in Photoshop for RGB colour work, but it is all down to personal preference. Of course, as already explained, due to the time period elapsing between the red and blue video runs, the features on the planet will be misaligned by roughly half an arc second at the disk centre. But this is easy to spot and moving the images by a few pixels, with a common atmospheric feature as a reference, matches them up. The combined Red + Blue average, when tweaked in brightness, makes a convincing green mono frame. We now have a Red BMP, a Blue BMP and a synthetic Green BMP, which can all be aligned with the RGB combine command in Maxim DL (or by using various other programs), which, as with the creation of the synthetic green frame, allows individual frames to be registered accurately. With a bit of brightness histogram tweaking you can then end up with a reasonable RGB colour image looking like Jupiter.

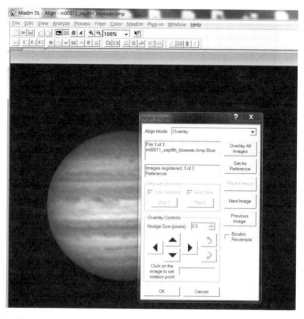

Figure 11. Maxim DL's RGB alignment process.

However, there is still plenty more tweaking to do. Some imagers prefer to use a real green filter, but it all depends on how much time you have when changing filters.

The final colour image produced this way might look a bit flat and maybe not as sharp as ideally you would like it to be. So, if you load it into a standard graphics package like Paintshop Pro or Photoshop, you can play with the gamma setting to make Jupiter look more like a sphere. At this stage you can also try a bit more sharpening with a mild unsharp mask routine. After the red and blue and synthetic green images have been combined, most images will actually tolerate a bit more sharpening. If the image then looks a tad noisy, you can run a mild Gaussian blur filter over it with a radius of maybe one pixel or so. You can also play with the colour balance to remove any unwanted blue or red tint and maybe saturate the colours a bit more. You will also have a blue fringe on one side of the Jovian disk and a red fringe on the other side, due to the difference in time between the two image runs and your alignment on the disk features. There are various ways to

Figure 12. Jupiter imaged by the author on 15 October 2011 with the 12-inch f/5.3 Newtonian, 5x Powermate and a Lumenera SKYnyx 2-0 camera.

Figure 13. A sequence of images (top left to bottom right) by the author taken on 28 September 2011 in a spell of good atmospheric seeing, showing the Great Red Spot, Io and its shadow at 01:40, 02:09, 02:21 and 02:39 UT.

remove these fringes. Away from Jovian opposition, the disk of the planet will lose one of these fringes in the terminator shadow, leaving just one to cope with. I find that the blue fringe is easier to remove without affecting Jupiter, whose features are mainly red. So, a crafty trick is to image Jupiter with the red filter first, before opposition, and with the blue filter first, after opposition. This always leaves the red fringe in the darkness and so the blue fringe can be removed with Photoshop's eyedroppers in the Enhance/Adjust Color/Adjust Hue-Saturation box. Just set the colour to blue, click the eyedropper on the limb, and reduce the lightness slider to zero. Of course, in practice, everyone owns and prefers different software. RegiStax and AutoStakkert! are freeware, but the other packages are not, so these techniques need tailoring to the imagers' own software preferences.

GOING EVEN FURTHER

In the last couple of years, the world's most advanced imagers have been trying to raise the bar even higher in their quest for the perfect image. One hardware technique being employed is the aforementioned anti-dispersion prism method, in which two thin Risley prisms are rotated in the telescope drawtube to neutralize the prismatic effect of the Earth's atmosphere. If done perfectly, white-light luminance videos can then be captured at extremely high frame rates. This is by no means a simple process and the prism angles have to be rotated every hour or so as the planet changes in altitude and azimuth because of the way the telescope view rotates with respect to the Earth's horizon. For many amateurs this is a step too far, especially with Jupiter being so high up from the UK in 2014. Nevertheless, many amateurs now own the Astro Systemes Holland (ASH) dispersion correcting device.

The other technique is perhaps even more daunting and is known as de-rotation. Because Jupiter rotates rapidly it may still look noisy, even after thousands of images have been stacked. If only it could be imaged over, say, a ten-minute period, rather than a few minutes, the result would be even smoother. Well, in the powerful WinJUPOS software it is, remarkably, now possible to de-rotate the planet, minute by minute, so that images can be stacked over a much longer time frame. It goes without saying that the extra complexity and processing power involved in this procedure is nothing short of mind-boggling, and is an indication of just how far amateurs are prepared to go to improve image quality and beat their main rivals. However, this technique is not for the squeamish, rather for those who already have a few years of Jupiter processing behind them and are prepared to spend a solid day of spare time processing one night's set of images. It also means that for it to work you need more than a few minutes of clear sky without cloud interruption, which is often a challenge in the UK. Also, as one might expect, de-rotation can produce subtle limb artefacts where the highly foreshortened features disappear and emerge from the hidden hemisphere and terminator of Jupiter over the ten-minute window, so it is certainly not all plain sailing.

In recent years, a number of amateurs have recorded impact flashes in the Jovian atmosphere when small asteroidal or cometary fragments have hit the giant planet's atmosphere. So, as a final thought, before you erase last night's Jupiter videos, it might be worth letting them run through at video speed just in case you have bagged one of these events. At the time of writing, two astronomers from Spain, namely Juan Carlos Moreno and Luis Calderon, have developed software to check Jupiter videos for impact flashes, as described at: www.pvol. ehu.es/software/.

MARS IN 2014

As a final thought, the planet Mars is also well placed this April, just after Jupiter sinks westward, and many of the imaging methods already discussed are suitable for this much smaller world. Mars is predominantly red in colour and although red light has a longer wavelength (meaning poorer telescopic resolution), the red end of the spectrum is far less affected by dispersion. Atmospheric seeing is usually better at red wavelengths too. Also, because Mars has a higher surface brightness than Jupiter, far faster frame rates can be used and longer f-ratios, too. Many modern imaging cameras allow imaging rates higher than 100 frames per second to be captured if a small ROI (region of interest) is selected and those higher-frame rates freeze the seeing far better. Also, because Mars is so small, and also rotates a lot more slowly than Jupiter, much longer imaging windows can be used, meaning that there are more frames to stack and the imager can be much more fussy about choosing how many frames to accept, with far more low-quality frames able to be rejected. With so much more time available the imager may choose to use a green filter instead of synthesizing the colour. For Mars at opposition this year the planet will be fifteen arc seconds in diameter. The planet rotates in 24 hours 37 minutes and so the centre of the disk will move at 1.9 arc seconds per hour, or take ten minutes to move by one third of an arc second, which is a factor of eight more leisurely than distant Jupiter's centre appears to drift with respect to the limb. So, you can casually spend a couple of minutes imaging at more than a hundred frames per second, for each Red, Green and Blue filter, and not even worry about colour fringing at the limb. With so many frames captured, though, you need to find out how many frames your PC and software can process in one chunk. It may be necessary to capture several smaller videos per colour once you start capturing multi-gigabyte videos. Good luck!

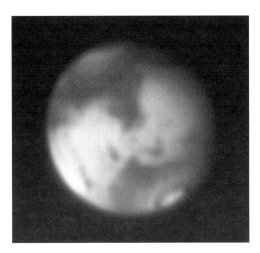

Figure 14. Mars, imaged by the author, on 1 April 2012, when it was just over twelve arc seconds in diameter.

My Mentor, Sir Patrick Moore

William Sheehan
Astronomer, author and historian

As with so many, Patrick Moore was my mentor when I first became interested in astronomy. One day (in February 1964), when I was not yet ten years old, I was walking home from school; it was early spring, and the snow was melting and forming puddles. I was splashing through them and came to a spot where, on seeing the Sun reflecting dazzlingly from the water, it suddenly dawned on me that the Sun was a star, and the stars were suns. I already knew this in a certain sense; but it had never been real to me until that moment. Immediately on returning home, I looked up every term I could think of in *Webster's Seventh New Collegiate Dictionary* – Sun, Moon, planet, star – and was 'hooked' on astronomy.

There was a small branch library maybe a half-mile or so from where I lived. The astronomy bookshelf became my haunt; many of the books were by Patrick – including the book that really captivated me more than any other, the lavishly illustrated *Story of Astronomy*. Patrick reeled me in with his inimitable style – he wrote as if conversing with you, and emphasized what could be experienced for oneself. I trawled the heavens for the objects he pointed me to. He was an eccentric and encouraged me – whose Asperger's tendencies were then quite marked – that it was all right to be different; I gained an enormous boost of self-esteem once I made the connection. Like Edwin Hubble in an earlier day, I affected Britishisms for a good long while.

I read Patrick's books with the greatest interest – I couldn't put them down, and, before long, I came to think of Patrick as a close friend (even though I had never met him). I read his *Guide to the Moon*, *How to Make and Use a Telescope* (with H. P. Wilkins), *Guide to the Planets*, *Guide to Mars*, *The Planet Venus*, *The Amateur Astronomer*, etc. In particular, I remember his summons to do 'useful work'.

Following his instructions, I sketched, made estimates of the times that various spots on Jupiter crossed the CM, monitored sunspots, observed variable stars. Was anything I did truly useful? Not, in a Douglas Adams sense, cosmically so; but useful to myself. Patrick was the high priest of amateur astronomy but also as approachable as an old shoe. I stood on the shore of the universe, and stuck my toes in and found that the temperature was 'just right'; before long, I wanted to plunge in.

Many years later, in 1987, when I was in medical school, I was still smitten with a smidgen of hero-worship for the grand old man, and found myself rereading his *Guide to the Moon* (the 1963 edition). He mentioned Wilhelm Beer and Johann von Mädler, and made the point that, 'for some strange reason', *Der Mond* had never been translated into English. I was conversant in German, and devised a strategy of making contact with him. I wrote to him, sending a specimen of what I could do with *Der Mond*. I can still remember the thrill of getting his personal response (in a BBC envelope): 'This is marvellous! All my life I have wanted to read Beer and Mädler. I can't wait to read the rest.'

Eventually, the Beer and Mädler project lapsed – most of it is actually pretty tedious – but it was a calling card for me, and it led to a meeting with Patrick. I visited Selsey in 1993 – I was on my way to Cambridge to personally deliver the manuscript of my biography of E. E. Barnard, but before heading to Cambridge, I went south from Paddington Station (as Patrick advised) to Chichester by train. At the station, Patrick met my wife and me – he was dressed unpretentiously in one of his plaid shirts – in his 1949 car; it was driven by a chauffeur. As soon as we arrived at his home he prepared a chicken dinner, which could not have been more savoury. He was then still in vigorous health, and later, when we were walking, I remember the Moon was low (it was September) and orange. With a sweeping gesture above the hedge as he indicated the Moon to me, he regaled me about his discovery, as an amateur astronomer, of 'Mare Orientale'. It was his proudest moment. By then I was keenly aware (alas!) that he had not actually discovered it; it had been seen by Wilkins (and referred to as 'Mare X') in the 1930s, and even earlier by the German Julius Franz, who had even named it 'Mare Orientale' as far back as 1906, but I hadn't the heart to tell him. Too, he was holding forth about the volcanic theory of the formation of lunar craters (and admitted that even Peter Cattermole had by then given up). These were eccentricities. I didn't care.

During that visit, he presented me with the typescripts of his two-volume translation of Flammarion's *La Planète Mars*, which he had completed around 1980. He wanted me to take them and see if I could get them published. I tried for years, and came very close to doing so in the early 2000s, when Willmann-Bell agreed to do it. In the end, Perry Remaklus backed out. He didn't think there would be sufficient interest. Sadly, it was only after Patrick's death that I was able to interest Springer in the project. It will appear after all – I hope to see it through the press by early 2014 – my only regret being that Patrick did not live to see it.

After my first visit to Selsey in 1993, I corresponded often with Patrick (including from New Zealand, where he sent faxes that electrified the staff of the mental health unit where I was working at the time). I returned to dear old Selsey again in 2004 – I was then *en route* to see the transit of Venus from South Africa, where I had agreed to participate in a conference on barred spirals. I should never have left England; the transit from Selsey was a media event, and Patrick – doing a *Sky at Night* broadcast, and joined by a cast that included Brian May – was in rare form. He had not lost his touch; his amazing ability to improvise on camera, and his impeccable timing, were undiminished.

I saw him once more, in 2006; by then his health was failing, and his speech was slurred. Nevertheless, he was still toiling on. I knew that it was likely that I would not see him again. Alas, I never would.

Farewell, dear Patrick; gone but never forgotten.

V. M. Slipher, Percival Lowell and the Discovery of the High Radial Velocities of the Spiral Nebulae

WILLIAM SHEEHAN

In 1901, after a hiatus of nearly four years, Percival Lowell, astronomer, mathematician, world traveller and businessman (Figure 1), was back on 'Mars Hill', the low mesa just west of the small ranching and lumbering town of Flagstaff, Arizona Territory, where he had built his observatory. After a sensational beginning in 1894, when Lowell and his assistants had kept Mars under scrutiny for months, amassing what seemed to be an impressive body of evidence for the existence of intelligent life on Mars, the observatory had gone through troubled times. Now, in 1901, it faced a critical turning point in its history.

PERCIVAL LOWELL, ASTRONOMER

By any measure, Lowell had followed a rather unorthodox route into astronomy. He was born in Boston in 1855 into a prominent New England family, then at the pinnacle of what passed for American aristocracy. He graduated with honours from Harvard in 1876, and at the commencement he gave an oration on the nebular hypothesis of Laplace. He remained enamoured of the nebular hypothesis for the rest of his life – not in Laplace's original formulation so much as in that of the English philosopher Herbert Spencer, whose system of 'Synthetic Philosophy' tried to explain how everything in the universe, including man, developed from a simple undifferentiated homogeneous state (i.e., nebula) to a complex, differentiated heterogeneity, through a

Figure 1. Percival Lowell, in profile, 1909, when he suggested that V. M. Slipher obtain spectrograms of the 'white' (spiral) nebulae. (Image courtesy of Lowell Observatory.)

principle of evolution. Indeed, Spencer's conceptual framework would fit Lowell snugly for the rest of his life.

After a Grand Tour of Europe with a cousin, travelling as far as Syria, Lowell settled down for several years of business in his grandfather's State Street office, which included managing the textile mills of the city of Lowell, Massachusetts. Until the Civil War, the mills were dependent on a supply of cheap cotton from the slave-tilled fields of the South and were the basis of the family's fortune. In the 1820s, before even so much as a brick for the first textile factory had been laid, immigrant Irish canal cutters had dug canal beds and built granite walls to divert water from the Merrimack River to power the mills; by 1850, six miles of them, operating on two levels, powered 320,000 spindles and almost 10,000 looms – so that canals, which Percival was later to transpose to another planet, were already an important theme in the Lowell household even before he was born.

By the time he was twenty-eight, Lowell had made enough money to live comfortably, and to never have to work another day in his life. Then he shocked his family (especially his father) by quitting the business, breaking off an engagement with an unidentified Brahmin[1] woman (probably a cousin), and after hearing a stimulating talk on Japan at the Lowell Institute given by zoologist Edward S. Morse, took his leave of Boston, which he called 'the most austere society the world has ever known'. He set sail in 1882 on a romantic adventure to the Far East, spending the next decade in travel and literary activity – writing four books of which the most important, *The Soul of the Far East*, was inspired by the broad Spencerian generalizations which Lowell found so appealing. (Here Lowell contrasted Western and Japanese societies, arguing that the latter, for all its simplicity, beauty and fragility, could not survive in competition with the more developed, vigorous, and individualistic West.)

Eventually, the romance and adventure of the Far East faded, and Lowell, with the same abandon with which he had embarked on his Oriental sojourn, switched careers again – this time to astronomy. His imagination had been fired by Camille Flammarion's *La Planète Mars*, which he received as a gift from an aunt for Christmas in 1893. Flammarion offered detailed descriptions of a network of bluish channels (canals) covering the surface of the planet as mapped by the Italian astronomer Giovanni Schiaparelli. As soon as he read Flammarion's book, Lowell 'fell under the spell of these non-existent phenomena and spent the rest of his career in increasingly elaborate attempts to map and interpret "these lines [that] run for thousands of miles in an unswerving direction, as far relatively as from London to Bombay, and as far actually as from Boston to San Francisco".'[2]

With the help of Harvard astronomer (and sometime Beacon Hill neighbour) William Henry Pickering, just back from Mars-observing adventures in the Andes of Peru, Lowell borrowed two telescopes, a 12-inch Clark refractor from Harvard and an 18-inch refractor whose lens had been fashioned by Pittsburgh optician John Brashear. He then sent Pickering's assistant Andrew E. Douglass to the Arizona Territory, where Pickering expected atmosheric conditions to be of nearly Andean quality for planetary observations. Before Douglass could survey more than a few sites (and just as he was about to head to Tucson), Lowell's impatience to get underway led to the perhaps overly hasty selection of Flagstaff. In its favour was the fact that it was on a railroad line. Pickering sent in advance by rail a prefabricated dome built to his specification. It was, however, not only the dome that was prefabricated. So were Lowell's views about Mars. In a talk to the Boston Scientific Society on 22 May 1894, Lowell stated the purpose, and expected findings, of his expedition: 'if the nebular hypothesis is correct, and there is good reason at present for believing in its general truth, then to develop life more or less distinctly resembling our own must be the destiny of every member of the solar family which is not prevented by purely physical conditions, size and so forth, from doing so.'

As for Schiaparelli's canals, Lowell stated that 'the most self-evident explanation from the markings themselves is probably the true one: namely, that in them we are looking upon the result of the work of some sort of intelligent beings . . . the amazing blue network on Mars hints that one planet besides our own is actually inhabited now.'

For Lowell, as historian Robert W. Smith has quipped, 'it was not just nebula to man but nebula to Martian'.[3]

Lowell entered astronomy just as the field was undergoing dramatic transformations. He was a well-educated generalist in an era of increasing specialization in the sciences. At the very moment he founded his observatory to study Mars by peering at it through his telescopes and rendering its appearance in sketches on paper, as astronomers had done going back to Galileo, the initiative had already passed to astrophysicists, who were combining the forces of spectroscopy and photography to advance the study of stars and nebulae. There were obvious reasons for the differences in technique. The photographic plate is an integrating detector; it builds up a cumulative impression of faint objects such as stars and nebulae. The human eye, on the other hand, is a differentiating detector. While lacking the ability to see faint objects, it is quick, and well-equipped for analyzing objects in motion.

A planet, because of the vicissitudes of seeing, has more in common with a motion picture than a still-life. When we look at a planet, say Mars, through the telescope, what we see is a staccato of fixed images, each immediately erased by the next one. A trick of the brain called flicker-fusion takes these static images and fuses them so that they appear to be a seamless continuum, which is what makes the illusion of 'motion pictures' so convincing. The problem in planetary astronomy is not just to detect motion, however, for one also wants to 'stop action', i.e., freeze the occasional high-definition frame from the series of the blurry ones. Unfortunately, the eye-brain system isn't designed to do that.

Astronomers in the era of the visual observations of planets were like the watchers of trotting and galloping horses in the pre-Eadweard Muybridge era. They had photography, but the photographic plate required an appreciable time – from 0.5 to 5 seconds and longer – just to 'see' the planet. This meant that detail in photographs of Mars was much more blurred than what the visual observer could make out. (Not until the late 1980s when CCD imaging techniques became available did the 'camera' finally catch up with and surpass the eye.) Also, since a planetary observation was made in private 'peepshow' fashion, rather than in a public format like a physics experiment, the testimony of different observers conflicted; planetary observations were 'subjective' in a way that photographs or spectrograms were not, and consensus could only be obtained by having different observers publish their drawings and negotiate over what they saw in the eyepiece. Eventually a reaction against planetary astronomy would take place, largely inspired by the antipathy of professional astronomers to what they thought were the unsound and amateurish methods of Percival Lowell.[4]

The observing campaign of his first season at Flagstaff was not even over before Lowell began blitzing the media, publishing his results in multiple journals all at once. A series of lectures given in Boston's Huntington Hall in February 1895 drew capacity audiences, and added to Lowell's celebrity. He must have made a strong impression. 'He was of medium height, slim and handsome, with an athletic build and an intense expression,' writes his biographer David Strauss. 'His erect bearing and fastidious dress contributed to a commanding presence.'[5] Lowell's vision of Mars – one that has enthralled and inspired humans ever since – was finally presented as a book, *Mars*, largely based on his articles and lectures; published in December 1895, it added fuel to the fire of late-nineteenth-century 'Mars fever' (Figure 2).

After Mars retreated out of range of surveillance in 1894 (Lowell's last observations were made in November, though Douglass continued to observe the planet into the following spring), the Brashear telescope returned to Pittsburgh. As a permanent replacement, Lowell ordered a 24-inch refractor from the Clark firm of Cambridgeport, Massachusetts. It was finished on schedule, and with the lens in tow, Lowell, together with Alvan G. Clark, the last surviving member of the Clark firm and responsible for making the lens, Clark's daughter, and Lowell's secretary, Wrexie Leonard, arrived at the Flagstaff train station (which still exists) on 22 July 1896. The lens was soon installed and

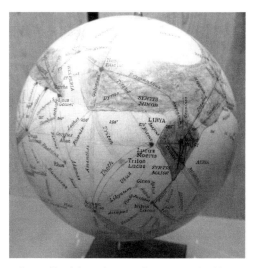

Figure 2. One of Lowell's globes of Mars, showing canals. (Photograph by William Sheehan, 2013.)

ready for testing. The iconic 24-inch Alvan Clark refractor (often nowadays referred to simply as the Clark telescope) was the first permanent telescope at Lowell Observatory (Figure 3). At this time, Lowell (and Douglass) expected that the Flagstaff observatory would be only temporary. They envisaged the observatory as a peregrinating affair, moving across latitudes and from point to point on the Earth's surface at successive oppositions of Mars so as always to enjoy the best possible locality and atmospheric conditions. In line with this philosophy, the Clark refractor, as soon as it had been checked out, was shipped to Tacubaya, outside Mexico City, for the 1 December opposition of Mars. Douglass served as frontman, arriving in Mexico in November, with Lowell himself arriving only in late December, well after the Martian opposition.

Miss Leonard joined the expedition, as did several new assistants, of whom the most notable was T. J. J. See, a Berlin-trained PhD who was on leave from the University of Chicago. See was then at the height of his fame as an expert on double stars. In addition, there were two young college grads, Daniel Drew and Wilbur A. Cogshall. See's inclusion indicates that, in addition to studying the objects of the Solar System, Lowell had decided to expand the observatory's programme of

Figure 3. The dome of the 24-inch Clark refractor at Lowell Observatory. The telescope was used both to observe the 'canals' of Mars and the 'hub and spokes' markings on Venus, and to obtain spectrograms of spiral nebulae. (Photograph by William Sheehan, 2013.)

research to stellar studies; but even before the telescope had moved to Mexico, See announced that on 30–31 August 1896 he had rediscovered the notoriously difficult 'companion' of Sirius, missing since 1890 in the glare of Sirius itself. It was not observed by other astronomers until November 1896, when it was seen at Lick Observatory, but in a different position to where See had made it out. The Lick director, E. S. Holden, citing a careful series of observations by double-star specialist Robert G. Aitken, concluded that, 'there is no object in the place reported by the astronomers of the Lowell Observatory'.[6]

STUDIES OF VENUS . . . AND CONTROVERSY

But it was Percival Lowell himself who provided the best news copy from the 1896–97 observing campaign. Ten days before See 'rediscovered' the companion of Sirius, Lowell (often in the company of Miss Leonard) began a study of the inner planets, Mercury and Venus. On Mercury, he made out linear details, which provided evidence supporting Schiaparelli's 1889 deduction that, as expected from the theory of tidal friction, Mercury rotated in the same period as it revolved about the Sun. More controversially, he supported Schiaparelli's conclusion that the same held for Venus – usually a notoriously bland object in the telescope. Lowell made out markings of a decided nature, and quite unlike those seen anywhere else: 'In the matter of contour, perfectly defined throughout, their edge being well marked … a large number of them … radiate like spokes from a certain center.'[7] In contrast to his observations of Mars (if not his deductions from them), Lowell's Venus markings were deeply disturbing to astronomers. Even before their existence was agreed, Lowell was going against the consensus that the Earth's sister-planet was shrouded in clouds, and instead claimed that his spoke-like markings had the appearance of 'ground and rock', which showed that its atmosphere, while extensive, was transparent. Their deadpan stare was what had led him to support the isosynchronous rotation – the rotation period was equal, he claimed, to the period of revolution of 225 days. One hemisphere was forever sun-lit, the other forever in night. He even went so far as to explain that the hub and spoke pattern was being produced by the 'funnel-like indraught of air from the dark side to the bright and then an umbrella-like return of it'. This, Lowell added, would 'necessarily' lead to the transport of all the water to the night side, where it would remain forever as ice.

The matter of Venus's rotation would not finally be settled until the 1960s, but in the 1890s, consensus remained elusive, and, opposing Lowell's endorsement of Schiaparelli's result, several other astronomers argued for a short Earthlike period of around twenty-four hours. From Lowell's point of view, a considerable advantage of the long period was its adaptability to his ready-made Spencerian frame of planetary evolution. Succumbing to relentless tidal friction from the Sun, the inner planets, Mercury and Venus, were supposed to have become 'bleached bones of worlds', 'planet corpses, circling unchanging, except for libration, around the Sun' (Percival Lowell, *Evolution of Worlds*, The Macmillan Company, New York, 1909). Though the leading authority of the theory of tidal friction, George Howard Darwin, giving the Lowell Institute Lectures in 1897, endorsed the result,[8] astronomers who had actually studied Venus through a telescope were openly hostile. Captain William Noble, first president of the British Astronomical Association, said that Lowell's map of Venus 'looks to me suspiciously like Mars. I do not know whether Mr Lowell has been looking at Mars until he has got Mars on the brain, and by some transference ... ascribed the markings to Venus.' His response was typical. The most celebrated observer of the day, E. E. Barnard of the Yerkes Observatory, using a 12-inch refractor to study the planet at George Ellery Hale's private Kenwood Observatory during the summer of 1897, wrote in his observing book: 'Venus – no markings seen – though there were the usual suggestions of large dusky regions. It seems to be fully steady enough to have seen Lowell's narrow markings.' Barnard, alas, never would succeed in making them out.

Lowell was evidently devastated by the ferocity of these criticisms. Before he could return to Flagstaff for another season of observing, he suffered a nervous breakdown that would sideline him, astronomically, for the next four years. A prolonged rest at his father's house in Brookline was recommended, and was tried for a month before Lowell, deciding the cure was worse than the disease, abandoned it, and went to Bermuda. He continued his convalescence in Virginia, Maine, New York, and – by early 1900 – on the French Riviera, where he enjoyed long talks with a fellow neurasthenic, the Harvard psychologist William James.

Lowell's illness meant the abandonment of the idea of a peregrinating observatory. For better or worse, the Lowell Observatory would remain in Flagstaff – even though evidence was accumulating that it did not quite enjoy the superiority of seeing that had been claimed. Douglass, whose first visit to the site had taken place in the spring, had failed to foresee that the winters at 7,000 feet elevation could be severe and see heavy snowfall. Though travel-brochure-style claims for the exceptional seeing at Flagstaff were often made by Lowell and his associates (and especially by See), Douglass himself later had to refute some of them:

> Speaking of our sky he [T. J. J. See] says it 'is commonly spoken of by us in daily conversation as Arizona blue,' a thing we have never mentioned and which was plainly gotten up for this article ... He says: 'We almost never have a Northeast wind here': one of the hardest winds ever experienced in this country was from the Northeast ... No wind records have ever been kept before other than for a very short time at this place or anywhere in this elevated region (short of Prescott, and I am doubtful of that) and there are heavy winds in this region that they never feel in Phoenix.[9]

These comments were made in a private letter from Douglass to the Boston investment banker William Lowell Putnam II, Lowell's brother-in-law, who took over administrative supervision of the observatory's affairs during Lowell's absence. Needless to say, they were kept private within the observatory's close circle. Officially, the superiority of Flagstaff's seeing was never to be called into question, and, as late as 1908, in his book *Mars as the Abode of Life* (The Macmillan Company, New York), Lowell was still maintaining: 'The object of the founding of the observatory at Flagstaff was the study of the planets ... The site chosen for the purpose enables it to prosecute this study to more advantage than is possible at any other observatory at present.'

Meanwhile, what might be called the 'T. J. J. See affair' was coming to a head. See proved to be egotistical and self-serving – among other things, he wrote and published grandiose reviews of his own work in which he described himself as a 'worthy successor of the Herschels' – while his behaviour towards his colleagues was reprehensible (and apparently included sexual improprieties). Nor, even apart from the fiasco over the companion of Sirius, did his double star measures inspire confidence. Cogshall informed Putnam, 'Many times he said, "That star looks double – certainly elongated – Look and see such a direction," I would look and to save my life I could see that it wasn't any longer one way than another, but he would say 'I am sure of it – strange you don't see it.'" One by one the assistants departed, and when, finally, in the fall of 1898, Putnam dismissed See, Douglass alone was left to carry on the observatory's work. The See affair not only demoralized Lowell's staff, it damaged the observatory's credibility at a time when it was already coming under attack, and for a brief time had the result of souring Lowell against hiring additional assistants.

Continuing his convalescence, Lowell generally avoided the stresses of astronomy, but in spite of the effect on his nerves, he puttered away, whenever he could, at a memoir on Venus for the American Academy of Arts and Sciences. Wrexie Leonard, Lowell's secretary, warned Douglass in June 1899: 'Do not allow yourself to break down. Mr Lowell's condition is a bad example. I can see that he is better but not well yet.' When Douglass himself visited Lowell in Boston near the end of 1899, he found, as he wrote to Daniel Drew, that Lowell 'wants to work away on the observations of Venus ... He is not working very hard but is nervous enough to have it worry him if all the material is not at hand.' Douglass, meanwhile, had begun to entertain serious doubts of the reality of some planetary markings reported at Flagstaff, especially those on Venus, and initiated a series of experiments in which artificial planet disks were observed through the telescope. The results were disturbing enough for Lowell to order their discontinuation on the grounds that they cast doubt on some of the observatory's publications.

Unable to leave the matter alone, Lowell (with Miss Leonard) at the end of 1899 began a series of observations of Venus with the 7-inch Merz refractor at Amherst Observatory, where David Peck Todd, an old friend, was director (Figure 4).

Figure 4. Amherst Observatory, whose 7-inch refractor was used by Percival Lowell and Miss Leonard to observe Venus in 1899–1900. Unfortunately, the telescope no longer exists; the lens was later broken by a ham-handed graduate student. (Photograph by William Sheehan.)

Though Mars came to opposition in December, Lowell does not seem to have paid any attention to it, but he and Miss Leonard made numerous drawings of Venus, with the 7-inch diaphragmed usually to an aperture of 4 inches (often with the image being viewed through a yellow glass). Despite the fact that Amherst was at sea-level rather than at 7,000 feet elevation like Flagstaff, the seeing seems to have been good enough, since the hub-and-spoke markings were in evidence once again (Figure 5).

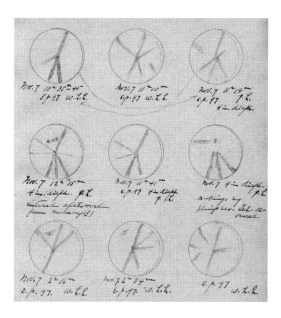

Figure 5. The spoke and hub system of Venus, as observed by Percival Lowell at Amherst. (Image courtesy of Lowell Observatory.)

The Amherst observations continued into early 1900. Meanwhile, Lowell's father Augustus, with whom Percival had always had a strained relationship, had died. Whether coincidence or not, Lowell's health now began decisively to improve! Henceforth, he was not quite as sensitive to criticism, and even changed his mind about the artificial planet work; he advised Douglass to carry on, making specific reference to the markings on Venus whose vindication had now become Lowell's first priority.

THE BRASHEAR SPECTROGRAPH

Just then, a devastating publication dropped into Lowell's in-box. Aristarch Belopolsky, a highly esteemed Russian astronomer at the Pulkova Observatory, had in April 1900 announced a spectrographic measure of Venus's rotation, giving it as twenty-four hours. 'Belopolsky's nut is a hard one to crack,' Lowell later quipped, and it led to a fateful decision, one that was eventually to lead to the very frontiers of cosmology. Realizing that the testimony of one spectroscope could only be answered by the testimony of another, and determined to spare no expense in defending his Venus work, Lowell, in December 1900, ordered (on Douglass's recommendation) a powerful spectrograph from John A. Brashear whose purpose was, he wrote, nothing less than 'to test spectrographically the rotation period of Venus' (Figure 6).

Figure 6. Percival Lowell and the Brashear spectrograph, early 1900s. (Image courtesy of William Sheehan collection.)

In making this commitment, Lowell signalled that he was planning to return full-time to astronomy. At the same time, he made a rather gutsy decision, since no one at the observatory at the time knew how to use such an instrument.

Indeed, the only astronomer in Flagstaff, after See's dismissal, was Douglass, who, after four years, had developed a strong independent streak; the artificial planet observations had led him to conclude that much of the surface detail reported on planets was fictitious. Shortly before Lowell's return (at the end of March 1901) and resumption of personal control of his institution, Douglass confided to his former mentor W. H. Pickering: 'It appears to me that Mr Lowell has a strong literary instinct and no scientific instinct.' He alluded to Lowell's 'strong personality, consisting chiefly of immensely strong convictions'. And then – making what would prove to be a fatal mistake – he continued in the same vein in a long letter to Lowell's cousin, Putnam:

> His work is not credited among astronomers because he devotes his energy to hunting up a few facts in support of some speculation instead of perseveringly hunting innumerable facts and then limiting himself to publishing the unavoidable conclusions, as all scientists of good standing do, in whatever line of work they may be engaged … I fear it will not be possible to turn him into a scientific man.

Douglass had sent these comments to Putnam 'in confidence'. Putnam seems to have kept the contents to himself until July 1901. Naturally, though, he felt obliged to share them with his brother-in law. His brother-in-law had a temper, and it was especially apt to flare up at perceived deficiencies in the loyalty or efficiency of hired help. Every inch an aristocrat, he had grown up surrounded by servants who were meant to glide about, providing service efficiently but without being visible themselves. In a fit of rage, he once threw a butler down the stairs of his Beacon Hill residence, and followed up by throwing the poor man's trunk after him! Though Douglass himself was no mere butler – he was descended from a wealthy and distinguished New England family and a professionally trained astronomer – Lowell would not tolerate such 'arrogant independence' in any employee. Douglass was fired immediately, without explanation. (For a time, Douglass was stuck in Flagstaff without a job; eventually, he did well, founding the science of dendochronology as well as the Steward Observatory at the University of Arizona in Tucson, where the seeing proved to be better even than that at Flagstaff!)

V. M. SLIPHER ARRIVES AT FLAGSTAFF

For a time, Lowell was without assistant astronomers, and he seems to have considered remaining so – enjoying a kind of solipsistic bliss in his Flagstaff redoubt. Fortunately, Wilbur A. Cogshall, one of the assistants who had left during the See affair and who was now director of Indiana University's Kirkwood Observatory, reminded Lowell of an earlier offer he had made to hire on a temporary basis a young Indiana graduate in astronomy and mechanics, Vesto Melvin Slipher – 'V. M.', as he was always known (Figure 7). Lowell replied to Cogshall: 'I shall be happy to have him come when he is ready. I have decided, however, that I shall not want another permanent assistant and take him only because I promised to do so; and for the term suggested. What it was escapes my memory. If, owing to this decision, he prefers not to come, let him please himself.' Apparently, Lowell never did recall what the term suggested was; Slipher arrived on Mars Hill that August, and would remain employed at the observatory until his retirement in 1954.

Figure 7. V. M. Slipher and family, on the porch of their house at Lowell Observatory. (Image courtesy of Lowell Observatory.)

When Slipher arrived, he found Lowell pointing his telescope at Venus, then blazing forth in the evening sky on the way to an evening elongation. Though it seems that Lowell again recovered the hub-and-spoke system – for some reason, his observing logbook for 1901 seems to have gone missing – he did not publish anything specifically about Venus that year. But clearly, the planet was still nagging at him, for just after Slipher's arrival, Lowell, now back in Boston, advised his new assistant, 'on the need for short exposures in photographing Venus', adding that experience had taught him that 'the markings grew more and more difficult as the phase increased'. In the last part of September 1901, the Brashear spectrograph arrived on schedule. At once, Lowell commanded his assistant to 'get the spectroscope [sic.] on and ... work as soon as you can. Perhaps – and I trust this may be the case – you have already done so.' To which he added, as an after-thought, 'How fare the squashes?' (Lowell was ever inordinately proud of his garden.)

Lowell's query about the squashes was not to be the last in that line. He appears in this correspondence as a fastidious micromanager who did not distinguish among specific roles for those he employed. Whenever he needed something, he turned to the nearest underling, no matter what the task or the employee's title, skills or experience, and never considered taking the time to match the employee to the task at hand. He often asked his secretary Miss Leonard to convey his displeasure over seemingly minor problems, like receiving the wrong cigars or a soup ladle with the wrong length of a handle; while at other times she was whisked over to take her place at the eyepiece to verify whatever planetary markings he was studying at the time (and it is notable that her drawings of Venus, alone among those of his assis-tants, capture with the same boldness and assurance the characteristic form of his hub-and-spoke system). In the same way, Slipher was not only expected to look after the squashes, but he was also (especially in the early years of his employment) asked to do some very non-astronomer tasks – such as measuring and creating drawings of all the new rooms in Lowell's sprawling residence – the 'Baronial Mansion' – or even purchasing a cow for the observatory (something which the native of Mulberry, Indiana, evidently managed to his employer's sat-isfaction). Some of Lowell's requests seem almost humorously trite; for instance, in one message, Lowell writes to Slipher from Chicago, 'Will you kindly see if shredded wheat biscuits are to be got at Flagstaff? If not please wire me at the Auditorium Annex [now the Congress Plaza Hotel].'

In similar fashion, by assigning Slipher the task of getting the spec-trograph in perfect running order, Lowell seems to have disregarded the fact that Slipher's degree in astronomy and mechanics had pro-vided no specific training in the use of such an instrument. (What he would have done with the spectrograph had he not decided to hire a new assistant, he seems not to have considered.) Though Slipher managed to 'get the spectroscope on' the 24-inch Clark refractor, within two weeks of Lowell's letter his first attempts to use it were, hardly surprisingly, ham-handed. A rather disgusted Lowell wrote to him that not only did Slipher's spectrograms of Jupiter, with a rapid rotation of ten hours, show the Doppler-shifted lines of a body in rotation, but so did those of the star Capella and Venus (obviously not the desired result!). Lowell then consulted with James McDowell at the Brashear firm, who suggested that Slipher's disappointing results were merely due to 'lack of adjustment'.

When, soon afterwards, Slipher suggested, not unreasonably, paying a visit to W. W. Campbell at the Lick Observatory, who was a leading authority in this line of work and busy measuring the radial velocities of stars with a Brashear spectrograph similar to the one Slipher was charged with putting into working order, Lowell hit the roof. Campbell, it turned out, had been one of Lowell's fiercest and most unrelenting critics (in a review of *Mars*, he had rather snidely said, 'Mr Lowell went direct from the lecture hall to his observatory, and how well his observations established his pre-observational views is to be read in this book.').[10] Lowell personalized such things, and so, forbidding Slipher to have contact with Campbell, the assistant had no choice but to soldier on, making do out of his own resources.

Fortunately, Slipher had grown up on a farm, and had great practical sense. His genius was in his hands. By mid-summer 1902, he had already come far and was producing spectrograms of Jupiter and Saturn that Lowell, having been appointed nonresident professor of astronomy at the Massachusetts Institute of Technology, was bragging up to its president Henry S. Pritchett as 'the first fruits of the new spectroscope, made by Brashear, in the hands of V. M. Slipher'. And Lowell added that Mr Brashear considered the spectroscope '"the finest and best instrument we have ever made" under the date of 21 September 1901. It was made so that I might be sure of the best possible instrument in the matter of Venus's rotation period.'

In 1902, Lowell seems to have been experiencing serious doubts about the spoke observations – he even did what was (for him) almost unprecedented in publishing a brief retraction in the German journal *Astronomische Nachrichten*, and when, in December 1902, he delivered a series of lectures on the Solar System at MIT, later published in book form, he discussed Mercury, Mars, Saturn and Its System, and Jupiter and Its Comets; Venus is noteworthy only by its absence.

SUCCESS WITH VENUS

But just as Lowell's confidence was beginning to fail, Slipher came through for him. By March 1903, Slipher had spectrograms of Venus that served as a 'nutcracker' to break the hard sentence of Belopolsky. Comparing the tilt of the lines at opposite sides of the visible disk of the planet, Slipher found practically a null value for the rotation effects; in his published report, he modestly claimed nothing more than evidence of a 'slow' rotation. But Lowell, committing a logical fallacy in the process, went further. In an article in the *Astronomische Nachrichten* reprinted in *Popular Astronomy*, he wrote, 'From the efficiency of the instrument and the unbiased manner in which the measurements were made we may, I think, conclude from the size of the probable error that the evidence of the spectroscope is against rotation of short duration and that so far as its measure of precision permits the investigation confirms a rotation period of 225 days.' To Pritchett at MIT he went even further. Slipher's result, he affirmed, 'which was got without any bias from me and with every precaution of his own to prevent unconscious bias on his part and to eliminate systematic errors, is completely confirmatory of Schiaparelli's period and of my visual work here in 1896–97 – the planet undoubtedly rotates in the time it revolves.'

There was never again any doubt in Lowell's mind about the rotation of Venus; nor was there about Earth's sister planet's place in his Spencerian scheme of planetary evolution. Indeed, he recovered the spoke-like markings again in 1903, 1910 and 1914. In October 1914, at the very moment that the bloody stand-off at Ypres was beginning in Flanders, he was photographed in the Clark dome with his bald pate covered with a newsboy cap turned back to front, peering through the Clark telescope in what has become one of the iconic images of astronomy (Figure 8). As time would tell, however, Slipher's spectrograms were less conclusive than Lowell thought; the spectrographic analysis of Venus's clouds was still failing to yield a specific result as late as the 1960s. Moreover, no entirely satisfactory explanation has ever been given for Lowell's spoke-like markings, though it may be significant

Figure 8. Percival Lowell observing Venus with the 24-inch Clark; photographed by Phillip Fox in October 1914. (Image courtesy of Lowell Observatory.)

that the radial pattern looks suspiciously like the pattern of vessels in the retina of the human eye![11]

Slipher's apparent conquest of Venus's rotation period with the spectrograph convinced Lowell that his assistant was indispensable, and soon Lowell charged him with other investigations that would support his programme of planetary studies, including the spectrographic confirmation of water vapour in the atmosphere of Mars. Though his results put him at odds with Lick Observatory astronomer W. W. Campbell, Slipher believed he had succeeded by 1909. And it was in pursuit of another of Lowell's planetological prizes that Slipher took up the problem which was to bring him immortal fame: that of getting spectrograms of the spiral nebulae.

Despite his long-standing allegiance to the nebular hypothesis, by 1905, Lowell had absorbed the *au courant* Chamberlin-Moulton hypothesis of the Solar System's formation, according to which, encounters among stars (many of them spent suns, dark stars roaming like 'tramps' through space, in Lowell's own vivid phrase) might pull filaments of gaseous material and debris from one of them to form a spiral nebula. The gases would subsequently condense into small particles – 'planetesimals' – which would then, by a process of accretion, form satellites and planets.

The Chamberlin-Moulton hypothesis challenged Lowell's Spencerian conviction of the inevitable advance of a nebula to planets in different stages of life and, during at least part of their life cycle, to life-forms, including intelligent ones, to planets in mid-career, like the Earth and Mars. Instead, it envisaged the Solar System beginning with a dramatic haphazard event. Not one to wed himself to strict consistency, Lowell, the literary man, sensed the inherent drama of the new scenario. He barely hinted at it when, a year after Chamberlin and Moulton published their hypothesis, he gave the Lowell Institute lectures in 1906 (published as *Mars as the Abode of Life*, he developed the idea fully in another series of MIT lectures given in February and March 1909, which was published as *The Evolution of Worlds*). Here, Lowell imagined a massive and ominous dark star approaching a sun-like star, raising gigantic tides, tearing it to pieces, and spreading the debris in antipodal directions along the line of their relative approach. And this, he claimed, was precisely what was attested to in the spiral nebulae:

> The form of the spiral nebulae proclaims their motion, but one of its particular features discloses more. For it implies the past cause which set this motion going. A distinctive detail of these spirals, which so far as we know is shared by all of them, is the two arms which leave the center from diametrically opposite sides. This indicates that the outward driving force acted only in two places, the one the antipodes of the other. Now what kind of force is capable of this peculiar effect? If we think of the matter we shall realize that tidal action would produce just this result ...[12]

OBTAINING SPECTRA OF THE SPIRAL NEBULAE

Keen to shore up his case, Lowell, in January and February 1909, suggested to V. M. that if the spiral nebulae were indeed incipient solar systems as he believed, they should show spectrographic similarities to solar system objects. With some of the same nonchalance with which he had requested his assistant to mind his squash or chase down shredded wheat for the breakfast table, he wrote from Boston on 8 February:

'I would like to have you take with your red sensitive plates the spectrum of a white nebula [i.e., a spiral] – preferably one that has marked centers of condensation.' At the bottom of the page as a gloss on 'condensation' he added further criteria: that the nebula should have a continuous spectrum and that Slipher should obtain the spectrum in parts. One gathers that he expected that the inner part of the nebula should show a sun-like spectrum while in the outer part the spectrum should show dark bands like those Slipher had observed in the spectra of the giant planets Jupiter, Saturn, Uranus and Neptune.

Though the wish might be father to the thought, it was not to its execution. Following up these terse hints, Slipher set to work. However, the technical problem that had been posed was exceedingly difficult, because of the extreme faintness of the nebulae. Previous investigations had been inconclusive. So far, the most ambitious (and successful) attempt to obtain spectrograms of the spiral nebulae had been made by E. A. Fath, a graduate student at Lick Observatory, with whom Slipher was in regular correspondence. Fath was doing his PhD dissertation on the topic, and designed and built a nebular spectrograph expressly for the purpose, which he attached to the 36-inch Crossley reflector on Mt Hamilton. In 1908, he obtained several spectrograms of spirals showing solar-type absorption lines, suggesting they consisted of stars. But, confusingly, he also obtained two spectrograms showing bright lines like those in the gaseous nebulae. Not having any reliable distances to the spirals (he was thrown off by a recent parallax measure by a Swedish astronomer, Bohlin, which suggested that the Andromeda Nebula was only nineteen light years away, obviously a gross error!), and receiving little encouragement from his conservative director W. W. Campbell, Fath did not pursue this investigation to any conclusion. In 1909, he left Lick to work as a fellow at Mt Wilson, and then, three years later, abandoned research altogether. (He spent most of his long career as a teacher at his *alma mater*, Carleton College in Northfield, Minnesota.)

The Crossley reflector, with its low ratio of focal-length to aperture, seemed to Slipher a more satisfactory instrument for such work than the 24-inch Clark. But Slipher continued to study the situation, and sought the advice of other astronomers. Fath in particular was free with advice. Together with the Lowell Observatory's machinist Stanley Sykes, Slipher incorporated what he learned into modifications of the Brashear spectrograph. He replaced the three-prism arrangement with a single prism, and realized (as had already been pointed out by James

E. Keeler of the Lick Observatory) that the focus-to-aperture ratio was not as important as he had thought and that what was more important was the speed of the camera lens. By the fall of 1912, Slipher was using the Lowell Observatory's modified Brashear spectrograph that was two hundred times faster than the three-prism version he had used to obtain the spectrograms of Venus in 1903. On 17 September 1912, he obtained a first spectrogram of Andromeda (Figure 9); it showed some detail. It made him hope that he might do what had never been done for a spiral nebula – obtain a radial velocity. He followed up with additional spectrograms of the object on 15–16 November and 3–4 December. Finally, on 28 December 1912, Slipher told Lowell that he hoped to get 'one good, carefully made spectrogram' of the Andromeda nebula. On the following night, he began an exposure on a plate that would run over three nights and into the pre-dawn hours of 1 January 1913 (Figure 10). On 2 January, he briefly perused the plate, and confided to Lowell a preliminary result: 'I feel safe to say here that the velocity bids fair to come out unusually high.'

Figure 9. M31, the Great Spiral in Andromeda. CCD image with a Ritchey-Chretien 10-inch telescope by William Sheehan.

With that understated comment, Slipher was announcing what would prove to be the germ of one of the most momentous findings in

Figure 10. V. M. Slipher, observing nebulae with the Brashear spectrograph. (Image courtesy of Lowell Observatory.)

astronomical history. Characteristically, he was at first thrown into a state of perplexity. Measuring in all four spectrograms the displacement of the nebular lines towards the violet with reference to such lines as those in the iron and vanadium comparison spectrum, he wrote to Fath, he found that the nebula was moving with a radial velocity three times that of any other object in the universe that had been measured thus far! For a moment, he was inclined to doubt whether the Doppler shift could be relied on as a valid indicator of radial velocity at all. He mulled his plates two more weeks until, on 3 February 1913, he announced to Lowell that the Andromeda Nebula was approaching the Earth at the then unheard-of speed of 300 kilometres per second. Lowell, whose mental flexibility and ability to adapt his views has perhaps been underestimated based on his earlier Mars and Venus work, replied: 'It looks as if you had made a great discovery. Try some other spiral nebulae for confirmation.'

HIGH VELOCITIES OF RECESSION

Now spring was approaching; the great nebulae of Virgo were coming into view. In April 1913, Slipher obtained spectrograms of NGC 4594, the dark-laned edge-on spiral sometimes known as the 'Sombrero' nebula (Figure 11). In contrast to the Andromeda nebula, which was approaching the Earth, NGC 4594 was rushing away at a fantastic speed of 1,000 kilometres per second. In August 1914, Slipher presented his results to the American Astronomical Society at its meeting in Evanston, Illinois (Figure 12). (Among those in the audience was a soon-to-be graduate student, Edwin P. Hubble.) Something unprecedented happened; he received a standing ovation (something not repeated again until W. W. Morgan announced his demonstration of the spiral-arm structure of the Milky Way in 1951). Slipher's paper, published during the next year, describes spectrograms giving radial velocities of fifteen spirals; all but two were receding at speeds of up to 1,100 kilometres per second, a circumstance which indicated to Slipher that there was 'a general fleeing from us or the Milky Way'. Though only a partial glimpse, these words contain the first hint of the expanding universe.

Figure 11. NGC 4594 (M104), whose large redshift astonished V. M. Slipher when he first discovered it in April 1913. CCD image with a Ritchey-Chretien 10-inch telescope by William Sheehan.

Figure 12. AAS meeting at Evanston, Illinois, August 1914. Slipher stands in the second row from the rear, second from left; E. A. Fath stands fifth from the right, wearing a hat, Edwin Hubble stands third from the right. At the centre of the picture, holding a book, is Harvard Observatory director E. C. Pickering. One would not guess from this group photograph that Slipher was the star of the meeting. (Photograph courtesy of Dearborn Observatory.)

Lowell himself seems to have been among the first to grasp the fact that Slipher's results were not consistent with the view that the spiral nebulae were solar systems in formation. Instead, he said, the high velocities of recession meant that the spiral nebulae must be systems outside the Solar System; indeed, 'island universes'.[13]

Unfortunately, Lowell did not have long to live, and after his sudden death (of a massive intracerebral haemorrhage) in November 1916, Slipher was left to continue his investigations without the stimulus and guidance of his director. In a 1917 paper, he expressed agreement with Lowell's surmise that the high radial velocities of the spirals strongly supported the view that 'the spiral nebulae are stellar systems seen at great distances'. But this was the end of Slipher's productive period. His close symbiotic relationship with Lowell had been highly productive, with each man contributing something that the other lacked.

Historian Joseph Tenn has said of Slipher, 'He needed Lowell to guide him, and Lowell's early death left him unprepared to face the future. Although a skilled spectroscopist, he lacked the imagination to innovate.'[14]

John S. Hall, a later Lowell director, in his obituary of V. M. in *Sky & Telescope*,[15] wrote: 'Slipher and Lowell had complementary temperaments. The latter was brilliant, enthusiastic, and a driving personality … Slipher, on the other hand, was deliberate, fastidious, patient, and showed a high order of technical knowledge.'

If Lowell had lived, it is possible that Slipher would have gone on to capitalize on his early results. In any case, by the time Lowell died, Slipher's spectrograms, which had been obtained to buttress Lowell's Venus observations and to confirm his belief that the spirals were nearby solar systems in formation, had led the Observatory far from its eccentric frontier beginnings. Much as Lowell and Slipher between them had accomplished, it is ironic that the discovery of the velocity-distance relationship – the graph on which the expansion of the universe was to be predicated – was to be the achievement of another, who combined in one person Lowell's driving personality and Slipher's technical knowledge. With a larger and better telescope, Edwin Hubble would see further than either. But he did so only by standing on the shoulders of giants.

FURTHER READING

Notes

1. A member of Boston's traditional upper class, families descended from the early settlers of the Plymouth and Massachusetts Bay colonies.
2. S. J. Gould, 'War of the Worldviews', *Natural History*, 12/1996–1/1997, pp. 22–3.
3. R. W. Smith, *The Road to Radial Velocities: V. M. Slipher and Mastery of the Spectrograph* (ASP Conference Series, 2013).
4. N. J. Woolf, 'The Impact of Space Studies on Astronomy', in: William E. Frye, ed., *Impact of Space Exploration on Society* (Tarzana, California: American Astronautical Society, 1966), pp. 180–1.
5. David Strauss, *Percival Lowell: The Culture and Science of a Boston Brahmin*, (Harvard University Press, Cambridge, Massachusetts, 2001).

6. William Graves Hoyt, *Lowell and Mars* (Tucson, Arizona: University of Arizona Press, 1976), p. 106.

7. P. Lowell, 'Detection of Venus's rotation period and fundamental physical properties of the planet's surface', *Popular Astronomy*, Vol. 4 (1896), pp. 281–5. See also: 'Determination of the rotation period and surface character of the planet Venus', *Monthly Notices of the Royal Astronomical Society*, Vol. 57 (1897), pp. 148–9; 'The rotation period of Venus', *Astronomische Nachrichten*, No. 3406 (1897), pp. 361–4; 'Venus in the light of recent discoveries', *Atlantic Monthly*, Vol. 5 (1897), pp. 327–43.

8. Sir G. H. Darwin, *The Tides and kindred phenomena in the Solar System: the substance of lectures delivered in 1897 at the Lowell Institute, Boston, Massachusetts* (London: John Murray, 3rd ed., 1911), pp. 302–3).

9. The personal correspondence between Lowell, Douglass, Putnam, Slipher, Wrexie Leonard, and Wilbur A. Cogshall, etc., cited here and on the following pages, is from the Lowell Observatory Archives.

10. W. W. Campbell, '[~]"Mars"[~]' by Percival Lowell, *Publications of the Astronomical Society of the Pacific*, 51 (1896), p. 207.

11. W. Sheehan and T. Dobbins, 'The spokes of Venus: an illusion explained', *Journal for the History of Astronomy*, Vol. 34 (2003), pp. 53–63.

12. P. Lowell, *The Evolution of Worlds* (New York: Macmillan, 1909), p. 24.

13. P. Lowell, 'The Genesis of Planets', *Journal of the Royal Astronomical Society of Canada* (1916), pp. 281–93.

14. Joseph S. Tenn, 'What Else did V. M. Slipher Do?', *Origins of the Expanding Universe 1912–1932*, Michael J. Way and Deirdre Hunter (eds.), ASP Conference Series Vol. 471, Astronomical Society of the Pacific (2013).

15. John S. Hall, 'V. M. Slipher's Trailblazing Career', *Sky & Telescope* 39, 84 (1970).

The Late Sir Patrick Moore

David M. Harland

Like many people of my generation, it was Patrick Moore's *The Sky at Night* programme on television that spurred my interest in astronomy. My first book on the subject, bought at the age of ten, was his *Guide to Mars*, which was published in 1965 just before the Mariner 4 flyby of the planet. Although a slim volume of just over one hundred pages, it provided an account of essentially everything that was known about the planet at that time.

I went on to study astronomy at university, and many years later I started to write on the subject myself. So my career derives directly from 'P', as he used to sign his letters. I met him a couple of times over the decades, when he was giving talks and signing books. On the occasion that I expressed my gratitude for his inspiration, he just grinned at me. I suppose it must have been something that he heard everywhere he went. As the saying goes, he 'made a difference'. He must have derived enormous satisfaction from having had such a positive influence on successive generations of youngsters.

The Nature of Mass and the Higgs Boson

DAVID M. HARLAND

INTRODUCTION

In recent years, the big issue in high-energy physics was whether the particle known as the 'Higgs boson' actually exists. This article reviews how the Standard Model of Elementary Particle Physics was derived, and how the early universe was once very hot and underwent a phase change as it cooled, at which time the Higgs boson manifested the property of mass.

PARTICLES

In 1897, when conducting experiments into the nature of electricity, J. J. Thomson realized that so-called 'cathode rays' were composed of individual particles, each of which bore the same charge and mass – the latter being one ten-thousandth that of the hydrogen atom, the lightest of elements. He called this particle the 'electron' and arbitrarily defined its electrical charge to be negative.

In 1914, after finding that there was a small nucleus deep within an atom, Ernest Rutherford suggested that the nucleus of the hydrogen atom was a single 'subatomic' particle which he named the 'proton'. Its charge was precisely equal and opposite to that of the electron. Overall, an atom was electrically neutral. A puzzling observation was that the masses of heavy elements (measured in units of the mass of hydrogen) were twice that of the number of protons that would be required to account for the electrical charge of the nucleus. Rutherford suggested that, for some reason, electrons were able to penetrate the nucleus and fuse with half of the protons to form neutral members of the nucleus. In 1921, W. D. Harkins proposed that this particle be named the 'neutron'. Its existence was confirmed in 1932 by James Chadwick, a former student of Rutherford.

It was then realized that if a neutron were to emit an electron, thereby becoming a proton, the change in the electrical charge of the nucleus would mean that it had been transmuted into another element. This went some way to explaining the form of radioactive decay in which an atom spontaneously emitted a highly energetic electron. In 1930, noting that the kinetic energy of such an electron did not precisely account for the change in state of the nucleus, Wolfgang Pauli speculated that the process by which a neutron transformed into a proton must also emit an electrically neutral particle that was massless. In 1934 Enrico Fermi suggested that this particle be named the 'neutrino'. Its existence was confirmed in 1956.

By the early 1950s, therefore, it seemed that the nature of atomic matter could be explained by the electron, proton and neutron, with the neutrino 'balancing the books' in radioactive decay. This was a remarkable exercise in reductionism, confirmed by empiricism.

But then an alarming number of other subatomic particles were discovered, and for a time chaos ruled. The zoo of particles which were subjected to the 'strong nuclear force', collectively known as 'hadrons', were rationalized by another exercise in reductionism. Enlightenment came in 1963 when Murray Gell-Mann described the hadrons in terms of symmetry groups involving either pairs or triplets of particles which he called 'quarks'. The theory remained a mathematical abstraction until 1968, when the Stanford Linear Accelerator found evidence that a proton was a cluster of particles, and, over the ensuing five years, various laboratories confirmed that these had the properties predicted for quarks.

In earlier developments, a particle named the muon was found in 1937. It was two hundred times heavier than the electron, and appeared to play no role in the structure of matter. Intriguingly, in 1962 it was established that there is a distinct neutrino associated with it. In 1976, the tauon, a particle similar to the electron but twice as heavy as the proton, was found, and in 2000, its neutrino was identified. The three kinds of electron and their neutrinos were collectively named 'leptons'.

Gell-Mann had envisaged three quarks, which he named 'up', 'down' and 'strange'. A fourth was found in 1974 by two teams of experimenters and named the 'charmed' quark. The fifth and sixth were identified in 1977 and 1998 and named 'bottom' and 'top' respectively.[1]

So this gave a nice balance between the leptons and the quarks, with six of each (Figure 1).

	quarks		
u up	c charm	t top
d down	s strange	b bottom

	leptons		
ν_e electron neutrino	ν_μ muon neutrino	ν_τ tauon neutrino
e electron	μ muon	τ tauon

Figure 1. The matching number of leptons and quarks.

FIELDS AND WAVES

In 1864, James Clerk Maxwell used the concept of a 'field' to derive a mathematical formalism that not only described all known properties of electricity and magnetism, including the way in which an electric current manifested a magnetic field and how a magnet induced an electric current, but also established that the electric and magnetic fields could not be considered in isolation since they were aspects of the single phenomenon of 'electromagnetism'. It was the change in the strength of a magnetic field that induced an electric current, and vice versa. In the electromagnetic field itself, a pair of transverse waves in mutually orthogonal planes were oscillating out of phase in a self-sustaining waveform (Figure 2). When Maxwell calculated the speed of an electromagnetic wave, it was the speed of light, measured by Ole Rømer in 1676 by timing the motions of the moons of Jupiter. Maxwell therefore made the bold inference that light was a manifestation of electromagnetism. His equations showed that when an electrically charged particle was accelerated, an electromagnetic wave would propagate outward from it in an ever-expanding spherical shell. Since the wave radiated away from its source, this phenomenon was called 'electromagnetic radiation'.

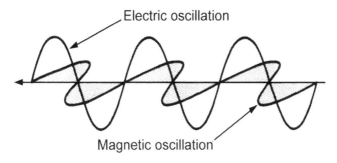

Figure 2. The oscillating electric and magnetic fields of electromagnetic radiation.

However, in 1900, Max Planck interpreted certain observations to explain light as a massless particle which he called a 'quantum'. In 1926, G. N. Lewis broadened the concept and suggested the name 'photon' for all electromagnetic radiation. It was therefore apparent that in certain circumstances light behaved as if it were a wave and in other cases as if it were a stream of particles.

In 1924, Louis de Broglie realized that this wave-particle duality ought also to apply to other particles. In other words, in the proper circumstances, an electron ought to behave as if it were a wave. The next year, G. P. Thomson (son of J. J. Thomson) demonstrated this, and Erwin Schrödinger devised a mathematical 'wave function' to describe the electron. Because electrons can travel at a significant fraction of the speed of light, Paul Dirac expanded Schrödinger's work in 1927 to take into account the theory of special relativity announced in 1905 by Albert Einstein. In 1929, Werner Heisenberg and Wolfgang Pauli independently generalized this into 'quantum field theory', with a separate field for each type of particle, and a particle being a concentration of energy arising from an oscillation in its field. Dirac's formulation suffered mathematical 'infinities' that made it impractical to perform calculations, but, in 1947, Julian Schwinger was able to eliminate them; as did S. I. Tomonaga and Richard Feynman, working independently the following year. In 1949, Freeman Dyson established that these three formulations were equivalent, and constituted a field theory which he called 'quantum electrodynamics'.

Earlier, Enrico Fermi had suggested in 1933 that it should be possible to describe the manner in which a neutron decayed by using a formalism similar to that devised by Dirac for the electromagnetic force. This 'weak' force, as it was dubbed, would require mediators as counterparts to the photon. To account for the short range of the force, these particles would have to possess large masses. In 1957, Julian Schwinger suggested a pair of mediators which he labelled the 'W' particles, one positively charged and the other negatively so. But his efforts to develop a formalism that directly related them to the photon suffered from infinities.

SYMMETRIES AND FORCES

If a transformation of a system yields no observable change, it is said to exhibit a symmetry. In 1915, Emmy Noether noticed that where a symmetry occurs in nature, a property is conserved. In fact, this serves as a definition: a symmetry is a property of a system that remains invariant with respect to a transformation of some kind.

The appearance of a snowflake is unchanged when it is rotated through 60 degrees, and 6 such transformations give a 360-degree rotation (Figure 3). This symmetry derives from the angle between the two hydrogen atoms that are bound to the oxygen atom in the water molecule. The distributions of electric charge within the atoms are rotationally symmetric prior to the formation of the molecule, then become polarized as they are bound together. The breaking of this symmetry manifests itself as a force that re-establishes the balance by locking the three atoms into an asymmetric composite structure. A water molecule is electrically neutral but its charge distribution is not uniform, and this creates an electrostatic force which enables neighbouring molecules to attract one another. These loose bonds give water the fluidic properties of a liquid. If water is heated to its boiling point, the random motions of the molecules are sufficient to break these loose bonds, and the liberated molecules act as a gas. In a similar way, if water is cooled to its freezing point, the molecules become sluggish and link up to produce a regular crystalline lattice. These three states of matter – gas, liquid and solid – are known as phases, with the transitions being called phase changes. Freezing is a spontaneously broken symmetry because the orientation of the molecules that initiate the process of crystallization randomly sets the orientation of the resulting lattice.

Figure 3. The symmetry of a snowflake.

In 1760, Joseph Black realized that when water freezes there is more energy in the collection of molecules of liquid water at 0°C than in the crystalline structure of ice at the same temperature. In a similar manner, there is more energy in steam at 100°C than water at the same temperature. This latent heat must be imparted to melt ice by breaking the crystals or to boil water by breaking the bonds that bind the molecules together. A phase change in which latent heat is required to reorganize the structure of a material is called a first-order phase change, and the physical properties of a material will change discontinuously.

In contrast, a second-order phase change, in which there is no physical restructuring and no latent heat, proceeds more smoothly. An atom is a tiny magnet because its electrons generate a magnetic moment. This effect is particularly strong in the case of iron. In 1895, Pierre Curie found that an iron magnet loses its magnetism upon being heated above 765°C and regains it upon cooling. As the melting point of iron is 1,540°C, this phase change occurs in the solid state. The individual atoms of hot iron are oriented randomly and there is no macroscopic magnetic field because their magnetic moments tend to cancel out. However, as the kinetic energy of the atoms declines as the metal cools, their individual motions slow sufficiently for the weak magnetic force between them to dominate (Figure 4). The atoms do not adopt another physical structure but they remain free to move, and by adopting a specific orientation they give up a component of their angular momentum. This is a smooth transition in which the macroscopic field created by the individual moments becoming mutually aligned strengthens gradually as the temperature nears the critical value. When an electrically charged particle is accelerated by a magnetic field, some of the energy in the field is converted into the kinetic energy of the particle, and the field is diminished. Conversely, the rotational energy that is given up as the iron atoms adopt the same orientation is transferred into the macroscopic magnetic field. There is no net change in energy in cooling through the 'Curie point', but the mutual realignment of the atoms redistributes the energy between the atoms and the magnetic field.

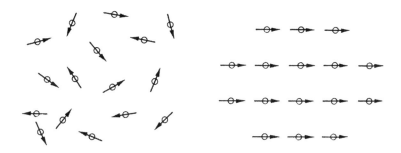

Figure 4. How the magnetic moments are randomized when iron atoms are hot and how they mutually align to create a macroscopic field when cold.

A hot iron bar could be magnetized, but this would require the application of an external magnetic field in order to force the atoms into a single orientation, and the symmetry breaking would not be spontaneous because the induced field would line up with the field that supplied the energy. In terms of magnetization, hot iron is in its lowest energy state since the randomly aligned magnetic moments of its atoms cancel out and the overall energy of the magnetic field is zero. Magnetization can be induced in hot iron only by adding energy to the system. As a result, the energy-versus-magnetization diagram is a U-shape in which the lowest energy state corresponds to zero magnetization (Figure 5). In the phase change that occurs on cooling through the Curie point, the zero of magnetization occurs at a positive energy state, and the lowest energy state has a non-zero magnetization (and as

Figure 6 shows, there are, in fact, two situations, corresponding to whether the field is aligned 'up' or 'down'). The transition is the switch from one relationship to another. A system will tend towards its minimum state for all forms of energy. The ground state for hot iron has zero magnetization at the minimum of energy, but cold iron has a non-zero magnetization. The energy that was transferred into the field during the phase change cannot be shed by further cooling, and this 'frozen' field is a 'false' ground state. This provides a useful insight into understanding the nature of mass.

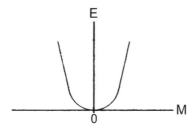

Figure 5. The field strength is zero when the energy is zero.

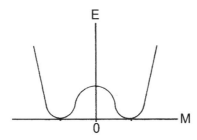

Figure 6. The field strength is non-zero when the energy is zero.

ELECTRO-WEAK UNIFICATION

The concept of 'gauge' (or scale) invariance was introduced in 1918 by H. K. H. Weyl, in an unsuccessful attempt to unify general relativity and electrodynamics. In 1929, after the development of quantum mechanics, he reformulated the concept of invariance to mean that the choice of phase of a wave function does not affect the wave equation.

This was of little interest until 1954, when C. N. Yang and Robert Mills, inspired by the newly completed theory of quantum electrodynamics, devised what they called a gauge theory that was invariant with respect to transformations in position and time and thus was insensitive to the manner in which its properties were measured; a requirement that they expressed as the Principle of Gauge Invariance. Yang and Mills realized that a field of force is how nature maintains an associated symmetry at every point in space – i.e., a local gauge symmetry. To put it another way, a force is simply nature's way of expressing a global symmetry in a local situation.

In fact, there are several kinds of field. A scalar field has a value at every point in space, but there is no intrinsic directionality. A particle in a uniform scalar field will not feel a force. But if there is a gradient in the field, this broken symmetry will manifest itself as a force which seeks to restore uniformity. Temperature is a scalar field. If there is a gradient in a temperature field, the resulting force will cause material to move from warm to cool regions. Similarly in mechanics, stress is the force induced by the gradient in a scalar strain field. On the other hand, a magnetic field has a vector, and an electrically charged particle in a uniform field will be accelerated along the line of force.

In 1960, Sheldon Glashow, a former student of Schwinger, had considered whether the electrodynamic and the weak forces could be unified in terms of symmetries. He found that there ought to be a third mediator of the weak force, this one electrically neutral. But his idea fell by the wayside for the lack of observational evidence. Another problem was that the theory required the mediating 'bosons' to be massless, whereas the short range of the force required them to be very heavy.[2] However, while studying spontaneous symmetry breaking in quantum fields, Jeffrey Goldstone found in 1960 that the process produced massless scalar bosons. A Mexican sombrero hat which has a small ball balanced upon its summit possesses a rotational symmetry, but if the ball rolls off and comes to rest in the annular brim, its presence spontaneously breaks the symmetry (Figure 7). This shape also describes the function of the potential energy of a quantum field that possesses an internal symmetry, one based on the intrinsic properties of the particles rather than on their position and motion in space. The particles subject to such a symmetry are interchangeable in some abstract space by the rotation of a 'selector arrow'. The spontaneous breaking of the symmetry of a quantum field is known as the

Goldstone Theorem. The object which breaks the exact (or 'perfect') symmetry is a Goldstone boson. Wherever the boson settles on the minimum-energy circle (equivalent to the annular brim of the hat), it is free to 'oscillate' with an arbitrarily small amount of energy, and therefore manifest itself as a massless particle.

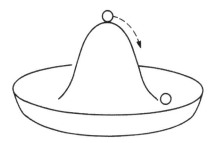

Figure 7. An illustration of broken symmetry.

In 1964, Peter Higgs made the startling discovery that the massless scalar bosons from the spontaneous symmetry breaking would 'combine with' and bestow mass upon the massless bosons of the gauge theory. The process was analogous to the phase change of spontaneous magnetization in which the profile of energy versus magnetization transitioned from a U-shaped to a W-shaped profile as the minimum energy state adopted a non-zero value (Figure 8). The process was different as the scalar 'Higgs field' (as it came to be known) froze, but the

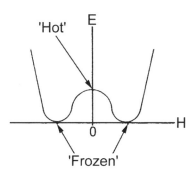

Figure 8. How the strength of the Higgs field has a non-zero value when its symmetry is broken and it 'freezes'.

effect was similar. In its 'hot' state, the field strength was zero (the ball was on top of the sombrero) but this symmetry was broken as the field 'froze' and adopted a non-zero value (the ball was in the rim). In magnetization, the released energy of angular momentum was transferred into the magnetic field and locked away so that it could not be shed by further cooling. When the Higgs field froze, it 'biased' the related fields. The minimum energy of a particle is its 'rest mass'. By giving particles energies that they could not shed, the freezing of the Higgs field gave them masses, with the actual mass of each particle depending upon the degree of coupling between its field and the Higgs field.[3]

In 1967, Steven Weinberg used the 'Higgs mechanism' (as it has become known) to explain how the massless bosons envisaged by Glashow would have acquired mass. But the theory still suffered infinities. These were resolved in 1971 by Gerard 't Hooft. With a consistent theory for a unified 'electro-weak' force, experimenters set out to find the three mediators. The 'W' particles proved to be about 80 GeV and the single 'Z' particle was 91 GeV.[4]

The profound implication of the electro-weak symmetry having been spontaneously broken in a phase change was that the universe was

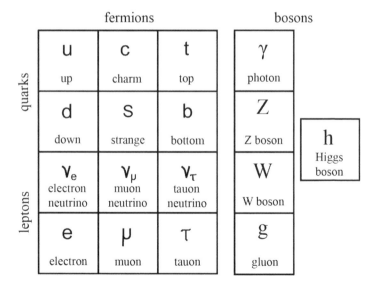

Figure 9. The Standard Model of Elementary Particle Physics.

once incredibly hot. This was consistent with the Big Bang theory. When the electro-weak symmetry applied, the electron and the neutrino had similar properties, and the photon and the three mediators of the weak force were all massless. When the symmetry was broken as the universe cooled, the photon remained massless and mediates the electromagnetic relic of the force, but the others gained so much mass by the Higgs mechanism that the weak force is limited to a very short range. Since the electro-weak force and the force that confines quarks inside hadrons so thoroughly explained particle interactions,[5] their underlying symmetries effectively constituted a Standard Model of Elementary Particle Physics (Figure 9).

SEEKING THE HIGGS BOSON

Verifying that it was the Higgs mechanism that spontaneously broke the electro-weak symmetry became the 'Holy Grail' of particle physics. This meant identifying the boson of the Higgs field. The theory specified many of its properties, but unfortunately not its mass, which made searching for it rather difficult. Early estimates based on circumstantial factors spanned the range 10–300 GeV, but it could be much higher. Only the lower region of this energy range was accessible to contemporary particle accelerators.

The primary objective of the Superconducting Super Collider that was to have been built in Texas was to confirm the existence of the Higgs boson, but this project was cancelled in the early 1990s. However, the Fermi National Accelerator Laboratory (Fermilab) at Batavia near Chicago, Illinois, was able to collect useful data while the Large Hadron Collider (LHC) was being built by the European Organization for Nuclear Research (CERN) on the French–Swiss border (Figure 10). The LHC is a circular tunnel with a circumference of twenty-seven kilometres that is buried, on average, one hundred metres below ground level. It houses a tube whose interior is kept at one ten-trillionth of sea-level pressure, which is as good a vacuum as nature has to offer anywhere in the Solar System. Sixteen hundred superconducting magnets distributed around the track are chilled to a few degrees above absolute zero by one hundred tonnes of liquid helium, and accelerate counter-rotating beams of protons. When the beams intersect at one of the experimental stations, this generates hundreds of millions of collisions per second. The collisional energies give rise to cascades of short-lived particles in the detectors.

The two instruments used in the search for the Higgs boson were ATLAS and CMS. They are both general-purpose detectors. There are others for more specialized research. ATLAS (A Toroidal LHC Apparatus) weighs 7,000 tonnes, and is 25 metres in diameter and 45 metres in length. CMS (Compact Muon Solenoid) weighs in at a hefty 12,500 tonnes, and is 15 metres in diameter and 25 metres in length. Overall, the two projects involve some five thousand people from universities and laboratories around the world (Figure 11).

Figure 10. The location of the Large Hadron Collider facility on the Franco-Swiss border. (CERN-Science Photo Library.)

The LHC was first activated on 10 September 2008, but a fault involving its magnets meant that it was not able to start taking data until November 2009, with a cautious 450 GeV per beam. But by March 2010, it was running with 3.5 TeV beams, making it the most powerful collider in the world. At this point, it began its search for the Higgs boson.

On 13 December 2011, CERN announced that both ATLAS and CMS suggested that there was a particle with a mass of about 125 GeV. In March 2012, analysis of data obtained by the Tevatron prior to its

Figure 11. Peter Higgs alongside the CMS detector of the LHC. (CERN-Science Photo Library.)

shut-down in September 2011 implied that the mass of the Higgs boson would be in the range of 115–152 GeV. On 4 July 2012, CERN announced that its two experiments had confirmed the existence of a new particle with a mass of 125 GeV, and as further data became available this particle was found to have properties consistent with those predicted for the Higgs boson. At the end of the year, the LHC was shut down for a two-year upgrade that will enable it to achieve its design target of 7.5 TeV beams.

THE FUTURE

Although identifying the Higgs boson completed the Standard Model of Elementary Particle Physics and explained how particles acquired their rest masses, there remains much research to be done because the Standard Model does not include gravity and does not explain either dark matter or dark energy. And, of course, physicists are eager to seek evidence of a 'supersymmetry' that would unify bosons with the two fermion families of quarks and leptons.

FURTHER READING

P. W. Anderson, 'Plasmons, Gauge Invariance, and Mass', *Physical Review*, Vol. 130 (April 1963), pp. 439–42.

F. Englert and R. Brout, 'Broken Symmetry and the Mass of Gauge Vector Mesons', *Physical Review Letters*, Vol. 13 (August 1964), pp. 321–3.

Jeffrey Goldstone, 'Field theories with superconductor solutions', *Nuovo Cimento*, Vol. 19 (January 1961), pp.154–64.

G. S. Guralnik, C. R. Hagen and T. W. B. Kibble, 'Global Conservation Laws and Massless Particles', *Physical Review Letters*, Vol. 13 (November 1964), pp. 585–7.

P. W. Higgs, 'Broken symmetries, massless particles and gauge fields', *Physical Review Letters*, Vol. 12 (September 1964), pp. 132–3.

P. W. Higgs, 'Broken symmetries and the Masses of Gauge Bosons', *Physical Review Letters*, Vol. 13 (October 1964), pp. 508–9.

Steven Weinberg, 'A Model of Leptons', *Physical Review Letters*, Vol. 19 (November 1967), pp. 1264–6.

Notes

1. Some people call the latter two quarks 'beauty' and 'truth'.

2. Subatomic particles are classified as 'bosons' or 'fermions', depending on a property known as 'spin'. In simple terms, fermions are the matter particles and bosons mediate the fundamental forces that act upon them.

3. In fact, this 'mechanism' was independently discovered in 1962 by Philip Anderson of Bell Laboratories whilst on sabbatical at the Cavendish Laboratory in Cambridge, England; in 1964 by Robert Brout and François Englert of the University of Brussels; also in 1964 by Peter Higgs at Edinburgh University and by Gerald Guralnik, Richard Hagen and Tom Kibble at Imperial College, London.

4. The masses of subatomic particles are measured as equivalent energies, in terms of 'electron Volts'. The rest mass of an electron is roughly 0.5 MeV, and that of a proton is 938 MeV. The weak force mediators are therefore about a hundred times heavier than the proton. 1 MeV = 10^6 electron Volts; 1 GeV = 10^9 electron Volts; 1 TeV = 10^{12} electron Volts.

5. The theory of 'quantum chromodynamics' was developed to explain how quarks were confined within hadrons by a force that was carried by mediators called 'gluons'.

6. As this yearbook went to press, it was announced that Peter Higgs, from the UK, and François Englert, from Belgium, would share the 2013 Nobel prize in physics for their work on the theory of the Higgs boson. In the 1960s, they were among several physicists who proposed a mechanism to explain why the most basic building blocks of the Universe have mass. The official citation for Higgs and Englert read: 'For the theoretical discovery of a mechanism that contributes to our understanding of the origin of mass of subatomic particles, and which recently was confirmed through the discovery of the predicted fundamental particle, by the ATLAS and CMS experiments at CERN's Large Hadron Collider.'

Sir Patrick Moore

Allan Chapman
Wadham College, Oxford

I did not meet Patrick in person until around 1970, when he opened
the Lancaster University Astronomical Society Observatory, but I had
been a great admirer since the early days of *The Sky at Night*. I, like so
many youngsters, had been fascinated by him – by his masterly knowledge of astronomy, his clarity as a writer, his brilliance as a TV science
presenter, and his very persona.

As a boy I read *The Amateur Astronomer* (1957), borrowed from the
local library and later proudly owned. I followed his instructions on
making a simple refracting telescope from a spectacle lens and a watch-
maker's eyeglass, and will never forget my first telescopic views of the
Moon, and my delight in showing it to chums and passers-by in the
street.

Around 1960, my geography teacher, Monty Phillips, used to amuse
us with hilarious impersonations of the young Patrick. Monty – who
maintained that Patrick 'had his suits cut with a circular saw' – would
ruffle his hair, set one eye higher than the other, stand with his jacket
half off one shoulder, and say, 'Good evening, welcome to *The Sky at
Night*.' For even in those days, Patrick was a larger-than-life figure and
an inspiration. And so he remained, for the next fifty-odd years, down
to his passing in December 2012.

I first got acquainted with Patrick personally in the 1980s, when we
found ourselves sharing lecture venues. He was unfailingly courteous,
modest and great fun. Travelling with him on a train was like being in a
goldfish bowl: strangers would stare from station platforms, nudge a
companion and wave. And Patrick would always smile and wave back.
Unlike a later generation of so-called 'celebs', Patrick, the *true* celebrity,
was always keen to engage with and compliment admirers.

I suppose I got to know Patrick best at the RAS, and, after 1990, at
club dinners at the Athenaeum. As a dinner companion he was a hoot,
especially if his old wartime chum Colin Ronan was dining as well. As

Patrick and Allan in the garden of Patrick's home in Selsey, which was often used for the filming of various TV programmes. (Image courtesy of Jane Fletcher, BBC *Sky at Night.*)

an astronomical historian, my ears were wagging, for I knew I was in the presence of a historic figure.

It was a great privilege to make eleven *Sky at Night* programmes with Patrick, for he was a master of broadcasting technique, from whom I learned a lot. I was honoured in 2003 when he 'moonlighted' from the BBC to do guest appearances in my own Channel 4 *Gods in the Sky* series.

I have given much thought to Patrick's place in history. And of one thing I am certain: he will endure. I have traced his 'intellectual ancestry' as a great science communicator back 370 years. Back through Sir Arthur Eddington (Radio), Sir Robert Ball (Victorian lecturer) and Michael Faraday (Royal Institution Children's Lectures) to the Revd Dr John Wilkins, who in 1640 first popularized the discoveries of Copernicus and Galileo in plain language for English readers.

To know Sir Patrick was to know a truly great man. God bless him.

Mapping and Understanding the Moon: From Thomas Harriot to Sir Patrick Moore

ALLAN CHAPMAN

Sir Patrick Alfred Caldwell Moore, CBE, FRS, had many claims to distinction, spanning a public career of sixty years. But if there was one area of his achievement that ran from his youth, before the Second World War, down to the very end of his life on 9 December 2012, it lay in his being a 'Moon man'. As with so many astronomers, Patrick Moore's fascination with the heavens began with the Moon; and I shall never forget the early hours of 19 May 1992, when he and I were observing the Moon together with the fifteen-inch 'Fullerscopes' reflector in his garden at Selsey. Patrick had focussed on the crater Aristarchus with a high magnification, and having studied it carefully for several minutes, without uttering a word, he invited me to look through the eyepiece and, in a neutral tone, asked what I could see. I said I felt sure that there was some reddish stain inside the crater – very conspicuous against the stark monochrome moonscape. 'Exactly!' he said. He believed that we had seen a Transient Lunar Phenomenon, or TLP. Over the course of the next hour, the reddish hue simply died away to leave the usual black and white terrain. Patrick said that it was very rare indeed for a person who was *not* a regular TLP watcher, such as myself, to see one, and I was honoured when in his official logging of the event he recorded my name as his co-observer.

As things stand at present, Patrick was the last great naked-eye lunar observer. The last great 'eye and pencil' observer, who did not use some kind of camera or, more lately, imaging technology and associated software, to depict the lunar surface. Yet in spite of Patrick's protests of being unable to draw a straight line and being devoid of artistic gifts, in reality he was a superlative lunar (and planetary) draughtsman. Portraits, landscapes and buildings may not have been his forte, but

348

show him a piece of the heavens, and a region of the Moon in particular, through an eyepiece, and he would render it in stunning detail. And his skill as a selenographer had been polished and perfected over a lifetime, beginning – at the age of fourteen, in 1937 – with his first paper to the British Astronomical Association, on the small craterlets in the Mare Crisium.

THOMAS HARRIOT AND THE BIRTH OF SELENOGRAPHY

When did people first become interested in observing and drawing the lunar surface, creating the art and science of 'selenography' (from the Greek words *selene*, 'moon', and *graphein*, 'to draw'), or Moon-drawing? For while there had been good naked-eye drawings, I would be so bold as to date selenography proper to 9.00 p.m. on the evening of 26 July 1609. For it was then that the Englishman Thomas Harriot directed his newly acquired 'Dutch truncke', or telescope, to the five-day-old Moon in the twilight of a summer's evening. This drawing (Figure 1) still survives in the West Sussex County Record Office in Chichester, along with Harriot's subsequent lunar maps and some two

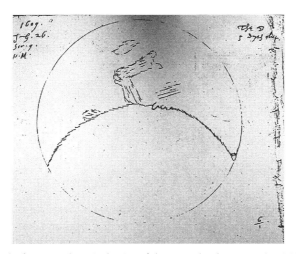

Figure 1. The first ever telescopic drawing of the Moon, by Thomas Harriot: 9.00 p.m., 26 July 1609, ×6 magnification. Notice that the Moon's 'horns' have not been included. (Image courtesy of Petworth House Archive and Lord Egremont.)

hundred sunspot drawings. I myself have handled this very first telescopic drawing of the Moon, which was executed in pen and ink, on a piece of good-quality foolscap paper. I even made a brief BBC TV news slot on it (broadcast at the very beginning of the 'Year of the Telescope' in 2009) to remind people that it had been an Englishman, Harriot, then living at Sion House in Sion Park, near Brentford, London, who had made the very first fully authenticated telescopic drawing of the Moon in July 1609 – four months ahead of Galileo, I might mention.

Of course, there was no shortage of naked-eye Moon sketches long before this time, and even pieces of prehistoric art contain items which have been interpreted as representing the Moon, its phases, and the light and dark patches upon it. By 1600, almost a decade before the first telescopes, various scientifically minded persons had made some remarkably good drawings of the Moon's light and dark regions: such as Dr William Gilbert, physician to Queen Elizabeth I and the founding father of geomagnetism.

But it was the invention of the telescope that was to become the crucial catalyst in the creation of the art and science of selenography, for that totally transformed our entire threshold of perception.

Harriot's July 1609 drawing is quite rudimentary, showing only the central part of the five-day Moon, with the horns cut off. This has led some people to suggest that Harriot was a poor draughtsman, but I would suggest a different explanation. As the lunar 'horns' in Harriot's ×6 'Dutch truncke' would have been washed-out brilliant white with no discernible detail (not to mention the likelihood that he was struggling to make sense of what he saw in this first ever recorded telescopic image of the lunar surface in human experience), he concentrated his efforts on what he *could* see. Namely, the curiously part-smooth and part-jagged terminator separating the brilliantly lit lunar 'day' from the lunar 'night' regions, still in black shadow. For if the Moon was a brilliant, partially tarnished silvery ball, as the hugely influential Aristotle had argued, and astronomers over the next two thousand years had generally accepted, why was it smooth in some places and rough in others? And why were what would soon be called the lunar 'seas' or *maria* so much more distinct when seen through the telescope than they appeared to the naked eye?

Harriot, I hasten to add, does not *write* about these features, but they are clearly visible in his drawing. And if you try temporarily to forget all that we now know about the Moon, and observe it through a reconstructed telescope like Harriot's, with its 'right way up' image and tiny field of view, as I have done, then his original drawing makes a lot more sense.

The jagged nightly terminator was especially problematic because one of the main reasons why some early telescopic astronomers bothered to look at the Moon in the first place was to establish the exact moment of dichotomy, or perfect half-Moon. By this means they hoped to be able to obtain a more accurate measure of the Earth-Moon-Sun distances, using a method originally outlined by Aristarchus (in c. 250 BC). But instead of the telescope being an aid towards making a more accurate triangulation, they found what they did not expect: namely, that the rough surface of the magnified Moon needed to be made sense of in its own right. We will return to Harriot shortly, but we must now look at the man whose observations, made with his *cannocchiale*, or 'little tube', and begun some months later around 30 November 1609, blazed the 'new world in the Moon' across Europe: Galileo.

GALILEO'S 'NEW WORLD IN THE MOON'

Having heard of the new device for magnifying distant objects in a letter from France in the spring of 1609, and having made several instruments for himself in Padua, near Venice, Italy, Galileo's first act was to demonstrate its usefulness as a military and naval aid to an influential group of Venetian Senators, and obtain a handsome reward! But he rapidly latched on to how the *cannocchiale* could give him an advantage in his dispute with Padua's more traditional scholars who defended the wisdom of the ancient Greek writers; for if Aristotle postulated a smooth Moon on philosophical grounds, based on the theory of planetary perfection, and he, Galileo, could show that our satellite was indeed rough and even mountainous, then he could seize the high ground in debate.

However, Galileo's original sepia watercolour paintings of the Moon from 30 November 1609, which formed the basis of the woodcut engravings he was to publish in *Sidereus Nuncius* ('The Starry Messenger') in March 1610, were *not* topographically accurate maps. Their primary purpose was to depict the rough, broken and variegated lunar surface, and to undermine the idea that it was smooth. His relative unconcern about the exact positions of lunar topographical features is evident from how depictions of the very conspicuous crater – perhaps Copernicus, Hipparchus or Albategnius – often vary in size and even in position with relation to the lunar diameter. For by Christmas 1609, Galileo viewed the telescope primarily as a powerful polemical device for undermining the conservative classical philosophers of Padua rather than an instrument of fundamental discovery in its own right. I would suggest that its true discovery potential only really dawned on Galileo in early January 1610 when he first glimpsed Jupiter's moons. But that is part of another story which does not directly concern us here.

THE FATHER OF LUNAR CARTOGRAPHY

Thomas Harriot, who made no efforts whatsoever to publicize his lunar and subsequent solar telescopic researches, obtained a copy of *Sidereus Nuncius* in England in June 1610. And far from being angry that Galileo was winning all the laurels for what he, Harriot, had seen first, he openly *admired* Galileo. This is evident from his letters to his friend Sir William Lower and his circle of astronomical friends – Mr Vaughan, Mr Prothero and others – at Trafenti, south-west Wales – all of whom had been observing the heavens with telescopes since Christmas 1609. True, Lower tried to persuade Harriot to publish, but to no effect, and it was not until 1784 that Harriot's Moon maps and astronomical correspondence first saw the light of day, when the visiting German astronomer Baron von Zach was going through Harriot's surviving papers!

I say Moon *maps*, rather than sketches, because that is what Harriot started to produce in a series of tantalizingly undated charts, generally about six inches in diameter, between his first sketch of 26 July 1609 and about 1613. For let us be clear about one important fact: Thomas Harriot was the true father of lunar cartography, or selenography. Unlike Galileo, he had no academic axe to grind, although he accepted the Copernican theory as a fact. But the fifty-year-old Harriot of 1610 was a very well-off bachelor, who, in addition to being one of the greatest mathematicians of the day, knew all about cartography and the importance of drawing accurate maps. Twenty-five years previously, for instance, he had taught navigation and cartography to his older

Oxford contemporary and lifelong friend Sir Walter Raleigh's sea captains, and had spent a year on the Roanoke, Virginia survey expedition of 1585–6.

Harriot, therefore, knew all about accurate cartography, and his pen-and-ink drawings of the Moon, made using his various 'Galilean'-style telescopes of around ×30 magnification (these were subsequently made by Harriot's technician Christopher Tooke – Great Britain's first telescope-maker), which were more powerful than his original ×6 'Dutch truncke', are, frankly, stunning. Harriot delineated the 'seas' with great accuracy and then added numerous crater and related topographical features, most of which we can tie up quite precisely with formations present on modern Moon maps (Figure 2). It is also clear that his polished six-inch Moon charts were not, after that of 26 July 1609, drawn from observations taken on a single night. Their detail is too rich, and one suspects that they were composed after several nights of terminator observation.

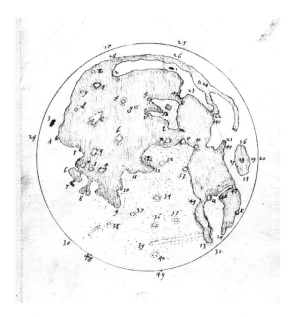

Figure 2. One of Harriot's detailed Moon maps. Probably made after reading Galileo's *Sidereus Nuncius*, but vastly more accurate than Galileo's moon pictures. (Image courtesy of Petworth House Archive and Lord Egremont.)

But as Harriot in 1609 had no sort of micrometer or eyepiece measuring device (the first was invented in around 1640 by William Gascoigne of Leeds, some eighteen years after Harriot's death in 1621), one assumes that he must have had a remarkably good eye for position and proportion. For generally he made features roughly the right size and put them in more or less the right place, despite the fact that he was working with a telescope with such a small field of view that he could only have seen about one-third or one-half of the full disk at any one position. In short, he must have had a cartographic visual memory that enabled him to see separate pieces of detail and then put them all together as one chart – probably checking their respective positions at full Moon.

Yet, as we saw, Harriot's selenographical work remained unknown until 1784, though his maps were not published in detail until the late-twentieth-century 'space race' made anything to do with the Moon headline-grabbing news. And by that time, 'the man who beat Galileo' was known only in specialist circles: either among academic mathematicians or historians of early-seventeenth-century science. But while Galileo has no real claim to being a cartographic selenographer, we must remain eternally indebted to him for two reasons. First, it was he who first blazed the news of the rough, mountainous, 'oceanic', variegated surface of the Moon across Europe in *Sidereus Nuncius*, which inspired countless others to examine our satellite and draw and describe it with ever increasing sophistication. And second, in 1637, at the age of seventy-three, he discovered its rocking motion, or libration, noticing that he could see a bit further round the edge or limb of the Moon at some times than he could at others. A 'rock' which would stimulate planetary dynamic researches and, by the 1680s, contribute to Sir Isaac Newton's definition of the 'three bodies problem', as the Sun, Moon and Earth exerted changing gravitational forces upon one another.

But why did Harriot never publish? It certainly had nothing whatsoever to do with Copernicanism or the Church, and we must remember that when Galileo published his own lunar observations in 1610 many Jesuit and other Roman Catholic astronomers *applauded* his discoveries, and confirmed them with their own telescopes. Besides, Harriot was an English Protestant, and had no fear at all of the Catholic Church. So let me suggest a reason: it was primarily political, for two of his closest high-profile friends were currently under arrest in the Tower of London with the executioner's axe hovering above their necks. One was his old friend Sir Walter Raleigh, against whom the new King James I had taken a violent dislike in 1603; the other was his patron and friend Henry Percy, Ninth Earl of Northumberland, who in 1609 was still being held on suspicion of involvement in Guy Fawkes's Gunpowder Plot of 1605. Harriot himself had been arrested, held and cross-examined for three weeks in 1605. So, I would suggest, it was in the interests of a wealthy private gentleman like Harriot not to make himself too conspicuous!

THE DEVELOPMENT OF SELENOGRAPHY

Selenography began to develop in a serious way in the 1640s, as optical technology was making slightly larger-aperture, longer-focal-length object glasses possible. Longer focal lengths meant larger prime-focus images, and the potential for much higher magnifications, especially when the concave eyeglasses of the early 'Galilean' telescopes were eventually replaced by the convex eyepieces first described by Johannes Kepler in 1611. By 1645, therefore, telescopic images could be bigger, brighter, clearer – and, when using a Keplerian eyepiece, upside down.

Michel Florent van Langren produced the first 'good quality' Moon map in 1645, finely engraved and printed from copper plates, and even today one cannot fail to be impressed by the fine detail which he included. Van Langren (often referred to in the Latin version of his name, Langrenius) was one of the first to wrestle with the problem of how to name the features he recorded. Being a Roman Catholic priest-astronomer, he named many features after Christian saints and other religious persons in the Catholic, but not in the Protestant, tradition.

Indeed, what to call lunar features was becoming an important issue, as better telescopes were revealing more and more detail, and the man whose system of nomenclature has left its permanent mark, with many of his names still in use today, is the Italian Jesuit priest-astronomer Giambattista Riccioli. His *Almagestum Novum* ('New Almagest') of 1651 divided the earth-facing side of the Moon into eight 'octants' or regions. Riccioli also worked out a coherent and impartial scheme for naming the three principal classes of lunar features: *maria*, or 'seas'; *terrae*, or 'lands'; and craters.

Riccioli tended to designate the 'seas', or dark regions, according to meteorological conditions – hence the seas of Crisis, Serenity (*Serenitatis*), Storm (*Procellarum*), Cold (*Frigoris*), and such – with a few more fanciful ones, such as the seas of 'Nectar' and 'Fecundity'. The 'lands', or higher and whiter-looking regions, he named after Heat (*Caloris*), Sterility (*Sterilitatis*) and even Vitality (*Vitae*).

Riccioli named the craters after famous human beings – invariably men, as most famous humans would have been in 1651. Here we encounter Greek philosophers, Roman poets, scientists, soldiers, statesmen, and other eminent personages from the classical world. Then in another 'octant' were more modern figures, from medieval and contemporary times. There are medieval Europeans, and even eminent Arabic scientists of the Middle Ages, such as Albategnius. And then one encounters the very moderns, such as Copernicus, Kepler, and Galileo.

But what, one might ask, was a Jesuit priest like Riccioli doing naming craters after outstanding Protestants like Kepler, or even 'heretics' like Copernicus and Galileo? I would suggest that we revise our modernist myth which has the Church trying to suppress scientific progress. For while Riccioli did *not* believe that the Earth moved around the Sun – on what were still very good evidential grounds in 1651 – such figures as Copernicus, Kepler, and Galileo were universally recognized as men of outstanding scientific brilliance, and while their heliocentricism may have been regarded as suspect, their other work as astronomers and physicists was seen as warranting the highest respect. Hence their inclusion on an Italian Jesuit's map. Indeed, Riccioli's map included Greek and Roman pagans, medieval Muslims, Christian saints, Protestants and even 'heretics'!

But the early Moon surveyor I know Sir Patrick Moore particularly admired was Johannes Hevelius of Dantzig (Gdansk), Poland. I know that Patrick held him in such esteem, for we discussed his achievement on several occasions, and I wrote my historical chapter on Hevelius's wider astronomical researches in the 2013 yearbook. But what about Hevelius the selenographer?

Hevelius's *Selenographia* (1647) was one of the foundational documents of lunar study. For one thing, he provides us with a detailed account of his telescopes and working procedures, describing not only his twelve-foot focus and other telescopes, but also the optical bench used to manufacture their optics, and his methods of mounting them. Then there is that sequence of forty lunar plates: made from his original drawings, then engraved onto copper plates for their publication as prints. In this sequence, we can trace the course of a whole lunation on a nightly basis, with craters, mountains and 'seas' emerging from the dark. And then there are the full-Moon charts, made up from all the nightly phase charts, to provide a stunning depiction of the lunar surface.

Selenographia is a scientific, intellectual and artistic masterpiece. A hefty folio volume, printed on the highest-quality paper, which is just as crisp, white and fresh as when it was new. (I personally am familiar with the copies in the Royal Society, London, and Bodleian Library, Oxford. The Bodleian copy once belonged to Sir Christopher Wren who, as a young man, had been an Oxford Professor of Astronomy.)

THE FIRST DETAILED SURVEYS

Before leaving the intensely scientifically fertile seventeenth century, however, I must mention two important figures: both friends of Sir Christopher Wren. The first was the Revd Dr John Wilkins, Warden of Wadham College, Oxford, and later Bishop of Chester, who, I would suggest, had two ancestral connections with Sir Patrick. First, he was a scientific educator of genius whose books, written in English, not Latin, took Copernican and Galilean astronomy to English-language readers. Second, in one of his books of 1638 (reprinted in 1640 when he was still only twenty-six), Wilkins began a serious discussion not only about the likely inhabitants of the Moon – 'Selenites' – but also about how humans might fly there by means of a mechanically propelled 'flying chariot', or space vehicle. Which makes Wilkins a pioneer both of popular astronomical education, and of space flight! And in 1660 Wilkins was instrumental in founding the Royal Society, to which Sir Patrick was elected an Honorary Fellow in 2001.

The other figure was Wilkins's Oxford pupil Dr Robert Hooke. Now while Hooke was not a selenographer like Hevelius and Riccioli, he was the first astronomer to make a detailed topographical survey of a single lunar formation, the crater Hipparchus (as Riccioli had named it), and the area around it, about ninety arc seconds across. Hooke tells us that he made the drawing, probably from Gresham College, London, where he was soon to be elected Professor of Geometry, in October 1664, using two long refracting telescopes of 30 and 60 feet focal length with single-element object glasses of around 3.5 inches in diameter and

Keplerian eyepieces, though Hooke does not tell us which aspects of the drawing he made with which telescope. My friend Tony Morris (of the Mexborough and Swinton, South Yorkshire Astronomical Society) calculated from the described optical characteristics of one of these telescopes that it would have given a magnification of around ×173.

Hooke's survey of Hipparchus is simply stunning in its accuracy and detail, and one need only compare it to a modern photograph of this same region, at the same lunation light angle, to realize this fact (Figure 3).

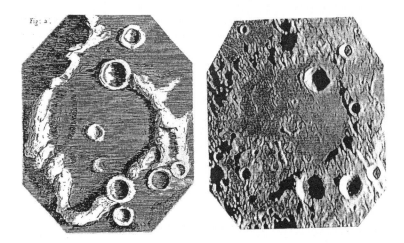

Figure 3. Left: Robert Hooke's drawing of the crater Hipparchus, October 1664, published in his *Micrographia* (1665). Right: Photograph of Hipparchus, by Gain Lee, of Huddersfield, Yorkshire, 28 March 2004, at 8.30 p.m.

But Hooke was also an experimental scientist of genius, and next went on to ask how the lunar surface could have come about. He not only proposed two possible processes, but also attempted to model them in the laboratory – perhaps the first attempt at astronomical modelling! To test his *volcanic* theory, Hooke prepared a tub of viscous pipe-clay mixture and blew into it with a pair of bellows. As the bubbles broke on the surface they left crater-like depressions. Then, asked Hooke, could the craters have been formed by *bombardment* from space? To test this idea, he dropped lead pistol bullets into the pipe-clay mixture from a great height. And not only did the bullets produce lovely crater-like depressions, but sometimes even central peaks as well. Hooke published his Hipparchus drawing and crater-forming experiments in his massively influential *Micrographia* (1665).

Some years ago, Sir Patrick and I reconstructed Hooke's bombardment model of crater formation for a *Sky at Night* programme, filmed in Patrick's garden. Standing on top of a tall step ladder, I used a catapult to shoot glass marbles into a tub of thick modelling clay. We got some lovely craters, though Patrick's suit unfortunately got liberally splattered with 'lunar debris'!

Lunar vulcanism has been a subject of much discussion over the years, and while modern research, based primarily on space-probe and lunar landing evidence, tells us that the Moon has been geologically dead and inert for millions of years, there have been several accounts of brilliant and sustained lights seen on the Moon's dark side which continue to puzzle us.

Sir William Herschel, for example, reported seeing several such spots to the Royal Society in April 1787, as published in his paper 'An Account of Three Volcanoes on the Moon', in the *Philosophical Transactions* of that year. Then in 1858, Mr Samuel Horton, who worked in Dr John Lee's private observatory near Aylesbury, reported seeing another bright, glowing spot on the dark part of the crescent.

Of course the one often referred to from the Middle Ages dates from 18 June 1178, when monks enjoying the summer evening air in the garden of the Canterbury monastery saw the new Moon's upper cusp suddenly split apart, spewing flames and cinders and shaking violently in the sky for some minutes thereafter. But was the *Chronicle* of Gervaise of Canterbury merely recording a silly superstition? Personally, I think not. For one thing, we know that Gervaise tried to be as precise as he could in his other celestial reports, such as those of the aurora borealis. Yet, surely, the Moon's northern cusp could not explode in flames and cinders? In 1976, however, Jack B. Hartung suggested that what *could* have happened on that June evening was that a meteoritic object struck the Moon, perhaps producing the crater Giordano Bruno.

However, what I suspect Gervaise's Canterbury monks had witnessed was a great meteor, or fireball, plunging acutely into the Earth's atmosphere in their direct, local, line of sight to the lunar cusp. Anyone who has seen such a dramatic burn-up, about eighty miles above our heads, as I have, is aware of a sudden brilliant flash, even colours, followed by a snaking, writhing vapour trail. Of course, this would have had nothing whatsoever to do with the Moon, which is 239,000 miles away; but what a spectacular line-of-sight effect it could have been!

After sixty or seventy years of intense, creative and detailed lunar study following 1609, things became very quiet for a long time. Indeed, one gets a sense of how far selenography had 'gone off the boil', as it were, from the very long delays in actually publishing new Moon maps. Giovanni Domenico Cassini's Moon map of 1679, for instance, was not published until 1787 – despite Cassini's enormous eminence as an astronomer and his family's dominance of the Paris Observatory for over a hundred years – while the Göttingen astronomer Tobias Mayer's 1749 map only appeared in 1775, some thirteen years after his death. Yes, people still looked at the Moon, and, as the nearest of all astronomical bodies, it was always an object of wonder to beginners in astronomy – just as it is today. But academic and research 'grand amateur' astronomer interest had moved elsewhere by 1730, as angle-measuring for Newtonian dynamical purposes dominated the science, and, after 1775, Sir William Herschel's 'surveys' of the deep sky.

It was a German 'grand amateur', Johann Hieronymus Schröter, who re-focussed serious attention back upon the Moon in the 1780s. Schröter was a private gentleman and chief magistrate of the north German town of Lilienthal, near Bremen, Saxony, in north Germany. And like his fellow German William Herschel, now living in Bath, then Slough, Schröter recognized the potential for light-grasp and high magnifications offered by the speculum metal reflecting telescope. Indeed, he had several fine ones, built by the Keil University physicist Johann Gottlieb Schrader and William Herschel, including one of 1793 with an 18.5-inch-diameter mirror of 27 feet focal length.

What fascinated Schröter about the Moon was the sheer complexity of detail that one could see at high magnification: far more, of course, than on anything else in the heavens. And as a meticulous researcher, he set about the task of not only observing and drawing hundreds of different features, at different phase-angles of light and over many years, but also of *measuring* them with micrometers. Knowing the exact angular diameter (preferably pole to pole) of the Moon on any given night, Schröter could then measure the angular size of any feature on its surface, such as mountains or craters.

This measuring was done with an eyepiece micrometer, in which two thin hairs (stretched pieces of spider's web was best) were set upright and parallel to each other in the telescope's field of view inside the micrometer. Each hair was attached to a very fine-pitched adjusting screw, so that as the observer rotated the screw from an outside knob, the hair would move smoothly across the field of view. In this way, an astronomer could 'sandwich' any suitably small lunar feature between the two hairs. A graduated dial on the head of the adjusting screw would tell him exactly how many full and part-turns had been necessary to enclose a given crater.

Then, knowing the exact focal length of his primary mirror, or lens, and the exact size of a lunar feature in, let us say, thousandths of an inch as measured with the eyepiece micrometer screw, he could calculate the precise angular size of the feature as a fraction of the whole lunar diameter. In this way, it became possible to produce a very accurate topographical study of the Moon. Of course, Schröter was in no way unique in his use of the micrometer to measure lunar features, for as we have seen, the device had been around since William Gascoigne invented it in around 1640, and Robert Hooke had popularized it before the Royal Society in 1667, while the instrument had been used by both Cassini and Mayer to construct their maps. I would suggest that what made Schröter's maps so much better was the superior quality of his telescopes, and the fact that Schröter, as a private gentleman, unlike Cassini and Mayer who were very much *professional* astronomers with state or academic duties to attend to, could devote as much time as he pleased to his beloved Moon-mapping project. His great *Selenotopografisches Fragmentum* was published in two volumes, in 1791 and 1802.

It says much about the popular myth of French Revolutionary and Napoleonic love of culture and civilized values, however, that when Bonaparte's troops arrived at Lilienthal in 1813, they destroyed Schröter's observatory!

SELENOGRAPHY IN THE VICTORIAN AGE

The rapidly expanding science of terrestrial geology may well have played a significant part in a return of astronomical interest in the Moon in the nineteenth century. Volcanoes, and the marks of vulcanism on the earth's surface in particular, became an object of intense fascination by 1825, especially in the wake of the spectacular eruptions of Skaftareldar in Iceland (1783–4), Tambora in Indonesia (1815) and Vesuvius (1794, 1822 and 1834), along with the writings of early vulcanologists, such as James Hutton, Alexander von Humbolt and Charles Daubeny. One had only to glance through a modest telescope to see jagged peaks, lava flows, extinct cones and great fissures (the 'Rilles' of Schröter) and cracks, running sometimes for hundreds of miles across the stark moonscape.

Yet why did the Earth have abundant oceans, a dense atmosphere, a surface shaped by intense erosion over *millions* of years (as they realized by 1830), teeming life forms, and climatic extremes, whereas the Moon was long dead and utterly changeless? These questions, and the stark incongruity between the Earth and the Moon, fascinated the scientists of the 'Romantic Era'; and as private ladies and gentlemen were avidly 'geologizing' the Scottish Highlands and once-volcanic Lake District by 1830, and a veritable explosion of 'grand' and more modest amateur astronomy was getting under way at exactly the same time, the Moon was coming to be seen in a new light.

Indeed, the 'Victorian Age' became a time of rapidly advancing selenography, especially in Great Britain and Germany: two countries which thought of themselves as cousins in the nineteenth century, with their strong mutual affinities of monarchy, commerce, military allegiance (against France), religion, education and love of science.

After Schröter, the next great selenographer was Wilhelm Lohrmann, whose 1824 Leipzig chart raised the level of selenographic excellence to new heights once more. And by Lohrmann's time, big, powerful, equatorially mounted, clock-driven achromatic refractors were becoming the norm for serious astronomical research, in the wake of Josef Fraunhofer's innovations at the Munich glassworks and telescope factory. Indeed, Fraunhofer's balanced 'German mount' would dominate telescopic engineering until the advent of computer-controlled tracking systems in the late twentieth century.

For while it was John Dollond in London who had invented the achromatic refractor around 1758, it was Fraunhofer who improved glass manufacture, and had fundamentally re-engineered the instrument by his death in 1824. And soon after, French, English and American opticians were following where Fraunhofer had led, to make the big refractor the most influential telescope of the nineteenth century.

One of the most famous Moon maps of all time was the fruit of both private scientific innovation and improved refractor technology. Wilhelm Beer was a banker of Berlin, with a passion for astronomy, and took upon himself the re-surveying of the Moon. Beer was really the enthusiastic patron who provided the money and resources, and Johann Heinrich von Mädler was a university-trained astronomer who needed a job, and who did much of the painstaking observing. Their *Mappa Selenographica totam Lunae hemisphaeram visibilem complectans* ('Moon map covering the whole visible hemisphere of the Moon') was published in four great sheets between 1834 and 1836, and rapidly became a classic in its minute study of detailed and delicate lunar formations. Formations which, to a geological eye, just might suggest certain parallels to earthly features, except for the absence of terrestrial craters. Yet why were the Earth and the Moon so profoundly different, scientists were beginning to ask, despite their close proximity in space? When the Revd Thomas W. Webb produced his *Celestial Objects for Common Telescopes* (1859), which was destined to become the 'bible' of Victorian popular amateur astronomy (and the natural ancestor to Sir Patrick's *The Amateur Astronomer* (1957)), he reproduced a reduced-size, fold-out version of Beer's and Mädler's 1836 map, which in 1859 was still the definitive Moon chart.

One Victorian 'grand amateur' in particular, also an informed amateur geologist, cast a geological eye upon our satellite. James Nasmyth was a great iron-master and engineer by profession, an Edinburgh native who made his fortune in Industrial Revolution Manchester, and so was ideally placed to see the Moon as a once-molten body that had slowly cooled. Nasmyth tells us that he had been fascinated by the behaviour of molten metal in his Patricroft, Manchester ironworks: its movement, and the islands of 'scum' or scoria that formed upon its surface, and which had visual parallels to lunar formations.

Nasmyth, moreover, was not only a serious lunar observer, but also an innovative telescope designer and builder in his own right. Using the resources of his great factory, with its metal-casting shops and steam-powered precision machinery (his firm built railway locomotives and marine engines), he built a far-reaching twenty-inch speculum-metal geared iron-mounted reflecting telescope in 1848–50 which showed the lunar surface with breathtaking clarity. He also built big reflector optics for grand amateur friends, such as William Lassell and Warren de la Rue, including an exquisite four-foot-diameter mirror for Lassell.

As Nasmyth was the son of a distinguished Scottish artist, Alexander Nasmyth, and was himself an accomplished artist, draughtsman and model-maker, he not only drew the lunar surface, but also made spectacularly detailed plaster of Paris models of features that particularly interested him (Figure 4). Many of these he photographed, and used to illustrate his and his co-author James Carpenter's *The Moon: considered as A Planet, A World, And A Satellite* (1874).

Figure 4. Aristotle and Eudoxus lunar craters. Note: these are *not* photographs of the craters, but of James Nasmyth's meticulous plaster models, built up from careful drawing at the telescope and photographed from above. The plaster models, about twelve inches across, are in the Science Museum, South Kensington. (From Nasmyth and Carpenter, *The Moon* (1874).)

Nasmyth developed a global 'model' of the origin of the Moon's geological formations and current appearance (Figure 5). He proposed that the Moon had once been molten. Then, as it cooled, a crust or skin formed upon the still-molten interior. Further cooling led to this crust warping, buckling and cracking to form the mountains, lunar *maria*, *Rilles*, the 'ray' systems of craters such as Tycho, and so on. He even had a glass globe made, which he subjected to thermal changes, and recorded the formation of very lunar-like cracks developing within it, generally radiating from particular stress points. Like Robert Hooke two hundred years before, James Nasmyth took selenography into the laboratory.

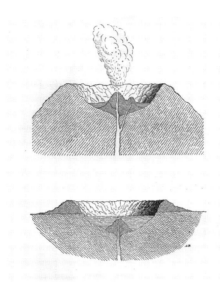

Figure 5. James Nasmyth's volcanic model of lunar crater formation. (From Nasmyth and Carpenter, *The Moon* (1874).)

Although it had been the Anglo-American physician and 'grand amateur' astronomer John William Draper who obtained the first photograph of the Moon with the new daguerreotype process in 1840, it was Nasmyth's Guernsey-born stationer and paper-manufacturer friend and client, Warren de la Rue, who really developed astronomical photography. Using an equatorial reflecting telescope designed primarily to work in those optical wavelengths to which the new and much superior 'wet collodian' photographic plates were most sensitive, de la Rue was obtaining some astonishingly good photographs of the Moon by the mid-1850s. And as Sir John Herschel observed to his 'grand amateur' friends, photography would be the future not only of selenography, but also of the whole of astronomical recording and measurement – although many optical, chemical, and mechanical hurdles would have to be surmounted in the meanwhile.

By the 1860s, therefore, lunar photography was becoming the way forward for astronomers on both sides of the Atlantic, as custom-built photographic telescopes were being constructed and experimented with. And in the wake of John William Draper's original experiments of 1840, both he, and then his son Dr Henry Draper, were taking stunning lunar photographs using improved instruments and processes, from just outside New York, by the 1860s.

So did 'grand amateur' photography consign traditional 'eye at the telescope' selenography to oblivion? Far from it. For one thing, early lunar photography was often far from easy to use when it came to securing really clear *cartographic* quality images. A good selenographical camera had not only to have the highest-grade optics, but also a well-nigh-perfect tracking mechanism, capable of staying fixed on one tiny area for maybe, in some cases, twenty or thirty seconds – quite a demand on the technology of 1865. And not only could early emulsions sometimes be unreliable for really critical work, but capturing fine detail could be infuriatingly elusive. Let us not forget that the amply resourced James Nasmyth chose to illustrate his great *The Moon* treatise with photographs of his visually derived, minutely detailed plaster models of lunar formations, rather than by direct photographs. And even in 1886, Sir Robert Stawell Ball would use the photographs of Nasmyth models to illustrate his *Story of the Heavens* and other popular astronomy books.

In many ways, the 'eye at the telescope' approach to selenography was less technically demanding. So long as one's optics were good, then telescope guidance systems could even be altazimuth, for an experienced visual observer tended to have developed a whole raft of skills, knacks and instincts whereby they could pretty well observe and draw at the same time: as could Sir Patrick Moore.

The real 'growth industry' in serious amateur lunar study began in 1859 with the Revd Thomas W. Webb's *Celestial Objects for Common Telescopes*, mentioned earlier. It was Webb's book, combined with the recent advent of the silver-on-glass reflecting telescope, which a skilled amateur could often make for himself for a few pounds, and even set up in an elegant, home-made 'telescope house' in the garden, that contributed to this 'growth industry'. Six-, eight- and ten-inch glass reflectors were proliferating by 1875, and Webb became a staunch advocate for the instrument.

This was the tradition out of which the British Astronomical Association Lunar Section was born in the early 1890s, not to mention the burgeoning astronomical societies of Liverpool, Leeds, South Wales, Belfast, Manchester, Newcastle and elsewhere, with their ever more keen lunar observers. Even the expatriate British colony at Pernambucco, Brazil had an astronomical society by 1890, and there were a growing number around the British Empire, the United States and Europe. The Moon was invariably the route into astronomy for amateurs worldwide.

LUNAR CHARTS AND THE 'SPACE RACE'

Lunar charts, many of very high quality, proliferated in the late nineteenth and twentieth centuries, inspired largely by Beer's and Mädler's classic charts. There were the charts of Julius Schmidt (1878) and Thomas Gwyn Elger (1895), and Walter Goodacre's classic chart of 1910. And then there was Hugh Percy Wilkins's great 300-inch-diameter chart of 1950.

But what brought the Moon to centre stage not merely for the scientific community but also for the world at large was the 'space race' between the United States of America and the Soviet Union in the late 1950s. After the collapse of the Nazi regime in 1945, German (and not necessarily Nazi) V1 and V2 rocket scientists were taken prisoner by the Americans and Russians. The great Werner von Braun ended up in America – where the young Patrick Moore met and talked with him on several occasions – and by 1957, when the Russians successfully launched their Earth-orbiting satellite Sputnik, the 'race to the Moon' was firmly on.

It was the Russians who led the way in the early years of the 'race', and in 1959, they sent their unmanned probe Lunik III around the Moon, securing the first-ever pictures of the 'dark side', or the side permanently turned away from the earth. All this was at the height of the Cold War, when Soviet Russia and the United States of America were detonating increasingly large hydrogen bombs, and whole sections of Eastern Europe were already either occupied by Communist forces or under imminent threat of invasion. Berlin, after all, was a divided city, and Germany a divided country, and Russian achievements of any kind were seen as pregnant with menace. Some people were even claiming that the Lunik III photographs were propaganda forgeries – and some 'experts' claimed they could see paintbrush marks on them – but Cold

War fears apart, they were, in fact, genuine. The far side of the Moon was dark no longer.

The first *Atlas of the Far Side of the Moon*, edited by N. P. Barbashov, A. A. Mikhailov and Y. N. Lipsky, was published in Moscow in 1960. What is so strikingly obvious about the 'dark side', even from the first relatively low-definition Russian photographs, however, was the over-whelming preponderance of bright 'land' areas, and the relative small-ness of the dark 'seas' or *maria*. Quite unlike the topography of the 'light side', in fact. Indeed, there appeared to be half a dozen 'seas', and far from being 'seas' like those on the 'light side', they were more like small, dark lakes; some of them, moreover, could be seen from the Earth side when the Moon's libration, or axial rocking motion, permit-ted. The names of certain features were clearly redolent of Russian propaganda, such as the 'Montes Sovietici' ('Soviet Mountains'), whereas some recognized truly great Russian scientists, such as the early pre-Soviet pioneer of rocket science, Konstantin Tsiolkovsky. Others acknowledged great non-Soviets, such as Louis Pasteur, Jules Verne, and even Thomas A. Edison. Then from 1960 onwards, a succession of United States' craft began to fill in the finer detail, as under President J. F. Kennedy in particular, the Moon became a focus of American aspiration, spearheaded by NASA, and culminating in a global sensation on 20–21 July 1969, when the American astronauts Buzz Aldrin and Neil Armstrong walked upon the lunar surface, leaving Michael Collins in the Moon-orbiting Command Module.

After 350 years in which self-funded amateur astronomers in vari-ous states of 'grandeur' had studied, mapped and classified the Moon's complex and variegated surface, the initiative finally passed to the pro-fessionals in the 1960s, as the US and Russia threw all they had at the Moon. Yet one man bridged those two worlds: Mr Patrick Moore, as he then was (Figure 6).

For one thing, Patrick's international reputation as a meticulous lunar observer, and as an expert on the limb-edge of the Moon and what could be seen in the 9 per cent of the 'dark side' visible from the Earth at the various librations, aroused both Russian and American interest. His careful drawings of 'Mare Orientale', or 'Eastern Sea', best visible on the extreme lunar libration, reported to the British Astronomical Association some years previously, got him an out-of-the-blue request from Russia in the wake of the Lunik III photographs. They wanted to see his Mare Orientale and other limb drawings to

Figure 6. Patrick Moore in the garden of his home in Selsey with 'Oscar', his 12½-inch reflecting telescope on an altazimuth mount. It was with this instrument that he did so much of his early lunar drawing. (Photograph courtesy of Chris Doherty.)

assist them in cartographically linking the Earth side with the 'dark' side of the Moon. And some years later, as the Americans surged ahead with the 'space race', they, too, requested drawings from Patrick and from other amateurs containing fine detail of tiny parts of the Earth-side of the Moon to help them select possible landing sites for the 1969 *Apollo 11* manned landing.

For while high-quality professional photographs of the Moon had long been available by the 1960s, it was still the practised, patient eye of the visual observer that was best able to catch the really fine detail, as even the clearest atmosphere thickened and thinned in a way that could obscure it. But a patient eye, and a long-trained visual memory at the eyepiece, could often capture the minutiae which a photographic plate might miss. For all this was well before 'smart' computer processing packages enabled an observer to take and stack hundreds of images of a given feature, and then analyse them so as to build up a micro-detailed image based on the clearest seconds of seeing from, perhaps, several hours of digital observing.

It was not for nothing that Patrick would come to know several astronauts and Moonwalkers as personal friends, and it speaks volumes of the high regard in which he was held that the *Apollo 11* astronaut Buzz Aldrin was delighted to fly over from the US to present Patrick with his TV BAFTA Award in 2001.

And, of course, it was also through television that Sir Patrick would form a link between the amateur and professional worlds of astronomy. *The Sky at Night*, quite by chance, would coincide with the success of the Russian Sputnik in 1957, and as the 'race for the Moon' grew apace, it was Patrick, more than any other TV presenter, who became the people's 'man on the Moon'. What a jaw-dropping moment it was on the evening of 24 October 1959, when the monthly number of *The Sky at Night* was five minutes into transmission and the Russians had just beamed an on-board spacecraft-scanned image of the 'dark side' of the Moon to the BBC and the amazing image appeared on the nation's TV screens with Patrick doing an 'off-the-cuff' commentary upon it!

The Lunik III probe would herald a fundamental shift in selenography, as Russian and then American orbiting spacecraft photographed the entire Moon, to a level of detail and cartographic accuracy that would be impossible through a 100-mile blanket of terrestrial atmosphere and at a distance of 239,000 miles. When it became possible for human beings to walk on the lunar surface, this sent the potential for detail straight through the roof, as lunar volcanoes and tectonics undreamed of by James Nasmyth became readily discernible, while lasers enabled us to monitor the peculiarities of the lunar orbit to a level of accuracy unimaginable for a conventional optical observatory.

In 1969, ten years after the launch of Lunik III, Patrick Moore issued his own 'outline' map of the Moon, manually scribed by Patricia A. Cullen. But it in no way drew a line under that tradition of visual, amateur lunar observing and draughtsmanship that began at 9.00 p.m. on the evening of 26 July 1609, when Thomas Harriot made his first sketch of the five-day Moon through his 'Dutch truncke'. For while modern amateur lunar observers may no longer expect to make major discoveries with their 10-, 15- or 24-inch-aperture telescopes, even when coupled to state-of-the-art analytical software, the Moon is still an object of delight. Quite simply, people's jaws still drop when they see the lunar surface with their own eyes for the first time. Children especially are fired to a serious interest in astronomy by looking at our satellite, and just as there are now many excellent amateur lunar photographers, so there are people who take pride in their superb pencil drawings of particular lunar formations and regions.

So the Moon is still very much with us as a source of astronomical inspiration. And, in our own time, perhaps no one has done more to make it so than Sir Patrick Moore, CBE, FRS.

FURTHER READING

Joseph Ashbrook (edited by Leif J. Robinson), *The Astronomical Scrapbook: Sky Watchers, Pioneers, and Seekers in Astronomy* (Cambridge, Massachusetts: Sky Publishing Corporation and CUP, 1984), for eight lunar-related articles, originally published by Ashbrook in *Sky and Telescope.*

Allan Chapman, '[~]"A World in the Moon": John Wilkins and his lunar voyage of 1640', *Quarterly Journal of the Royal Astronomical Society*, Vol. 32 (1991), pp. 121–32.

Allan Chapman, 'James Nasmyth: Astronomer of Fire', in Patrick Moore (ed.), *1997 Yearbook of Astronomy* (London: Macmillan, 1996), pp. 143–67.

Allan Chapman, 'A new perceived reality: Thomas Harriot's Moon maps', *Astronomy and Geophysics*, Vol. 50 (February 2009), pp. 27–33.

Allan Chapman, 'Johannes Hevelius (1611–1687): Instrument Maker, Lunar Cartographer and Surveyor of the Heavens', in Patrick Moore and John Mason (eds), *Patrick Moore's Yearbook of Astronomy 2013* (London: Macmillan, 2012), pp. 343–70.

Galileo Galilei, *Sidereus Nuncius* ('The Starry Messenger'), 1610, translated and introduced by Stillman Drake, in Drake (ed.), *Discoveries and Opinions of Galileo* (New York: Doubleday, Anchor Books, 1957), pp. 1–58.

Thomas Harriot, Moon drawings: see Google images and online pictures published by the Galileo Project.

Jack B. Hartung, 'Was the formation of a 20-km-diameter impact crater on the Moon observed on June 18, 1178?', *Meteoritics and Planetary Science*, Vol. 11, Issue 3 (1976), p. 187.

John Heilbron, *Galileo* (OUP, 2011).

William Herschel, 'An Account of Three Volcanoes on the Moon', *Philosophical Transactions* Vol. 72 (1787), pp. 229–32. Herschel makes the original notification to his friend Sir Joseph Banks, P.R.S., in a letter dated 25 April 1787, now in private hands, but whose owner, Mrs Morris in Scotland, has generously supplied scanned copies to the Royal Society and the R.A.S. See also A. Chapman, 'Sir William Herschel and a letter about lunar volcanoes', *The Speculum* (the journal of the William Herschel Society), Vol. 9, No. 2 (autumn 2010), pp. 26–8. Also Nigel Barnes and Andrew Watkinson-Trim, 'Exploring Herschel's volcanoes', *The Speculum*, Vol. 10, No. 2 (summer 2011), pp. 17–27, for a more detailed account of Herschel's and other observers' sightings of bright spots on the dark moon.

Robert Hooke, *Micrographia* (1665), Hipparchus crater drawing, pp. 242–6 (New York: Dover reprint edition).

Samuel Horton, bright spot on the moon, in an article from an unspecified magazine pasted in John Lee's 'Scrapbook', Museum of the History of Science, Oxford, Gunther 38.7. See A. Chapman, *The Victorian Amateur Astronomer: Independent Astronomical Research in Britain, 1820–1920* (John Wiley/Praxis Publishing, 1998), pp. 88–9, p. 339 (n. 95).

H. C. King, *A History of the Telescope* (London, 1955).

Patrick Moore, *Guide to the Moon* (London: Eyre and Spottiswoode, 1953).

Patrick Moore with H. P. Wilkins, *The Moon* (London: Faber and Faber, 1955).

Patrick Moore, *On the Moon* (London: Cassell, 2001).

Patrick Moore, *80 Not Out. The Autobiography* (London: Contender, 2003).

James Nasmyth and James Carpenter, *The Moon: Considered as a Planet, a World, and a Satellite* (London, 1874).

James Nasmyth, *James Nasmyth Engineer: An Autobiography* (ed. Samuel Smiles, London, 1889).

Faith K. Pizor and T. Allen Camp (eds), *The Man in the Moon* (London, 1971): sections from John Wilkins, pp. 41–58.

Stephen P. Rigaud, 'Account of Harriot's papers', published as a supplement to *The Miscellaneous Works of the Revd James Bradley* (Oxford, 1832–3).

William Sheehan and Richard Baum, 'Observation and inference: Johann Hieronymus Schröter, 1745–1816', *Journal of the British Astronomical Association*, Vol. 105 (1995), p. 171.

Reg Turnill, *The Moonlandings: An Eyewitness Account* (CUP, 2003).

Ewen A. Whitaker, *Mapping and Naming the Moon: A History of Lunar Cartography and Nomenclature* (CUP, 1999).

John Wilkins, *The Mathematical and Philosophical Works of the Right Reverend John Wilkins* (London, 1802), Frank Cass reprint (London, 1970), for full text of Wilkins's lunar writings, 'Selenites' and 'Flying Chariots'.

Thoughts on Patrick

Bill Leatherbarrow
BAA President and Director, BAA Lunar Section

My first encounter with Patrick was one that so many astronomers – amateur and professional – will recognize: a warm, encouraging, prompt (and, frankly, unexpected) response to a youthful letter from yet another tyro. How did he find the time and patience to write so many such letters over so many years, each one individualized and making the recipient feel very special?

My subsequent encounters with him grew out of the work of the Lunar Section of the British Astronomical Association. Patrick became director of that section when I first joined the BAA, and the fact that I am now privileged to hold the same office neatly bookends the years of our friendship, years that hold so many fond memories. Patrick served two stints as director in the 1960s and 1970s, and he was a perfect leader. He brought excitement (and a touch of stardust) to amateur lunar studies at a time of great interest and change, as the *Apollo* programme culminated in the manned lunar landings. He kept a belief in the value of amateur observations alive when they could so easily have been dismissed as redundant alongside professional efforts. He started new programmes of study to replace old-style cartography, including a sustained campaign to detect transient lunar phenomena, or TLPs, the reality of which is still a subject of much debate.

The Lunar Section was a stimulating place to be during Patrick's directorship, perhaps more so than at any time before or after. Patrick himself had served a long apprenticeship for the role, acting as a loyal and efficient lieutenant to H. P. Wilkins in the 1940s and 1950s. He travelled with Wilkins on those famous expeditions to Meudon to use the great 33-inch refractor for detailed mapping work, as well as co-authoring with him the classic text *The Moon*, which accompanied Wilkins's 300-inch map.

When Patrick assumed the directorship in 1964, he arrived like a whirlwind and the section became a hotbed of activity. Membership grew to over three hundred, a regular monthly circular was started, and section meetings were held throughout the country – all of which Patrick made a point of attending, despite his numerous other commitments. By that time he had become a 'celebrity' as a result of his television appearances, but this in no way impinged on the way he ran the Lunar Section, which for him was always a serious and scientific organization whose members, together with Patrick, believed that what they did counted. Patrick's own contribution to lunar cartography was immense, even if his resistance to the impact theory of crater formation turned out to be misplaced. But it was his ability to inspire others that was really telling: a great many subsequent students of the Moon, amateur and professional, owed so much to his influence, even when they disagreed with his views.

What will I remember of those amazing years, apart from the privilege of working under the guidance of such a figure?

The pleasure and excitement of finding regular letters or postcards from Patrick on the doormat, all addressed to W. Leatherbarrow, *Esqre* (a true Mooreism, and surely the most inefficient abbreviation ever coined); the visits to Selsey, when the anticipation of being met by Patrick at Chichester station was offset by apprehension at the thought of the subsequent drive to Farthings in '*The Ark*', during which all intervening obstacles, whether natural or man-made, were blithely ignored; his generosity of spirit; the way he filled every room he entered; the warmth he conjured for everyone he spoke to; his irreverent sense of fun; and, of course, those parties at his home.

Patrick's clarity of mind, energy and enthusiasm for his work endured to the end, but it was painful indeed to witness the diminution of his physical powers in his last years, along with the frustration it caused him.

But that's not the Patrick I will remember. The one I shall carry in my mind was a towering and inspirational figure, a true and unrepeatable force of nature, and I shall never forget him.

Sir Patrick Moore:
A True Knight

Ann Mills
Chairman of Trustees, South Downs Planetarium, Chichester

When you think of a knight of the realm, you might think of someone in shining armour with a strength and passion greater than us normal mortals. To the South Downs Planetarium in Chichester, Sir Patrick was our true knight. Patrick played a critical role in setting up the initial project over twenty years ago, and he was a constant motivator and inspiration to the team. His support continued from the day the planetarium opened in 2001 to his most recent visits in 2012. We were privileged to have him as our patron, and his regular visits to see us were always times of warmth and awe.

I remember a special visit by the Chief Inspector of Schools, Sir David Bell, with a group of sixty schoolchildren. Patrick was there with the planetarium's volunteer team, and David recalled vividly how he had sat up watching Patrick describing the Moon landings on TV and how inspired he had been. The happiest times at the planetarium were when we celebrated Patrick's birthday each year. As the number of candles on his cake grew so did the warmth and affection we all had for him.

Patrick was so very generous – most especially with his time. We worked together on a couple of projects over the last ten years and it was always a wonderful feeling coming into his study at Farthings, his home in Selsey. What a truly magical room it was! One project was the preparation of a small book on Thomas Harriot for the planetarium. When I told Patrick of our plan, he was delighted to help and wrote the foreword for us. When the writing and research got tedious, he would always keep me going by a short phone call – 'How's the book going?' – followed by an update of news. The most lasting memory for me was preparing an exhibition of Patrick's observational work for display at the planetarium. We sat on Saturday afternoons looking through his

Ann and Patrick at the South Downs Planetarium in Chichester (which Patrick helped to found) with a copy of Ann's little book on Thomas Harriot. (Image courtesy of Gavin Myers and South Downs Planetarium.)

notebooks and recalling his observations from before the Second World War and through the fifties and onwards. His drawings and notes for each observation were made in remarkable detail. When you read Patrick's notes, you can hear him speaking the words; he wrote as he spoke. Many of the notes contained his customary sense of mischief. I am sure that Patrick would have preferred it if I'd drunk a glass of wine on my visits, but, always the gentleman, he would arrange a mug of his other favourite drink, Earl Grey tea.

For Patrick's last birthday I made him a large star-covered cushion. He told me that within a couple of weeks his beloved cat Ptolemy had requisitioned it for his use. Patrick loved his cats and their comfort always came before his!

The planetarium in Chichester will no longer enjoy Patrick's many visits but it holds, and will continue to hold, a lasting memory of a very kind and remarkable man. We have lost our knight but he has left a tangible and visible mark on the planetarium and our work. I miss the gentleman, the twinkle in his eye, and his kindness.

Part Three

Miscellaneous

Some Interesting Variable Stars

JOHN ISLES

All variable stars are of potential interest, and hundreds of them can be observed with the slightest optical aid – even with a pair of binoculars. The stars in the list that follows include many that are popular with amateur observers, as well as some less well-known objects that are nevertheless suitable for study visually. The periods and ranges of many variables are not constant from one cycle to another, and some are completely irregular.

Finder charts are given after the list for those stars marked with an asterisk. These charts are adapted with permission from those issued by the Variable Star Section of the British Astronomical Association. Apart from the eclipsing variables and others in which the light changes are purely a geometrical effect, variable stars can be divided broadly into two classes: the pulsating stars, and the eruptive or cataclysmic variables.

Mira (Omicron Ceti) is the best-known member of the long-period subclass of pulsating red-giant stars. The chart is suitable for use in estimating the magnitude of Mira when it reaches naked-eye brightness – typically from about a month before the predicted date of maximum until two or three months after maximum. Predictions for Mira and other stars of its class follow the section of finder charts.

The semi-regular variables are less predictable, and generally have smaller ranges. V Canum Venaticorum is one of the more reliable ones, with steady oscillations in a six-month cycle. Z Ursae Majoris, easily found with binoculars near Delta, has a large range, and often shows double maxima owing to the presence of multiple periodicities in its light changes. The chart for Z is also suitable for observing another semi-regular star, RY Ursae Majoris. These semi-regular stars are mostly red giants or supergiants.

The RV Tauri stars are of earlier spectral class than the semi-regulars, and in a full cycle of variation they often show deep minima and double maxima that are separated by a secondary minimum. U Monocerotis is one of the brightest RV Tauri stars.

Among eruptive variable stars is the carbon-rich supergiant R Coronae Borealis. Its unpredictable eruptions cause it not to brighten, but to fade. This happens when one of the sooty clouds that the star throws out from time to time happens to come in our direction and blots out most of the star's light from our view. Much of the time R Coronae is bright enough to be seen in binoculars, and the chart can be used to estimate its magnitude. During the deepest minima, however, the star needs a telescope of 25-cm or larger aperture to be detected.

CH Cygni is a symbiotic star – that is, a close binary comprising a red giant and a hot dwarf star that interact physically, giving rise to outbursts. The system also shows semi-regular oscillations, and sudden fades and rises that may be connected with eclipses.

Observers can follow the changes of these variable stars by using the comparison stars whose magnitudes are given below each chart. Observations of variable stars by amateurs are of scientific value, provided they are collected and made available for analysis. This is done by several organizations, including the British Astronomical Association (see the list of astronomical societies in this volume), the American Association of Variable Star Observers (49 Bay State Road, Cambridge, Massachusetts 02138, USA), and the Royal Astronomical Society of New Zealand (PO Box 3181, Wellington, New Zealand).

Star	RA		Declination		Range	Type	Period	Spectrum
	h	m	°	′			(days)	
R Andromedae	00	24.0	+38	35	5.8–14.9	Mira	409	S
W Andromedae	02	17.6	+44	18	6.7–14.6	Mira	396	S
U Antliae	10	35.2	−39	34	5–6	Irregular	—	C
Theta Apodis	14	05.3	−76	48	5–7	Semi-regular	119	M
R Aquarii	23	43.8	−15	17	5.8–12.4	Symbiotic	387	M+Pec
T Aquarii	20	49.9	−05	09	7.2–14.2	Mira	202	M
R Aquilae	19	06.4	+08	14	5.5–12.0	Mira	284	M
V Aquilae	19	04.4	−05	41	6.6–8.4	Semi-regular	353	C
Eta Aquilae	19	52.5	+01	00	3.5–4.4	Cepheid	7.2	F–G
U Arae	17	53.6	−51	41	7.7–14.1	Mira	225	M

Some Interesting Variable Stars

Star	RA		Declination		Range	Type	Period	Spectrum
	h	m	°	′			(days)	
R Arietis	02	16.1	+25	03	7.4–13.7	Mira	187	M
U Arietis	03	11.0	+14	48	7.2–15.2	Mira	371	M
R Aurigae	05	17.3	+53	35	6.7–13.9	Mira	458	M
Epsilon Aurigae	05	02.0	+43	49	2.9–3.8	Algol	9892	F+B
R Boötis	14	37.2	+26	44	6.2–13.1	Mira	223	M
X Camelopardalis	04	45.7	+75	06	7.4–14.2	Mira	144	K–M
R Cancri	08	16.6	+11	44	6.1–11.8	Mira	362	M
X Cancri	08	55.4	+17	14	5.6–7.5	Semi-regular	195?	C
R Canis Majoris	07	19.5	−16	24	5.7–6.3	Algol	1.1	F
VY Canis Majoris	07	23.0	−25	46	6.5–9.6	Unique	—	M
S Canis Minoris	07	32.7	+08	19	6.6–13.2	Mira	333	M
R Canum Ven.	13	49.0	+39	33	6.5–12.9	Mira	329	M
*V Canum Ven.	13	19.5	+45	32	6.5–8.6	Semi-regular	192	M
R Carinae	09	32.2	−62	47	3.9–10.5	Mira	309	M
S Carinae	10	09.4	−61	33	4.5–9.9	Mira	149	K–M
l Carinae	09	45.2	−62	30	3.3–4.2	Cepheid	35.5	F–K
Eta Carinae	10	45.1	−59	41	-0.8–7.9	Irregular	—	Pec
R Cassiopeiae	23	58.4	+51	24	4.7–13.5	Mira	430	M
S Cassiopeiae	01	19.7	+72	37	7.9–16.1	Mira	612	S
W Cassiopeiae	00	54.9	+58	34	7.8–12.5	Mira	406	C
Gamma Cas.	00	56.7	+60	43	1.6–3.0	Gamma Cas.	—	B
Rho Cassiopeiae	23	54.4	+57	30	4.1–6.2	Semi-regular	—	F–K
R Centauri	14	16.6	−59	55	5.3–11.8	Mira	546	M
S Centauri	12	24.6	−49	26	7–8	Semi-regular	65	C
T Centauri	13	41.8	−33	36	5.5–9.0	Semi-regular	90	K–M
S Cephei	21	35.2	+78	37	7.4–12.9	Mira	487	C
T Cephei	21	09.5	+68	29	5.2–11.3	Mira	388	M
Delta Cephei	22	29.2	+58	25	3.5–4.4	Cepheid	5.4	F–G
Mu Cephei	21	43.5	+58	47	3.4–5.1	Semi-regular	730	M
U Ceti	02	33.7	−13	09	6.8–13.4	Mira	235	M
W Ceti	00	02.1	−14	41	7.1–14.8	Mira	351	S
*Omicron Ceti	02	19.3	−02	59	2.0–10.1	Mira	332	M
R Chamaeleontis	08	21.8	−76	21	7.5–14.2	Mira	335	M
T Columbae	05	19.3	−33	42	6.6–12.7	Mira	226	M
R Comae Ber.	12	04.3	+18	47	7.1–14.6	Mira	363	M
*R Coronae Bor.	15	48.6	+28	09	5.7–14.8	R Coronae Bor.	—	C
S Coronae Bor.	15	21.4	+31	22	5.8–14.1	Mira	360	M
T Coronae Bor.	15	59.6	+25	55	2.0–10.8	Recurrent nova	—	M+Pec
V Coronae Bor.	15	49.5	+39	34	6.9–12.6	Mira	358	C
W Coronae Bor.	16	15.4	+37	48	7.8–14.3	Mira	238	M

Star	RA		Declination		Range	Type	Period	Spectrum
	h	m	°	′			(days)	
R Corvi	12	19.6	−19	15	6.7−14.4	Mira	317	M
R Crucis	12	23.6	−61	38	6.4−7.2	Cepheid	5.8	F−G
R Cygni	19	36.8	+50	12	6.1−14.4	Mira	426	S
U Cygni	20	19.6	+47	54	5.9−12.1	Mira	463	C
W Cygni	21	36.0	+45	22	5.0−7.6	Semi-regular	131	M
RT Cygni	19	43.6	+48	47	6.0−13.1	Mira	190	M
SS Cygni	21	42.7	+43	35	7.7−12.4	Dwarf nova	50±	K+Pec
*CH Cygni	19	24.5	+50	14	5.6−9.0	Symbiotic	—	M+B
Chi Cygni	19	50.6	+32	55	3.3−14.2	Mira	408	S
R Delphini	20	14.9	+09	05	7.6−13.8	Mira	285	M
U Delphini	20	45.5	+18	05	5.6−7.5	Semi-regular	110?	M
EU Delphini	20	37.9	+18	16	5.8−6.9	Semi-regular	60	M
Beta Doradûs	05	33.6	−62	29	3.5−4.1	Cepheid	9.8	F−G
R Draconis	16	32.7	+66	45	6.7−13.2	Mira	246	M
T Eridani	03	55.2	−24	02	7.2−13.2	Mira	252	M
R Fornacis	02	29.3	−26	06	7.5−13.0	Mira	389	C
R Geminorum	07	07.4	+22	42	6.0−14.0	Mira	370	S
U Geminorum	07	55.1	+22	00	8.2−14.9	Dwarf nova	105±	Pec+M
Zeta Geminorum	07	04.1	+20	34	3.6−4.2	Cepheid	10.2	F−G
Eta Geminorum	06	14.9	+22	30	3.2−3.9	Semi-regular	233	M
S Gruis	22	26.1	−48	26	6.0−15.0	Mira	402	M
S Herculis	16	51.9	+14	56	6.4−13.8	Mira	307	M
U Herculis	16	25.8	+18	54	6.4−13.4	Mira	406	M
Alpha Herculis	17	14.6	+14	23	2.7−4.0	Semi-regular	—	M
68, u Herculis	17	17.3	+33	06	4.7−5.4	Algol	2.1	B+B
R Horologii	02	53.9	−49	53	4.7−14.3	Mira	408	M
U Horologii	03	52.8	−45	50	6−14	Mira	348	M
R Hydrae	13	29.7	−23	17	3.5−10.9	Mira	389	M
U Hydrae	10	37.6	−13	23	4.3−6.5	Semi-regular	450?	C
VW Hydri	04	09.1	−71	18	8.4−14.4	Dwarf nova	27±	Pec
R Leonis	09	47.6	+11	26	4.4−11.3	Mira	310	M
R Leonis Minoris	09	45.6	+34	31	6.3−13.2	Mira	372	M
R Leporis	04	59.6	−14	48	5.5−11.7	Mira	427	C
Y Librae	15	11.7	−06	01	7.6−14.7	Mira	276	M
RS Librae	15	24.3	−22	55	7.0−13.0	Mira	218	M
Delta Librae	15	01.0	−08	31	4.9−5.9	Algol	2.3	A
R Lyncis	07	01.3	+55	20	7.2−14.3	Mira	379	S
R Lyrae	18	55.3	+43	57	3.9−5.0	Semi-regular	46?	M
RR Lyrae	19	25.5	+42	47	7.1−8.1	RR Lyrae	0.6	A−F
Beta Lyrae	18	50.1	+33	22	3.3−4.4	Eclipsing	12.9	B

Some Interesting Variable Stars

Star	RA h	m	Declination °	′	Range	Type	Period (days)	Spectrum
U Microscopii	20	29.2	−40	25	7.0−14.4	Mira	334	M
*U Monocerotis	07	30.8	−09	47	5.9−7.8	RV Tauri	91	F−K
V Monocerotis	06	22.7	−02	12	6.0−13.9	Mira	340	M
R Normae	15	36.0	−49	30	6.5−13.9	Mira	508	M
T Normae	15	44.1	−54	59	6.2−13.6	Mira	241	M
R Octantis	05	26.1	−86	23	6.3−13.2	Mira	405	M
S Octantis	18	08.7	−86	48	7.2−14.0	Mira	259	M
V Ophiuchi	16	26.7	−12	26	7.3−11.6	Mira	297	C
X Ophiuchi	18	38.3	+08	50	5.9−9.2	Mira	329	M
RS Ophiuchi	17	50.2	−06	43	4.3−12.5	Recurrent nova	—	OB+M
U Orionis	05	55.8	+20	10	4.8−13.0	Mira	368	M
W Orionis	05	05.4	+01	11	5.9−7.7	Semi-regular	212	C
Alpha Orionis	05	55.2	+07	24	0.0−1.3	Semi-regular	2335	M
S Pavonis	19	55.2	−59	12	6.6−10.4	Semi-regular	381	M
Kappa Pavonis	18	56.9	−67	14	3.9−4.8	W Virginis	9.1	G
R Pegasi	23	06.8	+10	33	6.9−13.8	Mira	378	M
X Persei	03	55.4	+31	03	6.0−7.0	Gamma Cas.	—	O9.5
Beta Persei	03	08.2	+40	57	2.1−3.4	Algol	2.9	B
Zeta Phoenicis	01	08.4	−55	15	3.9−4.4	Algol	1.7	B+B
R Pictoris	04	46.2	−49	15	6.4−10.1	Semi-regular	171	M
RS Puppis	08	13.1	−34	35	6.5−7.7	Cepheid	41.4	F−G
L^2 Puppis	07	13.5	−44	39	2.6−6.2	Semi-regular	141	M
T Pyxidis	09	04.7	−32	23	6.5−15.3	Recurrent nova	7000±	Pec
U Sagittae	19	18.8	+19	37	6.5−9.3	Algol	3.4	B+G
WZ Sagittae	20	07.6	+17	42	7.0−15.5	Dwarf nova	1900±	A
R Sagittarii	19	16.7	−19	18	6.7−12.8	Mira	270	M
RR Sagittarii	19	55.9	−29	11	5.4−14.0	Mira	336	M
RT Sagittarii	20	17.7	−39	07	6.0−14.1	Mira	306	M
RU Sagittarii	19	58.7	−41	51	6.0−13.8	Mira	240	M
RY Sagittarii	19	16.5	−33	31	5.8−14.0	R Coronae Bor.	—	G
RR Scorpii	16	56.6	−30	35	5.0−12.4	Mira	281	M
RS Scorpii	16	55.6	−45	06	6.2−13.0	Mira	320	M
RT Scorpii	17	03.5	−36	55	7.0−15.2	Mira	449	S
Delta Scorpii	16	00.3	−22	37	1.6−2.3	Irregular	—	B
S Sculptoris	00	15.4	−32	03	5.5−13.6	Mira	363	M
R Scuti	18	47.5	−05	42	4.2−8.6	RV Tauri	146	G−K
R Serpentis	15	50.7	+15	08	5.2−14.4	Mira	356	M
S Serpentis	15	21.7	+14	19	7.0−14.1	Mira	372	M
T Tauri	04	22.0	+19	32	9.3−13.5	T Tauri	—	F−K
SU Tauri	05	49.1	+19	04	9.1−16.9	R Coronae Bor.	—	G

Star	RA		Declination		Range	Type	Period	Spectrum
	h	m	°	′			(days)	
Lambda Tauri	04	00.7	+12	29	3.4–3.9	Algol	4.0	B+A
R Trianguli	02	37.0	+34	16	5.4–12.6	Mira	267	M
R Ursae Majoris	10	44.6	+68	47	6.5–13.7	Mira	302	M
T Ursae Majoris	12	36.4	+59	29	6.6–13.5	Mira	257	M
*Z Ursae Majoris	11	56.5	+57	52	6.2–9.4	Semi-regular	196	M
*RY Ursae Majoris	12	20.5	+61	19	6.7–8.3	Semi-regular	310?	M
U Ursae Minoris	14	17.3	+66	48	7.1–13.0	Mira	331	M
R Virginis	12	38.5	+06	59	6.1–12.1	Mira	146	M
S Virginis	13	33.0	−07	12	6.3–13.2	Mira	375	M
SS Virginis	12	25.3	+00	48	6.0–9.6	Semi-regular	364	C
R Vulpeculae	21	04.4	+23	49	7.0–14.3	Mira	137	M
Z Vulpeculae	19	21.7	+25	34	7.3–8.9	Algol	2.5	B+A

V CANUM VENATICORUM   13h 19.5m +45° 32′ (2000)

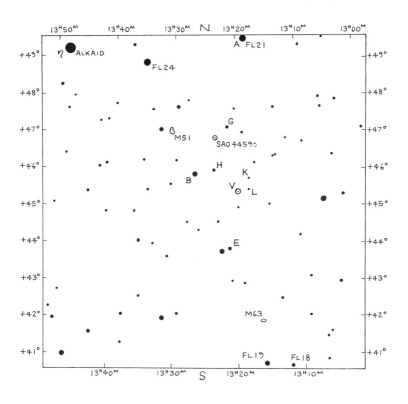

A 5.1	H 7.8
B 5.9	K 8.4
E 6.5	L 8.6
G 7.1	

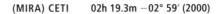

(MIRA) CETI   02h 19.3m −02° 59′ (2000)

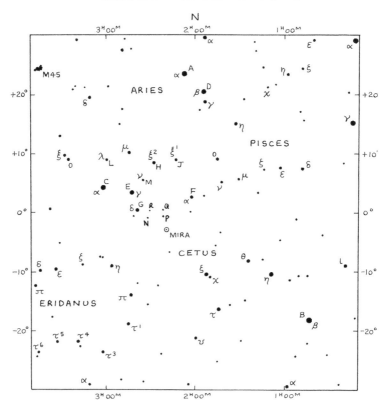

A 2.2	J 4.4
B 2.4	L 4.9
C 2.7	M 5.1
D 3.0	N 5.4
E 3.6	P 5.5
F 3.8	Q 5.7
G 4.1	R 6.1
H 4.3	

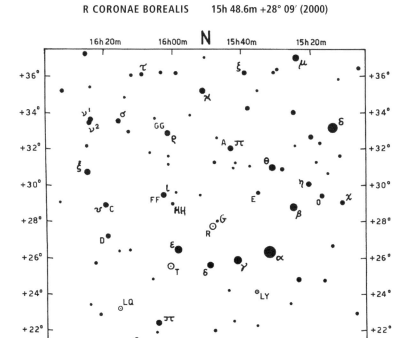

R CORONAE BOREALIS   15h 48.6m +28° 09′ (2000)

FF	5.0	C	5.8
GG	5.4	D	6.2
A	5.6	E	6.5
		HH	7.1
		G	7.4

CH CYGNI   19h 24.5m +50° 14′ (2000)

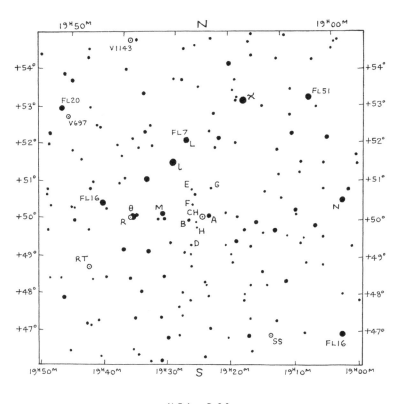

N 5.4	D 8.0
M 5.5	E 8.1
L 5.8	F 8.5
A 6.5	G 8.5
B 7.4	H 9.2

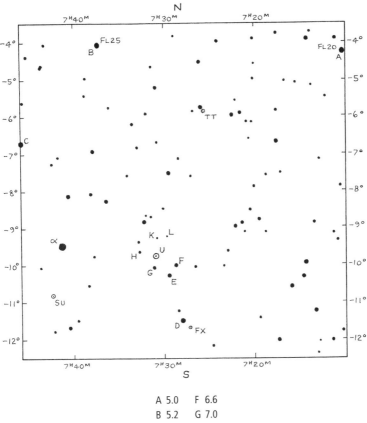

U MONOCEROTIS   **07h 30.8m −09° 47′ (2000)**

A 5.0	F 6.6
B 5.2	G 7.0
C 5.7	H 7.5
D 5.9	K 7.8
E 6.0	L 8.0

RY URSAE MAJORIS   12h 20.5m +61° 19′ (2000)
Z URSAE MAJORIS   11h 56.5m +57° 52′ (2000)

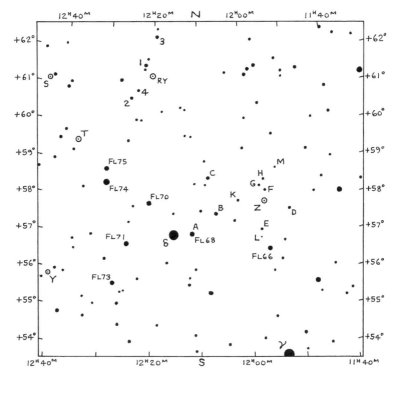

A	6.5	F	8.6	M	9.1
B	7.2	G	8.7	1	6.9
C	7.6	H	8.8	2	7.4
D	8.0	K	8.9	3	7.7
E	8.3	L	9.0	4	7.8

Mira Stars: Maxima, 2014

JOHN ISLES

Below are the predicted dates of maxima for Mira stars that reach magnitude 7.5 or brighter at an average maximum. Individual maxima can in some cases be brighter or fainter than average by a magnitude or more, and all dates are only approximate. The positions, extreme ranges and mean periods of these stars can be found in the preceding list of interesting variable stars.

Star	Mean magnitude at maximum	Dates of maxima
R Andromedae	6.9	22 Jan
W Andromedae	7.4	13 Dec
R Aquarii	6.5	25 Feb
R Aquilae	6.1	11 Mar, 20 Dec
R Boötis	7.2	22 June
R Cancri	6.8	27 July
S Canis Minoris	7.5	8 July
R Carinae	4.6	22 Mar
S Carinae	5.7	4 May, 30 Sept
R Cassiopeiae	7.0	3 Dec
R Centauri	6.0	21 Aug (secondary max.)
T Cephei	6.0	14 Apr
U Ceti	7.5	12 Feb, 4 Oct
Omicron Ceti	3.4	12 June
T Columbae	7.5	10 Feb, 23 Sept
S Coronae Borealis	7.3	22 Aug
V Coronae Borealis	7.5	5 Nov
R Corvi	7.5	23 Apr
R Cygni	7.5	22 Oct
RT Cygni	7.3	4 Apr, 11 Oct

Star	Mean magnitude at maximum	Dates of maxima
Chi Cygni	5.2	5 July
R Geminorum	7.1	12 Jan
U Herculis	7.5	23 Mar
R Horologii	6.0	24 July
R Hydrae	4.5	28 Dec
R Leonis	5.8	20 Oct
R Leonis Minoris	7.1	20 Mar
R Leporis	6.8	12 Nov
RS Librae	7.5	25 Apr, 29 Nov
V Monocerotis	7.0	16 Nov
R Normae	7.2	10 May
T Normae	7.4	22 Apr
V Ophiuchi	7.5	14 Jan, 7 Nov
X Ophiuchi	6.8	24 July
U Orionis	6.3	25 Mar
R Sagittarii	7.3	27 Apr
RR Sagittarii	6.8	18 June
RT Sagittarii	7.0	15 July
RU Sagittarii	7.2	18 June
RR Scorpii	5.9	11 Aug
RS Scorpii	7.0	12 June
S Sculptoris	6.7	1 Jan, 29 Dec
R Serpentis	6.9	5 Aug
R Trianguli	6.2	20 Sept
R Ursae Majoris	7.5	10 Mar
R Virginis	6.9	9 May, 2 Oct
S Virginis	7.0	7 Mar

Some Interesting Double Stars

BOB ARGYLE

The positions, angles and separations given below correspond to epoch 2014.0.

No.	RA	Declin-ation	Star	Magni-tudes	Separa-tion	PA	Cata-logue	Comments
	h m	° ′			arcsec	°		
1	00 31.5	−62 58	β Tuc	4.4,4.8	27.1	169	LCL 119	Both stars again difficult doubles.
2	00 49.1	+57 49	η Cas	3.4,7.5	13.3	324	Σ60	Easy. Creamy, bluish. P = 480 years.
3	00 55.0	+23 38	36 And	6.0,6.4	1.1	328	Σ73	P = 168 years. Both yellow. Slowly opening.
4	01 13.7	+07 35	ζ Psc	5.6,6.5	23.1	63	Σ100	Yellow, reddish-white.
5	01 39.8	−56 12	p Eri	5.8,5.8	11.7	187	Δ5	Period = 484 years.
6	01 53.5	+19 18	γ Ari	4.8,4.8	7.5	1	Σ180	Very easy. Both white.
7	02 02.0	+02 46	α Psc	4.2,5.1	1.8	262	Σ202	Binary, period = 933 years.
8	02 03.9	+42 20	γ And	2.3,5.0	9.6	63	Σ205	Yellow, blue. Relatively fixed.
			γ² And	5.1,6.3	0.1	87	OΣ38	BC now beyond range of amateur instruments.
9	02 29.1	+67 24	ι Cas AB	4.9,6.9	2.6	229	Σ262	AB is long-period binary. P = 620 years.
			ι Cas AC	4.9,8.4	7.1	117		
10	02 33.8	−28 14	ω For	5.0,7.7	10.8	245	HJ 3506	Common proper motion.
11	02 43.3	+03 14	γ Cet	3.5,7.3	2.3	298	Σ299	Not too easy.
12	02 58.3	−40 18	θ Eri	3.4,4.5	8.3	90	PZ 2	Both white.

No.	RA	Declin-ation	Star	Magni-tudes	Separa-tion	PA	Cata-logue	Comments
	h m	° ′			arcsec	°		
13	02 59.2	+21 20	ε Ari	5.2,5.5	1.3	210	Σ333	Closing very slowly. P = 1216 years? Both white.
14	03 00.9	+52 21	Σ331 Per	5.3,6.7	12.0	85	–	Fixed.
15	03 12.1	−28 59	α For	4.0,7.0	5.3	300	HJ 3555	P = 269 years. B variable?
16	03 48.6	−37 37	f Eri	4.8,5.3	8.2	215	Δ16	Pale yellow. Fixed.
17	03 54.3	−02 57	32 Eri	4.8,6.1	6.9	348	Σ470	Fixed. Deep yellow and white.
18	04 32.0	+53 55	1 Cam	5.7,6.8	10.3	308	Σ550	Fixed.
19	04 50.9	−53 28	ι Pic	5.6,6.4	12.4	58	Δ18	Good object for small apertures. Fixed.
20	05 13.2	−12 56	κ Lep	4.5,7.4	2.0	357	Σ661	Visible in 7.5 cm. Slowly closing.
21	05 14.5	−08 12	β Ori	0.1,6.8	9.5	204	Σ668	Companion once thought to be close double.
22	05 21.8	−24 46	41 Lep	5.4,6.6	3.4	93	HJ 3752	Deep yellow pair in a rich field.
23	05 24.5	−02 24	η Ori	3.8,4.8	1.8	77	DA 5	Slow-moving binary.
24	05 35.1	+09 56	λ Ori	3.6,5.5	4.3	44	Σ738	Fixed.
25	05 35.3	−05 23	θ Ori AB	6.7,7.9	8.6	32	Σ748	Trapezium in M42.
			θ Ori CD	5.1,6.7	13.4	61		
26	05 40.7	−01 57	ζ Ori	1.9,4.0	2.2	167	Σ774	Can be split in 7.5 cm. Long-period binary.
27	06 14.9	+22 30	η Gem	var,6.5	1.6	254	β1008	Well seen with 20 cm. Primary orange.
28	06 46.2	+59 27	12 Lyn AB	5.4,6.0,	1.9	67	Σ948	AB is binary, P = 908 years.
			12 Lyn AC	5.4,7.3	8.8	308	–	
29	07 08.7	−70 30	γ Vol	3.9,5.8	14.1	298	Δ42	Very slow binary.
30	07 16.6	−23 19	h3945 CMa	4.8,6.8	26.8	51	–	Contrasting colours. Yellow and blue.

Some Interesting Double Stars

No.	RA h m	Declin-ation ° ′	Star	Magni-tudes	Separa-tion arcsec	PA °	Cata-logue	Comments
31	07 20.1	+21 59	δ Gem	3.5,8.2	5.5	228	Σ1066	Not too easy. Yellow, pale blue.
32	07 34.6	+31 53	α Gem	1.9,2.9	5.0	56	Σ1110	Widening. Easy with 7.5 cm.
33	07 38.8	−26 48	κ Pup	4.5,4.7	9.8	318	H III 27	Both white.
34	08 12.2	+17 39	ζ Cnc AB	5.6,6.0	1.1	24	Σ1196	Period (AB) = 59.6 years. Near maximum separation.
			ζ Cnc AB-C	5.0,6.2	5.9	67	Σ1196	Period (AB–C) = 1115 years.
35	08 46.8	+06 25	ε Hyd	3.3,6.8	2.9	308	Σ1273	PA slowly increasing. A is a very close pair.
36	09 18.8	+36 48	38 Lyn	3.9,6.6	2.6	226	Σ1334	Almost fixed.
37	09 47.1	−65 04	υ Car	3.1,6.1	5.0	129	RMK 11	Fixed. Fine in small telescopes.
38	10 20.0	+19 50	γ Leo	2.2,3.5	4.6	126	Σ1424	Binary, period = 510 years. Both orange.
39	10 32.0	−45 04	s Vel	6.2,6.5	13.5	218	PZ 3	Fixed. Both white.
40	10 46.8	−49 26	μ Vel	2.7,6.4	2.6	57	R 155	P = 138 years. Near widest separation.
41	10 55.6	+24 45	54 Leo	4.5,6.3	6.6	111	Σ1487	Slowly widening. Pale yellow and white.
42	11 18.2	+31 32	ξ UMa	4.3,4.8	1.7	183	Σ1523	Binary, 59.9 years. Needs 7.5 cm.
43	11 23.9	+10 32	ι Leo	4.0,6.7	2.1	97	Σ1536	Binary, period = 186 years.
44	11 32.3	−29 16	N Hya	5.8,5.9	9.4	210	H III 96	Both yellow. Long-period binary.
45	12 14.0	−45 43	D Cen	5.6,6.8	2.8	243	RMK 14	Orange and white. Closing.
46	12 26.6	−63 06	α Cru	1.4,1.9	4.0	114	Δ252	Glorious pair. Third star in a low power field.

No.	RA	Declin-ation	Star	Magni-tudes	Separa-tion	PA	Cata-logue	Comments
	h m	° ′			arcsec	°		
47	12 41.5	−48 58	γ Cen	2.9,2.9	0.2	194	HJ 4539	Period = 84 years. Nearing periastron. Both yellow.
48	12 41.7	−01 27	γ Vir	3.5,3.5	2.1	8	Σ1670	Now widening quickly. Beautiful pair for 10 cm.
49	12 46.3	−68 06	β Mus	3.7,4.0	0.9	58	R 207	Both white. Closing slowly. P = 194 years.
50	12 54.6	−57 11	μ Cru	4.3,5.3	34.9	17	Δ126	Fixed. Both white.
51	12 56.0	+38 19	α CVn	2.9,5.5	19.3	229	Σ1692	Easy. Yellow, bluish.
52	13 22.6	−60 59	J Cen	4.6,6.5	60.0	343	Δ133	Fixed. A is a close pair.
53	13 24.0	+54 56	ζ UMa	2.3,4.0	14.4	152	Σ1744	Very easy. Naked-eye pair with Alcor.
54	13 51.8	−33 00	3 Cen	4.5,6.0	7.7	102	H III 101	Both white. Closing slowly.
55	14 39.6	−60 50	α Cen	0.0,1.2	4.4	275	RHD 1	Finest pair in the sky. P = 80 years. Closing.
56	14 41.1	+13 44	ζ Boo	4.5,4.6	0.5	291	Σ1865	Both white. Closing – highly inclined orbit.
57	14 45.0	+27 04	ε Boo	2.5,4.9	2.9	344	Σ1877	Yellow, blue. Fine pair.
58	14 46.0	−25 27	54 Hya	5.1,7.1	8.3	122	H III 97	Closing slowly. Yellow and reddish.
59	14 49.3	−14 09	μ Lib	5.8,6.7	1.8	6	β106	Becoming wider. Fine in 7.5 cm.
60	14 51.4	+19 06	ξ Boo	4.7,7.0	5.7	304	Σ1888	Fine contrast. Easy. P = 151.6 years.
61	15 03.8	+47 39	44 Boo	5.3,6.2	1.1	65	Σ1909	Period = 210 years. Closing more quickly.
62	15 05.1	−47 03	π Lup	4.6,4.7	1.7	65	HJ 4728	Widening. Both pale yellow.

Some Interesting Double Stars

No.	RA h m	Declin- ation ° ′	Star	Magni- tudes	Separa- tion arcsec	PA °	Cata- logue	Comments
63	15 18.5	−47 53	μ Lup AB	5.1,5.2	0.9	300	HJ 4753	AB closing. Under-observed.
			μ Lup AC	4.4,7.2	22.7	127	Δ180	AC almost fixed.
64	15 23.4	−59 19	γ Cir	5.1,5.5	0.8	358	HJ 4757	Closing. Needs 20 cm. Long-period binary.
65	15 34.8	+10 33	δ Ser	4.2,5.2	4.0	172	Σ1954	Long-period binary.
66	15 35.1	−41 10	γ Lup AB	3.5,3.6	0.8	277	HJ 4786	Binary. Period = 190 years. Needs 20 cm.
67	15 56.9	−33 58	γ Lup AB–C	5.3,5.8	10.2	49	PZ 4	Fixed. Both pale yellow?
68	16 14.7	+33 52	σ CrB	5.6,6.6	7.2	238	Σ2032	Long-period binary. Both white.
69	16 29.4	−26 26	α Sco	1.2,5.4	2.6	277	GNT 1	Red, green. Difficult from mid-northern latitudes.
70	16 30.9	+01 59	λ Oph	4.2,5.2	1.4	40	Σ2055	P = 129 years. Fairly difficult in small apertures.
71	16 41.3	+31 36	ζ Her	2.9,5.5	1.2	145	Σ2084	Period = 34.5 years. Now widening. Needs 20 cm.
72	17 05.3	+54 28	μ Dra	5.7,5.7	2.5	4	Σ2130	Period 812 years. Both stars white.
73	17 14.6	+14 24	α Her	var,5.4	4.6	103	Σ2140	Red, green. Long-period binary.
74	17 15.3	−26 35	36 Oph	5.1,5.1	5.0	141	SHJ 243	Period = 471 years.
75	17 23.7	+37 08	ρ Her	4.6,5.6	4.1	319	Σ2161	Slowly widening.
76	17 26.9	−45 51	HJ 4949 AB	5.6,6.5	2.1	251	HJ 4949	Beautiful coarse triple. All white.
			Δ 216 AC	7.1	105.0	310		
77	18 01.5	+21 36	95 Her	5.0,5.1	6.5	257	Σ2264	Colours thought variable in C19.
78	18 05.5	+02 30	70 Oph	4.2,6.0	6.2	127	Σ2272	Opening. Easy in 7.5 cm. P = 88.4 years.
79	18 06.8	−43 25	H5014 CrA	5.7,5.7	1.7	0	–	Period = 450 years. Needs 10 cm.

No.	RA		Declin-ation	Star	Magni-tudes	Separa-tion	PA	Cata-logue	Comments
	h	m	° ´			arcsec	°		
80	18	25.4	−20 33	21 Sgr	5.0,7.4	1.7	279	JC 6	Slowly closing binary, orange and green.
81	18	35.9	+16 58	OΣ358 Her	6.8,7.0	1.5	147	–	Period = 380 years.
82	18	44.3	+39 40	ε¹ Lyr	5.0,6.1	2.4	346	Σ2382	Quadruple system with ε2. Both pairs visible in 7.5 cm.
83	18	44.3	+39 40	ε² Lyr	5.2,5.5	2.4	76	Σ2383	
84	18	56.2	+04 12	θ Ser	4.5,5.4	22.4	104	Σ2417	Fixed. Very easy. Both stars white
85	19	06.4	−37 04	γ CrA	4.8,5.1	1.4	354	HJ 5084	Beautiful pair. Period = 122 years.
86	19	30.7	+27 58	β Cyg AB	3.1,5.1	34.3	54	Σ I 43	Glorious. Yellow, blue-greenish.
				β Cyg Aa	3.1,5.2	0.4	86	MCA 55	Aa. Very difficult. Period = 214 years
87	19	45.0	+45 08	δ Cyg	2.9,6.3	2.7	218	Σ2579	Slowly widening. Period = 780 years.
88	19	48.2	+70 16	ε Dra	3.8,7.4	3.0	19	Σ2603	Slow binary. Yellow and blue
89	19	54.6	−08 14	57 Aql	5.7,6.4	36.0	170	Σ2594	Easy pair. Contrasting colours.
90	20	46.7	+16 07	γ Del	4.5,5.5	9.0	265	Σ2727	Easy. Yellowish. Long-period binary.
91	20	59.1	+04 18	ε Equ AB	6.0,6.3	0.4	283	Σ2737	Fine triple. AB a test for 30 cm. P = 101.5 years
				ε Equ AC	6.0,7.1	10.3	66		
92	21	06.9	+38 45	61 Cyg	5.2,6.0	31.5	152	Σ2758	Nearby binary. Both orange. Period = 678 years.
93	21	19.9	−53 27	θ Ind	4.5,7.0	7.0	271	HJ 5258	Pale yellow and reddish. Long-period binary.
94	21	44.1	+28 45	μ Cyg	4.8,6.1	1.6	320	Σ2822	Period = 789 years.
95	22	03.8	+64 37	ξ Cep	4.4,6.5	8.4	273	Σ2863	White and blue. Long-period binary.

Some Interesting Double Stars

No.	RA		Declination	Star	Magnitudes	Separation	PA	Catalogue	Comments
	h	m	° ′			arcsec	°		
96	22	14.3	−21 04	41 Aqr	5.6,6.7	5.1	113	H N 56	Yellowish and purple?
97	22	26.6	−16 45	53 Aqr	6.4,6.6	1.3	56	SHJ 345	Long-period binary; periastron in 2023.
98	22	28.8	−00 01	ζ Aqr	4.3,4.5	2.2	166	Σ2909	Period = 487 years. Slowly widening.
99	23	19.1	−13 28	94 Aqr	5.3,7.0	12.3	351	Σ2988	Yellow and orange. Probable binary.
100	23	59.5	+33 43	Σ3050 And	6.6,6.6	2.3	338	–	Period = 717 years. Visible in 7.5 cm.

Some Interesting Nebulae, Clusters and Galaxies

Object	RA		Declina-tion		Remarks
	h	m	°	′	
M31 Andromedae	00	40.7	+41	05	Andromeda Galaxy, visible to naked eye.
H VIII 78 Cassiopeiae	00	41.3	+61	36	Fine cluster, between Gamma and Kappa Cassiopeiae.
M33 Trianguli	01	31.8	+30	28	Spiral. Difficult with small apertures.
H VI 33–4 Persei, C14	02	18.3	+56	59	Double cluster; Sword-handle.
Δ142 Doradûs	05	39.1	−69	09	Looped nebula round 30 Doradûs. Naked eye. In Large Magellanic Cloud.
M1 Tauri	05	32.3	+22	00	Crab Nebula, near Zeta Tauri.
M42 Orionis	05	33.4	−05	24	Orion Nebula. Contains the famous Trapezium, Theta Orionis.
M35 Geminorum	06	06.5	+24	21	Open cluster near Eta Geminorum.
H VII 2 Monocerotis, C50	06	30.7	+04	53	Open cluster, just visible to naked eye.
M41 Canis Majoris	06	45.5	−20	42	Open cluster, just visible to naked eye.
M47 Puppis	07	34.3	−14	22	Mag. 5.2. Loose cluster.
H IV 64 Puppis	07	39.6	−18	05	Bright planetary in rich neighbourhood.
M46 Puppis	07	39.5	−14	42	Open cluster.
M44 Cancri	08	38	+20	07	Praesepe. Open cluster near Delta Cancri. Visible to naked eye.
M97 Ursae Majoris	11	12.6	+55	13	Owl Nebula, diameter 3′. Planetary.
Kappa Crucis, C94	12	50.7	−60	05	'Jewel Box'; open cluster, with stars of contrasting colours.
M3 Can. Ven.	13	40.6	+28	34	Bright globular.
Omega Centauri, C80	13	23.7	−47	03	Finest of all globulars. Easy with naked eye.
M80 Scorpii	16	14.9	−22	53	Globular, between Antares and Beta Scorpii.
M4 Scorpii	16	21.5	−26	26	Open cluster close to Antares.

Some Interesting Nebulae, Clusters and Galaxies

Object	RA		Declina-tion		Remarks
	h	m	°	′	
M13 Herculis	16	40	+36	31	Globular. Just visible to naked eye.
M92 Herculis	16	16.1	+43	11	Globular. Between Iota and Eta Herculis.
M6 Scorpii	17	36.8	−32	11	Open cluster; naked eye.
M7 Scorpii	17	50.6	−34	48	Very bright open cluster; naked eye.
M23 Sagittarii	17	54.8	−19	01	Open cluster nearly 50′ in diameter.
H IV 37 Draconis, C6	17	58.6	+66	38	Bright planetary.
M8 Sagittarii	18	01.4	−24	23	Lagoon Nebula. Gaseous. Just visible with naked eye.
NGC 6572 Ophiuchi	18	10.9	+06	50	Bright planetary, between Beta Ophiuchi and Zeta Aquilae.
M17 Sagittarii	18	18.8	−16	12	Omega Nebula. Gaseous. Large and bright.
M11 Scuti	18	49.0	−06	19	Wild Duck. Bright open cluster.
M57 Lyrae	18	52.6	+32	59	Ring Nebula. Brightest of planetaries.
M27 Vulpeculae	19	58.1	+22	37	Dumb-bell Nebula, near Gamma Sagittae.
H IV 1 Aquarii, C55	21	02.1	−11	31	Bright planetary, near Nu Aquarii.
M15 Pegasi	21	28.3	+12	01	Bright globular, near Epsilon Pegasi.
M39 Cygni	21	31.0	+48	17	Open cluster between Deneb and Alpha Lacertae. Well seen with low powers.

(M = Messier number; NGC = New General Catalogue number; C = Caldwell number.)

Our Contributors

Nick James B.Sc., C.Eng. is the papers secretary of the British Astronomical Association and Assistant Director of its Comet Section. Professionally he is an engineer working in the space industry responsible for a team developing space communication and tracking systems. He has had a long-term interest in astronomical imaging starting with film and progressing more recently to CCDs and digital cameras. He is joint author, with Gerald North, of *Observing Comets*, published by Springer in 2003.

Dr Stephen Webb is the author of several books, including *Where Is Everybody?* (winner of the Contact in Context award, and shortlisted for the 2003 Aventis Prize for science books) and the recently published *New Eyes on the Universe: Twelve Cosmic Mysteries and the Tools We Need To Solve Them* (which gives an overview of the many observatories that are planned or are already in construction – ALMA is just one of many amazing instruments that will soon be observing the universe!). He blogs on these and other topics in science at http://stephen webb.info/.

Dr David A. Rothery is a planetary scientist at the Open University, where he chairs a course on 'Planetary Science and the Search for Life'. He is a member of the BepiColombo science team, and heads ESA's Mercury Surface and Composition Working Group.

Richard Myer Baum is a former Director of the Mercury and Venus Section of the British Astronomical Association, an amateur astronomer and an independent scholar. He is author of *The Planets: Some Myths and Realities* (1973), (with W. Sheehan) *In Search of Planet Vulcan: The Ghost in Newton's Clockwork Universe* (1997) and *The Haunted Observatory* (2007). He has contributed to the *Journal of the British Astronomical Association, Journal for the History of Astronomy,*

Sky & Telescope and many other publications including *The Dictionary of Nineteenth-Century British Scientists* (2004), and *The Biographical Encyclopedia of Astronomers* (2007).

Martin Mobberley is one of the UK's most active imagers of comets, planets, asteroids, variable stars, novae and supernovae and served as President of the British Astronomical Association from 1997 to 1999. In 2000, he was awarded the Association's Walter Goodacre Award. He is the sole author of seven popular astronomy books published by Springer as well as three children's 'Space Exploration' books published by Top That Publishing. In addition he has authored hundreds of articles in *Astronomy Now* and numerous other astronomical publications.

Dr William Sheehan has been an amateur astronomer since the age of nine. He has written several books, including *The Planet Mars: A History of Observation and Discovery* (1996) and *The Immortal Fire Within* (2007), a biography of pioneer Milky Way photographer Edward Emerson Barnard. He was named a 2001 Guggenheim Fellow for his research on the structure and evolution of the Galaxy. He lives in Willmar, Minnesota in the US.

Dr David M. Harland gained his BSc in astronomy in 1977 and a doctorate in computational science. Subsequently, he has lectured in computer science, worked in industry and managed academic research. In 1995, he 'retired' and has since published many books on space themes.

Dr Allan Chapman, of Wadham College, Oxford, is probably Britain's leading authority on the history of astronomy. He has published many research papers and several books, as well as numerous popular accounts. He is a frequent contributor to the *Yearbook*.

Astronomical Societies in the British Isles

Association for Astronomy Education
Secretary: Teresa Grafton, The Association for Astronomy Education, c/o The Royal Astronomical Society, Burlington House, Piccadilly, London W1V 0NL.

Astronomical Society of Edinburgh
Secretary: Horst Meyerdierks, Edinburgh EH16 4TF.
Website: www.astronomyedinburgh.org; *Email:* asewww@roe.ac.uk
Meetings: City Observatory, Calton Hill, Edinburgh. 1st Friday each month, 8 p.m.

Astronomical Society of Glasgow
Secretary: Mr David Degan, 5 Hillside Avenue, Alexandria, Dunbartonshire G83 0BB.
Website: www.astronomicalsocietyofglasgow.org.uk
Meetings: Royal College, University of Strathclyde, Montrose Street, Glasgow. 3rd Thursday each month, Sept.–Apr., 7.30 p.m.

Astronomical Society of Haringey
Secretary: Jerry Workman, 91 Greenslade Road, Barking, Essex IG11 9XF.
Meetings: Palm Court, Alexandra Palace, 3rd Wednesday each month, 8 p.m.

Astronomy Ireland
Secretary: Tony Ryan, PO Box 2888, Dublin 1, Eire.
Website: www.astronomy.ie; *Email:* info@astronomy.ie
Meetings: 2nd Monday of each month. Telescope meetings every clear Saturday.

British Astronomical Association
Assistant Secretary: Burlington House, Piccadilly, London W1V 9AG.
Meetings: Lecture Hall of Scientific Societies, Civil Service Commission Building, 23 Savile Row, London W1. Last Wednesday each month (Oct.–June), 5 p.m. and some Saturday afternoons.

Federation of Astronomical Societies
Secretary: Clive Down, 10 Glan-y-Llyn, North Cornelly, Bridgend, County Borough CF33 4EF.
Email: clivedown@btinternet.com

Junior Astronomical Society of Ireland
Secretary: K. Nolan, 5 St Patrick's Crescent, Rathcoole, Co. Dublin.
Meetings: The Royal Dublin Society, Ballsbridge, Dublin 4. Monthly.

Society for Popular Astronomy
Secretary: Guy Fennimore, 36 Fairway, Keyworth, Nottingham NG12 5DU.
Website: www.popastro.com; *Email:* SPAstronomy@aol.com
Meetings: Last Saturday in Jan., Apr., July, Oct., 2.30 p.m. in London.

Webb Deep-Sky Society
Membership Secretary/Treasurer: Steve Rayner, 11 Four Acres, Weston, Portland, Dorset DT5 2JG.

Email: stephen.rayner@tesco,net
Website: www.webbdeepsky.com

Aberdeen and District Astronomical Society
Secretary: Ian C. Giddings, 95 Brentfield Circle, Ellon, Aberdeenshire AB41 9DB.
Meetings: Robert Gordon's Institute of Technology, St Andrew's Street, Aberdeen.
Fridays, 7.30 p.m.

Abingdon Astronomical Society (was **Fitzharry's Astronomical Society**)
Secretary: Chris Holt, 9 Rutherford Close, Abingdon, Oxon OX14 2AT.
Website: www.abingdonastro.org.uk; *Email:* info@abingdonastro.co.uk
Meetings: All Saints' Methodist Church Hall, Dorchester Crescent, Abingdon, Oxon.
2nd Monday Sept.–June, 8 p.m. and additional beginners' meetings and observing
evenings as advertised.

Altrincham and District Astronomical Society
Secretary: Derek McComiskey, 33 Tottenham Drive, Manchester M23 9WH.
Meetings: Timperley Village Club. 1st Friday Sept.–June, 8 p.m.

Andover Astronomical Society
Secretary: Mrs S. Fisher, Staddlestones, Aughton, Kingston, Marlborough, Wiltshire
SN8 3SA.
Meetings: Grately Village Hall. 3rd Thursday each month, 7.30 p.m.

Astra Astronomy Section
Secretary: c/o Duncan Lunan, Flat 65, Dalraida House, 56 Blythswood Court,
Anderston, Glasgow G2 7PE.
Meetings: Airdrie Arts Centre, Anderson Street, Airdrie. Weekly.

Astrodome Mobile School Planetarium
Contact: Peter J. Golding, 53 City Way, Rochester, Kent ME1 2AX.
Website: www.astrodome.tv; *Email:* astrodome@clara.co.uk

Aylesbury Astronomical Society
Secretary: Alan Smith, 182 Marley Fields, Leighton Buzzard, Bedfordshire LU7 8WN.
Meetings: 1st Monday in month at 8 p.m., venue in Aylesbury area. Details from
Secretary.

Bassetlaw Astronomical Society
Secretary: Andrew Patton, 58 Holding, Worksop, Notts S81 0TD.
Meetings: Rhodesia Village Hall, Rhodesia, Worksop, Notts. 2nd and 4th Tuesdays of
month at 7.45 p.m.

Batley & Spenborough Astronomical Society
Secretary: Robert Morton, 22 Links Avenue, Cleckheaton, West Yorks BD19 4EG.
Meetings: Milner K. Ford Observatory, Wilton Park, Batley. Every Thursday, 8 p.m.

Bedford Astronomical Society
Secretary: Mrs L. Harrington, 24 Swallowfield, Wyboston, Bedfordshire MK44 3AE.
Website: www.bedsastro.co.uk
Meetings: Bedford School, Burnaby Rd, Bedford. Last Wednesday each month.

Bingham & Brooks Space Organization
Secretary: N. Bingham, 15 Hickmore's Lane, Lindfield, West Sussex.

Birmingham Astronomical Society
Contact: P. Bolas, 4 Moat Bank, Bretby, Burton-on-Trent DE15 0QJ.
Website: www.birmingham-astronomy.co.uk; *Email:* pbolas@aol.com
Meetings: Room 146, Aston University. Last Tuesday of month, Sept.–June (except
Dec., moved to 1st week in Jan.).

Blackburn Leisure Astronomy Section
Secretary: Mr H. Murphy, 20 Princess Way, Beverley, East Yorkshire HU17 8PD.
Meetings: Blackburn Leisure Welfare. Mondays, 8 p.m.

Blackpool & District Astronomical Society
Secretary: Terry Devon, 30 Victory Road, Blackpool, Lancashire FY1 3JT.
Website: www.blackpoolastronomy.org.uk; *Email:* info@blackpoolastronomy.org.uk
Meetings: St Kentigern's Social Centre, Blackpool. 1st Wednesday of the month,
7.45 p.m.

Bolton Astronomical Society
Secretary: Peter Miskiw, 9 Hedley Street, Bolton, Lancashire BL1 3LE.
Meetings: Ladybridge Community Centre, Bolton. 1st and 3rd Tuesdays Sept.–May,
7.30 p.m.

Border Astronomical Society
Secretary: David Pettitt, 14 Shap Grove, Carlisle, Cumbria CA2 5QR.
Website: borderastronomicalsociety.com; *Email:* davidpettitt@supanet.com
Meetings: Trinity School Observatory, Strand Road, Carlisle. 2nd and 4th Thursdays
each month, Sept.–May, 7.30–9 p.m.

Boston Astronomers
Secretary: Mrs Lorraine Money, 18 College Park, Horncastle, Lincolnshire LN9 6RE.
Meetings: Blackfriars Arts Centre, Boston. 2nd Monday each month, 7.30 p.m.

Bradford Astronomical Society
Contact: Mrs J. Hilary Knaggs, 6 Meadow View, Wyke, Bradford BD12 9LA.
Website: www.bradfordastronomy.co.uk
Meetings: Eccleshill Library, Bradford. Alternate Mondays, 7.30 p.m.

Braintree, Halstead & District Astronomical Society
Secretary: Mr J. R. Green, 70 Dorothy Sayers Drive, Witham, Essex CM8 2LU.
Meetings: BT Social Club Hall, Witham Telephone Exchange. 3rd Thursday each
month, 8 p.m.

Breckland Astronomical Society (was **Great Ellingham and District Astronomy Club**)
Contact: Martin Wolton, Willowbeck House, Pulham St Mary, Norfolk IP21 4QS.
Meetings: Great Ellingham Recreation Centre, Watton Road (B1077), Great
Ellingham, 2nd Friday each month, 7.15 p.m.

Bridgend Astronomical Society
Secretary: Clive Down, 10 Glan-y-Llyn, Broadlands, North Cornelly, Bridgend
County CF33 4EF.
Email: clivedown@btinternet.com
Meetings: Bridgend Bowls Centre, Bridgend. 2nd Friday, monthly, 7.30 p.m.

Bridgwater Astronomical Society
Secretary: Mr G. MacKenzie, Watergore Cottage, Watergore, South Petherton,
Somerset TA13 5JQ.
Website: dbown100.tripod.com/BWASTRO.htm
Meetings: Room D10, Bridgwater College, Bath Road Centre, Bridgwater. 2nd
Wednesday each month, Sept.–June.

Bridport Astronomical Society
Secretary: Mr G. J. Lodder, 3 The Green, Walditch, Bridport, Dorset DT6 4LB.
Meetings: Walditch Village Hall, Bridport. 1st Sunday each month, 7.30 p.m.

Brighton Astronomical and Scientific Society
Secretary: Ms T. Fearn, 38 Woodlands Close, Peacehaven, East Sussex BN10 7SF.
Meetings: St John's Church Hall, Hove. 1st Tuesday each month, 7.30 p.m.

Bristol Astronomical Society
Secretary: Dr John Pickard, 'Fielding', Easter Compton, Bristol BS35 5SJ.
Meetings: Frank Lecture Theatre, University of Bristol Physics Dept., alternate Fridays in term time, and Westbury Park Methodist Church Rooms, North View, other Fridays.

Callington Community Astronomy Group
Secretary: Dale Moore *Tel:* 01752 319259
Website: www.callington-astro.org.uk; *Email:* enquiries@callington-astro.org.uk
Meetings: St Dominick Parish Hall, St Dominick, Saltash, Cornwall, PL12 6TD. 2nd Friday each month, Sept.–June, 7.30 p.m.

Cambridge Astronomical Society
Secretary: Brian Lister, 80 Ramsden Square, Cambridge CB4 2BL.
Meetings: Institute of Astronomy, Madingley Road. 3rd Friday each month.

Cardiff Astronomical Society
Secretary: D.W.S. Powell, 1 Tal-y-Bont Road, Ely, Cardiff CF5 5EU.
Meetings: Dept. of Physics and Astronomy, University of Wales, Newport Road, Cardiff. Alternate Thursdays, 8 p.m.

Castle Point Astronomy Club
Secretary: Andrew Turner, 3 Canewdon Hall Close, Canewdon, Rochford, Essex SS4 3PY.
Meetings: St Michael's Church Hall, Daws Heath. Wednesdays, 8 p.m.

Chelmsford Astronomers
Secretary: Brendan Clark, 5 Borda Close, Chelmsford, Essex.
Meetings: Once a month.

Chester Astronomical Society
Secretary: John Gilmour, 2 Thomas Brassey Close, Chester CH2 3AE.
Tel: 07974 948278
Email: john_gilmour@ouvip.com
Website: chesteras.blogspot.co.uk
Meetings: Burley Memorial Hall, Waverton, near Chester. Last Wednesday of each month except August and December at 7.30 p.m.

Chester Society of Natural Science, Literature and Art
Secretary: Paul Braid, 'White Wing', 38 Bryn Avenue, Old Colwyn, Colwyn Bay LL29 8AH.
Email: p.braid@virgin.net
Meetings: Once a month.

Chesterfield Astronomical Society
President: Mr D. Blackburn, 71 Middlecroft Road, Stavely, Chesterfield, Derbyshire S41 3XG. *Tel:* 07909 570754.
Website: www.chesterfield-as.org.uk
Meetings: Barnet Observatory, Newbold, each Friday.

Clacton & District Astronomical Society
Secretary: C. L. Haskell, 105 London Road, Clacton-on-Sea, Essex.

Cleethorpes & District Astronomical Society
Secretary: C. Illingworth, 38 Shaw Drive, Grimsby, South Humberside.
Meetings: Beacon Hill Observatory, Cleethorpes. 1st Wednesday each month.

Cleveland & Darlington Astronomical Society
Contact: Dr John McCue, 40 Bradbury Rd., Stockton-on-Tees, Cleveland TS20 1LE.

Meetings: Grindon Parish Hall, Thorpe Thewles, near Stockton-on-Tees. 2nd Friday, monthly.

Cork Astronomy Club
Website: www.corkastronomyclub.com
Email: astronomycork@yahoo.ie
Meetings: UCC, Civil Engineering Building, 2nd Monday each month, Sept.–May, 8.00 p.m.

Cornwall Astronomical Society
Secretary: J. M. Harvey, 1 Tregunna Close, Porthleven, Cornwall TR13 9LW.
Meetings: Godolphin Club, Wendron Street, Helston, Cornwall. 2nd and 4th Thursday of each month, 7.30 for 8 p.m.

Cotswold Astronomical Society
Secretary: Rod Salisbury, Grove House, Christchurch Road, Cheltenham, Gloucestershire GL50 2PN.
Website: cotswoldas.org.uk/cas/
Meetings: Shurdington Church Hall, School Lane, Shurdington, Cheltenham. 2nd Saturday each month, 8 p.m.

Coventry & Warwickshire Astronomical Society
Secretary: Steve Payne, 68 Stonebury Avenue, Eastern Green, Coventry CV5 7FW.
Website: www.covastro.org.uk; *Email:* sjp2000@thefarside57.freeserve.co.uk
Meetings: The Earlsdon Church Hall, Albany Road, Earlsdon, Coventry. 2nd Friday, monthly, Sept.–June.

Crawley Astronomical Society
Secretary: Ron Gamer, 1 Pevensey Close, Pound Hill, Crawley, West Sussex RH10 7BL.
Meetings: Ifield Community Centre, Ifield Road, Crawley. 3rd Friday each month, 7.30 p.m.

Crayford Manor House Astronomical Society
Secretary: Roger Pickard, 28 Appletons, Hadlow, Kent TM1 0DT.
Meetings: Manor House Centre, Crayford. Monthly during term time.

Crewkerne and District Astronomical Society (CADAS)
Chairman: Ron Westmaas
Website: www.cadas.net
Meetings: St. Bartholomew's Church Hall, Abbey Street, Crewkerne, TA18 7HY, third Wednesday of every month, 7.30 p.m. All welcome.

Croydon Astronomical Society
Secretary: John Murrell, 17 Dalmeny Road, Carshalton, Surrey.
Meetings: Lecture Theatre, Royal Russell School, Combe Lane, South Croydon. Alternate Fridays, 7.45 p.m.

Derby & District Astronomical Society
Secretary: Ian Bennett, Freers Cottage, Sutton Lane, Etwall.
Website: www.derbyastronomy.org
Email: bennett.lovatt@btinternet.com
Meetings: Friends Meeting House, Derby. 1st Friday each month, 7.30 p.m.

Doncaster Astronomical Society
Secretary: A. Anson, 15 Cusworth House, St James Street, Doncaster DN1 3AY
Website: www.donastro.org.uk; *Email:* secretary@donastro.org.uk
Meetings: St George's Church House, St George's Church, Church Way, Doncaster. 2nd and 4th Thursday of each month, commencing at 7.30 p.m.

Dumfries Astronomical Society
Secretary: Klaus Schiller, lesley.burrell@btinternet.com.
Website: www.dumfriesastronomysociety.org.uk
Meetings: George St Church Hall, George St, Dumfries. 2nd Tuesday of each month, Sept.–May.

Dundee Astronomical Society
Secretary: G. Young, 37 Polepark Road, Dundee, Tayside DD1 5QT.
Meetings: Mills Observatory, Balgay Park, Dundee. 1st Friday each month, 7.30 p.m. Sept.–Apr.

Easington and District Astronomical Society
Secretary: T. Bradley, 52 Jameson Road, Hartlepool, Co. Durham.
Meetings: Easington Comprehensive School, Easington Colliery. Every 3rd Thursday throughout the year, 7.30 p.m.

East Antrim Astronomical Society
Secretary: Stephen Beasant
Website: www.eaas.co.uk
Meetings: Ballyclare High School, Ballyclare, County Antrim. First Monday each month.

Eastbourne Astronomical Society
Secretary: Peter Gill, 18 Selwyn House, Selwyn Road, Eastbourne, East Sussex BN21 2LF.
Meetings: Willingdon Memorial Hall, Church Street, Willingdon. One Saturday per month, Sept.–July, 7.30 p.m.

East Riding Astronomers
Secretary: Tony Scaife, 15 Beech Road, Elloughton, Brough, North Humberside HU15 1JX.
Meetings: As arranged.

East Sussex Astronomical Society
Secretary: Marcus Croft, 12 St Mary's Cottages, Ninfield Road, Bexhill-on-Sea, East Sussex.
Website: www.esas.org.uk
Meetings: St Mary's School, Wrestwood Road, Bexhill. 1st Thursday of each month, 8 p.m.

Edinburgh University Astronomical Society
Secretary: c/o Dept. of Astronomy, Royal Observatory, Blackford Hill, Edinburgh.

Ewell Astronomical Society
Secretary: Richard Gledhill, 80 Abinger Avenue, Cheam SM2 7LW.
Website: www.ewellastro.org
Meetings: St Mary's Church Hall, London Road, Ewell. 2nd Friday of each month except August, 7.45 p.m.

Exeter Astronomical Society
Secretary: Tim Sedgwick, Old Dower House, Half Moon, Newton St Cyres, Exeter, Devon EX5 5AE.
Meetings: The Meeting Room, Wynards, Magdalen Street, Exeter. 1st Thursday of month.

Farnham Astronomical Society
Secretary: Laurence Anslow, 'Asterion', 18 Wellington Lane, Farnham, Surrey GU9 9BA.
Meetings: Central Club, South Street, Farnham. 2nd Thursday each month, 8 p.m.

Foredown Tower Astronomy Group
Secretary: M. Feist, Foredown Tower Camera Obscura, Foredown Road, Portslade, East Sussex BN41 2EW.
Meetings: At the above address, 3rd Tuesday each month. 7 p.m. (winter), 8 p.m. (summer).

Greenock Astronomical Society
Secretary: Carl Hempsey, 49 Brisbane Street, Greenock.
Meetings: Greenock Arts Guild, 3 Campbell Street, Greenock.

Grimsby Astronomical Society
Secretary: R. Williams, 14 Richmond Close, Grimsby, South Humberside.
Meetings: Secretary's home. 2nd Thursday each month, 7.30 p.m.

Guernsey: La Société Guernesiasie Astronomy Section
Secretary: Debby Quertier, Lamorna, Route Charles, St Peter Port, Guernsey GY1 1QS, and Jessica Harris, Keanda, Les Sauvagees, St Sampson's, Guernsey GY2 4XT.
Meetings: Observatory, Rue du Lorier, St Peter's. Tuesdays, 8 p.m.

Guildford Astronomical Society
Secretary: A. Langmaid, 22 West Mount, The Mount, Guildford, Surrey GU2 5HL.
Meetings: Guildford Institute, Ward Street, Guildford. 1st Thursday each month except Aug., 7.30 p.m.

Gwynedd Astronomical Society
Secretary: Mr Ernie Greenwood, 18 Twrcelyn Street, Llanerchymedd, Anglesey LL74 8TL.
Meetings: Dept. of Electronic Engineering, Bangor University. 1st Thursday each month except Aug., 7.30 p.m.

The Hampshire Astronomical Group
Contact: Graham Bryant
Website: www.hantsastro.org.uk; *Email:* graham.bryant@hantsastro.org.uk
Meetings: 2nd Friday, Clanfield Memorial Hall, all other Fridays Clanfield Observatory.

Hanney & District Astronomical Society
Secretary: Bob Church, 47 Upthorpe Drive, Wantage, Oxfordshire OX12 7DG.
Meetings: Last Thursday each month, 8 p.m.

Harrogate Astronomical Society
Secretary: Brian Bonser, 114 Main Street, Little Ouseburn TO5 9TG.
Meetings: National Power HQ, Beckwith Knowle, Harrogate. Last Friday each month.

Havering Astronomical Society
Secretary: Frances Ridgley, 133 Severn Drive, Upminster, Essex RM14 1PP.
Meetings: Cranham Community Centre, Marlborough Gardens, Upminster, Essex. 3rd Wednesday each month except July and Aug., 7.30 p.m.

Heart of England Astronomical Society
Secretary: John Williams, 100 Stanway Road, Shirley, Solihull B90 3JG.
Website: https://sites.google.com/site/hoeastro/Home/; *Email:* secretary@hoeas.co.uk
Meetings: Furnace End Village, over Whitacre, Warwickshire. Last Thursday each month, except June, July & Aug., 8 p.m.

Hebden Bridge Literary & Scientific Society, Astronomical Section
Secretary: Peter Jackson, 44 Gilstead Lane, Bingley, West Yorkshire BD16 3NP.
Meetings: Hebden Bridge Information Centre. Last Wednesday, Sept.–May.

Herefordshire Astronomical Society
Secretary: Paul Olver, The Buttridge, Wellington Lane, Canon Pyon, Hereford
HR4 8NL.
Email: info@hsastro.org.uk
Meetings: The Kindle Centre, ASDA Supermarket, Hereford. 1st Thursday of every
month (except August) 7 p.m.

Herschel Astronomy Society
Secretary: Kevin Bishop, 106 Holmsdale, Crown Wood, Bracknell, Berkshire
RG12 3TB.
Meetings: Eton College. 2nd Friday each month, 7.30 p.m.

Highlands Astronomical Society
Secretary: Richard Green, 11 Drumossie Avenue, Culcabock, Inverness IV2 3SJ.
Meetings: The Spectrum Centre, Inverness. 1st Tuesday each month, 7.30 p.m.

Hinckley & District Astronomical Society
Secretary: Mr S. Albrighton, 4 Walnut Close, The Bridleways, Hartshill, Nuneaton,
Warwickshire CV10 0XH.
Meetings: Burbage Common Visitors Centre, Hinckley. 1st Tuesday Sept.–May,
7.30 p.m.

Horsham Astronomy Group (was **Forest Astronomical Society**)
Secretary: Dan White, 32 Burns Close, Horsham, West Sussex RH12 5PF.
Email: secretary@horshamastronomy.com
Meetings: 1st Wednesday each month.

Howards Astronomy Club
Secretary: H. Ilett, 22 St George's Avenue, Warblington, Havant, Hampshire.
Meetings: To be notified.

Huddersfield Astronomical and Philosophical Society
Secretary: Lisa B. Jeffries, 58 Beaumont Street, Netherton, Huddersfield, West
Yorkshire HD4 7HE.
Email: l.b.jeffries@hud.ac.uk
Meetings: 4a Railway Street, Huddersfield. Every Wednesday and Friday, 7.30 p.m.

Hull and East Riding Astronomical Society
President: Sharon E. Long
Email: charon@charon.karoo.co.uk
Website: http://www.heras.org.uk
Meetings: The Wilberforce Building, Room S25, University of Hull, Cottingham
Road, Hull. 2nd Monday each month, Sept.–May, 7.30–9.30 p.m.

Ilkeston & District Astronomical Society
Secretary: Mark Thomas, 2 Elm Avenue, Sandiacre, Nottingham NG10 5EJ.
Meetings: The Function Room, Erewash Museum, Anchor Row, Ilkeston. 2nd
Tuesday monthly, 7.30 p.m.

Ipswich, Orwell Astronomical Society
Secretary: R. Gooding, 168 Ashcroft Road, Ipswich.
Meetings: Orwell Park Observatory, Nacton, Ipswich. Wednesdays, 8 p.m.

Irish Astronomical Association
President: Terry Moseley, 31 Sunderland Road, Belfast BT6 9LY, Northern Ireland.
Email: terrymosel@aol.com
Meetings: Ashby Building, Stranmillis Road, Belfast. Alternate Wednesdays,
7.30 p.m.

Irish Astronomical Society
Secretary: James O'Connor, PO Box 2547, Dublin 15, Eire.
Meetings: Ely House, 8 Ely Place, Dublin 2. 1st and 3rd Monday each month.

Isle of Man Astronomical Society
Secretary: James Martin, Ballaterson Farm, Peel, Isle of Man IM5 3AB.
Email: ballaterson@manx.net
Meetings: Isle of Man Observatory, Foxdale. 1st Thursday of each month, 8 p.m.

Isle of Wight Astronomical Society
Secretary: J. W. Feakins, 1 Hilltop Cottages, High Street, Freshwater, Isle of Wight.
Meetings: Unitarian Church Hall, Newport, Isle of Wight. Monthly.

Jersey Astronomy Club
Secretary: Jodie Masterman, *Tel:* 07797 813681
Email: jodiemasterman@yahoo.co.uk
Chairman: Martin Ahier, *Tel:* (01534) 732157
Meetings: Sir Patrick Moore Astronomy Centre, Les Creux Country Park, St Brelade, Jersey, 2nd Monday of every month (except August), 8.00 p.m.

Keele Astronomical Society
Secretary: Natalie Webb, Department of Physics, University of Keele, Keele, Staffordshire ST5 5BG.
Meetings: As arranged during term time.

Kettering and District Astronomical Society
Asst. Secretary: Steve Williams, 120 Brickhill Road, Wellingborough, Northamptonshire.
Meetings: Quaker Meeting Hall, Northall Street, Kettering, Northamptonshire. 1st Tuesday each month, 7.45 p.m.

King's Lynn Amateur Astronomical Association
Secretary: P. Twynman, 17 Poplar Avenue, RAF Marham, King's Lynn.
Meetings: As arranged.

Lancaster and Morecambe Astronomical Society
Secretary: Mrs E. Robinson, 4 Bedford Place, Lancaster LA1 4EB.
Email: ehelenerob@btinternet.com
Meetings: Church of the Ascension, Torrisholme. 1st Wednesday each month except July and Aug.

Knowle Astronomical Society
Secretary: Nigel Foster, 21 Speedwell Drive, Balsall Common, Coventry, West Midlands CV7 7AU.
Meetings: St George & St Theresa's Parish Centre, 337 Station Road, Dorridge, Solihull, West Midlands B93 8TZ. 1st Monday of each month (+/– 1 week for Bank Holidays) except August.

Lancaster University Astronomical Society
Secretary: c/o Students' Union, Alexandra Square, University of Lancaster.
Meetings: As arranged.

Layman's Astronomical Society
Secretary: John Evans, 10 Arkwright Walk, The Meadows, Nottingham.
Meetings: The Popular, Bath Street, Ilkeston, Derbyshire. Monthly.

Leeds Astronomical Society
Secretary: Mark A. Simpson, 37 Roper Avenue, Gledhow, Leeds LS8 1LG.
Meetings: Centenary House, North Street. 2nd Wednesday each month, 7.30 p.m.

Leicester Astronomical Society
Secretary: Dr P. J. Scott, 21 Rembridge Close, Leicester LE3 9AP.
Meetings: Judgemeadow Community College, Marydene Drive, Evington, Leicester.
2nd and 4th Tuesdays each month, 7.30 p.m.

Letchworth and District Astronomical Society
Secretary: Eric Hutton, 14 Folly Close, Hitchin, Hertfordshire.
Meetings: As arranged.

Lewes Amateur Astronomers
Secretary: Christa Sutton, 8 Tower Road, Lancing, West Sussex BN15 9HT.
Meetings: The Bakehouse Studio, Lewes. Last Wednesday each month.

Limerick Astronomy Club
Secretary: Tony O'Hanlon, 26 Ballycannon Heights, Meelick, Co. Clare, Eire.
Meetings: Limerick Senior College, Limerick. Monthly (except June and Aug.), 8 p.m.

Lincoln Astronomical Society
Secretary: David Swaey, 'Everglades', 13 Beaufort Close, Lincoln LN2 4SF.
Meetings: The Lecture Hall, off Westcliffe Street, Lincoln. 1st Tuesday each month.

Liverpool Astronomical Society
Secretary: Mr K. Clark, 31 Sandymount Drive, Wallasey, Merseyside L45 0LJ.
Meetings: Lecture Theatre, Liverpool Museum. 3rd Friday each month, 7 p.m.

Norman Lockyer Observatory Society
Secretary: G. E. White, PO Box 9, Sidmouth EX10 0YQ.
Website: www.normanlockyer.com
Meetings: Norman Lockyer Observatory, Sidmouth. Fridays and 2nd Monday each
month, 7.30 p.m.

Loughton Astronomical Society
Secretary: Brian Morton
Website: www.las-astro.org.uk
Meetings: 1st Theydon Bois Scout Hall, Loughton Lane, Theydon Bois. Weekly on
Thursdays.

Lowestoft and Great Yarmouth Regional Astronomers (LYRA) Society
Secretary: Simon Briggs, 28 Sussex Road, Lowestoft, Suffolk.
Meetings: Community Wing, Kirkley High School, Kirkley Run, Lowestoft. 3rd
Thursday each month, 7.30 p.m.

Luton Astronomical Society
Secretary: Mr G. Mitchell, Putteridge Bury, University of Luton, Hitchin Road, Luton.
Website: www.lutonastrosoc.org.uk; *Email:* user998491@aol.com
Meetings: Univ. of Luton, Putteridge Bury (except June, July and August), or
Someries Junior School, Wigmore Lane, Luton (July and August only), last Thursday
each month, 7.30–9.00 p.m.

Lytham St Anne's Astronomical Association
Secretary: K. J. Porter, 141 Blackpool Road, Ansdell, Lytham St Anne's, Lancashire.
Meetings: College of Further Education, Clifton Drive South, Lytham St Anne's. 2nd
Wednesday monthly Oct.–June.

Macclesfield Astronomical Society
Secretary: Mr John H. Thomson, 27 Woodbourne Road, Sale, Cheshire M33 3SY
Website: www.maccastro.com; *Email:* jhandlc@yahoo.com
Meetings: Jodrell Bank Science Centre, Goostrey, Cheshire. 1st Tuesday of every
month, 7 p.m.

Maidenhead Astronomical Society
Secretary: Tim Haymes, Hill Rise, Knowl Hill Common, Knowl Hill, Reading RG10 9YD.
Meetings: Stubbings Church Hall, near Maidenhead. 1st Friday Sept.–June.

Maidstone Astronomical Society
Secretary: Stephen James, 4 The Cherry Orchard, Haddow, Tonbridge, Kent.
Meetings: Nettlestead Village Hall. 1st Tuesday in the month except July and Aug., 7.30 p.m.

Manchester Astronomical Society
Secretary: Mr Kevin J. Kilburn FRAS, Godlee Observatory, UMIST, Sackville Street, Manchester M60 1QD.
Website: www.manastro.co.uk; *Email:* enquiry@manastro.org
Meetings: At the Godlee Observatory. Thursdays, 7 p.m., except below.
Free Public Lectures: Renold Building UMIST, third Thursday Sept.–Mar., 7.30 p.m.

Mansfield and Sutton Astronomical Society
Secretary: Angus Wright, Sherwood Observatory, Coxmoor Road, Sutton-in-Ashfield, Nottinghamshire NG17 5LF.
Meetings: Sherwood Observatory, Coxmoor Road. Last Tuesday each month, 7.30 p.m.

Mexborough and Swinton Astronomical Society
Secretary: Mark R. Benton, 14 Sandalwood Rise, Swinton, Mexborough, South Yorkshire S64 8PN.
Website: www.msas.org.uk; *Email:* mark@masas.f9.co.uk
Meetings: Swinton WMC. Thursdays, 7.30 p.m.

Mid-Kent Astronomical Society
Secretary: Peter Parish, 30 Wooldeys Road, Rainham, Kent ME8 7NU.
Meetings: Bredhurst Village Hall, Hurstwood Road, Bredhurst, Kent. 2nd and last Fridays each month except August, 7.45 p.m.
Website: www.midkentastro.org.uk

Milton Keynes Astronomical Society
Secretary: Mike Leggett, 19 Matilda Gardens, Shenley Church End, Milton Keynes MK5 6HT.
Website: www.mkas.org.uk; *Email:* mike-pat-leggett@shenley9.fsnet.co.uk
Meetings: Rectory Cottage, Bletchley. Alternate Fridays.

Moray Astronomical Society
Secretary: Richard Pearce, 1 Forsyth Street, Hopeman, Elgin, Moray, Scotland.
Meetings: Village Hall Close, Co. Elgin.

Newbury Amateur Astronomical Society (NAAS)
Secretary: Mrs Monica Balstone, 37 Mount Pleasant, Tadley RG26 4BG.
Meetings: United Reformed Church Hall, Cromwell Place, Newbury. 1st Friday of month, Sept.–June.

Newcastle-on-Tyne Astronomical Society
Secretary: C. E. Willits, 24 Acomb Avenue, Seaton Delaval, Tyne and Wear.
Meetings: Zoology Lecture Theatre, Newcastle University. Monthly.

North Aston Space & Astronomical Club
Secretary: W. R. Chadburn, 14 Oakdale Road, North Aston, Sheffield.
Meetings: To be notified.

Northamptonshire Natural History Society (Astronomy Section)
Secretary: R. A. Marriott, 24 Thirlestane Road, Northampton NN4 8HD.

Email: ram@hamal.demon.co.uk
Meetings: Humfrey Rooms, Castilian Terrace, Northampton. 2nd and last Mondays, most months, 7.30 p.m.

Northants Amateur Astronomers
Secretary: Mervyn Lloyd, 76 Havelock Street, Kettering, Northamptonshire.
Meetings: 1st and 3rd Tuesdays each month, 7.30 p.m.

North Devon Astronomical Society
Secretary: P. G. Vickery, 12 Broad Park Crescent, Ilfracombe, Devon EX34 8DX.
Meetings: Methodist Hall, Rhododendron Avenue, Sticklepath, Barnstaple. 1st Wednesday each month, 7.15 p.m.

North Dorset Astronomical Society
Secretary: J. E. M. Coward, The Pharmacy, Stalbridge, Dorset.
Meetings: Charterhay, Stourton, Caundle, Dorset. 2nd Wednesday each month.

North Downs Astronomical Society
Secretary: Martin Akers, 36 Timber Tops, Lordswood, Chatham, Kent ME5 8XQ.
Meetings: Vigo Village Hall. 3rd Thursday each month. 7.30 p.m.

North-East London Astronomical Society
Secretary: Mr B. Beeston, 38 Abbey Road, Bush Hill Park, Enfield EN1 2QN.
Meetings: Wanstead House, The Green, Wanstead. 3rd Sunday each month (except Aug.), 3 p.m.

North Gwent and District Astronomical Society
Secretary: Jonathan Powell, 14 Lancaster Drive, Gilwern, nr Abergavenny, Monmouthshire NP7 0AA.
Meetings: Gilwern Community Centre. 15th of each month, 7.30 p.m.

North Staffordshire Astronomical Society
Secretary: Duncan Richardson, Halmerend Hall Farm, Halmerend, Stoke-on-Trent, Staffordshire ST7 8AW.
Email: dwr@enterprise.net
Meetings: 21st Hartstill Scout Group HQ, Mount Pleasant, Newcastle-under-Lyme ST5 1DR. 1st Tuesday each month (except July and Aug.), 7–9.30 p.m.

Northumberland Astronomical Society
Contact: Dr Adrian Jametta, 1 Lake Road, Hadston, Morpeth, Northumberland NE65 9TF.
Email: adrian@themoon.co.uk
Website: www.nastro.org.uk
Meetings: Hauxley Nature Reserve (near Amble). Last Thursday of every month (except December), 7.30 pm. Additional meetings and observing sessions listed on website.
Tel: 07984 154904

North Western Association of Variable Star Observers
Secretary: Jeremy Bullivant, 2 Beaminster Road, Heaton Mersey, Stockport, Cheshire.
Meetings: Four annually.

Norwich Astronomical Society
Secretary: Dave Balcombe, 52 Folly Road, Wymondham, Norfolk NR18 0QR.
Website: astronomicalsociety.org.uk
Meetings: Seething Observatory, Toad Lane, Thwaite St Mary, Norfolk. Every Friday, 7.30 p.m.

Nottingham Astronomical Society
Secretary: C. Brennan, 40 Swindon Close, The Vale, Giltbrook, Nottingham NG16 2WD.
Meetings: Djanogly City Technology College, Sherwood Rise (B682). 1st and 3rd Thursdays each month, 7.30 p.m.

Oldham Astronomical Society
Secretary: P. J. Collins, 25 Park Crescent, Chadderton, Oldham.
Meetings: Werneth Park Study Centre, Frederick Street, Oldham. Fortnightly, Friday.

Open University Astronomical Society
Secretary: Dr Andrew Norton, Department of Physics and Astronomy, The Open University, Walton Hall, Milton Keynes MK7 6AA.
Website: www.physics.open.ac.uk/research/astro/a_club.html
Meetings: Open University, Milton Keynes. 1st Tuesday of every month, 7.30 p.m.

Orpington Astronomical Society
Secretary: Dr Ian Carstairs, 38 Brabourne Rise, Beckenham, Kent BR3 2SG.
Meetings: High Elms Nature Centre, High Elms Country Park, High Elms Road, Farnborough, Kent. 4th Thursday each month, Sept.–July, 7.30 p.m.

Papworth Astronomy Club
Contact: Keith Tritton, Magpie Cottage, Fox Street, Great Gransden, Sandy, Bedfordshire SG19 3AA.
Email: kpt2@tutor.open.ac.uk
Meetings: Bradbury Progression Centre, Church Lane, Papworth Everard, nr Huntingdon. 1st Wednesday each month, 7 p.m.

Peterborough Astronomical Society
Secretary: Sheila Thorpe, 6 Cypress Close, Longthorpe, Peterborough.
Meetings: 1st Thursday every month, 7.30 p.m.

Plymouth Astronomical Society
Secretary: Alan G. Penman, 12 St Maurice View, Plympton, Plymouth, Devon PL7 1FQ.
Email: oakmount12@aol.com
Meetings: Glynis Kingham Centre, YMCA Annex, Lockyer Street, Plymouth. 2nd Friday each month, 7.30 p.m.

PONLAF
Secretary: Matthew Hepburn, 6 Court Road, Caterham, Surrey CR3 5RD.
Meetings: Room 5, 6th floor, Tower Block, University of North London. Last Friday each month during term time, 6.30 p.m.

Port Talbot Astronomical Society (formerly **Astronomical Society of Wales**)
Secretary: Mr J. Hawes, 15 Lodge Drive, Baglan, Port Talbot, West Glamorgan SA12 8UD.
Meetings: Port Talbot Arts Centre. 1st Tuesday each month, 7.15 p.m.

Preston & District Astronomical Society
Secretary: P. Sloane, 77 Ribby Road, Wrea Green, Kirkham, Preston, Lancashire.
Meetings: Moor Park (Jeremiah Horrocks) Observatory, Preston. 2nd Wednesday, last Friday each month, 7.30 p.m.

Reading Astronomical Society
Secretary: Mrs Ruth Sumner, 22 Anson Crescent, Shinfield, Reading RG2 8JT.
Meetings: St Peter's Church Hall, Church Road, Earley. 3rd Friday each month, 7 p.m.

Renfrewshire Astronomical Society
Secretary: Ian Martin, 10 Aitken Road, Hamilton, South Lanarkshire ML3 7YA.

Website: www.renfrewshire-as.co.uk; *Email:* RenfrewAS@aol.com
Meetings: Coats Observatory, Oakshaw Street, Paisley. Fridays, 7.30 p.m.

Rower Astronomical Society
Secretary: Mary Kelly, Knockatore, The Rower, Thomastown, Co. Kilkenny, Eire.

St Helens Amateur Astronomical Society
Secretary: Carl Dingsdale, 125 Canberra Avenue, Thatto Heath, St Helens, Merseyside WA9 5RT.
Meetings: As arranged.

Salford Astronomical Society
Secretary: Mrs Kath Redford, 2 Albermarle Road, Swinton, Manchester M27 5ST.
Meetings: The Observatory, Chaseley Road, Salford. Wednesdays.

Salisbury Astronomical Society
Secretary: Mrs R. Collins, 3 Fairview Road, Salisbury, Wiltshire SP1 1JX.
Meetings: Glebe Hall, Winterbourne Earls, Salisbury. 1st Tuesday each month.

Sandbach Astronomical Society
Secretary: Phil Benson, 8 Gawsworth Drive, Sandbach, Cheshire.
Meetings: Sandbach School, as arranged.

Sawtry & District Astronomical Society
Secretary: Brooke Norton, 2 Newton Road, Sawtry, Huntingdon, Cambridgeshire PE17 5UT.
Meetings: Greenfields Cricket Pavilion, Sawtry Fen. Last Friday each month.

Scarborough & Ryedale Astronomical Society
Secretary: Andy Exton, FRAS, 59 Norwood Street, Scarborough, North Yorkshire, YO12 7EG.
Website: www.scarborough-ryedale-as.org.uk; *Email:* saras.secretary@gmail.com
Meetings: Ayton Village Hall, Wilsons Lane, East Ayton, Scarborough, YO13 9HY. 3rd Friday each month (except Aug. and Dec.), 7 p.m.

Sheffield Astronomical Society
Secretary: Darren Swindels, 102 Sheffield Road, Woodhouse, Sheffield, South Yorkshire S13 7EU.
Website: www.voyagerdome.co.uk/sas/
Meetings: Twice monthly at Mayfield Environmental Education Centre, David Lane, Fulwood, Sheffield S10, 7.30–10 p.m.

Shetland Astronomical Society
Secretary: Peter Kelly, The Glebe, Fetlar, Shetland ZE2 9DJ.
Email: theglebe@zetnet.co.uk
Meetings: Fetlar, Fridays, Oct.–Mar.

Shropshire Astronomical Society
Contact: Mr David Woodward, 20 Station Road, Condover, Shrewsbury, Shropshire SY5 7BQ.
Website: http://www.shropshire-astro.com; *Email:* jacquidodds@ntlworld.com
Meetings: Quarterly talks at the Gateway Arts and Education Centre, Chester Street, Shrewsbury and monthly observing meetings at Rodington Village Hall.

Sidmouth and District Astronomical Society
Secretary: M. Grant, Salters Meadow, Sidmouth, Devon.
Meetings: Norman Lockyer Observatory, Salcombe Hill. 1st Monday in each month.

Solent Amateur Astronomers
Secretary: Ken Medway, Flat 4, Foyes Court, Shirley Road, Southampton SO15 3SG.
Website: www.delscope.demon.co.uk/society/home.htm

Email: ken@medway1875.freeserve.co.uk
Meetings: Kestrel Room, Eastpoint Centre, Bursledon Road, Thornhill, Southampton SO19 8BR. 3rd Tuesday each month, 7.30 p.m.

Southampton Astronomical Society
Secretary: John Thompson, 4 Heathfield, Hythe, Southampton SO45 5BJ.
Website: sas-astronomy.org.uk
Meetings: Conference Room 3, The Civic Centre, Southampton. 2nd Thursday each month (except Aug.), 7.30 p.m.

South Downs Astronomical Society
Secretary: J. Green, 46 Central Avenue, Bognor Regis, West Sussex PO21 5HH.
Website: www.southdowns.org.uk
Meetings: Chichester High School for Boys. 1st Friday in each month (except Aug.).

South-East Essex Astronomical Society
Secretary: C. P. Jones, 29 Buller Road, Laindon, Essex.
Email: cpj@cix.co.uk
Meetings: Lecture Theatre, Central Library, Victoria Avenue, Southend-on-Sea. Generally 1st Thursday in month, Sept.–May, 7.30 p.m.

South-East Kent Astronomical Society
Secretary: Andrew McCarthy, 25 St Paul's Way, Sandgate, near Folkestone, Kent CT20 3NT.
Meetings: Monthly.

South Lincolnshire Astronomical & Geophysical Society
Secretary: Ian Farley, 12 West Road, Bourne, Lincolnshire PE10 9PS.
Meetings: Adult Education Study Centre, Pinchbeck. 3rd Wednesday each month, 7.30 p.m.

Southport Astronomical Society
Secretary: Patrick Brannon, Willow Cottage, 90 Jacksmere Lane, Scarisbrick, Ormskirk, Lancashire L40 9RS.
Meetings: Monthly Sept.–May, plus observing sessions.

Southport, Ormskirk and District Astronomical Society
Secretary: J. T. Harrison, 92 Cottage Lane, Ormskirk, Lancashire L39 3NJ.
Meetings: Saturday evenings, monthly, as arranged.

South Shields Astronomical Society
Secretary: c/o South Tyneside College, St George's Avenue, South Shields.
Meetings: Marine and Technical College. Each Thursday, 7.30 p.m.

South-West Hertfordshire Astronomical Society
Secretary: Len Mann. *Email:* the.secretary@swhas.org.uk
Website: www.swhas.org.uk
Meetings: The Royal Masonic School, Rickmansworth. See website for details.

Stafford and District Astronomical Society
Secretary: Miss L. Hodkinson, 6 Elm Walk, Penkridge, Staffordshire ST19 5NL.
Meetings: Weston Road High School, Stafford. Every 3rd Thursday, Sept.–May, 7.15 p.m.

Stirling Astronomical Society
Website: www.stirlingastronomicalsociety.org.uk
Email: stirlingastronomicalsociety@gmail.com
Meetings: 2nd Friday each month in the Smith Museum & Art Gallery, Dumbarton Road, Stirling.

Stoke-on-Trent Astronomical Society
Secretary: M. Pace, Sundale, Dunnocksfold, Alsager, Stoke-on-Trent.
Meetings: Cartwright House, Broad Street, Hanley. Monthly.

Stratford-upon-Avon Astronomical Society
Secretary: Robin Swinbourne, 18 Old Milverton, Leamington Spa, Warwickshire CV32 6SA.
Meetings: Tiddington Home Guard Club. 4th Tuesday each month, 7.30 p.m.

Sunderland Astronomical Society
Contact: Don Simpson, 78 Stratford Avenue, Grangetown, Sunderland SR2 8RZ.
Meetings: Friends Meeting House, Roker. 1st, 2nd and 3rd Sundays each month.

Sussex Astronomical Society
Secretary: Mrs C. G. Sutton, 75 Vale Road, Portslade, Sussex.
Meetings: English Language Centre, Third Avenue, Hove. Every Wednesday, 7.30–9.30 p.m., Sept.–May.

Swansea Astronomical Society
Secretary: Dr Michael Morales, 238 Heol Dulais, Birch Grove, Swansea SA7 9LH.
Website: www.swanastro.org.uk
Meetings: Lecture Room C, Science Tower, University of Swansea. 2nd and 4th Thursday each month from Sept.–June, 7 p.m.

Tavistock Astronomical Society
Secretary: Mrs Ellie Coombes, Rosemount, Under Road, Gunnislake, Cornwall PL18 9JL.
Meetings: Science Laboratory, Kelly College, Tavistock. 1st Wednesday each month, 7.30 p.m.

Thames Valley Astronomical Group
Secretary: K. J. Pallet, 82a Tennyson Street, South Lambeth, London SW8 3TH.
Meetings: As arranged.

Thanet Amateur Astronomical Society
Secretary: P. F. Jordan, 85 Crescent Road, Ramsgate.
Meetings: Hilderstone House, Broadstairs, Kent. Monthly.

Torbay Astronomical Society
Secretary: Tim Moffat, 31 Netley Road, Newton Abbot, Devon TQ12 2LL.
Meetings: Torquay Boys' Grammar School, 1st Thursday in month; and Town Hall, Torquay, 3rd Thursday in month, Oct.–May, 7.30 p.m.

Tullamore Astronomical Society
Secretary: Seanie Morris, 'Anstee', Daingean Rd, Tullamore, Co. Offaly, Ireland.
Website: www.tullamoreastronomy.com; *Email:* midlandsastronomy@gmail.com
Meetings: Order of Malta Lecture Hall, Tanyard, Tullamore, Co. Offaly, Eire. Mondays at 8 p.m., every fortnight.

Tyrone Astronomical Society
Secretary: John Ryan, 105 Coolnafranky Park, Cookstown, Co. Tyrone, Northern Ireland.
Meetings: Contact Secretary.

Usk Astronomical Society
Secretary: Bob Wright, 'Llwyn Celyn', 75 Woodland Road, Croesyceiliog, Cwmbran NP44 2OX.
Meetings: Usk Community Education Centre, Maryport Street, Usk. Every Thursday during school term, 7 p.m.

Vectis Astronomical Society
Secretary: Rebecca Mitchelmore
Website: www.wightastronomy.org
Email: secretary@wightastronomy.org
Meetings: Newport Parish Church Centre, Newport. 4th Friday each month except Dec., 7.30 p.m.

Vigo Astronomical Society
Secretary: Robert Wilson, 43 Admers Wood, Vigo Village, Meopham, Kent DA13 0SP.
Meetings: Vigo Village Hall. As arranged.

Walsall Astronomical Society
Secretary: Bob Cleverley, 40 Mayfield Road, Sutton Coldfield B74 3PZ.
Meetings: Freetrade Inn, Wood Lane, Pelsall North Common. Every Thursday.

Wealden Astronomical Society
Secretary: K.A. Woodcock, 24 Emmanuel Road, Hastings, East Sussex TN34 3LB.
Email: wealdenas@hotmail.co.uk
Meetings: Herstmonceux Science Centre. Dates, as arranged.

Wellingborough District Astronomical Society
Secretary: S. M. Williams, 120 Brickhill Road, Wellingborough, Northamptonshire.
Meetings: Gloucester Hall, Church Street, Wellingborough. 2nd Wednesday each month, 7.30 p.m.

Wessex Astronomical Society
Contact details and programme to be found at: www.wessex-astro.org.uk
Meetings: first Tuesday monthly at 7.30 p.m. in the Allendale Centre, Hanham Road, Wimborne Minster, Dorset BH21 1AS
Observatory: Durlston Country Park, Swanage, Dorset

West Cornwall Astronomical Society
Secretary: Dr R. Waddling, The Pines, Pennance Road, Falmouth, Cornwall TR11 4ED.
Meetings: Helston Football Club, 3rd Thursday each month, and St Michall's Hotel, 1st Wednesday each month, 7.30 p.m.

West of London Astronomical Society
Secretary: Duncan Radbourne, 28 Tavistock Road, Edgware, Middlesex HA8 6DA.
Website: www.wolas.org.uk
Meetings: Monthly, alternately in Uxbridge and North Harrow. 2nd Monday in month, except Aug.

West Midlands Astronomical Association
Secretary: Miss S. Bundy, 93 Greenridge Road, Handsworth Wood, Birmingham.
Meetings: Dr Johnson House, Bull Street, Birmingham. As arranged.

West Yorkshire Astronomical Society
Secretary: Pete Lunn, 21 Crawford Drive, Wakefield, West Yorkshire.
Meetings: Rosse Observatory, Carleton Community Centre, Carleton Road, Pontefract. Each Tuesday, 7.15 p.m.

Whitby and District Astronomical Society
Secretary: Rosemary Bowman, The Cottage, Larpool Drive, Whitby, North Yorkshire YO22 4ND.
Meetings: Whitby Mission, Seafarers' Centre, Haggersgate, Whitby. 1st Tuesday of the month, 7.30 p.m.

Astronomical Societies in the British Isles

Whittington Astronomical Society
Secretary: Peter Williamson, The Observatory, Top Street, Whittington, Shropshire.
Meetings: The Observatory. Every month.

Wiltshire Astronomical Society
Chair: Mr Andrew J. Burns, The Knoll, Lowden Hill, Chippenham, SN15 2BT; 01249 654541
Website: www.wasnet.co.uk; *Email:* angleburns@hotmail.com
Secretary: Simon Barnes, 25 Woodcombe, Melksham, Wiltshire SN12 6HA.
Meetings: The Field Pavilion, Rusty Lane, Seend, Nr Devizes, Wiltshire. 1st Tuesday each month, Sept.–June. Viewing evenings 4th Friday plus special events, Lacock Playing Fields, Lacock, Wilsthire.

Wolverhampton Astronomical Society
Secretary: Dr Julian Cooper
Website: www.wolvas.org.uk; *Email:* secretary@wolvas.org.uk *Twitter:* @wolvasuk
Meetings: The Environmental Centre, Highfields School, Boundary Way, Penn, Wolverhampton, WV4 4NT. Alternate Mondays, Sept.–Apr., extra dates in summer, 7.30 p.m.

Worcester Astronomical Society
Secretary: Mr S. Bateman, 12 Bozward Street, Worcester WR2 5DE.
Meetings: Room 117, Worcester College of Higher Education, Henwick Grove, Worcester. 2nd Thursday each month, 8 p.m.

Worthing Astronomical Society
Contact: G. Boots, 101 Ardingly Drive, Worthing, West Sussex BN12 4TW.
Website: www.worthing-astronomical-society.com
Email: gboots@observatory99.freeserve.co.uk
Meetings: Heene Church Rooms, Heene Road, Worthing. 1st Wednesday each month (except Aug.), 7.30 p.m.

Wycombe Astronomical Society
Secretary: Mr P. Treherne, 34 Honeysuckle Road, Widmer End, High Wycombe, Buckinghamshire HP15 6BW.
Meetings: Woodrow High House, Amersham. 3rd Wednesday each month, 7.45 p.m.

The York Astronomical Society
Contact: Hazel Collett, Public Relations Officer
Tel: 07944 751277
Website: yorkastro.org.uk
Meetings: The Knavesmire Room, York Priory Street Centre, Priory Street, York. 1st and 3rd Friday of each month (except Aug.), 8 p.m.

The William Herschel Society maintains the museum established at 19 New King Street, Bath BA1 2BL – the only surviving Herschel House. It also undertakes activities of various kinds. New members would be welcome; those interested are asked to contact the Membership Secretary at the museum.

The South Downs Planetarium (Kingsham Farm, Kingsham Road, Chichester, West Sussex PO19 8RP) is now fully operational. For further information, visit www.southdowns.org.uk/sdpt or telephone (01243) 774400.

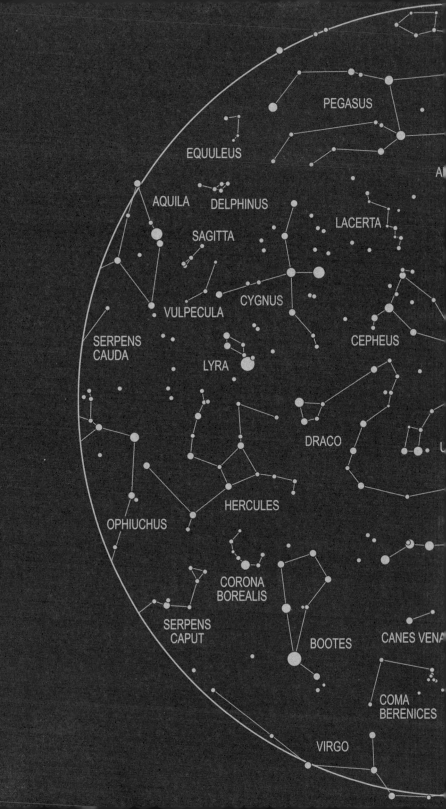